Handbook of Accessible Instruction and Testing Practices

Stephen N. Elliott · Ryan J. Kettler
Peter A. Beddow · Alexander Kurz
Editors

Handbook of Accessible Instruction and Testing Practices

Issues, Innovations, and Applications

Second Edition

Editors
Stephen N. Elliott
Arizona State University
Tempe, AZ, USA

Peter A. Beddow
Accessible Hope, LLC
Nashville, TN, USA

Ryan J. Kettler
Rutgers
The State University of New Jersey
Piscataway, NJ, USA

Alexander Kurz
Arizona State University
Tempe, AZ, USA

ISBN 978-3-030-10017-9   ISBN 978-3-319-71126-3   (eBook)
https://doi.org/10.1007/978-3-319-71126-3

© Springer International Publishing AG 2011, 2018
Softcover re-print of the Hardcover 2nd edition 2018
This work is subject to copyright. All rights are reserved by the Publisher, whether the whole or part of the material is concerned, specifically the rights of translation, reprinting, reuse of illustrations, recitation, broadcasting, reproduction on microfilms or in any other physical way, and transmission or information storage and retrieval, electronic adaptation, computer software, or by similar or dissimilar methodology now known or hereafter developed.
The use of general descriptive names, registered names, trademarks, service marks, etc. in this publication does not imply, even in the absence of a specific statement, that such names are exempt from the relevant protective laws and regulations and therefore free for general use.
The publisher, the authors and the editors are safe to assume that the advice and information in this book are believed to be true and accurate at the date of publication. Neither the publisher nor the authors or the editors give a warranty, express or implied, with respect to the material contained herein or for any errors or omissions that may have been made. The publisher remains neutral with regard to jurisdictional claims in published maps and institutional affiliations.

Printed on acid-free paper

This Springer imprint is published by the registered company Springer International Publishing AG part of Springer Nature
The registered company address is: Gewerbestrasse 11, 6330 Cham, Switzerland

To all the teachers who make learning accessible for children often assumed to not understand and for all the future teachers who aspire to do the same. Your efforts make a difference for many.

                 Stephen N. Elliott

To Cary Cherniss, Susan Forman, Stanley Messer, and Linda Reddy, for giving me the job I love, and to Kelly and Austin, the family I love.

                   Ryan J. Kettler

To all the students for whom school experiences have wounded your hope and stolen your natural joy of learning: you are infinitely valuable. And to all the teachers: may your love of teaching return to you a thousandfold.

                   Peter A. Beddow

To Gavin and Zak, the sons I love and always wanted. To Madison and Ariza, the girls I love and never knew I needed. And to Kaylee, the woman I love and laugh with.

                   Alexander Kurz

Preface

The fundamental premise for this book is that *access is an essential part of high-quality instruction and fair testing*. When access is denied or poorly managed, learning suffers and assessment of that learning is inaccurate.

This book is an update and expansion of *Handbook of Accessible Achievement Tests for All Students* published by Springer in 2011. It has been motivated by the increasing demand for accessible instruction and testing practices from the professional community. Specifically, in 2014, the American Educational Research Association, the American Psychological Association, and the National Council on Measurement in Education published a new set of *Standards for Educational and Psychological Testing* and in it included an entire chapter on fairness with accessibility and opportunity to learn (OTL) as critical concepts. In addition, national testing consortia such as the Smarter Balanced Assessment Consortium and the Partnership for Assessment of Readiness for College and Careers now require a high level of access for their interim and summative tests and are pushing the envelope with innovative computerized assessments that have embraced a number of accessibility innovations. Practitioners have also begun to include opportunity to learn data in their teacher evaluation and professional development efforts, as evidenced by projects such as the School System Improvement Project in New Jersey. Finally, the Center for Applied Special Technology (CAST) has continued to advance Universal Design for Learning principles and has gained substantial traction in mainstream education with teachers of all types of students, not just students with disabilities.

There is a growing national and international interest in making education – both instruction and testing – highly accessible and equitable for all students. With advances in technology, strong professional endorsements, and growing legal expectations for accessibility, the publication of a more expansive and updated account of accessibility research and practices was needed. Throughout this book, *accessibility is defined as the extent to which a product, environment, or system eliminates barriers and permits equal access to all components and services for all individuals.* In summary, this book is the collective response by 30 dedicated scholar educators motivated to do more to improve accessibility for learners to valued lessons, tests, and educational outcomes.

Tempe, AZ, USA	Stephen N. Elliott
Piscataway, NJ, USA	Ryan J. Kettler
Antioch, TN, USA	Peter A. Beddow
Tempe, AZ, USA	Alexander Kurz

Contents

1. **Accessible Instruction and Testing Today** 1
   Ryan J. Kettler, Stephen N. Elliott, Peter A. Beddow, and Alexander Kurz

2. **US Policies Supporting Inclusive Assessments for Students with Disabilities: A 60-Year History** 17
   Susan C. Weigert

3. **International Policies that Support Inclusive Assessment** 37
   Michael Davies

4. **Fair Testing and the Role of Accessibility** 59
   Elizabeth A. Stone and Linda L. Cook

5. **Designing, Developing, and Implementing an Accessible Computer-Based National Assessment System** 75
   Magda Chia and Rachel Kachchaf

6. **The Accessibility Needs of Students with Disabilities: Special Considerations for Instruction and Assessment** 93
   Jennifer R. Frey and Carrie M. Gillispie

7. **Assessing Students with Autism: Considerations and Recommendations** 107
   Peter A. Beddow

8. **Moving Beyond Assumptions of Cultural Neutrality to Improve Accessibility and Opportunity to Learn for English Language Learners** 119
   Tim Boals, Mariana Castro, and Lynn Shafer Willner

9. **Confronting the Known Unknown: How the Concept of Opportunity to Learn Can Advance Tier 1 Instruction** 135
   Alexander Kurz

10. **Response-to-Intervention Models and Access to Services for All Students** 157
    Todd A. Glover

11	**Accurate and Informative for All: Universal Design for Learning (UDL) and the Future of Assessment** 167
	David H. Rose, Kristin H. Robinson, Tracey E. Hall, Peggy Coyne, Richard M. Jackson, William M. Stahl, and Sherri L. Wilcauskas

12	**Item Development Research and Practice** 181
	Anthony D. Albano and Michael C. Rodriguez

13	**Cognitive Load Theory for Test Design** 199
	Peter A. Beddow

14	**Testing Adaptations: Research to Guide Practice** 213
	Leah Dembitzer and Ryan J. Kettler

15	**Promoting Valid Assessment of Students with Disabilities and English Learners** 231
	Stephen G. Sireci, Ella Banda, and Craig S. Wells

16	**Recent Advances in the Accessibility of Digitally Delivered Educational Assessments** 247
	Michael Russell

17	**Accessibility Progress and Perspectives** 263
	Stephen N. Elliott, Ryan J. Kettler, Peter A. Beddow, and Alexander Kurz

Index 269

Contributors

Anthony D. Albano University of Nebraska-Lincoln, Lincoln, NE, USA

Ella Banda University of Massachusetts Amherst, Amherst, MA, USA

Peter A. Beddow Accessible Hope LLC, Nashville, TN, USA

Tim Boals University of Wisconsin-Madison, Madison, WI, USA

Mariana Castro University of Wisconsin-Madison, Madison, WI, USA

Magda Chia Stanford University, Understanding Language/Stanford Center for Assessment, Learning, and Equity, Stanford, CA, USA

Linda L. Cook Educational Testing Services, Princeton, NJ, USA

Peggy Coyne Lexia Learning Systems, Concord, MA, USA

Michael Davies Education and Professional Studies, Griffith University, Brisbane, Australia

Leah Dembitzer Center for Health Education, Medicine, and Dentistry, Lakewood, NJ, USA

Stephen N. Elliott Arizona State University, Tempe, AZ, USA

Jennifer R. Frey The George Washington University, Washington, DC, USA

Carrie M. Gillispie The George Washington University, Washington, DC, USA

Todd A. Glover Rutgers University, Piscataway, NJ, USA

Tracey E. Hall CAST, Wakefield, MA, USA

Richard M. Jackson CAST, Wakefield, MA, USA

Rachel Kachchaf University of California Los Angeles, Smarter Balanced Assessment Consortium, Los Angeles, CA, USA

Ryan J. Kettler Rutgers, The State University of New Jersey, Piscataway, NJ, USA

Alexander Kurz Arizona State University, Tempe, AZ, USA

Kristin H. Robinson CAST, Wakefield, MA, USA

Michael C. Rodriguez University of Minnesota-Twin Cities, Minneapolis, MN, USA

David H. Rose CAST, Wakefield, MA, USA

Michael Russell Boston College, Chestnut Hill, MA, USA

Stephen G. Sireci University of Massachusetts Amherst, Amherst, MA, USA

William M. Stahl CAST, Wakefield, MA, USA

National Center on Accessible Educational Materials, Wakefield, MA, USA

Elizabeth A. Stone Educational Testing Services, Princeton, NJ, USA

Susan C. Weigert US Department of Education, Office of Special Education Programs, Washington, DC, USA

Craig S. Wells University of Massachusetts Amherst, Amherst, MA, USA

Sherri L. Wilcauskas CAST, Wakefield, MA, USA

Lynn Shafer Willner University of Wisconsin-Madison, Madison, WI, USA

About the Editors

Stephen N. Elliott the senior editor, is a Mickelson Foundation Professor at Arizona State University. Steve teaches courses on measurement and assessment of academic and social behavior and codirects two USDE research grants concerning opportunity to learn and the achievement growth of students. Steve has authored more than 250 journal articles, books, and chapters as well as 6 widely used behavior-rating scales.

Ryan J. Kettler is an associate professor in the School Psychology program of the Graduate School of Applied and Professional Psychology at Rutgers University. He conducts research in data-based decision making, including issues related to screening, inclusive assessment, rating scale technology, and reliability and validity. Ryan has authored more than 50 articles and chapters.

Peter A. Beddow is the president of Accessible Testing, LLC, the mission of which is to facilitate the development of tests that are free from barriers for students with a broad range of abilities and needs. He is the senior author of the Test Accessibility and Modification Inventory and has authored numerous articles and chapters on accessibility theory. He also operates Accessible Behavior, LLC, through which he works with teachers, parents, and other caregivers and leaders to understand and manage child behavior and facilitate positive behavior change for individuals with behavior problems. Pete lives in Nashville, Tennessee.

Alexander Kurz is an assistant research professor in the T. Denny Sanford School of Social and Family Dynamics and director of the AzPREP Office at Arizona State University. He conducts research on opportunity to learn, instructional coaching, and collective impact. Alex codirects several USDE research grants concerning opportunity to learn, the achievement growth of students, school improvement, educator evaluation, as well as research with community nonprofits such as Valley of the Sun United Way. Alex has authored more than 20 articles and chapters and codeveloped a widely used OTL measure.

Accessible Instruction and Testing Today

Ryan J. Kettler, Stephen N. Elliott, Peter A. Beddow, and Alexander Kurz

Accessibility – defined as the extent to which a product, environment, or system eliminates barriers and permits equal use of components and services for a diverse population of individuals – is necessary for effective instruction and fair testing. To the extent that instruction, instructional materials, and tests are not accessible to any portion of the student population, learning is likely to be incomplete, and inferences made from observations and test results are likely to be inaccurate. Optimal accessibility is implicitly promised to all students. Delivering on the promise of accessible instruction and testing practices, therefore, is a shared responsibility for educational stakeholders, including teachers, school leaders, policy makers, software developers, textbook authors, test designers, and many others.

Access is a fundamental educational principle that involves more than participation in general education classes with common curricula and assessments. Access involves removing obstacles that limit students' opportunities to learn the intended and tested curriculum, deny or disrupt their receipt of individualized accommodations for learning and testing, and reduce the degree to which tests provide accurate information about their knowledge and skills (Elliott & Kettler, 2015). Unfortunately, barriers exist for many students with disabilities and their teachers. Strategies and resources to remove these access barriers are grounded in educational legislation, universal design theory, and professional testing practices; these strategies are at the heart of quality instruction, meaningful learning, and fair testing practices (Elliott, Kurz, & Schulte, 2015; *Smarter Balanced Usability, Accessibility, and Accommodations Guidelines*, 2016).

With the publication of the *Standards for Educational and Psychological Testing* (American Educational Research Association [AERA], National Council on Measurement in Education [NCME], and American Psychological Association [APA], 2014), access became a central tenet in fair testing practices. From an instructional perspective, access is the opportunity for a student to learn the content of the intended curriculum. In the current educational framework, this means each student has the appropriate opportunities to acquire the knowledge and skills featured in the content standards of her state and to ultimately perform on

R. J. Kettler (✉)
Rutgers, The State University of New Jersey, Piscataway, NJ, USA
e-mail: r.j.kettler@rutgers.edu

S. N. Elliott · A. Kurz
Arizona State University, Tempe, AZ, USA
e-mail: steve_elliott@asu.edu; Alexander.Kurz@asu.edu

P. A. Beddow
Accessible Hope, LLC, Nashville, TN, USA

the state's end-of-year achievement tests. Teachers are encouraged to teach to the content standards, rather than to the test, and to create engaging instruction for all students to increase the opportunity for learning to occur. From an educational testing perspective, access is manifest when a test-taker is able to show the degree to which he knows the tested content (Kettler, Elliott, & Beddow, 2009). Test accessibility is optimized when "all test takers have an unobstructed opportunity to demonstrate their standing on the construct(s) being measured" (AERA et al., 2014, p. 49). Collectively, this access to instruction and testing should minimize bias and increase fairness for students.

This chapter focuses on accessibility issues along the journey from an individual content standard or set of standards to the inferences that can be drawn from an item or test score about the performance of a student, teacher, and school. We highlight accessibility to instruction and testing, as well as the barriers that preclude this access, using Kettler's (2015) Interpretation of Achievement Test Scores (IATS) Paradigm. In addition, the chapter provides a context of legal and policy issues around accessibility and methods of measuring relevant components. In closing, we introduce the sections and chapters of the *Handbook of Accessible Instruction and Testing Practices*. Now let's get started with Item 1.

You have 40 seconds to solve Item 1.
Solve.

1.

$$\begin{array}{r} 3\ 6\ 5 \\ -1\ 1\ 9 \\ \hline \end{array}$$

a. 246
b. 254
c. 256
d. 484

Most of us have been asked to solve an item like this one at some point in our lives and have probably done so without considering many of its properties. Those properties include the content, difficulty, intended population, and target construct, to name a few.

Per the common core standards for mathematics, within the domain Number and Operations in Base Ten (NBT) at the third-grade level, standard A.2 states: *Fluently add and subtract within 1000 using strategies and algorithms based on place value, properties of operations, and/or the relationship between addition and subtraction* (Common Core State Standards Initiative, 2013, http://www.corestandards.org/Math/Content/3/NBT). Item 1 could be one of many items included on a third-grade mathematics test, designed to address the narrow construct described in A.2, as well as the broader construct labeled NBT. The item involves the subtraction of two three-digit numbers. The answer choices include three distractors (i.e., incorrect answer choices): one (choice b) that would be attractive if the smaller digit was always subtracted from the larger digit; one (choice c) that would be attractive if 10 was added to make the 5 in 365 a 15, but 1 was *not* subsequently subtracted from the 6; and one (choice d) that would be attractive if the numbers were added together. Answer choice "a" is the correct answer.

We do not know how good item 1 is, nor do we know how accessible it is for a diverse population of test-takers. Can students from all groups show what they know and can do via Item 1 or might some groups do poorly on it for reasons unrelated to the intended constructs (i.e., triple-digit subtraction, NBT, mathematics)? Can Item 1 be adapted in any way that increases its accessibility, without compromising its effectiveness for measuring the intended constructs? Let us consider these issues and others within the context of a case study.

Case Study

Jessica is a third-grade student who is struggling in mathematics and who does poorly on tests. Her intelligence is near the normative mean for her age, and her processing speed is about one standard deviation below the mean. Jessica's academic fluency (i.e., reading fluency, mathematics fluency, writing fluency) scores are nearly two standard deviations below the mean, reflecting a clear difficulty with timed tasks. A primary concern in Jessica's case is that a functional impairment (i.e., a deficit in a skill needed for access) in fluency could keep her from learning what she needs to know in subtraction, NBT, and mathematics and from subsequently showing what she knows and can do. Jessica may not be able to learn this material if it is presented at a pace and in a time frame that is intended for students with typical fluency. Her score from a timed test of NBT may be as reflective or more reflective of her fluency as it is of NBT.

Two types of adaptations may increase accessibility for Jessica. Instructional adaptations may assist Jessica in learning NBT and mathematics, and testing adaptations may assist her in subsequently showing what she has learned. Given Jessica's low fluency, more time will likely need to be provided for her to learn new concepts. When teaching a concept such as NBT, Jessica's teacher may present the new content more slowly, to the extent possible, and this adaptation could benefit a number of students. Her teacher also may check for understanding more often, perhaps nonverbally during the introduction on the construct and afterward with Jessica during practice time. As part of differentiated instruction, Jessica may be placed in a mathematics group with other students whose fluency is low. This group may receive more direct instruction, scaffolding, and guided feedback and receive less independent practice, compared to other groups. Jessica could also benefit from additional academic time, perhaps through extended resource opportunities during school or afterschool tutoring. Such adaptations would be provided with the intent to help Jessica learn content she is able to master, with the assumption she simply needs a little more time compared to other students.

Jessica could also benefit from an extra time adaptation on achievement tests. Consider Item 1 with Jessica provided 50% extra time, so she has 60 seconds rather than 40 seconds. Given her functional impairment, the added time could allow Jessica to respond to Item 1 similarly to how students without such impairments perform in the standard 40 seconds. Gathering evidence that this adaptation would improve measurement of the construct (i.e., act as an accommodation) rather than change the construct (i.e., act as a modification) is possible using multiple similar items and multiple examinees with similar functional impairments. For the sake of this example, we will assume Jessica did everything exactly the same way a student without a functional impairment would, except it took her 50% longer due to lower fluency.

Access Skills, Target Skills, and Adaptations

Access skills are those skills one needs to learn and perform on tests, but which are not the constructs being taught during the lesson or measured during the test. Access skills are the prerequisite skills students are assumed to have obtained prior to learning the lesson or taking the test (Elliott, Braden, & White, 2001). Jessica's mathematics instruction was not designed to increase her academic fluency, nor was her timed mathematics assessment designed to be a measure of fluency. The lesson and the test were, however, designed for a group of examinees that are at or above a minimal threshold on fluency, an access skill for the test. Targeted skills or knowledge, by contrast, are the constructs that are intended to be taught during the lesson and intended to be measured by the test. Sufficient levels of all access skills allow the lesson to be learned and allow the subsequent score on the test to be reflective of the target construct. The target constructs of Jessica's lesson and test were triple-digit subtraction, NBT, and mathematics achievement.

In the case of Jessica, some assumptions would be necessary to draw the conclusion the adaptations were accommodations rather than modifications. Specifically, we postulated extra time would improve Jessica's learning of mathematics and would also improve the test's reflection of that learning. This assumption can be tricky, particularly in the case of testing adaptations. The content standard does not specify any time limit within which Jessica is supposed to learn the skill, other than the implication she must master it during her third-grade year. It would be highly unusual if such a time limit were indicated in achievement content standards (by contrast, it is common for intelligence tests to have controlled learning tasks with strict parameters about time and other characteristics for teaching). While time is not limited by the content standard and not likely to be an issue for teaching the construct, time can be a very important issue around testing the construct.

The assertion that extra time on tests is an accommodation for Jessica rather than a modification is based on a three-step process using questions about (a) access skills, (b) available accommodations, and (c) targeted skills or knowledge identified by Kettler (2012). The first question addresses access skills: *Does the student have a functional impairment in an area that is an access skill for the test being considered?* With fluency scores about two standard deviations below the normative mean, Jessica has a functional impairment in a skill needed to access any timed test. The next question addresses available accommodations: *Are any accommodations available to address the impairment?* In Jessica's case, extra time accommodations are a logical match for an impairment in fluency. The last question addresses targeted skills or knowledge: *If selected, will the accommodation or accommodations change the construct being measured by the test?* Given Item 1 has a time limit, as does the achievement test that would likely contain it, fluency is a part of the construct being measured. At issue is whether providing extra time to Jessica will change the construct being measured or simply increase precision and accuracy of measurement of the intended construct. The intent of providing Jessica extra time as an accommodation is that the test would then measure fluency for her to the same extent it measures fluency for students who do not have a functional impairment and do not receive an accommodation.

In cases in which access skills are not sufficient for a student to show what she knows on the test, and appropriate adaptations are not provided, the score from the test reflects in part deficiencies in these skills rather than on the construct being measured. If Jessica is not provided extra instructional and practice time, she may not learn the content as well as she could. Even if Jessica learns the content as well as her fellow students, if she completes Item 1 without extra time, she may not have as good of a chance to be successful. Over the course of an entire test, administered under standard time conditions, Jessica may attain a lower score than other students who have mathematics achievement similar to hers and have fluency that is better than hers. Jessica's subsequent low score on the test could be more reflective of her fluency than of her triple-digit subtraction, NBT, or mathematics achievement. The impact of access skills deficits and other threats to the relationship between the construct and the test score can be conceptualized using the paradigm described in the next section.

The Interpretation of Achievement Test Scores (IATS) Paradigm

Since the passage of the No Child Left Behind (NCLB) Act of 2001, educator effectiveness has been evaluated primarily based on student test scores in reading and mathematics. This practice makes sense from the standpoint that the ultimate goal of our teachers and schools is to increase student learning, and growth in achievement can be a good indicator of learning. One criticism of this approach is that much more goes into learning than just instruction, so it is an imperfect practice to draw inferences about teaching based solely on student achievement, even for situations in which achievement is measured based on growth rather than status. Instruction and learning are related and distinct variables. There is simply too much happening in a student's life – both within the classroom and beyond it – that affects learning for even the best measures of student achievement outcomes to be used as sole indicators of the effectiveness of teachers'

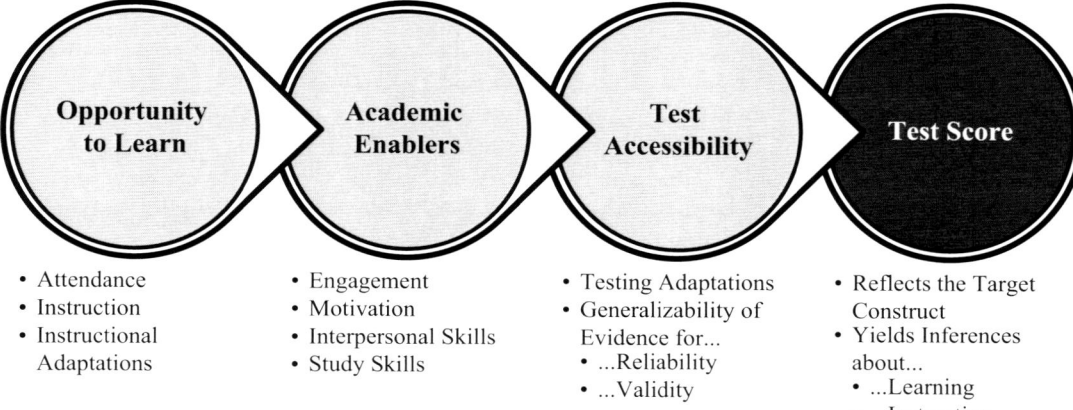

Fig. 1.1 The Interpretation of Achievement Test Scores (IATS) Paradigm addresses the components that substantially impact the inferences that can be drawn about teachers, schools, and districts (Kettler, 2015; reprinted by permission of SAGE Publications, Inc.)

instructional processes. The NCLB requirement to include large-scale testing in reading and mathematics at many grade levels was a positive step. The logical next step is to use a model with a diverse set of measures that allows more sophisticated inferences to be drawn from the resulting scores. The IATS Paradigm (Kettler, 2015), depicted in Fig. 1.1, addresses this issue.

The IATS Paradigm focuses on the *within-classroom* variables involved in the educational process, from a student entering a classroom being afforded an opportunity to learn (OTL) to inferences being drawn about the teacher's instruction based on the student's test score. Following OTL and preceding the test score, two other broad classes of variables (academic enablers and test accessibility) must be considered in order to draw many valid inferences. Each of these four components is necessary to determining whether a teacher or school has successfully taught the constructs, as delineated in the content standards, to each student.

Opportunity to Learn

OTL generally refers to the opportunities schools afford their students to learn what they are expected to know (Herman, Klein, & Abedi, 2000; Kurz, 2011) and is widely considered a teacher effect. Such a definition highlights issues such as the "who," the "what," and the "how well" of instruction. Consequently, the basic definition of OTL by Herman et al. has been refined and expanded to cover instructional time, content coverage, and quality of instruction (Kurz, 2011). These three dimensions of instructional time, content coverage, and instructional quality have a substantial history in education research, and each has been found to account for a meaningful portion of the differences in students' achievement as measured by tests (Kurz, 2011; Kurz, Elliott, & Schulte, 2015). Kurz, Elliott, Lemons, et al. (2014) further provided an operational definition of OTL, which has been applied in subsequent research across a variety of settings (e.g., Heafner & Fitchett, 2015; Roach, Kurz, & Elliott, 2015): OTL is "the degree to which a teacher dedicates instructional time and content coverage to the intended curriculum objectives emphasizing higher-order cognitive processes, evidence-based instructional practices, and alternative grouping formats" (p. 27).

The IATS Paradigm includes three basic factors that affect OTL: attendance, instruction, and instructional adaptations. Often neglected in our consideration of inferences drawn from test scores, attendance is a starting point for contextualizing educator performance, in that it is illogical to hold teachers responsible for opportunities lost during times that students are absent from class. That noted, Kurz et al. (2014) do not explicitly include attendance in their definition of OTL, because OTL is considered an educator factor (for an elaboration of this perspective, see Kurz's Chap. 9 of the current volume). Their definition does include instructional time, and, as such, attendance enters the model as a function of reduced instructional time. The IATS Paradigm focuses on within classroom variables, a definition that also puts attendance in a debatable position, since it refers to the gate between variables outside the classroom and variables within the classroom. Regardless of the position of attendance in the model, it is important to recognize that attending school is a prerequisite to everything else in the model and that considering attendance is critical when interpreting scores to evaluate teachers and schools.

Next, instruction is included because its quality directly affects student test scores. Instruction on grade-level content standards is the central variable about which we are often trying to draw inferences from achievement test scores, and in contrast to attendance, the concern is that changes in scores (i.e., learning) are often overly attributed to instruction. Lastly, instructional adaptations are used by effective educators to complement high-quality instruction by differentiating for learners with a diverse set of needs (Ketterlin-Geller & Jamgochian, 2011). Instructional adaptations should be selected to address functional impairments, to ensure barriers (e.g., working memory load, distractions, complex language) do not keep the target construct from being learned.

Universal Design for Learning Universal Design for Learning (UDL) is one framework through which to consider the quality of instruction. Universal design (UD), as defined in the Assistive Technology Act (P.L. 105–394, 1998), is "a concept or philosophy for designing and delivering products and services that are usable by people with the widest possible range of functional capabilities…" (§3(17)). UDL has influenced the design of instructional materials and practices and is considered a scientifically valid framework for guiding educational practice (Higher Education Opportunity Act of, 2008). Benefits of UDL include that the framework (a) provides flexibility in the ways students are presented information, students respond or demonstrate knowledge and skills, and students are engaged; (b) reduces barriers in instruction by incorporating appropriate accommodations and supports; and (c) challenges students by maintaining high achievement expectations. These expectations apply equally to students with disabilities and to students with limited English proficiency.

The UDL framework is described in *Teaching Every Student in the Digital Age* (Rose & Meyer, 2002), *The Universally Designed Classroom* (Rose, Meyer, & Hitchcock, 2005), and Chap. 11 of this volume. Out of these contributions has emanated a set of UDL Guidelines that can assist teachers planning lessons of study or developing curricula to reduce barriers, optimizing levels of challenge and support, and meeting the needs of all learners. They also can help educators identify the barriers found in existing curricula. The UDL Guidelines are organized according to three main principles: (a) Provide Multiple Means of Representation, (b) Provide Multiple Means of Action and Expression, and (c) Provide Multiple Means of Engagement. For each of these principles, specific "Checkpoints" are provided, followed by examples of practical suggestions. For example, Checkpoint 1.3 under the principle Provide Multiple Means of Representation specifies to "Offer alternatives for visual information." Implementation examples include to provide text or spoken descriptions, use touch equivalents, provide physical objects or models, and provide auditory cues for key concepts and transitions. The website for the National Center on Universal Design for Learning (http://www.udlcenter.org) provides implementation examples for each checkpoint, as well as a summary of the research evidence in support of each checkpoint.

Instructional Learning Opportunities Guidance System OTL can be measured using the Instructional Learning Opportunities Guidance System (MyiLOGS; Kurz, Elliott, & Shrago, 2009). MyiLOGS is an online teacher self-report measure connecting content standards to actual performance. Teachers log their practices daily, indicating the amount of time spent on each content standard, cognitive process, instructional practice, and grouping format. MyiLOGS subsequently reports indices reflective of instructional time and content coverage, as well as the percentage of time spent on higher-order thinking skills, empirically supported practices, and individual or small group formats. Research findings on MyiLOGS are documented in the literature (Kurz, Elliott, Lemons et al., 2014; Kurz, Elliott, Kettler, & Yel, 2014) and at the measure's website (www.myilogs.com). MyiLOGS is one measure that may be used to represent OTL for persons interested in its influence on instruction and student achievement (For a case study involving this measure, see Kurz's Chap. 9 of the current volume).

Academic Enablers

Academic enablers (e.g., social skills, engagement behaviors, motivation, study skills) are skills that facilitate students' interest and engagement in instructional and learning activities. Interest and engagement are part of meaningful access to instructional and testing events. The concept of academic enablers evolved from the work of researchers who explored the relationship between students' nonacademic behaviors (e.g., social skills and motivation) and their academic achievement (Gresham & Elliott, 1990; Wentzel, 1993). For example, in a 5-year longitudinal study, Caprara and colleagues found the social skills of third-grade students were better predictors of eighth-grade academic achievement, compared to the academic skills of third-grade students (Caprara, Barbaranelli, Pastorelli, Bandura, & Zimbardo, 2000). Even stronger findings were reported by Malecki and Elliott (2002), who showed social skills correlated approximately 0.70 with end-of-year academic achievement as measured by high-stakes tests. Finally, DiPerna and colleagues' (DiPerna, Volpe, & Elliott, 2001; DiPerna, Volpe, & Elliott, 2005) findings as summarized in Fig. 1.2 indicated social skills (i.e., interpersonal skills) play a significant role in predicting the achievement of elementary students in language arts and mathematics. As noted in the illustrated structural model, interpersonal skills work through motivation to influence both engagement and study skills, which are proximal influences directly on academic achievement.

As documented in the work of DiPerna and others, academic enablers can influence learning across a range of content areas, including language arts, mathematics, and science. Therefore, academic enabling skills are included within the IATS Paradigm because they impact the degree to which the OTL can be converted into the learning of target constructs. That is, academic enablers facilitate student interest and engagement in instruction about new content or material, allowing students to capitalize on OTL events in schools.

Academic Competence Evaluation Scales DiPerna and Elliott (2002) included a measure of academic enablers on the Academic Competence Evaluation Scales, a teacher-report and self-report measure designed to provide information on students' strengths and weaknesses in both academic skills and enablers. Academic enablers subscales include interpersonal skills, engagement, motivation, and study skills. Teachers and students completing the ACES evaluate the frequency for enablers on a 5-point scale (1 = *Never*, 2 = *Seldom*, 3 = *Sometimes*, 4 = *Often*, and 5 = *Almost Always*). Evidence regarding the validity of both forms of the ACES is available in the *ACES Manual* (DiPerna & Elliott, 2002). Persons interested in the influence of academic enablers on achievement test scores may use the ACES to estimate this relationship. Academic enabling skills can be taught and measured and have been found to facilitate engagement in learning. When provided opportunities to learn accessible material, academic enablers serve to advance learning and academic performance.

Test Accessibility

Accessibility in assessment refers to the degree to which a test permits the examinee to demonstrate achievement on the targeted construct. Test accessibility is included within the IATS

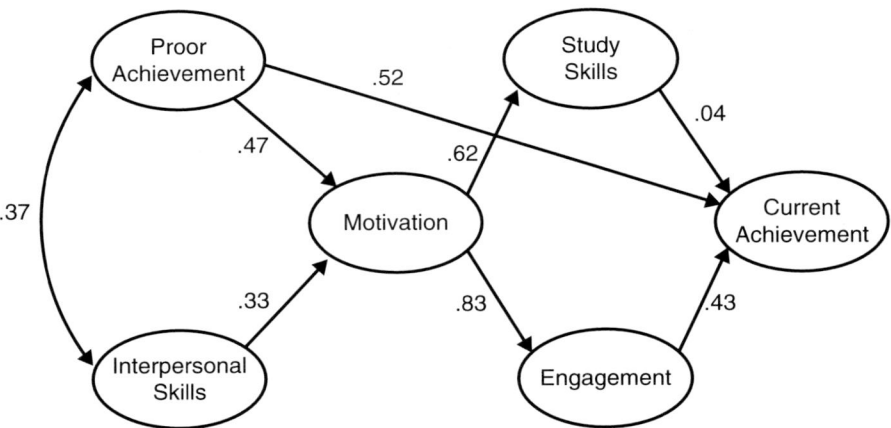

Fig. 1.2 Interpersonal skills work through motivation to influence both engagement and study skills, which are proximal influences directly on academic achievement (DiPerna et al., 2005; reprinted by permission of Elsevier.)

Paradigm because it has clear implications for interpretation of the test score; a student for whom a test event contains access barriers may not attain a meaningful score – that is, the inferences drawn from her test score may be invalid. Kettler et al. (2009) indicated "Access, therefore, must be understood as an interaction between individual test-taker characteristics and features of the test itself" (p. 530). Because of this, the accessibility of a test ultimately varies from student to student. Therefore, accessibility as a test characteristic may describe the degree to which the test allows all individuals within the intended population to demonstrate what they know and can do on the target construct. To illustrate, consider two test items: the first includes on a single page the necessary content for solving the item and the second includes the same content but presents it across several pages. The two items may be equally accessible for individuals with above-average working memory, but for individuals with working memory limitations, the first item may be significantly more accessible.

Universal Design for Assessment Just as UDL offers a framework for considering the quality of instruction, its principles can be applied for Universal Design in Assessment (UDA), which is a framework for considering the quality of tests and other assessment tools. Many achievement test items written by teachers and professional test developers can be improved to reduce access barriers (see Elliott et al., 2010; Kettler et al., 2011) and enhance measurement of the target construct. Accessible items, therefore, should contain little or no content that requires a test-taker to demonstrate skills that are irrelevant to the construct intended for measurement – lest these "access skills" impact test score interpretations. This is of particular importance in cases in which access skills are challenging for the examinee. A common example is the need to read narrative text to solve a mathematics problem. For an examinee with low reading ability, complex text in such a test item may represent an access barrier that precludes him from fully demonstrating his mastery of the target construct of the item. Across the range of items on a test, inferences about his knowledge, skills, and abilities in the mathematics domain may be negatively biased.

The inclusion of extraneous and/or construct irrelevant demands, therefore, must be addressed at both the item and test levels to ensure the resulting scores represent, to the greatest extent possible, a measure of the target skills or knowledge that is free from the influence of ancillary interactions due to access barriers. To this end, cognitive load theory (CLT; Chandler & Sweller, 1991), a model for understanding the effects of various features of instructional task demands on learning outcomes, offers a useful lens through which to understand and evaluate the accessibility of items and tests. (In Chap. 13 of the current volume, Beddow details how CLT can be used to design and evaluate tests and items to enhance their accessibility.) With the limitations of human working memory in mind, CLT indicates for optimal learning efficiency designers of instructional materials and test items should aim to eliminate extraneous load while maximizing intrinsic load. This helps a learner allocate her cognitive resources to the primary objectives of the item or test and not be burdened by extraneous material irrelevant to the process of solving the problem.

Using CLT, UDA guidelines, and knowledge of information processing challenges of many students with disabilities, Beddow, Kettler, and Elliott (2008) created tools for educators to develop accessible test items that yield scores from which inferences are equally valid for all examinees. Specifically, Beddow et al. (2008) developed the Test Accessibility and Modification Inventory (TAMI) and the TAMI Accessibility Rating Matrix (ARM; Beddow, Elliott, & Kettler, 2009). These tools are available to teachers and test developers at http://www.accessibletesting.com/tami/ for the design and evaluation of items on classroom and large-scale tests.

Test Accessibility and Modification Inventory
The TAMI (Beddow et al. 2008) is a tool for evaluating the accessibility of a test prior to pilot testing for reliability and validity evidence. The TAMI includes an inventory of considerations across six elements (e.g., passage, answer choices) for paper and pencil tests and four additional elements (e.g., test delivery system, audio) for computer-based tests, designed to systematically evaluate the accessibility of items. The inventory is applied to items and tests to estimate accessibility across a broad range of students. The TAMI includes 57 considerations such as the following: (a) paragraphs are appropriate in length, (b) text includes all requisite information for responding, and (c) there is sufficient space between lines. The TAMI can be used to effectively screen for the barriers to accessibility that keep students from showing what they know. If used consistently, the TAMI can improve the overall process of item writing and development.

Testing Adaptations Because accessibility refers to an interaction between the student and the test, testing adaptations are also included in this section of the IATS Paradigm. The TAMI may be used initially to evaluate item and test accessibility and subsequently to inform which adaptations are necessary for individuals and groups of test-takers. All adaptations to be provided should be selected with the intent of increasing accessibility. Because instructional adaptations and assessment adaptations are selected using the same logic, there should be a great deal of overlap between the two sets. In cases in which adaptations are needed and not provided, test accessibility may be depressed, and the degree to which desired inferences can be drawn from the test score is reduced (In Chap. 14 of the current volume, Dembitzer & Kettler examine in detail the relationship between testing adaptations and accessibility).

Historically, access barriers in testing have been addressed primarily with the use of testing accommodations, testing adaptations that improve measurement of the construct rather than changing the construct being measured. Testing accommodations are changes in the administration procedures of a test to address the special needs of individual test-takers (Hollenbeck, 2002). This definition of testing accommodations is consistent with major research reviews (Laitusis, Buzick, Stone, Hansen, & Hakkinen, 2012; Sireci, Scarpati, & Li, 2005). Testing accommodations, applied individually based on specific student needs, should provide teachers and stakeholders with the same amount of information about a student's skill level on the target construct as is provided for students not receiving accommodations. Research indicates effect sizes (the amount of change, or difference between an adapted mean score and an un-adapted mean score, divided by the pooled standard deviation of the means) of most testing adaptations on students' test scores are small, though there is evidence they are practically meaningful. These results suggest for some students, testing adaptations may function as accommodations, reducing barriers and yielding more accurate measures of achievement and in some cases higher test scores.

Based on these reviews of research and an examination of all students' needs during testing, leading testing entities such as the Smarter Balanced Assessment Consortium (*Usability, Accessibility, and Accommodations Guidelines*, Smarter Balanced Assessment Consortium, 2015) have developed a broad conceptualization of accessibility resources that includes the use of universal tools (e.g., calculator, English dictionary, spell check), designated supports (e.g., color contrast, glossary for translations), and accommodations (e.g., text to speech and read aloud for ELA reading passages, multiplication tables). This array of accessibility tools can be used to reduce access barriers that are likely to have a negative effect on students' test scores.

Reliability and Validity While the TAMI can be used to measure accessibility prior to test administration, any barriers to access that remain in a test will result in depressed reliability and validity indices across various evidence categories such as internal consistency, test-retest reliability, internal structure, and relations to other variables. For cases in which test accessibility is low, variance in the test scores reflects error, rather than variance in the target construct. The ultimate evidence for test accessibility is high-quality reliability and validity research findings. For cases in which the accessibility of tests for certain subgroups (e.g., students with functional impairments) is questioned, the evidence should be collected and analyzed on homogenous samples from these subgroups, to determine whether the test meets psychometric standards. For cases in which adaptations are used with certain subgroups, reliability and validity evidence should be collected on homogenous samples from those subgroups using those same adaptations. Historically, too much research on testing adaptations has focused on *performance* of the students, rather than on the *precision* and *accuracy* of measurement for these students. As a field, it is important to prioritize establishing the meaning of a score, prior to interpreting its magnitude.

Reliability refers to the consistency of scores and can be considered the proportion of variance that is systematic, rather than random error score variance. Reliability is estimated using a number of techniques, often based on correlation coefficients. Internal consistency is a type of reliability that addresses the homogeneity of a set of items. One common indicator of internal consistency is Cronbach's Alpha, which is the average of all of the possible split half correlations within a set of items. Test stability, alternate-form reliability, and inter-rater or inter-scorer reliability address the consistency of test scores across time, forms, and raters (if applicable) or scorers. Each estimate of reliability is sensitive to variance in at least one variable (e.g., test stability is sensitive to change over time, alternate-form reliability is sensitive to differences between forms), so it is important for a test to have reliability evidence in multiple forms and for interpretation of that evidence to be logical. For example, test-retest stability would be expected to be higher for a relatively stable construct (e.g., working memory among elementary school students) compared to a relatively fluid construct (e.g., oral reading fluency among elementary school students).

The proportion of variance in scores that is systematic rather than random can be further subdivided into true score variance and systematic error score variance. Construct validity refers to the proportion of score variance that is true score variance, or variance in the actual characteristic being measured, and can be considered the degree to which accurate inferences can be made from the score. Whereas reliability indices may not reveal that for a group of students with functional impairments in reading, scores from a test of story problems reflect reading fluency more so than mathematical calculations, validity indices should disaggregate systematic measurement of the target construct (mathematical calculations) from systematic measurement of any other construct (reading fluency).

The *Standards for Educational and Psychological Testing* (AERA et al., 2014) identify four forms of evidence that collectively reflect construct validity: content validity, validity based on response processes, internal structure validity, and validity based on relations to other variables. Content validity is the degree to which test items and their constituent parts (e.g., passage, stem, graphics, answer choices) reflect the intended construct. Content validity evidence is typically collected through expert review. Validity evidence based on response processes addresses whether respondents answer items using the strategies intended by the test developers. Such evidence may be collected through think-aloud laboratories and posttest surveys. Internal structure validity evidence is the degree to which the various parts of a test fit together as represented by the theory on which it is based. Internal structure validity evidence is often characterized using factor analysis and correlations among subscales of a test. Validity evidence based on relations to other variables is the degree to which scores positively relate with similar constructs, negatively relate with opposing constructs, and share non-relationships with unrelated constructs. Relations to other variables are often characterized using correlations with scores from similar tests. As with the various types of reliability evidence, each of these types of construct validity evidence has limitations, so the strongest validity arguments feature a combination of evidence types evaluated in a strategic manor. Once one has sufficient evidence of the validity of inferences that can be drawn from a test score, it is possible to work backward through the IATS Paradigm and consider the relative contribution of the previously described variables to that score, a process we illustrate next.

Test Scores and Subsequent Inferences

At the end of the IATS Paradigm, there are scores on items and tests to be interpreted. Jessica answered "b" to Item 1, earning an item score of 0, as part of a set of items she completed for a raw test score of 7. That raw score converted to a percentile rank of 12, indicating that Jessica's score was equal to or greater than only 12% of her statewide peers on the third-grade mathematics examination. We can draw the inference – with some level of confidence dictated by the reliability and variance of the test – that Jessica is equal to or better than about 12% of her statewide peers at performing on the third-grade mathematics test. There is not much more we can infer from this score alone.

Some primary inferences that we would like to make from Jessica's performance address the quality of instruction provided by her teacher, classroom, school, and district. We cannot draw these conclusions with confidence because we have not established the test was accessible, reliable, and valid for drawing inferences about Jessica. We do not even know the score reflected Jessica's achievement in mathematics. For example, if Jessica did not receive the extra time adaptation, her functional impairment in fluency may have kept her from showing what she knew in mathematics. The test may have had a time limit that made it inaccessible for her, and that time limit may make the scores from the test unreliable for students that have functional impairments in fluency. These are just a couple examples of issues that may have made the test inaccessible for Jessica.

Assuming that the test was accessible for Jessica, so that it reliably and validly yielded scores and subsequent inferences about her mathematics achievement, we can conclude Jessica is better than about 12% of her statewide peers at mathematics. We have not addressed the reason or reasons she has only learned that much mathematics. Without accounting for academic enablers, we cannot be sure Jessica's struggles are based on difficulty understanding the material; her struggles may be attributable to inability to get motivated and engaged in the material, to positively interact in the classroom, or to study effectively. For example, a lack of engagement in the classroom could be a barrier that keeps Jessica from learning the lessons the teacher is presenting. Such issues would internally impede Jessica's ability to learn.

Assuming Jessica has sufficient academic enablers, the within-classroom explanation for her performance is most likely based on OTL. Failure to attend class, lack of high-quality instruction, or omission of any necessary instructional adaptations could have stunted learning and caused poor performance on the examination. It is also possible that Jessica's OTL has been high, and her performance is attributable to factors outside the school or classroom, such as family distress. Recall achievement is the intended outcome of effective instruction, but the two are only related variables; they are not one in the same variable. A situation in which a score is low while indicators of OTL (e.g., MyiLOGS), academic enablers (e.g., ACES), and test accessibility (e.g., TAMI) are high may be the exception. Such a finding does not necessarily imply one of the indicators is wrong. Additional hypotheses and data collection may be necessary to identify the barriers to learning and demonstrating proficiency. A nuanced view of test score interpretation is particularly important because the impact of policy on accessibility – the topic of next section – is increasing.

Legislative Basis for Access

Access to education, and in particular the grade-level curriculum, lies at the heart of virtually all educational legislation and sound instruction for students with disabilities. The Rehabilitation Act of 1973 (Section 504) and the Individuals with Disabilities Education Act of 1975 as well as its subsequent reauthorizations served as the foundation for the inclusion of students with disabilities in standards-based reform and test-based accountability under the No Child Left Behind Act (NCLB) of 2001. The access to the general curriculum mandates in the reauthorization of IDEA in 1997 (a) provided all students with disabilities access to a challenging curriculum, (b) yielded high expectations for all students with disabilities, and (c) ensured all students with disabilities were included in test-based accountability mechanisms such as large-scale testing, progress monitoring, and public performance reporting. A few years later, the universal accountability provisions of NCLB continued to underscore and expand access for students with disabilities by mandating academic content that is aligned with the local and statewide grade-level standards of students without disabilities (Kurz & Elliott, 2011).

The Every Student Succeeds Act (ESSA) of 2016 continued this emphasis by providing funding for states to develop and demonstrate innovative assessment systems that are "accessible to all students, such as by incorporating the principles of universal design for learning" (Section 1204 (e)(2)(A)(vi)). The ESSA also allotted funds "for the purposes of enriching the academic experience of students by promoting…school readiness through the development and dissemination of accessible instructional programming for preschool and elementary school children and their families" (Section 4616(a)). This dual emphasis on accessibility in learning and accessibility in assessment is a positive step toward a more comprehensive view of test results, consistent with the IATS Paradigm (Kettler, 2015) and the foundation of the *Handbook of Accessible Instruction and Testing Practices*.

We conclude this introductory chapter with an introduction to the sections and chapters of this text, which go into greater detail about the accessibility considerations identified in this chapter.

Introduction to the Handbook of Accessible Instruction and Testing Practices

The *Handbook of Accessible Instruction and Testing Practices* is divided into four sections based on their intended application to accessibility in learning and achievement. The first section, Professional Policies and Considerations, addresses the broad policy influences that affect accessibility practices in the United States and abroad. *Weigert's* "U.S. Policies Supporting Inclusive Assessments for Students with Disabilities: A 60-Year History" is a thorough review of American educational policy from legislation of the 1950s and 1960s through the ESSA of 2016. In "International Policies that Support Inclusive Assessments," *Davies* compares the policies of the United States, Australia, and China to provide a global context for issues we often consider solely in a domestic context. *Stone and Cook* provide a technical and theoretical analysis of access and related assessment issues in "Fair Testing and the Role of Accessibility." Concluding this section, in "Designing, Developing, and Implementing an Accessible Computer-Based National Assessment System," *Chia and Kachchaf* elaborate on the Smarter Balanced Assessment Consortium's handling of accessibility considerations. Collectively these chapters allow the reader to explore accessibility concerns deeply with regard to policy and theory, as well as broadly across nations and decades, to draw conclusions about trends and the current state of instruction and assessment.

The next section on Special Populations recognizes that accessibility is often most observable in its absence. Chapters in this section describe the accessibility needs of special populations that share common functional impairments. *Frey and Gillispie* write about the needs of the largest of these special groups in "The Accessibility Needs of Students with Disabilities: Special Considerations for Instruction and Assessment." In "Assessing Students with Autism: Considerations and Recommendations," *Beddow* addresses the rapidly growing population of individuals with autism spectrum disorder. Concluding this section, *Boals, Castro, and Shafer-Willner* address accessibility needs shared by students who are learning English as a second language in "Moving beyond Assumptions of Cultural Neutrality to Improve Accessibility and Opportunity to Learn for English Language Learners." The chapters in this section provide specific guidelines for the groups they examine in depth and also highlight accessibility principles by discussing populations with whom they are extremely salient.

The third section on Classroom Connections pivots toward accessibility in the classroom, an area that has received increased attention over the past 5 years. *Kurz* provides a detailed explanation of OTL and uses the concept in the context of multitiered service delivery models to operationalize high-quality Tier 1 instruction in "Confronting the Known Unknown: How the Concept of Opportunity to Learn Can Advance Tier 1 Instruction." In "Response-to-Intervention Models and Access to Services for All Students," *Glover* goes beyond individual students and addresses instructional access on a systemic level. Concluding this section, *Rose, Robinson, Hall, Coyne, Jackson, Stahl, and Wilcauskas* provide a detailed explanation of UDL in "Accurate and Informative for All: Universal Design for Learning (UDL) and the Future of Assessment." Collectively, these chapters address the critical components of accessible instruction, including the provision of opportunities, universal design to support learners, and differentiated instruction for different learning needs.

The final section informs and updates readers on the area of accessibility that has received the most attention to date: Test Design Principles and Innovative Practices for More Accessible Tests. In *Albano and Rodriguez's* "Item Development Research and Practice," readers are introduced to guidelines for writing items, as well as to the research and theory that provide support for those practices. In "Cognitive Load Theory for Test Design," *Beddow* provides an intricate treatment of accessibility from a novel theoretical perspective with a focus on reducing access barriers for individuals with working memory limitations. *Dembitzer and Kettler* focus on the effect changes made to items and tests have on precision and accuracy in "Testing Adaptations: Research to Guide Practice." In "Promoting Valid Assessment of Students with Disabilities and English Learners," *Sireci, Banda, and Wells* address changes to improve measurement of the target construct in an environment that is increasingly computer-based. *Russell* delves into technological advances to increase test access in "Recent Advances in the Accessibility of Digitally Delivered Educational Assessments." Collectively, these chapters cover the importance of appropriately designing and providing accommodations for items and tests in both paper-and-pencil and computer formats.

The 4 sections and 17 chapters contained in this volume collectively address the issues relevant to accessibility of instruction and testing practices. We hope you find them exciting, fulfilling, and influential; for now we will leave you with some preliminary conclusions on issues that can be better understood through this handbook!

(Introductory) Conclusions

Much has been done and continues to be done to increase the likelihood all students have access to both instruction and assessments. Recent legislation, theory, and research have highlighted the importance of accessibility across the educational milieu. At the same time, technological advancements have brought the possibility of universal design and access for a diverse population of students within reach. These developments provide an optimistic outlook regarding the accessibility of assessments and instructional practices in the near future.

While advances in accessibility are being made, misconceptions about the concept persist. Accessibility may be most readily identified as an issue of fairness, but it has broader implications of efficacy, validity, and equal opportunity for all students. These concepts are interrelated and cannot be fully considered independently of each other. Also, accessibility has historically been associated with the *performance* of students, rather than with the *precision* and *accuracy* of measurement for these students. Such an association is at odds with the philosophy that the access we are providing is to learn material and to have that learning accurately measured. A third misconception is that individual characteristics create access barriers to instruction and testing. It is rather the case that access is a function of the sufficiency of design and implementation features of instructional scenarios and test events to interact with a diverse population of students.

We conclude this introductory chapter of the *Handbook of Accessible Instruction and Testing Practices* with a couple recommendations that may be reinforced, altered, and even challenged over the course of the next 16 chapters. The first is that as a field, it is important to prioritize establishing what a score means prior to interpreting its magnitude. The access we seek for students is first and foremost to enable them to learn and to achieve, rather than merely to attain equal mean scores across groups. The next conclusion is that the logical process for drawing inferences from test scores is to use a multiple-measure model to allow for increased sophistication of inferences about achievement. While the IATS Paradigm is one such model, it is more important to recognize the broad array of variables that impact a test score, rather than to agree on their organization and relative impact. Finally, access gaps in instruction and OTL must be eliminated. Although some students may not reach desired achievement levels, differences between groups in access to instruction and OTL are entirely unacceptable. These are the elements of a truly accessible free and appropriate public education to which all students are entitled.

References

American Educational Research Association, American Psychological Association, & National Council on Measurement in Education. (2014). *Standards for educational and psychological testing*. Washington DC: American Educational Research Association.

Assistive Technology Act, 29 U.S.C. § 3001 et seq. (1998).

Beddow, P. A., Elliott, S. N., & Kettler, R. J. (2009). *TAMI accessibility rating matrix*. Nashville, TN: Vanderbilt University. Available at http://peabody.vanderbilt.edu/tami.xml

Beddow, P. A., Kettler, R. J., & Elliott, S. N. (2008). *Test accessibility and modification inventory*. Nashville, TN: Vanderbilt University. Available at http://peabody.vanderbilt.edu/tami.xml

Caprara, G. V., Barbaranelli, C., Pastorelli, C., Bandura, A., & Zimbardo, P. G. (2000). Social foundations of children's academic achievement. *Psychological Science, 11*, 306–310.

Chandler, P., & Sweller, J. (1991). Cognitive load theory and the format of instruction. *Cognition and Instruction, 8*, 293–332.

Common Core State Standards Initiative. (2013). Retrieved from www.corestandards.org on May 2, 2017.

DiPerna, J. C., & Elliott, S. N. (2002). Promoting academic enablers to improve student achievement. *School Psychology Review, 31*, 293–298. Retrieved from http://www.nasponline.org/publications/spr/sprmain.aspx

DiPerna, J. C., Volpe, R., & Elliott, S. N. (2001). A model of academic enablers and elementary reading/language arts achievement. *School Psychology Review, 31*, 298–312.

DiPerna, J. C., Volpe, R., & Elliott, S. N. (2005). A model of academic enablers and mathematics achievement in elementary grades. *Journal of School Psychology, 43*, 379–392.

Elliott, S. N., Braden, J. P., & White, J. (2001). *Assessing one and all: Educational accountability and students with disabilities*. Alexandria, VA: Council for Exceptional Children.

Elliott, S. N., Kettler, R. J., Beddow, P. A., Kurz, A., Compton, E., McGrath, D., … Roach, A. T. (2010). Effects of using modified items to test students with persistent academic difficulties. *Exceptional Children, 76*(4), 475–495.

Elliott, S. N., & Kettler, R. J. (2015). Item and test design considerations for students with special needs. In S. Lane, T. M. Haladyna, & M. Raymond (Eds.), *Handbook of test development* (2nd ed., pp. 374–391). New York, NY: Routledge, Taylor and Francis.

Elliott, S. N., Kurz, A., & Schulte, A. (2015). Maximizing access to instruction and testing for students with disabilities: What we know and can do to improve achievement. *Smarter balanced assessment consortium spotlight series for teachers supporting students with disabilities*. UCLA: Los Angeles.

Every Student Succeeds Act, 20 U.S.C. § 6301 (2015).

Gresham, F. M., & Elliott, S. N. (1990). *Social skills rating system*. Circle Pines, MN: American Guidance Service.

Heafner, T. L., & Fitchett, P. G. (2015). An opportunity to learn US history: What NAEP data suggest regarding the opportunity gap. *High School Journal, 98*(3), 226–249. https://doi.org/10.1353/hsj.2015.0006

Herman, J. L., Klein, D. C., & Abedi, J. (2000). Assessing students' opportunity to learn: Teacher and student perspectives. *Educational Measurement: Issues and Practice, 19*(4), 16–24.

Higher Education Opportunity Act of 2008. 20 U.S.C. § 1001 (2008).

Hollenbeck, K. (2002). Determining when test alterations are valid accommodations or modifications for large-scale assessment. In G. Tindal & T. Haladyna (Eds.), *Large scale assessment programs for all students* (pp. 109–148). Mahwah, NJ: LEA.

Individuals With Disabilities Education Act, 20 U.S.C. § 1400 (1975).

Individuals With Disabilities Education Act, 20 U.S.C. § 1400 (1997).

Ketterlin-Geller, L. R., & Jamgochian, E. M. (2011). Instructional adaptations: Accommodations and modifications that support accessible instruction. In S. N. Elliott, R. J. Kettler, P. A. Beddow, & A. Kurz (Eds.), *Handbook of accessible achievement tests for all students: Bridging the gaps between research, practice, and policy* (pp. 131–146). New York: Springer.

Kettler, R. J. (2012). Testing accommodations: Theory and research to inform practice. *International Journal of Disability, Development, and Education, 5*(1), 53–66. https://doi.org/10.1080/1034912X.2012.654952

Kettler, R. J. (2015). Adaptations and access to assessment of common core content. *Review of Research in Education, 39*, 295–330. https://doi.org/10.3102/0091732x14556075

Kettler, R. J., Elliott, S. N., & Beddow, P. A. (2009). Modifying achievement test items: A theory-guided and data-based approach for better measurement of what students with disabilities know. *Peabody Journal of Education, 84*, 529–551. https://doi.org/10.1080/01619560903240996

Kettler, R. J., Rodriguez, M. R., Bolt, D. M., Elliott, S. N., Beddow, P. A., & Kurz, A. (2011). Modified multiple-choice items for alternate assessments: Reliability, difficulty, and differential boost. *Applied Measurement in Education, 24*(3), 210–234. https://doi.org/10.1080/08957347.2011.580620

Kurz, A. (2011). Access to what should be taught and will be tested: Students' opportunity to learn the intended curriculum. In S. N. Elliott, R. J. Kettler, P. A. Beddow, & A. Kurz (Eds.), *Handbook of accessible achievement tests for all students: Bridging the gaps between research, practice, and policy* (pp. 99–129). New York: Springer.

Kurz, A., & Elliott, S. N. (2011). Overcoming barriers to access for students with disabilities: Testing accommodations and beyond. In M. Russell (Ed.), *Assessing students in the margins: Challenges, strategies, and techniques*. Charlotte, NC: Information Age Publishing.

Kurz, A., Elliott, S. N., & Shrago, J. S. (2009). *MyiLOGS: My instructional learning opportunities guidance system*. Nashville, TN: Vanderbilt University.

Kurz, A., Elliott, S. N., Kettler, R. J., & Yel, N. (2014). Assessing students' opportunity to learn the intended curriculum using an online teacher log: Initial validity evidence. *Educational Assessment, 19*(3), 159–184. https://doi.org/10.1080/10627197.2014.934606

Kurz, A., Elliott, S. N., Lemons, C. J., Zigmond, N., Kloo, A., & Kettler, R. J. (2014). Assessing opportunity-to-learn for students with and without disabilities. *Assessment for Effective Intervention, 40*(1), 24–39. https://doi.org/10.1177/1534508414522685

Kurz, A., Elliott, S. N., & Schulte, A. (2015). *Opportunity to learn for all students: Enhancing access to what should be taught and will be tested*. Smarter balanced assessment series for teachers supporting students with disabilities. UCLA: Los Angeles.

Laitusis, C. C., Buzick, H. M., Stone, E., Hansen, E. G., & Hakkinen, M. T. (2012). *Accommodations and accessibility tools*. Commissioned Report for the Smarter Balanced Assessment Consortium.

Malecki, C. K., & Elliott, S. N. (2002). Children's social behaviors as predictors of academic achievement: A longitudinal analysis. *School Psychology Quarterly, 17*, 1–23. https://doi.org/10.1521/scpq.17.1.1.19902.

No Child Left Behind (NCLB) Act, 20 U.S.C.A. § 6301 et seq. (2001).

Rehabilitation Act, 29 U.S.C. § 701 (1973).

Roach, A. T., Kurz, A., & Elliott, S. N. (2015). Using personalized instructional feedback data to facilitate opportunity to learn for students with disabilities. *Preventing School Failure., 59*, 168. https://doi.org/10.1080/1045988X.2014.901288

Rose, D., & Meyer, A. (2002). *Teaching every student in the digital age*. Alexandria, VA: ASCD. Available online at: http://www.cast.org/teachingeverystudent/ideas/tes/

Rose, D. H., Meyer, A., & Hitchcock, C. (Eds.). (2005). *The universally designed classroom: Accessible curriculum and digital technologies* (pp. 13–35). Cambridge, MA: Harvard Education Press.

Sireci, S. G., Scarpati, S. E., & Li, S. (2005). Test accommodations for students with disabilities: An analysis of the interaction hypothesis. *Review of Educational Research, 75*(4), 457–490.

Smarter Balanced Assessment Consortium. (2015). *Usability, accessibility, and accommodations guidelines*. Author.

Smarter Balanced Assessment Consortium. (2016). *Smarter balanced assessment consortium: Usability, accessibility, and accommodations guidelines*. July 1, 2016: Author.

Wentzel, K. R. (1993). Does being good make the grade? Social behavior and academic competence in middle school. *Journal of Educational Psychology, 85*, 357–364.

US Policies Supporting Inclusive Assessments for Students with Disabilities: A 60-Year History

Susan C. Weigert

US Policies Supporting Inclusive Assessment of Students with Disabilities

This chapter provides an overview of the past 60 years of US policies pertaining to inclusive assessment practices for students with disabilities (SWDs). At the time of this writing, states have had an opportunity to twice administer the new multistate consortia-developed college- and career-ready assessments first released in 2015 and have adjusted their efforts in the face of several new Federal policies—the rescinding of the regulation on modified achievement standards, flexibility requests which called for higher expectations for the attainment of college and career readiness for all students, revised concepts of *test fairness* in the Standards for Educational and Psychological Testing (American Educational Research Association [AERA], American Psychological Association [APA], and National Council on Measurement in Education [NCME], 2014), and significant guidance from the Department of Education Office of Special Education and Rehabilitation clarifying the meaning of *access to the general education curriculum* for SWDs. Of equal importance, the *Every Student Succeeds Act* (ESSA) has handed accountability for testing results to states, providing some relief from the temptation for states to "game the system" by setting lower achievement standards or finding ways to exclude SWDs from participation. The newly reauthorized ESSA and Title I regulations have additionally encouraged state innovation in the format, accessibility, and timing of assessment through model demonstration authority that permits states to develop assessments that can be embedded into instruction—in place of high-stakes end-of-the-year assessments. Many of the flexibilities under the new law hold promise to support teachers in collecting useful information from assessments and in ensuring that appropriate access tools are provided for each SWD individually. In the following section, some of the key historical events that have brought about this new era of inclusive assessment will be revisited. Table 2.1 provides an advance overview of legislative milestones that have increased equity and raised expectations for SWDs in the USA over the past 60 years.

Note: the views expressed in this chapter are solely those of the author in her private capacity. No official support or endorsement by the US Department of Education is intended nor should it be inferred.

S. C. Weigert (✉)
US Department of Education, Office of Special Education Programs, Washington, DC, USA
e-mail: sweigert2@verizon.net

Table 2.1 Key legislative and regulatory events with implications for inclusion of SWDs in standards and assessments

Event	Year	Implication for inclusion
PL 93–112, section 504 of the Rehabilitation Act	1973	Required reasonable accommodations for students with physical or mental impairments. Required assessments to be provided in a child's "normal mode of communication" (including native language), whenever feasible
PL 93–380, ESEA	1974	Mandated access to a "free and appropriate" public education (FAPE) in the "least restrictive" environment deemed possible
PL 94–142, Education for All Handicapped Children Act	1975	Mandated that testing materials and procedures used for evaluation and placement not be the sole criterion for determining an appropriate educational program for a child with a disability
Regulations amending the Rehabilitation Act of 1973	1977	Educational tests were to be selected and administered to ensure that the results of testing accurately reflected the student's educational achievement level rather than merely reflecting the student's impaired skills (except when those skills were the factors measured by the test)
Regulations amending the Rehabilitation Act of 1977	1980	Assessment results used for college admissions were not to merely reflect the applicant's impaired sensory, manual, or speaking skills
PL 101–476, IDEA	1990	Inclusion focused on physical placement of SWDs in age- and grade-appropriate classrooms
PL 103–382, ESEA: Improving America's Schools Act	1994	Required states to have valid, reliable, and aligned assessments based on challenging content standards in the four core academic subjects by school year 2000–2001. Testing was only required three times in K-12. While SWDs were included, there were no consequences for failure to include them
PL 103–227 Goals 2000 Educate America Act	1994	Set forth requirements for state improvement plans, including voluntary adoption of standards for content, student performance, and opportunity to learn
PL 105–17 IDEA amendments	1997	Required SWDs to be included in all general state- and district-wide assessment programs and, for those who could not participate, required that states develop and implement alternate assessments by 2000. Employed the IEP as a tool to ensure inclusion in state standards and assessments
PL 107–110 The No Child Left Behind Act	2001	Required inclusion of 95% of SWDs in statewide accountability systems based on state reading and math standards, including annual testing for all students in grades 3–8 and annual statewide progress objectives
PL 108–446 IDEA	2004	Permitted new classroom-based assessments to be developed for the purpose of assisting with the identification of learning disability through the assessment of a student's response to tiered evidence-based interventions (RTI)
Joint Title I IDEA regulations	2007	Provided flexibility for states to administer an alternate assessment against a reduced performance standard (modified academic achievement standard—AA-MAS) for a small group of SWDs whose disability precluded them from achieving grade-level proficiency in the same time frame as other students
Title I regulations amending ESEA and IDEA	2015	Rescinded the authority of states to define modified academic achievement standards for eligible students with disabilities explaining that new research indicated that SWDs could make academic progress with evidence-based instructional strategies and supports and that new college- and career-ready assessments were designed to facilitate valid reliable and fair assessment of SWDs formerly eligible for the AA-MAS
PL 114–95 ESSA reauthorization	2015	States were required to establish achievement standards aligned to requirements for college and career readiness. Restricted participation in alternate assessment to 1% of the population. States were required to apply universal design for learning (UDL) in assessment development and ensure availability of appropriate accommodations such as assistive technology devices. Permitted assessment to be administered in the form of multiple interim assessments and adaptive assessments

Assessment Policies in the 1960s and 1970s: Inclusion with Protections

The history of inclusive assessment policies in the USA has been a product of many political and practical influences, but at the root of these developments has been the principle of equal protection. Title VI of the Civil Rights Act of 1964 prohibited discrimination on the basis of race, sex, color, or national origin, rather than on the basis of disability. The spirit of this law swept SWDs into the same political current and helped to ensure the equity of their educational opportunities. The passion for equal access to education as a civil right was best characterized by Chief Justice Warren's opinion on Brown v. Board of Education in 1954:

> In these days it is doubtful that any child may reasonably be expected to succeed in life if he is denied the opportunity of an education. Such an opportunity, where the State has undertaken to provide it, is a right that must be made available to all on equal terms. (Brown v. Board of Education, 347 U.S. 483, 1954, quoted in Russo & Osborne, 2008 p. 493)

While policies of inclusion were a widely accepted solution to problems of inequity in public education, compulsory education statutes during the 1960s and early 1970s left the authority to school districts to decide whether SWDs could "benefit" from instruction (Russo & Osborne, 2008). Yet the inclusion principles were eventually codified in PL 93–112, Section 504 of the Rehabilitation Act of 1973, which prohibited discrimination against individuals with disabilities in federally funded programs and required reasonable accommodations for students with physical or mental impairments that "substantially limited" them in one or more major life activities, including learning (29 USC § 706 (7) (B)). In addition to physical and sensory handicaps, Section 504 of the Rehabilitation Act applied to persons with 'mental' disabilities such as mental retardation, traumatic or organic brain syndromes, emotional disturbance, specific learning disabilities, and other cognitively disabling conditions (Phillips, 1994).

The Rehabilitation Act also defined the meaning of a free and appropriate public education (FAPE) and specified that appropriate education included educational services designed to meet the individual education needs of SWDs "as adequately" as the needs of students without disabilities were met. Yet the only assessment-related provisions of the Act were those that required that assessments be provided in a child's "normal mode of communication" (including native language) unless it was clearly not feasible to do so.

The principle of inclusion in the Rehabilitation Act was later incorporated into the ESEA amendments of 1974 (PL 93–380), which also mandated the "free and appropriate public education (FAPE)" in the "least restrictive environment (LRE)." These provisions were codified a year later in the Education for All Handicapped Children Act (PL 94–142). Yet at the time, FAPE simply meant access to special education and related services—in conformity with individualized academic and behavioral goals stated in the student's individualized education program (IEP), rather than connoting access to the general education curriculum. A new requirement for inclusive assessment of SWDs in PL 94–142 §612 (5) (C) mandated that testing and procedures used for evaluation and placement not be the sole criterion for determining an appropriate educational program for a child with a disability. Implied in this requirement was the desire to "protect" SWDs from the consequences of assessments that were designed more for the purposes of sorting and ranking students rather than for ensuring their access to an appropriate education.

The 1977 regulations amending the Rehabilitation Act of 1973 established further guidelines for evaluation and testing of children with impairments (§104.35) and required that tests and other evaluation materials meet requirements for validity for the specific purposes for which the tests were used and that they be administered by trained personnel in conformity with test developers' instructions. Further, the type of assessments to be used for educational evaluation of SWDs was to include those tailored to assess specific areas of educational need, not merely those designed to measure a student's IQ. Finally, educational tests were to be selected and administered to ensure that the results of testing accurately reflected the student's educational aptitude or achievement level (or whatever educational factor was to be measured by the test), rather than merely reflecting the student's impaired sensory, manual, or speaking skills (except when those skills were the factors measured by the test). In retrospect, these provisions of the 1977 regulations attempted to address what is now termed "ableism"–policies and expectations developed for nondisabled persons, applied to persons with disabilities in ways that disadvantage them (Hehir, 2005). As in the prior decade, the era of the 1970s was a time in which SWDs were given assessments that had never been designed with their access needs or their rate of learning in mind. The 1977 regulations provided protections against "disparate impact" of assessments for SWDs, yet this protection required that the student be "otherwise qualified"—capable of meeting the same standards required for nondisabled students. As US Supreme Court Justice Powell commented:

> Section 504 imposes no requirement upon an educational institution to lower or to effect substantial modifications of standards to accommodate a handicapped person. (Southeastern Community College v. Davis 442 U.S. 397, 1979 Supreme Court of United States)

The 1980s and 1990s: IEP as Curriculum

As had been the case in the 1977 regulations, regulatory changes to the Rehabilitation Act in 1980 required that assessments used for college admissions constitute validated predictors of college aptitude or college achievement, rather than merely reflecting the applicant's impaired sensory, manual, or speaking skills. Yet the 1980 regulations continued to permit use of tests with established disproportionate adverse effects on SWDs, provided that an alternate test with a less disproportionate effect was unavailable. That same year, when President Jimmy Carter established the Department of Education (ED) as a cabinet-level agency with a mission to ensure that educational opportunities were not denied on account of race, creed, color, national origin, or sex, disability was not included among the list of protected categories. In addition, Section 103 (a) of the Department of Education Organization Act (PL 96–88) prohibited ED from exercising any control over the curriculum or any program of instruction or selection of instructional materials by any school system or educational institution.

Soon after the establishment of the new agency, Education Secretary Terrel Bell created the National Commission on Excellence in Education which produced a report on the status of American education entitled *A Nation at Risk*. The report concluded that the country was threatened by a "rising tide of mediocrity", that over 10% of 17-year-olds were functionally illiterate, that SAT scores were declining across the country, and that many students required remediation courses even after entering college. The report concluded that comprehensive strategies to reform education across the country were needed (National Commission on Excellence in Education, 1983). The needed reforms were delayed pending a fuller picture of student performance, by instituting on a statewide, voluntary basis, the national assessment of all students (Ginsberg, Noell, & Plisko, 1988). During this decade and throughout the next, however, participation of SWDs in the national assessment (later, the National Assessment of Educational Progress or NAEP) remained minimal (Thurlow, Seyfarth, Scott, & Ysseldyke, 1997). In addition, most state assessment programs based their inclusion decisions on the basis of time spent in the regular classroom (Thurlow & Yesseldyke, 1993). Some factors that belied high exclusion rates on the NAEP cited by NCEO included unclear participation guidelines, sampling plans that systematically excluded students in separate schools or those not in graded classes, and "altruistic" motivation to reduce stress on students not expected to perform well (Zigmond & Kloo, 2009). Additionally, some states were unwilling to make accommodations to students to permit participation of SWDs in the NAEP (Ysseldyke, Thurlow, McGrew, & Shriner, 1994).

On the state assessment front, SWDs were included only slightly more often than in the NAEP. Shriner and Thurlow (1993) document that in the early 1990s, fewer than 10% of SWDs were being included in state assessments. As a consequence of the widespread assessment exclusion policies for the first two decades after the establishment of the Office of Special Education Programs (OSEP), there was very little known about the academic outcomes of SWDs (Ysseldyke et al., 1994).

When IDEA was reauthorized in 1990 as PL 101–476, the focus of the law remained on physical inclusion—greater inclusion in community schools, least restrictive placement of students, and transition services. Placements of SWDs in classes were to be age and grade appropriate with a minimum of placement in self-contained classrooms. Teaching methods for including SWDs in the general education classrooms began to involve cooperative learning and peer-instruction models. Nevertheless, the emphasis was placed on physical inclusion, as if being placed with nondisabled students was sufficient or even more important than the quality or effectiveness of their academic experience (Danielson, 2009). While teaching staff were expected to "adapt" the curricular content, in doing so, they were encouraged to choose a grade-level curriculum that was "developmentally" most suited to each SWD's typically below-grade level IEP goals, rather than to find ways to intensify supports and interventions to ensure the student could access grade-level standards (Simon, Karasoff, & Smith, 1991).

IDEA 1990 funded studies and investigations through which to collect information needed for program and system improvements by states and LEAs. The results of the National Longitudinal Transition Study became available to OSEP shortly before the 1997 authorization and helped to shed light on the degree to which inclusion efforts were failing to ensure the effective instruction of SWDs (Danielson, 2009).

Prior to the 1994 Elementary and Secondary Education Act (ESEA) reauthorization, Title I funds were to be distributed to schools on the basis of the poverty level and economic needs of students rather than on the basis of performance on state assessments. But the reauthorized 1994 ESEA shifted the focus to assessing outcomes for all children, including students with disabilities, in key disciplines: mathematics, science, history, geography, civics, English, the arts, and other languages. The reauthorized ESEA attempted to ensure that "all students," including "special needs" students, met high academic standards; that teaching and learning improved; that schools were provided flexibility coupled with responsibility for student performance; that schools and districts worked cooperatively with parents and the community; and that Federal aid went to the poorest students (US Department of Education, 1993).

The reauthorized ESEA endeavored to improve learning through reform approaches that were similar to other countries whose students were thought to be outperforming American students, particularly in the fields of science and mathematics. Accordingly, closely following ESEA 1994 the Goals 2000 Educate America Act (PL 103–227) was signed into law March 31, 1994. The objective of the Goals 2000 Act was to ensure that by the year 2000 "all students" would leave grades 4, 8, and 12 with competency in English, mathematics, science, foreign languages, civics and government, economics, arts, history, and geography. Every student was to be prepared for responsible citizenship, postsecondary learning, and productive employment. The reforms of Goals 2000 were grounded in the concept that states would voluntarily develop more challenging content and performance standards, design instruction and assessments aligned to these standards, and participate in accountability reporting on the extent to which schools and students were meeting state standards (National Academy of Education, 1998; The White House, 1990). For some states, this prompted a first attempt to develop a broad framework for a general education curriculum (National Academy of Education, 1998). Ultimately, under the Title I requirement, all states were expected to have valid, reliable, and aligned assessments based on their new content standards in each of the four core academic subjects by school year 2000–2001.

In spite of these advances, throughout the decade of the 1990s and the first decade of 2000, among disability advocates, it was acknowledged that there existed both an education gap and an "assessment gap" for SWDs (Danielson, 2009). The National Center on Educational Outcomes (NCEO) publicly posed the question of whether SWDs were seriously being considered in the standards-based reform and pointed out that when identifying sources of data for monitoring progress toward the national goals, in 1991, the National Education Goals Panel identified data collection programs that had excluded up to 50% of SWDs (McGrew, Thurlow, Shriner, & Spiegel, 1992). NCEO questioned whether, in its quest to become first in the world, the USA had forgotten its students with disabilities (Thurlow & Yesseldyke, 1993).

The Council for Exceptional Children (CEC) testified to Congress in 1992 that the standards themselves should be constructed so as to accommodate all students, and it called for an investigation into alternative forms of assessments as well as ways to ensure that when educators worked on standards for assessments, at least one member be included who had expertise in working with individuals with disabilities (CEC testimony before House Subcommittee on Elementary, Secondary, and Vocational Education, 1992a). By the time IDEA 1997 was reauthorized, most states had established content standards in the four core content areas, yet the question of which SWDs could access these standards and participate in assessments based upon them was a subject of considerable debate. Furthermore, the type of tests that were employed to measure student performance posed barriers of their own. States began moving away from the more flexible, "authentic" performance-based assessments, which had been more inclusive of a range of student ability levels, in order to find pragmatic ways of meeting the requirements of large-scale standardized testing. "Authentic" assessments were difficult to standardize across a large and diverse population of students. Further, while most special educators believed that performance-based assessments could provide more accurate descriptions of student achievement and student progress and that they were more helpful in informing classroom practice, their administration was expensive and time-consuming.

As the standards movement gained traction, there was growing concern that widely used norm-referenced assessments were not particularly appropriate to the goals of a standards-based reform, not just in the case of SWDs but for all students. Norm-referenced tests, which had primarily been useful for school boards in comparing the performance of their students with national norms, were not aligned to the curricula that students were to be taught under the new standards movement and provided little information other than "standing" in relation to comparison groups. During the mid-1990s, many states justified the exclusion of SWDs from standardized testing on the basis of fairness—that, because the IEP defined the content SWDs should be taught, SWDs had never received an opportunity to learn the material assessed on general assessments. Later, states began to justify the exclusion of SWDs on the basis of utility—arguing that, due to the tests' lack of sensitivity at the lower ranges of performance, assessment results did not provide any useful information about the academic performance or the educational needs of SWDs. Advocates complained that the use of norm-referenced testing, in which SWDs, as a group, invariably fell into the lower percentiles of performance, had perpetuated the assumption that SWDs were not capable of making academic progress.

While many in the special education field were divided as to how SWDs should participate in the standards-based accountability movement, most later came to agree, as one state policymaker commented, that "the removal of special education students from the 'accountability track' resulted in their removal from the 'curriculum track'" (Koehler, 1992). In the end, the shared concern over the inclusiveness of SWDs in the accountability movement gained the most traction and succeeded in uniting leaders across the special and general education fields for the next 30 years.

Following Goals 2000, many states developed assessment systems and attempted to define "what all students should know" in their new content standards. Most states gradually shifted to the use of criterion-referenced assessments which provided more useful information for teachers, and at least a percentage of SWDs were included in these assessments. In order to assist SWDs in accessing the new criterion-referenced assessments, states usually developed a list of "standard accommodations." The four classes of standard accommodations included *presentation format*, which pertained to changes in how tests were presented, including Braille versions of tests or orally reading the directions to students with dyslexia; *response format*, which were changes in how students gave responses, including pointing to a response or dictating to a scribe; *setting of the test* could be in small groups or with an aide; and finally, *timing of the test* could include time extensions or supervised breaks during the test. Typically, "nonstandard" accommodations resulted in a "flag" on the test score, indicating, for practical purposes, that the score was earned by the student given these accommodations were of questionable validity (for more information on testing accommodations and accessibility, the reader is directed to Dembitzer and Kettler's Chap. 14, as well as to Sireci, Banda, and Wells' Chap. 15, both in the current volume).

In response to questions about the attainability of performance standards for all SWDs, during this time, the Department of Education advised states to implement alternative assessments for a "small number" of students and to implement accommodations to ensure an "equal playing field" for those students. They explained, "Assessment accommodations help students show what they know without being placed at a disadvantage by their disability" (US Department of Education, 1997). Claims about the ability of accommodations alone to overcome the disadvantages on assessment created by a student's disability were accepted by most educators. Nevertheless, the implementation of test participation guidelines for SWDs became the object of great consternation across states.

Policy experts maintained, often based upon the Supreme Court ruling in Southeastern Community College v. Davis, that standards developed for "all students" could not be relaxed for SWDs even if those assessments were supposed to be useful in guiding instruction (Phillips, 2002). Disability advocates countered that, as SWDs were not included when the standards were developed, it seemed inappropriate to hold them to these standards. In actuality, the development of content standards (which reflected the prioritized academic content states had developed) was not so much in question as was the establishment of "achievement'" standards (cut points defining proficiency or mastery of the content). The distinction between "content standards" and "performance standards" had been articulated in the "Improving America's Schools Act" of 1994 (IASA). Yet the process of setting standards was and remains one that references "typical" performance on tests of mostly nondisabled students. During the decade between the IASA and the No Child Left Behind Act, SWDs were not substantially included in the pool of students from which performance standards were established. The inclusion methods which pertained to assessments during this time were entirely focused upon the provision of testing accommodations rather than modifications to test items themselves.

Testing accommodations also evolved to become more sensitive to a wider group of SWDs. While prior to the passage of the Americans with Disabilities Act of 1990, test developers provided accommodations predominantly for students with sensory impairments; following the passage of the ADA, advocates for persons with learning disabilities argued that Federal law should also require testing accommodations and modifications for cognitive disabilities such as dyslexia and other processing impairments. Policy-makers responded that accommodations for these types of cognitive disabilities threatened the valid interpretation of a student's test score. The disability community became embroiled in another debate over inclusion of SWDs in large-scale assessments.

IDEA 1997 and Options for Alternate Assessment

Significant policy input into the 1997 IDEA reauthorization came through David Hoppe, an aide to Senator Trent Lott who was a parent of a person with disabilities who brought a diverse group of disability advocates to consensus around the issue of test participation. While the field was nearly unanimous that accountability and assessments based entirely on IEP rubrics did not make sense, at the same time, there were debates about the validity of test scores for SWDs, especially those with cognitive impairments, who had never been exposed to the grade-level curriculum being assessed. Hoppe convinced policy-makers to sidestep the partisanship in reauthorizing IDEA 1997 and urged Congress to develop a bill which would please both sides of this debate (Danielson, 2009).

By providing funding opportunities, OSEP attempted to spur the field to go beyond what was technically considered feasible in assessment and to respond to the increasing demand for teaching tools and new approaches to the assessment of SWDs. The reauthorized IDEA (1997) provided for the development of new "curriculum-based measurement" (CBM) assessments, originally developed for the purpose of educational research, to measure progress among children with disabilities given educational "interventions." The new assessments were adapted to be used in classrooms for special education, related services, and/or early intervention under § 641, (1) (G) of the law. Funds were also to be made available for the development of alternative assessments—originally for the inclusion of non-native English speakers and other minority students, to prevent misidentification of such students as SWDs. IDEA (1997) attempted to spur the research and development community to develop new formative assessments for SWDs to track progress that could not be observed in large-scale state assessments. The new formative measures called for new approaches to data collection (e.g., Fuchs & Fuchs, 2004), the use of "probes" followed by intensive, evidence-based interventions, and the recording of change. The new CBMs could be individualized for students working across a broad continuum of skill levels. They also represented a new "scientific" approach to assessment and supported the monitoring of incremental progress over time (Stecker, 2005).

While CBM assessments had the advantage of accessibility and while they provided some tools for decision-making in the classroom, advocates maintained they often had the disadvantage of removing SWDs from the general education classroom, thus reducing their opportunity to learn grade-level content aligned to the state standards:

> These assessments frequently were conducted in isolation from the larger general education curriculum. The assessments focused on immediate and discrete skill deficits and IEPs often were a collection of isolated skill objectives that led to isolated instruction…Too often, the IEP *became* the curriculum for the student, instead of a tool for defining how to implement a general education curriculum. (Nolet & McLaughlin, 2000, p. 10)

The 1997 reauthorization of the IDEA was a turning point in inclusive assessment owing to its endorsement of the participation of all children with disabilities in state assessments as well as for the requirement that alternate assessments be made available, by July 2000, for any disabled student who could not meaningfully participate in the regular state assessment even with accommodations (US Department of Education, 2000). The advent of alternate assessments greatly influenced Federal policy-makers to move somewhat away from the idea that a single standard of performance on state standards, even for purposes of accountability, must be appropriate for "all students."

States slowly accepted the realization that new assessments based on the state's content standards would have to be developed for students with the most severe disabilities—these were the students labeled with "severe-profound disabilities" and the "trainable mentally handicapped" (Quenemoen, 2009). According to Browder, Wakeman, and Flowers (2009), prior to IDEA 1997, there were three groups of SWDs: those who pursued a general education curriculum with expectations for grade-level achievement, those who required a remedial curriculum (e.g., a 7th grader working on 4th grade math), and those who required functional life skills to prepare for independent living. While prior to 1997, teachers anticipated that only the first group of SWDs would be expected to participate in state assessments, after the 1997 reauthorization, a major policy shift took hold through inclusion of students with "significant cognitive disability" (a term which first appeared in the 1997 amendments) in alternate assessments (Browder et al., 2009; Browder, Wood, Thompson, & Ribuffo, 2014). While the new alternate assessments were to be aligned with the general curriculum standards set for all students, the 1997 amendments also maintained that they "should not be assumed appropriate only for those students with significant cognitive impairments" (34 CFR §200).

In spite of the more inclusive assessment practices introduced by the 1997 IDEA, the disability community remained divided for some time by the debate over the assessment of IEP goals as an appropriate response to the new standards movement. Other advocates worried that the substitution of assessments of the attainment of IEP goals for state and national test participation would violate the spirit of inclusion—especially since IEP goals were often selected based on a "catalogue approach" in which instructional goals were simply chosen from a list of common goals or goals that could be useful in skills of "everyday life" (Browder et al., 2009). Importantly, IEP goals were never designed to bring about the transitioning of SWDs into grade-level academic content standards but rather were developed to remediate delays in academic development more generally.

In response to the new mandate for alternate assessments, states developed many types of such assessments using a variety of approaches—from simple teacher checklists of functional skills to reports of progress toward IEP goals and to portfolios of student work or performance tasks related to academic content standards (Thompson &Thurlow, 2000).

Other new elements in the 1997 IDEA amendments included a requirement for the consideration of assistive technology needs for participation in state assessments, as well as for attention to the communication needs of children who were deaf or hard of hearing or those with limited English language proficiency. In cases when an IEP team or Section 504 team determined that standard assessments, even with reasonable accommodations, did not provide a student with an opportunity to demonstrate his or her knowledge and skills, the state or school district was to provide an alternate assessment. Yet whatever assessment approach was taken, the scores of SWDs were to be included in the assessment system for purposes of public reporting and school and district accountability.

In addition to the mandates for including SWDs in state assessments, the reauthorized IDEA 1997 established new technical requirements for assessments used to determine eligibility for special education, including the mandate to provide information that was "instructionally relevant" in the evaluation of disability. Assessment instruments used for disability evaluation were also required to assess the "relative contributions" of both cognitive and behavioral factors, in addition to physical or developmental factors, on academic performance. States were required to administer such assessments to SWDs in the child's native language or typical mode of communication. In addition, any standardized tests given to a child were required to be validated for the specific purposes for which they were to be used. Additional assessment tools and strategies that directly assisted teachers in determining the educational needs of the child were also to be provided under IDEA1997.

In response to these mandates, OSEP funded a variety of projects, such as supporting computer-adaptive assessments aligned to the state standards that would be capable of identifying, through "dynamic" assessment techniques, learning issues of students with learning disabilities in order to uncover the instructional gaps they were manifesting in general education settings (e.g. Tindal, 2009). It was known that the population of students with specific learning disability (SLD) consisted of slow learners who could eventually address all of the standards, though not necessarily in the time frame required to participate fairly in the summative end-of-year assessments. OSEP struggled with how to balance the inclusion of students with high-incidence SLD in state assessments. The answer OSEP formulated to best address this was to mandate that instruction be provided by skilled teachers specifically trained to work with the SLD population.

OSEP also funded the Access Center to help teachers adapt and individualize instruction aligned to the grade-level content standards, rather than providing "out-of-level" instruction, as was a common teaching practice prior to 1997. Yet, for many advocates in the field, the use of assessments based on content standards that many SWDs could not master in the same time frame was also considered "out-of-level" assessment, since it required a typical SLD student to make more than a year's worth of average progress to learn enough grade-level material to be fairly assessed on the new assessments (Danielson, 2009).

Another effect of the 1997 revision of IDEA was to shift reform efforts to the IEP, re-envisioning it not as a guide to what SWDs were to be learning but rather employing the IEP as a tool to ensure inclusion and progress in the grade-level general education curriculum by defining each student's present level of performance, including how the student's disability affected his or her ability to be involved in and make progress in the general education curriculum. Additionally, the law required a statement in the IEP about the program modifications and supports to be used by school personnel to enable the child to be involved in and make progress in the general education curriculum and to be educated and to participate with his or her peers without disabilities.

Subsequent to the IDEA Part B regulations in 1999, which mandated inclusion of all SWDs in standards-based reform programs, many state and local education agencies still had a difficult time trying to convince teachers to teach SWDs grade-level content standards in addition to remedial instruction based upon IEP goals.

2002 No Child Left Behind Act

Under the 1994 ESEA, states had been required to test only three times during a student's tenure in the K-12 educational system. For policymakers crafting the reauthorized ESEA, this left too many intervening years in which children's academic difficulties could go unaddressed, with the result that many children were being "left behind," academically. Under the *No Child Left Behind Act* (NCLB) of 2002, states were obliged to enhance their existing assessment systems to include annual assessments in reading/language arts and mathematics for all public school students in grades 3 through 8 and at least once in grades 10 through 12 by the 2005–2006 school year. Additionally, by the 2007–2008 school year, all states were to annually assess their students in science at least once in grades 3 through 5, once in grades 6 through 9, and once in grades 10 through 12 (US Department of Education, 2003).

The NCLB required annual testing in reading and mathematics, the demonstration of "adequate yearly progress" against state-specified performance targets, and the inclusion of all students in annual assessments. Secretary of Education, Rod Paige, later succeeded by White House domestic policy advisor, Margaret Spellings, emphasized that the purpose of the NCLB provisions was to ensure that every child was learning "on grade level." The accountability for the SWD subgroup also required steps to recruit, hire, train, and retain highly qualified personnel, research-based teaching methods, and the creation of improvement programs to address local systems that fell short of performance goals.

During the same year, President George W. Bush created the President's Commission on Excellence in Special Education, a program designed to improve the dropout rate among SWDs, who were leaving school at twice the rate of their peers and whose enrollment in higher education was 50% lower. Moreover, the SLD subgroup had grown over 300% since 1976, and 80% of those with SLD reportedly had never been taught to read (President's Commission on Education, 2002). Few children in special education were closing the achievement gap. A major finding of the Commission was that although special education was based in civil rights and legal protections, most SWDs were being left behind. Several findings of the Commission included criticisms that the reauthorized 1997 IDEA placed process above results and compliance above achievement and outcomes for SWDs. Further, special education did not appear to guarantee more effective instruction for struggling students. The identification process for special education services was also criticized for being based upon a "wait-to-fail" model. In this model, a student had to be significantly performing below his (IQ-determined) anticipated performance level before he could receive special education services. Criticism was also launched against the Department of Education for becoming two separate systems, at a time when many advocates felt that general education and special education should share responsibilities for the instruction of SWDs. Another recommendation of the report was a call for improved assessment policies to prevent the exclusion of SWDs from state and district-wide assessments, still a common practice in 2001.

2002–2003 Title I Regulations Permitting Alternate Achievement Standards in Accountability

The ESEA regulations of 2002 implementing the assessment provisions of NCLB authorized the use of alternate assessments in accountability and required that states make available alternate assessments for any student unable to participate in the state's general assessments, even with accommodations. The subsequent ESEA regulations of 2003 permitted states to develop and include in accountability alternate achievement standards for students with the most significant cognitive disabilities. The regulations required that the alternate assessment be aligned with the state's academic content standards (although not with grade-level academic content standards), promotes access to the general curriculum, and reflects professional judgment of the highest achievement standards possible (34 CFR§200.1). While the regulations forced most states to begin to revise, by the year 2000, the assessments they had originally created in response to the more lenient 1997 IDEA requirements, there was little knowledge in the field of the appropriate academic content on which to base such tests. While there had been some early work on how to teach general education curriculum content to students with severe disabilities (e.g., Downing & Demchak, 1996), the mandate for alternate achievement standards aligned to the state's academic content standards had yet to become a critical impetus to change in the curriculum for SWDs with severe disabilities. Over the next decade, teachers of students with low-incidence disabilities struggled to articulate a coherent academic curriculum appropriate to the diverse population of students with significant cognitive disabilities. Yet perhaps the most significant contributing factor in delaying the development of valid and aligned alternate assessments under the NCLB was the belief among special educators charged with developing these early assessments that academic content standards were not relevant to their students and that the more appropriate content for these students consisted of "life skills" for independent living (Wallace et al., 2008). While the life skills vs. academic skills debate was to become a recurrent theme in the NCLB era, the Department of Education attempted to hold alternate assessments to standards for technical adequacy through the peer review process. These expectations included content alignment to standards (which could be standards for a grade band rather than specific to a grade) and achievement standards (i.e., expectations for the level of performance considered proficient) that were appropriate and attainable for the majority of eligible students. Over the next decade, while the quality of many alternate assessments on alternate achievement standards (AA-AAs) improved somewhat, by 2010, many states still did not have alternate assessments that met the minimal technical requirements that had been established by the Federal government. Nevertheless, results obtained through the administration of state alternate assessments began to reveal some useful information about the population of students taking them: that many eligible students were able to communicate using symbolic representation (e.g., reference to persons, things, and ideas) and that a substantial portion could learn to read and reason with mathematics (Browder, Wakeman, Spooner, Ahlgrim-Delzell, & Algozzine, 2006; Kearns, Towles-Reeves, Kleinert, & Kleinter, 2009).

Throughout the first decade of the millennium, however, many students with significant cognitive disabilities, particularly those with no communication skills, continued to be excluded from participation in alternate assessments. One study of excluded students found that many of them were able to communicate if provided augmentative and assistive technologies and that approximately 75% were able to learn sight words and use calculators to perform mathematical calculations (Kearns et al., 2009). It was the opinion of Kearns et al. (2009) that problems with inclusiveness on alternate assessment during this era had most to do with the students' opportunities to learn the content on which the assessments were based rather than on the ability levels of students themselves.

An additional problem with the implementation of alternate assessments for students with the most significant cognitive disabilities during this era was the continued difficulty of establishing achievement standards for the full range of ability reflected in this population of students. While states were permitted under ESEA regulations in 2003 to develop alternate assessments with more than one alternate achievement standard (i.e., more than one level of proficiency), in practice, IEP teams in states that adopted multiple achievement standards were reluctant to assign students to the higher, more challenging standard. Instead, teachers assigned both high- and low-performing students to the assessments associated with the lowest achievement standards, in order to ensure higher passing percentages under NCLB accountability. As a result of this practice, which continued through the next decade, the proficiency rates on alternate assessments were always much higher than rates of SWDs on the general assessment—a finding that suggests the alternate assessments were never challenging enough for the majority of students taking them. More importantly, the establishment of the lower performance expectations for this population of students had the effect of disguising rather than promoting their potential to learn.

During the first decade of the millennium, alternate assessments varied in the extent to which they actually informed parents and teachers about student academic progress. While advances in the development of classroom-based formative assessments, such as CBM, had been available for students with high-incidence disabilities such as SLD since IDEA 1997, more useful, instructionally-embedded assessments were never available for students who took alternate assessments. At the foundation of the continued accessibility problem was the need for states and districts to more clearly articulate an appropriate academic curriculum for eligible students—one that was linked to the same grade-level content standards intended for all students, yet which reflected more appropriate performance standards—i.e., content and skills within a range of difficulty, which might encourage continual progress among eligible students at all levels of ability, and at any place in the performance continuum.

IDEA 2004 and Assessments Measuring Responsiveness to Intervention

The reauthorization of the IDEA 2004 (PL 108–446) reiterated the NCLB mandate for inclusion of all SWDs in state- and district-wide assessments and clarified that IEP goals were not to be the only foci of assessment. Yet the only vision for assessment-related changes to the 2004 IDEA was a new model pertinent to for determinations of SLD based on the earlier CBM assessments. These assessments were to be used to track "responses to interventions" (RTI) in the classroom and provided an alternative to the IQ performance discrepancy model of eligibility for special education that had been the subject of criticism in the Commission report. Under IDEA 2004, the CBM assessments could be used to identify SLD by recording a student's response to a tiered system of evidence-based interventions (RTI). Such assessments could be implemented for multiple purposes, including screening students in basic skills (such as literacy or mathematics), monitoring progress in significant areas of academic weakness, and decision-making in moving unresponsive students into more intensive remedial instruction. While RTI was widely attempted across states in the decade following its appearance in the law, the practice of implementing "tiered interventions" in schools was promoted by OSEP as an evidence-based "school-wide" method for remediating slow learners, rather than simply a method to confirm the classification of SLD. The reauthorized ESSA later adopted the term "multitiered system of supports" (MTSS) in place of the term "RTI," defining it as a "comprehensive continuum of evidence-based, systemic practices to support a rapid response to students' needs with regular observation to facilitate data-based instructional decision-making" (ESSA, Section 8002). While MTSS was implemented widely in states following IDEA 2004, concerns began to surface about its effective implementation following the 2015 publication on IES study of RTI which indicated that, in practice, students were not always carefully screened for participation in the tiers of MTSS and the placement in intervention was causing lower than expected outcomes for some students (Balu et al., 2015). A growing concern about the proliferation of MTSS models for SWDs was that it not become, as the IEP once was, an alternative to access to the general education curriculum (for more information on RTI and accessibility, the reader is directed to Glover's Chap. 10 in the current volume).

2007–2015 Joint Title I IDEA Regulations Permitting Modified Academic Achievement Standards in Accountability

Nearing the end of the George W. Bush' presidential term, Secretary of Education Margaret Spellings grew concerned about the slow pace with which states were advancing to the goal of "universal proficiency" by 2014 intended by the NCLB. The Spellings administration responded to concerns expressed by states and the special education community that a small group of SWDs who were enrolled in the regular education classrooms were unable to demonstrate progress on their state's general assessment by the end of the school year (US Department of Education, 2005). The administration responded by announcing a new assessment "flexibility" to permit "persistently low-performing" SWDs to take a new type of alternate assessment based on modified academic achievement standards (AA-MAS). States argued that the need for the new alternate assessments was justified by the presence of a group of special education students (some of whom had learning disabilities and others who had intellectual disabilities, autism, or other health impairments) who were not benefitting instructionally from being placed in the general assessments. When the 2007 Joint IDEA Title I regulations were published permitting 2% of students to take alternate assessments on modified achievement standards, OSEP invested 13 million dollars for states to develop the new assessments, Disability advocacy groups soon began to object to the assessment of SWDs against a lower standard of performance. The concern of advocates was that tracking of students into less challenging coursework was being done merely for the sake of state accountability and did not benefit the affected students. Finally, when several large states enrolled a large proportion of students with learning disabilities in the modified assessments, the disability community called for the revocation of the AA-MAS flexibility, even before any of the new assessments funded by the Federal investments had been completed or implemented. In 2008, as the Obama administration commenced, disability advocates heavily lobbied the new administration to revoke state options to create alternate assessments on modified achievement standards.

One positive outcome from the era of the "modified achievement standards" came from several studies conducted during their development (e.g., Elliott et al., 2010; Elliott, Kurz, Beddow, & Frey, 2009) that revealed important information about how to improve item accessibility for students with disabilities. In 2008,

Education Secretary Arne Duncan promised significant improvements in item accessibility features of new assessments to be funded under the "Race to the Top" assessment initiative which, they argued, would eliminate any need for a test on "modified achievement standards" for students with disabilities. Three years later, the 2% flexibility was rescinded in practice by the announcement of waivers of the NCLB accountability requirements which included a requirement that states wishing to take advantage of the waiver discontinue administering the AA-MAS. Final regulations that formally rescinded the AA-MAS were not issued until nearly the end of the Obama administration, in August 2015. In its justification for the reversal of policy on modified achievement standards, the Department explained that new and better assessment accessibility for students with disabilities would end the requirement for the "2%" option:

> …The Secretary believes that these amended regulations are needed to help refocus assessment efforts and resources on the development of new general assessments that are accessible to a broader range of students with disabilities….(US Department of Education, p. 50784)

"Race to the Top" Assessment Initiatives

During the initial years of the Obama administration, the "new generation" of standards and assessments was envisioned, and policy-makers hoped that American students would become more competitive in the global marketplace as a result of these changes. Many of the goals of the Race to the Top (RTT) assessment initiative seemed to reiterate those of the Goals 2000 era. The RTT initiative endeavored to create assessments aligned to higher state standards held in common by many states—standards that were not only more streamlined than those states had developed under previous assessment policies but were more focused in the intent to teach American students to reason and critically analyze informational and literary texts, as well as to become more facile with concepts and procedures of higher mathematics. Built upon a coherent framework that progresses from kindergarten through 12th grade, the standards lend themselves to continuity and coherence, as well as to being measured through adaptive assessments capable of identifying where a student is performing in the continuum of learning. The RTT assessment (RTTA) program supported the development of new assessments capable of measuring student growth in learning new college and career-ready standards—features that promised to help provide more useful information about the progress of lower-performing students, including SWDs. Secretary Duncan explained:

> … The Department plans to support consortia of states, who will design better assessments for the purposes of both measuring student growth and providing feedback to inform teaching and learning in the classroom. All students will benefit from these tests, but the tests are especially important for students with disabilities. (Duncan, 2010)

The new policies supporting the more inclusive RTTA assessments aspired to replace the need for modified achievement standards by promoting the development of assessments that would be designed from the beginning to incorporate the performance ranges of all students, including SWDs. OSEP, in turn, funded the development of new alternate assessments on alternate academic achievement standards for students with the most significant cognitive disabilities designed to promote higher achievement than had ever been ever envisioned for this group of students, to foster development of reading and mathematical skills that would help to support entrance into the workplace by the time of high school graduation.

To maximize the inclusion of SWDs in the development of the next-generation assessments, the state-run consortia funded under the Race to the Top Assessment Program made an effort to maximize the availability of supports and accommodations for online assessments for a wide class of students by the time they were released in 2014–2015. Two of the consortia developed adaptive assessments that permitted more targeted instructional interventions for students both above and below their tested grade level. Another feature of the college- and career-ready assessments was their measurement of higher-order thinking skills by means of extended performance tasks. However, as several researchers later pointed out (e.g., Mislevy, 2015), performance task results are affected by a student's opportunity to learn, as well as the effects of "construct-irrelevant" factors inherent in language demands (Linn, 1994, p. 6). Assessment results from the states using the new RTTA assessments pointed to the need to provide SWDs with instruction designed to promote their success on such extended performance tasks (for more information on accessibility considerations in development of an RTTA, the reader is directed to Chia and Kachchaf's Chap. 5 in the current volume).

Reauthorization of the ESEA: The "Every Student Succeeds Act"

There were several key changes in the reauthorized ESEA of 2016 that promised to affect the ways that SWDs would be assessed and instructed in the future. Table 2.2 depicts the menu of options for assessment allowed under the 2016 Act.

While the 2016 ESSA did not mention the possibility for states to develop alternate assessments on grade-level achievement standards, the ESSA-amended IDEA Section 612(a)(16)(C) (codified in 20 U.S.C. 1412(a)(16)(C) has been interpreted by some to prohibit any alternate assessment other than the alternate assessment on alternate academic achievement standards). Moreover, to date, no states have successfully developed alternate assessments on grade-level achievement standards that have met the requirements of the Department of Education's peer review process. The ESSA also provides for school districts to adopt nationally recognized tests in place of the regular state assessments for high school students, such as the ACT or SAT. In 2016, over half of all US states required the participation in nationally recognized college entrance tests such as the SAT or ACT. However, these testing companies have posed barriers in the past to SWDs in their effort to obtain needed accommodations. Students, parents, and states have complained about the denial of accommodations on ACT and SAT tests or the requirements for excessive amounts of documentation to obtain them (Scott, 2011). Questions of equal access eventually prompted the Department of Justice to issue technical assistance on testing accommodations later incorporated into the 2016 ESEA (see US Department of Justice, 2015). Importantly, unless states specifically negotiate agreements with the testing companies to provide assessment accommodations, using them may

Table 2.2 Assessment options for students with disabilities under the ESSA

General assessment requirements[a]

Reading/language arts (R/LA) and mathematics general assessments in grades 3–8 and once in high school

Science general assessments once in grade spans 3–5, 6–9, and 10–12

Reading/language arts (R/LA) and mathematics alternate assessments based on alternate academic achievement standards in grades 3–8 and once in high school

Science alternate assessments based on alternate academic achievement standards once in grade spans 3–5, 6–9, and 10–12

Optional assessment flexibilities

If a state allows it, an LEA may apply to the state to administer one nationally recognized high school assessment[b] across the district in lieu of the statewide assessment in high school

8th grade students who are taking a course related to the specific end-of-course test the state uses to meet the assessment requirements under Title I, Part A for high school students may take the end-of-course test, and the results are used for accountability purposes

[a]The ESSA and 2016 assessment regulations are silent on the use of alternate assessment on grade-level achievement standards. However, the ESSA amended IDEA Section 612(a)(16)(C) (codified in 20 U.S.C. 1412(a)(16)(C)), and this section, while ambiguous, has been interpreted to prohibit any alternate assessment other than the alternate assessment on alternate academic achievement standards.
[b]"Nationally recognized high school academic assessment" means an assessment of high school students' knowledge and skills that is administered in multiple states and is recognized by institutions of higher education in those or other states for the purposes of entrance or placement into courses in postsecondary education or training programs.

limit the opportunities for these students to receive college-reportable scores (e.g., see Lazarus, & Thurlow, 2016).

The 2015 reauthorization of the ESEA required that all assessments be developed, to the extent practicable, using principles of universal design for learning.[1] In addition, it gave states the right to administer computer-adaptive assessments, including both regular and alternate assessments, for accountability. However, participation in the alternate assessment on alternate academic achievement standards was restricted under the new law to one percent of enrolled students in the state per subject, although school districts whose enrollment exceeded the cap of 1% were permitted to apply for a waiver. ESEA Title I regulations published in December 2016 reiterated these requirements and required that all assessments met technical standards of fairness, in addition to validity and reliability. However, the Department's definition of fairness was limited to technical aspects of assessments rather than inclusive of 'opportunity to learn' the content being assessed. The Department addressed the issue of fairness in its nonregulatory guidance for peer review of state assessment systems in 2015, in standard 4.2, which stated:

> The State has taken reasonable and appropriate steps to ensure that its assessments are accessible to all students and fair across student groups in the design, development and analysis of its assessments. (US Department of Education, 2015, p. 40)

The 2015 peer review guidance for state assessments required evidence pertinent to the design, development, and analysis of assessments that support their accessibility and fairness but did not make reference to several areas of fairness addressed in the *Standards for Educational and Psychological Testing*, released in 2014. The aspects of fairness cited in the *Standards* included the concept of fairness as opportunity to learn the content covered by the test.

The Department's 2016 Title I assessment regulations, however, reiterated expectations for fairness in the ESSA, as well as the requirement that general assessments be aligned with entrance requirements for the state's higher education system and with career and technical education. Alternate assessments for students with the most significant cognitive disabilities were likewise required to be aligned to requirements for competitive, integrated employment, consistent with the Workforce Innovation and Opportunity Act. In effect, the requirements reflected in these regulations promoted the highest expectations for student achievement seen in 60 years.

Under the 2016 Title I assessment regulations, states were required to ensure appropriate accommodations, such as assistive technology devices for students who need them. Another advantage of the new requirements, reflected both in the ESEA and the regulations, was the option for states to develop interim assessments to be used in accountability determinations, in place of a single end-of-year summative assessments. Students whose disabilities create limitations in executive functions or stamina to sit for hours-long assessments may benefit from the new option. Further, the technical restrictions on adaptive assessments in NCLB, in which states were not permitted to develop items above and below grade level, in order to assess the performance of students performing at those levels, have also been lifted under the 2015 ESSA. Likewise, under the new 2016 Title I assessment regulations, while an adaptive test must continue to measure a student's academic proficiency based on the state academic standards for the grade in which the student is enrolled, the assessment of performance with items above and below grade level is now expressly permitted in the law. The requirement to retain high standards for proficiency and to promote college and career readiness also does not prevent states from establishing multiple levels of proficiency, including

---

[1] The term "universal design for learning" means a scientifically valid framework for guiding educational practice that (A) provides flexibility in the ways information is presented, in the ways students respond or demonstrate knowledge and skills, and in the ways students are engaged; (B) reduces barriers in instruction; provides appropriate accommodations, supports, and challenges; and maintains high achievement expectations for all students, including students with disabilities and students who are limited English proficient *(Section 8101(51) of the ESEA; Section 103 of the Higher Education Act (20 U.S.C. 1003).*

both grade-level competency and a higher level aligned to college and career readiness. Given these new flexibilities to measure student performance more frequently, and with a wider lens to reveal above and below grade-level proficiency, it is likely that newly permitted assessment systems may indeed prove more valid indicators of the true performance of SWDs than were the alternate assessments on modified academic achievement standards.

The 2016 ESSA has continued the long-standing efforts of Congress to oppose any reduction in the rigor of achievement standards that could be established for SWDs. Other than alternate academic achievement standards for students with the most significant cognitive disabilities, the ESSA expressly prohibits any other alternate achievement standards to be established on assessments for Title I accountability. In the transition to new accountability systems in 2017, IEP teams may continue to enroll some SWDs inappropriately in alternate assessments, but the waiver of the 1% cap requirement requires that states take steps to provide oversight of LEAs that exceed the threshold to improve implementation of guidelines for participation in alternate assessments, so that the state meets the 1.0 percent cap in future years. The incentive to over-enroll SWDs in alternate assessments may be rooted in continued struggle of general and special educators to provide instruction sufficient to ensure their success on a grade-level assessment within the time frame required to take the assessment. As the implementation of these new regulation provisions is underway, a clearer picture may emerge of the success of the Federal government's efforts to apply the "all students" performance expectations to 90% of SWDs.

Conclusion: The Search for a Path to Equity of Educational Benefit

Over the past 60 years, policies supporting inclusion in standards-based assessments have helped to promote educational equity and opportunity for SWDs in American public schools. Advances are apparent both in the increased rates of high school graduation and in enrollment in postsecondary education. While under GOALS 2000 barely a third of SWDs graduated high school with a regular diploma, 63 percent did so in 2014 (NCES, 2016). While, in 1987, only 1 in 7 SWDs enrolled in postsecondary education, 25 years later, nearly two-thirds of SWDs did so (Newman et al., 2011). As policies require incorporation of UDL in test development, along with the implementation of innovative assessments, improvements in the quality of information derived from tests about the performance of SWDs are much more likely.

An interesting lesson of the past 60 years has been that Federal accountability, with its efforts to shine a spotlight on academic performance among key subgroups of students, and to hold standards high, has succeeded in motivating changes in the behaviors of stakeholders at all levels of the system—administrators, teachers, and students themselves. But equity of opportunity for SWDs to achieve greater educational benefits continues to be a distant frontier of education policy. While opportunity to learn had been mentioned in the Goals 2000 Educate America Act 20 years ago, this term has disappeared from the policy radar. In 2017 the US Supreme Court considered whether public schools are required to provide SWDs a significant, or slightly above a "de minimis," standard of educational benefit. In March, 2017,

the Court unanimously rejected the 'de minimis' standard for educational benefit and ruled that schools must provide students an education that is "reasonably calculated to enable a child to make progress appropriate in light of the child's circumstances" (Endrew F. v. Douglas Co School District, 2017).

A persistent impediment to true equity in educational outcomes for SWDs remains the expectation that the most severely impaired of these students, most of whom require more time and more intensive instruction to learn the standards-based content for their grade, must meet performance expectations for their grade within the same time period as nondisabled students. Given that these SWDs are increasingly removed from grade-level instruction to receive MTSS or other interventions, or placed in inclusive general education classrooms without supplemental supports, expectations for their achievement of equivalent standards may appear unrealistic. Is it a new form of "ableism" to create policies that hold SWDs to standards for graduation that work well for nondisabled students, without also providing modifications that ensure SWDs a viable opportunity to attain a high school diploma? While the Federal government permits extended school years (ESYs) for SWDs (to prevent loss of skill or to respond to a low degree of progress toward IEP goals), given state restrictions on eligibility for ESYs, very few SWDs are able to utilize the option for extended time permitted under the IDEA regulations, regardless of the academic benefit they might gain from a "postgraduate year."[2] While some advocates may worry that extra instructional time, even during the school year, could incentivize a slowing down of efforts to teach SWDs, it seems more likely that not doing so will persistently ensure reduced educational outcomes for those who need more time to learn the same content as their nondisabled peers.

The past 60 years of Federal policies on assessment have withstood the tendency of states to reduce performance expectations for SWDs through alternate assessments. But if the United States is to realize its aspiration for equitable achievement outcomes for SWDs, policies will need to find other ways to promote the attainment of proficiency for SWDs who simply require more time to succeed. To promote equity of achievement for SWDs, it is necessary to recognize and support their individualized learning trajectories, as well as to support and promote the development of innovative, within-year assessments that can help teachers monitor academic progress toward proficiency. Innovative assessments grounded in learning progressions, which provide guidelines for individualized instruction toward the grade-level standard, may offer the best hope yet for the future of inclusive assessment and for the attainment of both equity and excellence.

---

[2] See US Department of Education, OSEP, 2003, Letter to Givens.

References

American Educational Research Association (AERA), American Psychological Association (APA), National Council on Measurement in Education (NCME). (2014). *Standards for edu- cational and psychological testing*. Washington, DC: Author.

Balu, R., Zhu, P., Doolittle, F., Schiller, E., Jenkins, J., & Gersten, R. (2015). *Evaluation of response to intervention practices for elementary school reading. NCEE 2016–4000*. National Center for Education Evaluation and Regional Assistance.

Browder, D., Wakeman, S., & Flowers, C. (2009). Which came first, the curriculum or the assessment? In W. D. Shafer & R. W. Lissitz (Eds.), *Alternate assessments based on alternate achievement standards: Policy, practice, and potential*. Baltimore, MD: Paul H Brookes Publishing.

Browder, D., Wakeman, S., Spooner, F., Ahlgrim-Delzell, L., & Algozzine, B. (2006). Research on reading instruction for individuals with significant cognitive disabilities. *Exceptional Children, 72*, 392–408.

Browder, D. M., Wood, L., Thompson, J., & Ribuffo, C. (2014). *Evidence-based practices for students with severe disabilities*. CEEDAR Document NO. IC-3. CEEDAR Center. Retrieved on August, 31, 2015. Chicago.

Brown v. Board of Education, 347 U.S. 483. (1954).

Danielson, L. (2009, October 22). Personal communication.

Downing, J. E., & Demchak, M. (1996). First Steps: Determining individual abilities and how best to support students. In J. E. Downing (Ed.), *Including students with severe and multiple disabilities in typical classrooms: Practical strategies for teachers* (pp. 35–61). Baltimore, MD: Paul H. Brookes Publishing.

Duncan, A. (2010). Keeping the promise to all america's children. Remarks made to the council for exceptional children, April 21, Arlington, VA.

Elliott, S. N., Kettler, R. J., Beddow, P. A., Kurz, A., Compton, E., McGrath, D., … Roach, A. T. (2010). Effects of using modified items to test students with persistent academic difficulties. *Exceptional Children., 76*(4), 475–495.

Elliott, S. N., Kurz, A., Beddow, P., & Frey, J. (2009). *Cognitive load theory: Instruction-based research with applications for designing tests*. Paper presented at the Annual Convention of the National Association of School Psychologists, Boston, MA. February 24.

Fuchs, L. S., & Fuchs, D. (2004). Determining adequate yearly progress from kindergarten through grade 6 with curriculum-based measurement. *Assessment for Effective Instruction, 29*(4), 25–37.

Ginsberg, A. L., Noell, J., & Plisko, V. W. (1988). Lessons from the wall chart. *Educational evaluation and policy analysis., 10*(1), 1–10.

Hehir, T. (2005). *New directions in special education: eliminating ableism in policy and practice*. Cambridge, MA: Harvard Education Press.

Kearns, J. F., Towles-Reeves, E., Kleinert, H. L., & Kleinter, J. (2009). Who are the children who take alternate achievement standards assessments? In W. D. Schafer & R. W. Lissitz (Eds.), *Alternate Assessments Based on Alternate Achievement Standards: Policy, Practice, and Potential*. Baltimore, MD: Paul H Brookes Publishing.

Koehler, P. D. (1992). Inclusion and adaptation in assessment of special needs students in Arizona. In M. L. Thurlow & J. E. Yesseldyke (Eds.), *Can "all" ever really mean "all" in defining and assessing student outcomes? (Synthesis report No. 5)*. Minneapolis, MN: University of Minnesota, National Center on Educational Outcomes.

Lazarus, S. S., & Thurlow, M. L. (2016). *2015–16 high school assessment accommodations policies: An analysis of ACT, SAT, PARCC, and Smarter Balanced (NCEO Report 403)*. Minneapolis, MN: University of Minnesota, National Center on Educational Outcomes.

Linn, R. L. (1994). Performance assessment: Policy promises and technical measurement standards. *Educational Researcher, 23*(9), 4–14.

McGrew, K. S., Thurlow, M. L., Shriner, J. G., & Spiegel, A. N. (1992). *Inclusion of students with disabilities in national and state data-collection programs. (Technical Report 2)*. Minneapolis, MN: University of Minnesota, National Center on Educational Outcomes.

Mislevy, R. M. (2015). *Resolving the paradox of rich performance tasks*. Paper presented at the Fifteenth Annual Maryland Conference: Test Fairness in the New Generation of Large- scale Assessment October 30, The University of Maryland at College Park.

National Academy of Education. (1998). *Goals 2000: Reforming education to improve student achievement*. Washington DC: National Academy of Education.

National Commission on Excellence in Education. (1983). *A Nation at risk: The imperative for educational reform*. Washington, D.C.: U.S. Government Printing Office.

Newman, L., Wagner, M., Knokey, A. M., Marder, C., Nagle, K., Shaver, D., & Wei, X. (2011). *The post-high school outcomes of young adults with disabilities up to 8 years after high school: A report from the national longitudinal transition study-2 (NLTS2). NCSER 2011–3005*. National Center for Special Education Research.

Nolet, V., & McLaughlin, M. J. (2000). *Accessing the general curriculum: Including students with disabilities in standards-based reform*. Thousand Oaks, CA: Corwin Press.

Phillips, S. E. (1994). High stakes testing accommodations: Validity versus disabled rights. *Applied Measurement in Education, 7*(2), 93–120. Lawrence Erlbaum, Associates, Inc.

Phillips, S. E. (2002). Legal issues affecting special populations in large-scale assessment programs. In G. Tindal & T. M. Haladyna (Eds.), *Large-scale assessment programs for all students: Validity, technical adequacy, and implementation*. Mahwah, NJ: Lawrence Erlbaum Associates.

President's Commission on Excellence in Special Education. (2002). *A new era: Revitalizing special education for children and their families*. Washington, DC: Author.

Quenemoen, R. (2009). The long and winding road of alternate assessments: Where we started, where we are now, and the road ahead. In W. D. Schafer & R. W. Lissitz (Eds.), *Alternate assessments based on alternate achievement standards: Policy, practice, and potential*. Baltimore, MD: Paul H Brookes Publishing Co..

Russo, C., & Osborne, A. (Eds.). (2008). *Essential concepts and school-based cases in special education law*. Thousand Oaks, CA: Corwin Press.

Scott, G. A. (2011). *Higher education and disability: Improved federal enforcement needed to better protect students' rights to testing accommodations (GAO-12-40, Report to Congressional Requesters)*. Washington, DC: US Government Accountability Office.

Shriner, J., & Thurlow, M. L. (1993). *State special education outcomes: A report on state Activities at the end of the century*. Minneapolis, MN: National Center on Educational Outcomes, University of Minnesota.

Simon, M, Karasoff, P., & Smith, A. (1991). *Effective practices for inclusion Programs: A technical assistance planning guide*. (unpublished paper supported by U.S. Department of Education Cooperative Agreements #GOO87C3056–91 and #GOO87C3058–91).

Skirtic, T. M. (1991). The special education paradox: Equity as the way to excellence. *Harvard Educational Review, 61*(2).

Stecker, P. M. (2005). Monitoring student progress in individualized educational programs using curriculum-based measurement. In U.S. Department of Education, Office of Special Education: IDEAS that Work: Toolkit on teaching and assessing students with disabilities. National Center on Student Progress Monitoring.

The Elementary and Secondary Education Act of 1965 (P.L. 89–10).

The White House. (1990). *National educational goals, Office of the Press Secretary*. Washington, DC: Author.

Thompson, S. J., & Thurlow, M. L. (2000). *State alternate assessments: Status as IDEA alternate assessment requirements take effect (Synthesis report 35)*. Minneapolis, MN: University of Minnesota, National Center on Educational Outcomes.

Thurlow, M. L., Seyfarth, A., Scott, D. L., & Ysseldyke, J. E. (1997). *State assessment policies on participation and accommodations for students with disabilities: 1997 update (Synthesis report No. 29)*. Minneapolis, MN: University of Minnesota, National Center on Educational Outcomes.

Thurlow, M. L., & Ysseldyke, J. E. (1993). *Can "all" ever really mean "all" in defining and assessing student outcomes? (Synthesis Report No.5)*. Minneapolis, MN: University of Minnesota, National Center on Educational Outcomes.

Tindal, G. (2009). Reflections on the Alternate Assessment in Oregon. In W. D. Shafer & R. W. Lissitz (Eds.), *Alternate assessments based on alternate achievement* standards: Policy, practice, and potential. Baltimore, MD: Paul H Brookes Publishing Co.

U.S. Department of Education. (1993). *The reauthorization of the elementary and secondary education act, executive summary, 1993*. U.S. Department of Education.

U.S. Department of Education. (1997). *Elementary and secondary education. Guidance on standards, assessments and accountability*. Retrieved Oct 2, 2009 from http://www2.ed.gov/policy/elsec/guid/standardsassessment/guidance_pg4.html#disabilities3.

U.S. Department of Education. (2003). *Standards and assessments non-regulatory guidance March 10, 2003*. Washington, DC: Author.

U.S. Department of Education. (2005). *Secretary spellings announces new flexibility for states raising achievement for students with disabilities, May 10, 2005*. Washington DC: U.S. Department of Education.

U.S. Department of Education. (2015). *Peer review of state assessment systems: Non-regulatory guidance for states for meeting requirements of the elementary and secondary education act of 1965, as amended*. Washington, DC: Author.

U.S. Department of Education, National Center for Education Statistics. (2016). *The condition of education 2016* (NCES 2016–144), Retrieved from: https://nces.ed.gov/ccd/tables/ACGR_RE_and_characteristics_2013-14.asp.

U.S. Department of Education, Office of Special Education Programs (2003). *Letter to givens*. Retrieved August 24, 2016 from http://www2.ed.gov/policy/speced/guid/idea/letters/2003–1/given020403iep1q2003.pdf. Washington, DC: Author.

U.S. Department of Justice. (2015). *Testing accommodations*. Washington, DC: author. Retrieved from: http://www.ada.gov/regs2014/testing_accommodations.html.

Wallace, T., Ticha, R., & Gustafson, K. (2008). *Study of General Outcome Measurement (GOMs) in reading for students with significant cognitive disabilities: Year 1*. RIPM Technical Report #27.

Ysseldyke, J., Thurlow, M. L., McGrew, K. S., & Shriner, G. J. (1994). *Recommendations for making decisions about the participation of students with disabilities in statewide assessment programs: A report on a working conference to develop guidelines for statewide assessments and students with disabilities (Synthesis report 15)*. Minneapolis, MN: National Center on Educational Outcomes.

Zigmond, N., & Kloo, A. (2009). The 'two percent students': Considerations and consequences of eligibility decisions. *Peabody Journal of Education, 84*(4), 478–495.

International Policies that Support Inclusive Assessment

Michael Davies

Assessment is integral to education and the instruction process. It determines, at different levels, how well the goals of education are being met, how well-planned teaching activities lead to the learning that was intended, and, from the student perspective, what they learned. It is hoped that all students are provided with the opportunity of a fair assessment. Under inclusive and accessible assessment policy, learners with special educational needs are expected to participate and progress in the general curriculum, albeit with appropriate modifications and adaptations. They are also increasingly being expected to participate in a country's national or state assessment regimes (Mitchell, 2015). Unfortunately, assessment is not always inclusive or accessible. Internationally, lack of accessibility is recognised in legislative enactments, by policy frameworks, and by implementation requirements by many overseeing organisations and systems, and by individual countries. Accountability of schools and school systems provides a complicating backdrop to these initiatives, and a wider concern that standards-based reform in education is dominating much of the educational and political discourse around the world (Mitchell, 2015).

Another background educational issue is to recognise the importance of applying inclusive assessment and accessibility in both special education and inclusive education settings. Hornby (2015) summarises the two approaches of inclusive education and special education by indicating that they are based on different philosophies and provide alternative, somewhat oppositional, views of education for children with special educational needs and disabilities. Hornby (2015) presents a theory of inclusive special education comprising a synthesis of the philosophy, values, and practices of inclusive education with the interventions, strategies, and procedures of special education. This unification aims to provide a vision and guidelines for policies, procedures, and teaching strategies that will facilitate the provision of effective education for all children with special educational needs and disabilities. For the purposes of reviewing inclusive assessment and accessibility internationally, inclusive special education is adopted as a unifying theoretical principle and inclusive of the two approaches.

This chapter provides an overview of the macro-policy initiatives that support inclusive assessment and then provides examples of countries that are at different levels in their development and application of policy in attempting to achieve inclusive assessment. Comparative studies have the potential to highlight strengths and

M. Davies (✉)
Education and Professional Studies,
Griffith University, Brisbane, Australia

Australian Institute of Professional Counsellors,
Griffith University, Brisbane, Australia
e-mail: michael@aipc.net.au;
m.davies@griffith.edu.au

weaknesses of systems, highlight the different manifestations of inclusive assessment current in each country, and explore how individual countries have managed various challenges as they attempt to align international policy with education systems, developed from their own legacy, interests, pressures, and priorities (Smyth et al., 2014). The United States has set the bar in terms of comprehensive legislation and policies that drive inclusive and accessible assessment for students, across inclusive and special education, at a number of levels – opportunity to learn, testing accommodations, and modifications to test items. Some other countries are working towards developing policies, and some are developing critical strategic approaches, but while the international intent may be there, the outcome is patchy to say the least. Australia is reviewed as an example of a country with the infrastructure and opportunity to achieve great improvement in inclusive and accessible assessment for students across inclusive special education but has not progressed as much as would be expected. China is very much the emerging international service provider and, as a signatory to the UN Convention on the Rights of Persons with Disabilities (2006), recognises the need for inclusive and accessible assessment but seems intent on developing the resources and infrastructure in special education as a first priority. These three examples provide an understanding of where many countries across the world are faring when it comes to understanding international inclusive assessment.

Macro-Policy Initiatives

Internationally, there are a number of policy initiatives that have the potential to drive individual countries to adopting and applying accessible and inclusive assessment. The United Nations Convention (United Nations, 2006), the United Nations Educational, Scientific and Cultural Organisation (UNESCO, 2016), the Organisation for Economic Co-operation and Development (OECD) student assessments (see D'Alessio & Cowan, 2013), the European Agency for Special Needs and Inclusive Education (see Watkins, 2007), and the Standards for Educational and Psychological Testing (see AERA, APA, & NCME, 2014) provide key components for countries to reflect on and implement legislatively, in policy and in practice. Each of these will now be briefly described.

United Nations Convention

Inclusive education depends on educators at all levels of the system being committed to its underlying philosophy and being willing to implement it (Mitchell, 2015). This means that education systems and schools should articulate an inclusive culture in which "there is some degree of consensus … around values of respect for difference and a commitment to offering all pupils access to learning opportunities" (Ainscow & Miles, 2012, p. 27). It means recognising the obligations into which most countries entered when they signed and ratified the *Convention on the Rights of Persons with a Disability* (United Nations, 2006), which includes a significant commitment to inclusive education. Article 24 states that signatories recognise the right of persons with disabilities to education, ensuring an inclusive education system at all levels. In realising this right, States Parties are to ensure that persons with disabilities are not excluded from the general education system on the basis of disability and that they can access an inclusive, quality, free education on an equal basis with others in the communities in which they live. Reasonable accommodation of the individual's requirements needs to be provided to facilitate their effective education, and effective individualised support measures also need to be provided. Article 24 of the Convention requires signatories to provide reasonable accommodations to meet the requirements of students with disabilities and to support them to facilitate effective education and provide individualised support measures in environments that maximise academic and social development. Over 160 nations are signatories to this Convention.

United Nations Educational Scientific and Cultural Organisation (UNESCO)

Global Education Reports are published annually by the United Nations Educational Scientific and Cultural Organisation. These comprehensive reports document progress towards achieving Sustainable Development Goals (SDG). Goal 4 aims to ensure inclusive and equitable quality education and promote lifelong learning opportunities for all, while sub-goal SDG 4.5 specifically commits all countries to ensure equal access to all levels of education and vocational training, regardless of disability status. Clearly these goals are works in progress, but they provide opportunities to reflect on movement towards achievement and the role of each country in this process.

The UNESCO (2016) report suggests that to ensure that education is inclusive, educators must be better prepared and school infrastructures properly adapted to address the needs of individuals with disabilities. Monitoring these aspects is important to ensure that schools and teachers address all learners. The quest for assessing student learning and gathering national data has increased across the world. In their most recent Education for All Global Monitoring Report (UNESCO, 2015), it was noted that "since 2000, countries' interest in improving their understanding of education system outcomes has rapidly expanded" (p 18). In the last decade of the last century, 34% of countries carried out at least one national learning assessment; however, between 2000 and 2013, the percentage grew to 69%. Particularly rapid improvement was observed in the Arab States, Central Asia, Central and Eastern Europe, and East Asia and the Pacific. As Watkins, Ebersold, and Lenart (2014) pointed out, all countries need to track the implementation of their educational policies and legislation and how policies lead towards greater educational inclusion through systematic data collection.

Organisation for Economic Co-operation and Development (OECD) Student Assessments

While national assessments were on the increase, involvement also increased in international comparative assessments across the world. Initially launched in 1997, the Organisation for Economic Co-operation and Development (OECD) Programme for International Student Assessment (PISA) has the largest coverage across countries and over time, enabling a systematic review of trends. Since 1997, PISA has been applied every 3 years to 15-year-old students across over 70 countries in the areas of mathematics, reading, science, financial literacy, and, in the last 4 years, problem-solving.

Of 38 countries where the mean score in reading can be compared over 2000–2009, 13 improved while 4 deteriorated, and 14 countries reduced the percentage of learners falling below a minimum proficiency threshold; PISA attempts to use inclusive assessment practices across international boundaries, a most difficult and complex task. As outlined in the technical notes of the PISA online site (PISA, 2016), PISA is an international test with items to which students have been exposed to a different extent in different schools, different countries, and different curricular contexts. The idea of PISA is not to reduce the assessment to the lowest common denominator of tasks that are taught in all countries in identical ways but rather to reflect the range of competencies that students aged 15 years across the world need to master to be successful in the different subject areas that are tested every 3 years. PISA applies strict technical standards for the sampling of schools and students within schools. The sampling procedures are quality assured, and the achieved samples and corresponding response rates are subject to an adjudication process that verifies that they have complied with the standards set or not. The technical section suggests that confidence in the robustness of PISA is based on the rigour which is applied to all technical aspects of item development, trialling, analysis, review, and selection in survey design, implementation, and analysis. However, despite these technical statements that indicate robustness, with all countries attempting to maximise the coverage of 15-year-olds enrolled in education in their national samples, the sampling standards permit the exclusion of up to a total of 5% of the relevant population. Predictably, permissible exclusions include students with a disability, as well as schools that are geographically inaccessible. While standardised international definitions of disability are not agreed upon, along with many other complications such as the use of adjustments or accommodations to testing, the inclusive assessment of students with disabilities will likely remain out of the scope of PISA.

PISA has come to influence the way in which governments worldwide perceive, assess, and measure the performance and value of their own education systems (D'Alessio & Cowan, 2013). Political pressure for tangible "improvements" has caused these methods of assessment, purportedly underpinned by "comparative" methodologies, to lead "to an intensification of pedagogies, teaching to the test, as well as a growth in hierarchically arranged accountabilities that burden classroom teachers with mountains of non-curricular paperwork. Such popularized research findings have influenced a drift toward students preparing for high attainment levels in standardized tests rather than in pedagogies which are centered round learning for life" (D'Alessio & Cowan, 2013, p.229–230).

Additionally, sharing data across international boundaries is fraught with difficulties (D'Alessio & Watkins, 2009). Countries and communities have different cultures and contexts and often do not share the same terminology or agree on what constitutes a disability or a "special educational need". Linguistic diversity contributes to complications such as differing understandings and uses of key terms (D'Alessio, Watkins, & Donnelly, 2010). We also need to question the adoption of data collection and classification systems that fail to capture the complexity of these fields and the social/educational contexts under investigation (D'Alessio & Cowan, 2013).

The European Agency for Special Needs and Inclusive Education

The European Agency for Special Needs and Inclusive Education was established in 1996 (as the European Agency for Development in Special Needs Education). "The Agency" is a unique organisation in the field of special needs education that attempts to facilitate the effective transfer of European and country-specific information relevant to individual countries' national contexts and to identify the strengths and weaknesses of various policies and their implementation.

All aspects of Agency work are aligned with key international statements related to equal opportunities and special needs education. The Agency is essentially a network of member country representatives and experts nominated by the respective ministries of education and is maintained by the Ministries of Education in Austria, Belgium, Cyprus, Czech Republic, Denmark, Estonia, France, the German Bundesländer, Greece, Hungary, Iceland, Italy, Latvia, Lithuania, Luxembourg, the Netherlands, Norway, Poland, Portugal, Spain, Sweden, Switzerland, and the United Kingdom (England only).

The Agency completed a comprehensive review of assessment in inclusive settings (Watkins, 2007) in all member countries from 2005 to 2007. Information from this project includes reports on each of the 23 participating countries describing their assessment policy and practice, a web database of country information, and a synthesis report of key findings in 19 languages. All of these and other project materials are available from www.european-agency.org/site/themes/assessment/. The Agency's continued work on inclusive assessment (Kyriazopoulou & Weber, 2009) provided specific crucial indicators:

- Indicator for policy: "assessment policies and procedures support and enhance the successful

inclusion and participation of all pupils vulnerable to under-achievement and exclusion" (p. 4).
- Indicator for legislation: "assessment legislation promotes a view of assessment as a tool for teaching and learning, not as a tool for classification, accountability or resource allocation" (p. 5).

The Agency work also provides the following associated preconditions that must be fulfilled for the above indicators to be effectively implemented:

- All policy statements concerning learners with special educational needs are integrated within general educational policies and support the principle of their inclusion within the least restrictive environment.
- The ultimate goal for assessment procedures specified in all policies is that of supporting teaching, learning, and progression for all learners. All assessment procedures are available for and accessible to all learners in ways that are adapted to their particular needs (e.g. Braille, via interpreters).
- Assessment policies ensure assessment methods are "fit for purpose", appropriate, and monitored. Monitoring of educational standards makes use of a variety of evidence (not just learner assessment information) and supports research and development of new assessment methods and tools.
- Assessment policies outline varied and flexible support, resources, and training that will be provided for teacher and school and multi-disciplinary team-level responsibilities to be fulfilled.
- All assessment policies promote a holistic/ecological view of learning considering environmental factors (within the school and family) and social and emotional skills as well as academic learning goals.
- Assessment policies account for and aim to facilitate necessary cooperation with other service sectors (i.e. health and social services).
- Legislation ensures that policy, provision, and support are consistent across geographical areas of a country/region (Watkins, 2007).

While these indicators and characteristics drive the overview agenda for the 23 member countries, they do not stipulate specific legislative beacons to drive inclusive policy and practices within these countries. As a result, evidence of inclusive assessment using the full range of available approaches is limited. Kefallinou and Donnelly (2016) provide a detailed account of the main policy issues and challenges that countries commonly face in implementing inclusive assessment and highlight ways to address these challenges. Meijer and Watkins (2016) suggest that the concept of inclusion differs across countries and is constantly changing. They suggest that a lack of shared understanding of core concepts and terminology relating to inclusion is based on four factors: language used (e.g. translation of the word "inclusion" between European languages and English is not direct); legislation related to general and special education varies in each country, and policy implementation is context driven; concepts such as special need or disability held by policy-makers vary across countries and policy terminology varies; and lastly, practitioner conceptions of inclusion are diverse and have expanded to include a wide range of learners vulnerable to exclusion and have a systemic component. This final factor has also been supported by D'Allessio and Cowan (2013). Each of the Agency members has its own laws, policies, and systems, and at least five countries – Belgium, Germany, Spain, Switzerland, and the United Kingdom – can be described as federal in nature, composed of smaller regions or countries. At the policy level, the key European and international statements provide a common frame of reference, but countries have evolved their own policies and practices. Smyth et al. (2014) compared the evolution of four EU countries (Ireland, Austria, Spain, and the Czech Republic), and the unique sociocultural, political, and economic context in each country shaped its journey towards "compliance" and a shared policy of intent that failed to result in common legislative or practice outcomes. However, details regarding inclusive assessment are not provided.

Each state within the EU is responsible for the design and delivery of educational provision and international standards. Many initiatives have not been incorporated into the legal systems of EU countries (Schoonheim & Ruebain, 2005). For instance, few European states have explicitly included reasonable accommodation clauses to guarantee equitable access to learning environments. If accommodations are not provided in the learning environment, it would be most unlikely that assessment would be afforded accommodations to make assessment inclusive.

While legislative changes in inclusive and special education can be recognised in some of the member countries (Meijer, 2003b; Watkins, 2007), Agency work indicates that a number of policy areas require further development. Meijer, Soriano, and Watkins (2007) first of all identify the *increasing tension* between schools' academic requirements and the capabilities of pupils with special education needs. While schools aspire to academic excellence, they also need to ensure that educational programmes and inclusive assessment practices are provided and driven by policy. Additionally, policy also needs to address the development of systematic *monitoring and evaluation procedures* within the framework of special needs education in inclusive and separate special settings. Inclusive assessment in many settings is not supported by appropriate policies and procedures. Finally, policy needs to address the development of flexible *frameworks of provision* that support inclusive practices and can be applied to all sectors of educational provision (Meijer, 2003a; Watkins, 2003).

Many EU and other countries need to take heed of internationally accepted principles that can guide the development of inclusive and accessible assessments. One set of principles is *the Standards for Educational and Psychological Testing* (American Educational Research Association [AERA], American Psychological Association [APA], & the National Council on Measurement in Education [NCME], 2014) which will be outlined next.

Standards for Educational and Psychological Testing

The Standards for Educational and Psychological Testing is a set of testing standards developed jointly by AERA, APA, and NCME. The 2014 edition pays attention to two elements relevant to inclusive and accessible assessment: (1) examining accountability issues associated with the uses of tests in educational policy and (2) broadening the concept of accessibility of tests for all examinees.

The *Standards* provide international guidelines for the evaluation, development, and use of assessment instruments. The guidelines provide standards for validity and outline the following sources of validity evidence: evidence based on test content; response processes; internal structure; relations to other variables such as convergent and discriminant evidence, test criterion relationships, and validity generalisation; and finally, evidence based on consequences of testing.

In the section on *standards on fairness and bias*, the focus is on the aspects of fairness and testing that are customarily the responsibility of those who make, use, and interpret tests, which are characterised by some level of professional and technical consensus. It does not examine the very broad issues related to regulations, statutes, and case law that govern test use and the remedies for harmful practice. The *Standards* describe fairness in the following four principle ways in which the term fairness should be used: fairness as a lack of bias; fairness as equitable treatment in the testing process; fairness as equality in outcomes of testing; and fairness as opportunity to learn. The *Standards* describe the term bias as construct-irrelevant components that result in systematically lower or higher scores for identifiable groups of examinees. Likewise, two main sources of bias are identified: content-related sources of bias and response-related sources of bias.

The *Standards* also focus on the testing of individuals with disabilities from a technical and professional perspective. However, test developers and users are also encouraged to become familiar with federal, state, and local laws and court and administrative rulings that regulate the testing and assessment of individuals with disabilities. The *Standards* do address issues regarding appropriate accommodations when testing individuals with disabilities, strategies of test modification, using modifications in different testing contexts, and reporting scores on modified tests. These standards provide international testing agencies, policy-makers, educational authorities, schools, and teachers with guidelines for how they should proceed with inclusive assessment.

More recently, these standards have been supported by the publishing of an International Handbook of Testing and Assessment by the International Test Commission (Leong, Bartram, Cheung, Geisinger, & Iliescu, 2016). Within this handbook, Geisinger and McCormick (2016) provide an overview of testing and assessing individuals with disabilities. It includes a definitional section, before discussing US legislation, and decision-making regarding the application of a range of inclusive strategies that are promoted as models of inclusive practice. While it is uncertain as to how influential the Standards for Educational and Psychological Testing and the new International Handbook of Testing and Assessment are internationally, it is suggested that these two sources provide a foundation to promote inclusive assessment practices to meet the needs of all students in inclusive and special education settings. Additionally, the following section proposes a framework for countries to consider and apply if inclusive assessment is to be achieved.

An Inclusive Assessment Framework

Inclusive assessment for national, state, and classroom assessment should be driven by *appropriate legislation* that drives *clearly stated policies* that realise *inclusive and accessible assessment practices*. Douglas, McLinden, Robertson, Travers and Smith (2016) proposed three key elements in their inclusive assessment framework that have been adapted for the purposes of this chapter, and that will form the basis of a comparative analysis between different countries. These elements are summarised in Table 3.1 and then further described.

1. *Assessments Should Include All Children and Young People*

Different countries vary in the strength of their legislation, policies, and practices in relation to assessing *all* students and vary in the way that they document all pupils' educational progress and outcomes.

2. *Assessments* Should Be Accessible and Appropriate

Legislation and policy should promote the use of inclusive learning and assessment strategies and procedures so that the diverse range of pupils within the educational system of each country are able to be assessed fairly and appropriately.

Table 3.1 Key elements of an inclusive assessment framework

Key elements	Description and components
Assessments should include all children and young people	All students are included
Assessments should be accessible and appropriate	Opportunity to learn the intended curriculum that is tested Accommodations and adjustments to both instruction and testing practices are applied Alternative assessments are available Universally designed assessment to reduce the need for accommodated and alternative versions
Assessments should measure and document areas of relevance	Measure progress and outcomes on the full breadth of the curriculum that an education system offers

There is a rich literature on inclusive assessment strategies (see Geenen & Ysseldyke, 1997; Watkins, 2007) that are often promoted in the context of national assessment practices but equally pertain to classroom contexts.

The major strategies for the inclusion of students with special needs in national, state, and classroom assessment include the following:

- Ensuring students have the *opportunity to learn* the intended curriculum that students are ultimately tested on (Kurz, 2011).
- *Accommodations and adjustments* to both instruction (Ketterlin-Geller & Jamgochian, 2011) and testing practices (Kettler, 2012) to include students with special needs. Modifications, or adjustments, or accommodations are required because standard instructional and assessment formats and procedures can present barriers to pupils with special needs and limit their capacity to learn and to demonstrate their abilities under normal assessment conditions. These assessment accommodations seek to make an assessment accessible while maintaining the same assessment criteria (e.g. Lazarus, Thurlow, Lail, & Christensen, 2009). This involves making changes to the assessment process, but not to the essential content. Assessors need to distinguish between accommodations necessary for students to access or express the intended learning content and the content itself. There are over 65 accommodations or adjustments for learning and assessment that can be categorised into motivational adjustments, scheduling adjustments, setting adjustments, assisting with directions, pretest assistance, equipment or assistive technology, and presentation formats for learning or assessment (Davies, Elliott, & Cumming, 2016). Accommodations or adjustments can be applied in classroom learning and assessment, and also in state and national assessments, providing the policy and procedures allow them.
- *Alternative assessments* based on Alternate Academic Achievement Standards. An alternative assessment is designed for relatively few students with disabilities who are unable to participate in the regular assessment with appropriate accommodations (US Department of Education, 2003). Alternative assessment aims to ensure that all pupils, irrespective of their ability, can be assessed appropriately in all inclusive and special education settings by creating a range of assessments with different assessment criteria. These students have need of an alternative assessment because of their inability to respond to the format and content of the standard assessment. That is, the required response mode, context, and content of the standard assessment may be too challenging or may be inappropriate for students with severe disabilities. Teacher observations, samples of student work, and standardised performance tasks are examples of alternative assessment (Douglas et al., 2016). Alternate assessment allows for different modes of responding, a different context of assessment, and different content that is still linked to state or national standards.
- Alternate assessments should have:
  - A clearly defined structure
  - Guidelines determining which students may participate
  - Clearly defined scoring criteria and procedures
  - A report format that clearly communicates student performance in terms of the academic achievement standards defined by the state
  - High technical quality, including validity, reliability, accessibility, and objectivity, which applies to regular state assessments as well
- *Universally designed systems* (Lazarus et al., 2009). Universally designed systems include those in which a single assessment method is suitable for all students. The approach argues that careful attention to assessment design will include all and reduce the need for accommodated and alternative versions (e.g. Lazarus et al., 2009). Douglas et al. (2016) see this as an important aspiration – with attention to such principles, the need for accommodated

and alternative assessments could be reduced, although, they could not find any examples of universally designed national assessments that include all students.

3. *Assessments Should Measure and Document Areas of Relevance*

   Assessments should seek to measure progress and outcomes on the full breadth of the curriculum that an education system offers. Douglas et al. (2016) suggest that the inclusion of a diverse range of students within the educational system means it will be necessary to assess areas of specific relevance to people with special needs across a wider or additional curriculum. Watkins (2007) indicated that inclusive assessment should "aim to "celebrate" diversity by identifying and valuing all pupils' individual learning progress and achievements" (p. 48) and assessing a wide coverage of nonacademic as well as academic subjects. Alternative assessments will be required for this to be effective. Additionally, systems need to be in place to record educational progress in these areas of interest, relevance, or concern to a range of given stakeholders.

Micro-Policy Initiatives: Individual Case Studies

Each country occupies its own level of legislative, policy, and practice on the inclusive and accessible assessment spectrum. To better understand current international status and challenges faced by various countries, this section will present some detail of three countries. Table 3.2 depicts the three countries' positions on a spectrum from least inclusive to most inclusive, across a range of considerations.

Table 3.2 Inclusive assessment spectrum

Low level of inclusive assessment/quality					High level of inclusive assessment/quality
Practices					*Practices*
No assessment of students with additional needs			ANB MSB	ASB	USB	Inclusive assessment consistently applied
Limited opportunities for assessment		ANB MSB			ASB USB	All students included across all opportunities
Limited opportunity to learn the intended tested curriculum/tested with no exposure			ANB MSB	ASB USB		Opportunity to learn the intended tested curriculum
Assessment offered however Family and Student not encouraged to participate						
	ANB MSB				ASB USB	Families and students encouraged
No universally designed assessments Measures progress and outcomes on narrow range of curriculum No adjustments/accommodations applied for instruction or testing		ANB MSB		USB	ASB		Learner at centre of assessment process, can influence assessment, ongoing consultation of learner, relevance to learner
			ANB	ASB USB		Universally designed assessments
		ANB MSB	USB		ASB	Measures progress and outcomes on full range of curriculum
		MSB	ANB		ASB USB	Apply adjustments/accommodations as required for both instruction and testing

(continued)

Table 3.2 (continued)

Low level of inclusive assessment/quality					High level of inclusive assessment/quality
Policy/procedures					*Policy/procedures*
Assessment for school/teacher accountability		ANB MSB		ASB USB	Assessment to support and enhance inclusion
Students can be exempted	ANB MSB			ASB USB	Participation of *all* students
Support inflexible assessment practices	MSB	ANB	USB	ASB	Support innovative creative flexible practices
Legislation					*Legislation*
SWDs not identified				ASB ANB USB MSB	SWDs identified
Inconsistent nationally		ASB		ANB USB MSB	Consistent nationally
Inconsistent regionally		ASB	ANB MSB	USB	Consistent regionally
Assessment as tool for accountability, resource allocation	ANB MSB	USB		ASB	Assessment as tool for learning and teaching

Note: First Letter indicates country: *A* Australia, *C* Mainland China, *U* USA
Following letter indicates setting: *S* School based; *NB* National based
For the USA and Mainland China, only school based was noted since school based also reflects national based for each element
Allocation of column level on the spectrum is an estimate of the relative level of inclusive assessment practice based on available documented evidence

United States of America

The United States is the third worlds' largest country (325 million) comprising fifty states. It has an education system of three levels of school education from K to 12 which includes elementary (kindergarten through fifth grade) school, middle or junior high (sixth through eighth grade), and high school (ninth through twelfth grade). About 87% of school-age children attend public schools, about 10% attend private schools, and roughly 3% are home-schooled. Public school curricula, budgets, and policies for K-12 schooling are set through locally elected school boards that have jurisdiction over school districts. State governments set overall educational standards, often mandate standardised tests for public school systems, and supervise state colleges and universities.

In the United States, education is not a specified federal responsibility but is essentially under control of the states. However, since states rely on federal funding, receipt of funding is reliant on states adhering to legislation and policy and participating in programmes such as the National Assessment of Educational Progress (NAEP) that captures samples of students across the states (Cumming, 2012). The United States has had policies that have promoted the development of inclusive assessment practices for students with disabilities (SWDs) for over 60 years. As indicated in Table 3.1, the United States has put in place the most complete system of legislation, policy, and practice to drive inclusive education. These policies and practices continue to evolve, and as Weigert (Chap. 2 in this volume) indicates, several new federal policies such as rescinding regulations on modified achievement standards and the "Every Student Succeeds Act" (ESSA) have eased requirements for high-stakes testing across states, reducing administrators' temptations to set lower achievement standards or to find ways to exclude SWDs from participation.

Until recently in the United States, accountability in special education was defined in terms of progress in meeting Individualised Education Program (IEP) goals (Mitchell, 2015). That all changed with the Individuals with Disabilities Education Act (IDEA, 97) which required all students, including those with disabilities, to participate in their states' accountability systems. Both IDEA 97 and the No Child Left Behind Act of 2002 required that alternate assessment be provided for students who could not participate in state or district assessments with or without accommodations. Prior to ESSA, states were permitted to measure up to 3% of their students using alternate assessments (1% against alternate achievement standards and 2% against modified standards).

The National Center on Educational Outcomes has published extensively on alternate assessment for students with significant cognitive disabilities (see Lazarus, Cormier, Crone, & Thurlow, 2010; Lazarus, Hodgson, & Thurlow, 2010). These documents provide information on states' accommodation policies on alternate assessments and guidelines for such assessments. Other useful guides to alternate assessment include Bolt and Roach (2009) and publications from the US Department of Education, particularly those relating to its policy for including students with disabilities in standards-based assessment used in determining "adequate yearly progress" (e.g. Technical Work Group on Including Students with Disabilities in Large Scale Assessments, 2006).

Summary of Inclusive Assessment Policies in the USA

Major Legislation and Policy:

Individuals with Disabilities Education Act (IDEA, 1997).
No Child Left Behind (NCLB)/Every Student Succeeds Act (ESSA)

1. *Assessments Should Include "All" Children and Young People*

   All students must be included in state assessments, and therefore strict requirements exist for states to provide accommodated and alternative versions of assessments to include students with disabilities. Required to assess *all* students and document all pupils' educational progress and outcomes.

2. *Assessments Should Be Accessible and Appropriate*
   - *Opportunity to Learn* (OTL)

     There is policy and practice intent and research and trialling of systems to document OTL that helps to ensure alignment of content standards, content taught, and content tested (see Kurz, 2011, as well as Kurz's Chap. 9 in the current volume), but there are no systematic practices to document whether students had the opportunity to learn the curriculum on which they were tested.

     However, as Weigert indicates in Chap. 2, the newly reauthorised ESSA encourages state innovation assessment that permits instructionally embedded, within-year assessments that will support teachers to better align instruction with content standards.

   - *Accommodations and Adjustments*

     Since all students with disabilities are to be included in state assessments, there are strict requirements for states to provide accommodated and alternative versions of assessments. Lazarus et al. (2009) and Weigert (Chap. 2 of the current volume) provide an analysis of accommodation procedures across the United States.

   - *Alternate Assessments*

     States are required to provide "alternate assessments" for students with significant cognitive disabilities and working at achievement standards at or below a basic level. Alternate achievement standards have an expectation that performance will differ in complexity from grade-level achievement standards. An analysis of approaches developed in different states is provided by Cameto et al. (2009).

- *Universally Designed Systems* (Lazarus et al., 2009): in which a single assessment method is suitable for all students. The approach argues that careful attention to assessment design will include all and reduce the need for accommodated and alternate versions (e.g. Lazarus et al., 2009). Douglas et al. (2016) see this as an important aspiration – with attention to such principles, the need for accommodated and alternative assessments could be reduced, although they could not find any examples of universally designed national assessments that include all students.

3. *Assessments Should Measure and Document Areas of Relevance*

   With standards-based education, schools and school districts are held accountable for progress towards state-defined learning standards – a key focus of the No Child Left Behind Act (NCLB). NCLB requires that states assess performance annually in grades 3–8 in reading/language arts, mathematics, and science with additional tests for grades 10–12.

   IDEA and NCLB require standards-based accountability monitoring for all students with special needs. States must assess student progress against these standards and high school graduation and employment outcomes, and these data are published. Analysis of these data allows some disaggregation of pupils by disability/SEN subgroups, although capacity varies from state to state (Altman et al., 2010). Douglas et al. (2016) also identify the National Assessment of Educational Progress (NAEP) as a sample-based annual assessment of a range of curriculum areas for grades 4, 8, and 12. While students with disabilities are included in NAEP, they can be excluded if teachers feel the assessment is inappropriate. Maxwell and Shah (2011) indicated that targets have been set to ensure that 85% of students with disabilities are included. Additionally, assessing progress and participation of 20 IDEA Part-B indicators across a range of curriculum areas defined by NCLB is also required, along with wider indicators such as post-school outcomes including high school graduation and drop-out rates and employment.

On an individual class learning level, pupils identified as having a disability have their learning and development assessed through an IEP. The US law requires schools to include a statement of the child's present level of performance, annual goals, and short-term objectives plus details of all special support that needs to be provided (McLaughlin & Thurlow, 2003).

As Douglas et al. (2016) indicate, the National Longitudinal Transition Study-2 (NLTS2) with a nationally representative sample of around 11,000 students receiving special education services is another significant source of data that includes educational progress and outcomes in a range of areas, including attainment as well as broader outcome areas for combined (Sanford et al., 2011) and for specific disability groups (e.g. Cameto & Nagle, 2007).

Australia

Australia is a small country (24 million) that has a federal parliamentary democracy comprising six states and two territories with a two-tier system of school education which includes primary education (generally to 12 years of age) and secondary education (generally to 18 years of age), with schooling compulsory between the ages of 6 and 15 or 16. State and territory educational authorities provide free public education that accommodates about two-thirds of the total student population. The remaining students attend fee-paying religious and secular private schools, which also receive substantial government funding (Davies & Dempsey, 2011). For students with a disability, states and territories generally provide three enrolment options: regular classes, support classes (separate classes in a regular school), and special schools. The Australian government has committed an additional $9.8 billion in needs-based school funding commencing 2015 for the next 6 years (Budget Overview; AG, 2013).

Under the *Disability Discrimination Act 1992* (DDA; Australasian Legal Information Institute, 2009), extended by specific Education Standards, it is unlawful for an educational authority to discriminate against a student on the grounds of disability by denying or limiting the student's access to any services or curriculum or exclude the student from participation, including assessment. In terms of assessment, since 1999, established national goals for schooling have driven broad directions for the achievement of socially just and comparable educational outcomes for all students including students with additional needs (see MCEECDYA, 2010). National goals are also embedded into a common commitment to a national curriculum and a national testing programme and the use of a common student academic grading system.

Key strategies for the strengthening of educational accountability and transparency include providing students, teachers, and schools with good-quality data on student performance to improve student outcomes, informing parents and families about the performance of their son or daughter at school, of the school their child attended, and of the larger education system. The National Assessment Program for Literacy and Numeracy (NAPLAN) has since 2008 aimed to assess all students in Years 3, 5, 7, and 9 using common national tests in reading, writing, spelling, grammar and punctuation, and numeracy. All Australian children are expected to complete NAPLAN tests for assessing student outcomes and needs for funding at a national level. The Australian Curriculum, Assessment and Reporting Authority policy (2011) states that, "while not all students with disabilities are expected to be able to access NAPLAN tests, even students with significant intellectual or complex disabilities should be given the opportunity to participate" (p. 12). However, each year 5–7% of students are exempted, withdrawn, or absent and do not participate in NAPLAN, despite its compulsory status (Davies, 2012). The lack of full participation in NAPLAN reduces the validity and utility of its results and means there is little or no accountability for the education of a substantial number of Australian students. Each year, nearly 40,000 students with additional needs (SWANs) do not participate in NAPLAN. SWANs who do participate are rarely supported by appropriate adjustments to the test setting and are assessed with items that have not been designed using accessibility principles. There is an immediate need for accurate benchmarking of all students, especially SWANs, to ensure funding is allocated to those most in need, for maximum community benefit. Additionally, many schools and classroom teachers do not apply the most accessible and effective assessment strategies to ensure accurate and fair testing for all students.

Many students do not have full access to the relevant curriculum and find test items unnecessarily difficult. Computer-adaptive testing, or tailored testing that adapts to the examinee's ability level, is currently being trialled in preparation for full computerisation of NAPLAN in the next few years.

Current data on adjustments provided in NAPLAN testing indicates that the adjustments are inadequate to fully support the participation of all students. The estimated 90,000 SWANs who complete NAPLAN have a very restricted range of test adjustments, in comparison with those normally used in classroom instruction or classroom assessment (Davies, Elliott, & Cumming, 2016). Assessment should allow students to demonstrate their learning, with adjustments provided to facilitate access (AG, 2005, 6.3). The purpose of test adjustments is to increase test reliability and the validity of inferences about the students' abilities. Students may have the required knowledge, skills, or abilities, but presentation of a question may preclude them from demonstrating that knowledge. Many students and especially SWANS are inappropriately tracked into lower levels of curriculum, reducing their opportunities to learn – a fundamental educational equity issue highlighted in the *Standards for Educational and Psychological Testing* (AERA, APA, & NCME, 2014). For most SWANs and many other students, NAPLAN does not yet meet professional testing standards for valid, fair, and equitable assessment. In fact, many SWANs do not receive the standard feedback on NAPLAN test performance because they are excluded from the test, devaluing the test process, the students, and their families. This disadvantages many students and schools and provides incomplete, inaccurate performance reports to the public (Davies, 2012; Dempsey & Davies, 2013), which then form the basis of needs-based funding.

In recent years, the Nationally Consistent Collection of Data on School Students with Disability (NCCDSS) has also taken place. The NCCDS is a joint initiative by all Australian government and non-government education authorities to annually collect data to identify the number of school students with disabilities and the level of reasonable educational adjustment provided for them (see https://www.education.gov.au/students-disability).

Summary of Inclusive Assessment Policies in Australia

Major Legislation and Policy:

Disability Discrimination Act (1992), Education Standards (2005)

1. *Assessments Should Include "All" Children and Young People*

    All students must be included in NAPLAN assessments for Years 3, 5, 7, and 9. Testing allows only a limited range of reasonable adjustments and accommodations to increase inclusion of students with disabilities and to document all pupils' educational progress and outcomes. Subsequently, 5–7 percent of students do not participate, and one-third of those who do not participate are students with a disability.

    Classroom assessments utilise a larger range of adjustments, but not as many as are provided in the instructional process.

2. Assessments Should Be Accessible and Appropriate
   - *Opportunity to Learn*

     While there is policy and practice intent, there are no specific practices to measure or review whether students had the opportunity to learn the curriculum they are tested on.
   - *Accommodations and Adjustments*

     A limited range of accommodations can be allowed for students with disabilities in national assessments, and this list is documented and followed by educational authorities.

     Teachers can provide accommodated and alternative versions of assessments as part of classroom assessment. Davies et al. (2016) provide a breakdown of the use of 67 adjustments in classrooms and in NAPLAN assessment. Data indicates that teachers apply more adjustments to students with additional needs as part of classroom instruction, but the application level is reduced in classroom assessments and reduced to a lower level in national testing.
   - *Alternate Assessments*

     NAPLAN does not currently permit the use of alternate assessments for students with significant cognitive disabilities working on achievement standards at or below a basic level. The application of computer-assisted formats that are being trialled for implementation in 2018 might bring in a capacity to scope and vary assessments. However, plans for alternate assessments for national testing have not been documented publicly.

     In many specialised classroom settings, alternate assessments are applied to achieve a valid teacher assessment of student learning.
   - *Universally Designed Systems*

     The application of a single assessment method that applies universally designed assessments to include all students was not evidenced.

3. *Assessments Should Measure and Document Areas of Relevance*

    NAPLAN produces an annual report that documents the student-, school-, and state-level outcomes based on results of tests of reading, writing, spelling, grammar and punctuation, and numeracy of all Year 3, 5, 7, and 9 students each year. This testing provides a snapshot of educational achievement in these central and key components, but is clearly not comprehensive or broad, and does not capture data in areas of relevance for all students. Teachers and schools are held accountable for progress towards state-defined goals for improvement, and school data is publicly listed.

There is no legislation that drives accountability monitoring for students with special needs. In fact, students with disability or additional learning needs are not separately recognised in the data. NAPLAN does not collect data on students with disabilities or special needs who participate or who are exempted or withdrawn. The only disaggregation that occurs in reporting is related to gender, indigeneity, and language background other than English. While other systems such as NCCDSS and the National Disability Insurance Scheme (NDIS) gather data on people with disabilities, this data is not connected to assessment of learning, achievement, or outcomes for students with a disability.

At an individual class learning level, students with a disability may have their learning and development assessed through an IEP, but there is no law nor legislation at a state or federal level to make this mandatory.

The Longitudinal Study of Australian Children (LSAC) does have a nationally representative sample of around 11,000 students, with a proportion having a disability. Monitoring of these students provides a source of data in relation to educational progress and outcomes in a range of areas, including attainment as well as broader outcome areas (Dempsey & Davies, 2013).

Mainland China

Mainland China is a populous (over 1.3 billion persons) nation that by sheer numbers has a significant impact on world education. Education in China is predominately a system of public education run and funded by the Ministry of Education. All children attend school for at least 9 years of compulsory education that includes 6 years of primary education (age six or seven to age twelve), followed by 3 years of junior secondary education (middle school) for ages 12 to 15.

Special education that focused on programmes for gifted children and for students with learning difficulties was recognised in the 1985 National Conference on Education. Gifted children could skip grades, and children with learning difficulties were encouraged to reach minimum standards. Children with severe learning problems and other special needs were usually not schooled and were the responsibilities of their families. Extra provisions were made for blind and severely hearing-impaired children; however, special schools enrolled fewer than 10% of all eligible children in those categories. No legislative attention was paid to special education in China until mainstreaming and inclusion were introduced in the late 1980s (Deng & Harris, 2008) through a national movement called "Learning in Regular Classrooms" (LRC) to serve students with special educational needs, mainly referring to children with intellectual disabilities, visual impairments, and hearing impairments (Deng & Poon-McBrayer, 2004). Essentially, LRC is China's version of inclusion and has led to huge changes in special education in China because it enrolled more children with disabilities into the general education system (Weng & Feng, 2014).

In addition to LRC, two landmark laws and regulations enacted in the 1980s led to better safeguarding of education rights of all children with disabilities (Gu, 1993). The Compulsory Education Law of People's Republic of China (National People's Congress of People's Republic of China, 1986) and the Law on the Protection of Persons with Disabilities (LPPD) of People's Republic of China (National People's Congress of People's Republic of China, 1990), revised in 2008 (National People's Congress, 2008). For this law to guarantee the rights of persons with disabilities to basic education, the State Council in 1994 issued the Regulation on Education of the Disabled that stipulated state obligations to educating those with a disability and that government at all levels should strengthen leadership, planning, and development of education for the disabled and increase financial inputs to improve educational provision for students with disabilities (UNESCO, 2011). The impetus behind these laws lead to more governmental special education regulations and guidelines for teacher preparation, inclusive education, early intervention, curriculum, diagnosis and classification, instructional education plans, and financial support.

Documentation indicates that 18% of students with disabilities in 1990 were in general education classrooms, but by 1996–1997, 55.7% of students with special needs were educated in mainstream schools (Center on International Education Benchmarking, 2016). By 2003, Learning in Regular Classrooms (LRC) programmes served approximately 67% of all students identified with disabilities (364,700) in regular schools (Ministry of Education of China, 2003). While these data indicate a move to inclusive education, the quality and accessibility of LRC is not known. Additionally, it was estimated that in 2007, 223,000 school-age students with disability did not attend school. Moreover, just more than half of teachers in special education had a qualification in special education (UNESCO, 2009). In 2014, China had 2000 schools for special education, with a total of 60,000 staff (48,125 full-time teachers) and 394,870 students enrolled (NBS, 2014). While LRC has progressed rapidly, so too has the growth in special schools. This growth has been tempered by concerns regarding quality of instruction due to "a lack of specialists, a shortage of personnel, inadequate funding, and limited technology" (Weng & Feng, 2014, p. 663). High instructional quality for students with special educational needs (SEN) in mainstream classrooms is not being realised because of lack of expertise, support and resources, and effective assessment measures (Deng & Pei, 2009).

Mainland China is a signatory to the United Nations Convention on the Rights of Persons with Disabilities. However, Hernandez (2008) indicated that while China adopted laws that encourage education for all, inclusive education is not mandated, universal education is not provided, and both funding and the teacher force are not sufficient to be able to deliver promised outcomes. Hernandez called for China to fulfil its obligations by revising existing and inadequate domestic laws to comply with the Convention, enforcing these laws, and building capacity by meeting funding needs and teacher training requirements (Davies, Elliott, Sin, Yan, & Yel, 2017).

In response to the points raised by Hernandez (2008), the People's Republic of China issued a People with Disabilities Education Ordinance (2011). Clause 20 outlined course designs, syllabus, and text resources suitable for students with disabilities. In terms of inclusive assessment, it also indicated the responsibilities of examination and approval of these elements by the educational administrative department of the government at or above province level. Clause 21 outlined how appropriate adjustments can be made on the learning requirement for courses, syllabus, and text resources. Finally, Clause 41 stipulated that teacher training colleges and universities should arrange required and selective courses on special education within their programme plans so that pre-service teachers could master the requisite essential knowledge and skills about special education to meet the needs of special students in the regular classroom.

Further regulations were issued in 2015 by the State Council outlining a number of adjustments that could be reasonably applied for people with disabilities completing the National Higher Education Entrance Examination (People's Republic of China, 2015). These adjustments included those for students with vision impairment, hearing impairment, physical impairment, and with other special educational needs. The China Disabled Persons' Federation also announced a scheme to implement adjustments to support classroom learning for special students studying in a normal class. Acceptable adjustments included adapting textbooks, content of courses, alternative teaching plans, and syllabi. While these regulations and ordinances have been published, the uptake of these adjustments and practices by teachers of students with SEN is uncertain. Some indication of the application of a comprehensive list of 67 adjustments in classroom instruction, classroom assessment, and national testing is documented in Davies et al. (2017). This analysis indicates that adjustments are more likely to be applied by teachers as part of instruction and less likely to be applied in classroom assessment and even less in national testing.

The lack of application of inclusive practices needs to be understood in light of the major characteristics of traditional education, examination, conformity, and competition (Lee, 1995), which reflect Chinese cultural values. Deng and Pei (2009) further explore cultural concerns for the application of inclusive education in Mainland China. Whole-class teaching that dominates Chinese classrooms was imported from the West in the early twentieth century (Wang & Wang, 1994), and this model has been integrated into and shaped by the philosophy of Confucian collectivism – a tradition supported by communist dogmatism (Zhou, 2002). This tradition values loyalty and obedience to authority, with the goals of collective more important than the individual and their interests and happiness. Under the collectivist philosophy, curriculum, instructional methods, and academic standards are identical for all students (Wang & Wang, 1994), and so the needs of students with diverse abilities and unique learning needs are often neglected under this teaching of uniformity (Deng & Poon-McBrayer, 2004). The LRC promoted individualised teaching, and new education reform promotes diversity and individuality into the Chinese education system. However, the whole class lecture model remains the dominant method, with individual students with SEN receiving tutoring after class (Deng & Pei, 2009). Some differentiated teaching provides some variation in teaching to identified groups of students labelled "key", "fast", "average", or "slow". However, the pressure to prepare high-standard students for college entrance examinations is so great that the "average" and "slow" students are often neglected (Lin, 1993), and this emphasis has continued (Deng & Poon-McBrayer, 2004).

Summary of Inclusive Assessment Policies in Mainland China

Major Legislation and Policy:

Learning in Regular Classrooms (LRC).
Compulsory Education Law of People's Republic of China (National People's Congress of People's Republic of China, 1986).

The Law on the Protection of Persons with Disabilities (LPPD) of People's Republic of China (National People's Congress of People's Republic of China, 1990), revised in 2008 (National People's Congress, 2008)

1. *Assessments Should Include "All" Children and Young People*

    China is a UN Convention signatory, so there appears to be intent to be inclusive. However, there are indications that many children with disabilities are not at school but are kept at home. For those at school, reports exist of a lack of effective assessment measures.

    In terms of assessment, the responsibilities of examination and approval are undertaken by the educational administrative department of the government at or above the province level.

    In 2015, the State Council outlined a number of adjustments that could be reasonably applied for people with disabilities completing the National Higher Education Entrance Examination (People's Republic of China, 2015).

2. *Assessments Should Be Accessible and Appropriate*
    - *Opportunity to Learn*

    While there is policy and practice intent, there are no specific practices to measure nor review whether students had the opportunity to learn the curriculum on which they were tested.
    - *Accommodations and Adjustments*

    A limited range of accommodations can be allowed for students with disabilities in national assessments and for students with vision impairment, hearing impairment, physical impairment, and with other special educational needs.

    The China Disabled Persons' Federation also announced a scheme to implement adjustments to support classroom learning for special students studying in a normal class. Acceptable adjustments included adapting textbooks, content of courses, alternative teaching plans, and syllabus. Davies et al. (2016) provide a breakdown of the use of 67 adjustments in classrooms and in NAPLAN assessment. Data indicates that teachers apply

more adjustments to students with additional needs as part of classroom instruction, but the application level is reduced in classroom assessments and reduced to a lower level in national testing.
- *Alternative Assessments*

  Plans for alternative assessments to classrooms and national testing have not been documented publicly.
- *Universally Designed Systems*

  The application of a single assessment method that applies universally designed assessments to include all students was not evidenced.
3. *Assessments Should Measure and Document Areas of Relevance*

   National testing takes place but it is unclear how comprehensive or broad it is to capture data in areas of relevance for all students. Teachers and schools are held accountable for progress towards state-defined goals for improvement, and school data is publicly listed.

   There is no legislation that drives accountability monitoring for students with special needs. At an individual class learning level, students with a disability may have their learning and development assessed, but it is not freely documented, and there is no law or legislation at a state or regional level to make this mandatory.

Discussion

This chapter has provided an overview of the macro-international initiatives that impact inclusive assessment and accessibility and has illustrated how these policies have influenced the evolution of inclusive assessment policies in three countries. The United States has provided the front running in the development of legislation, policy, and practices. Australia has followed the lead of both the United States and the United Kingdom in its unique development of inclusive assessment policy and practice. Mainland China, as the most populous nation in the world, has the largest population of students with disabilities and is beginning to place enormous resources into special and inclusive education. From this brief review, a number of significant issues have emerged, and these will now be briefly discussed.

1. In most countries, legislative enactments establish the intentions of policy frameworks that then indicate practice requirements for inclusive assessment (Cumming, 2012). The United States provides the best example of causal links between these three components. While many countries are UN declaration signatories, only some of these, such as Australia, have legislated for, and developed policies that are inclusive, but only recommend and not require equitable and accessible practices, and so the enacted practices fall short of being equitable. Some other signatories, such as Mainland China, have not specified accessible practices in their legislation or the policy-directed inclusive practices, except for documenting allowable adjustments in the national test. Many other signatories have not specified any legislation, policy, or practices.
2. When legislation and policy-driven practices are outlined, there appears to be a pecking order in what actual practices are put in place. There seems to be a tendency for inclusive practices related to instruction and curriculum to be prioritised, both in legislation and in relation to practices, before inclusive assessment. It would seem that inclusive assessment is only considered when the strategies and practices for inclusive curriculum and instruction are well in place. This is a false strategy, since inclusive and equitable assessment drives instruction and appropriate curriculum.
3. The United States leads the way in establishing mandated pubic laws that promote the rollout of inclusive assessment policies and practices and the development of new and creative strategies. Many practices and strategies, such as OTL, accommodations and adjustments, and adaptive assessment, have been developed and are being trialled in the United States. Other countries seem limited across legislation, policy, and practice.
4. Many countries do not seem to see inclusive assessment as an issue, let alone a priority.

5. Resourcing of special needs education seems to be a predictor of inclusive assessment across countries. The more the resources are applied to special education, the more likely that inclusive assessment is considered a priority that deserves attention.
6. National assessment also seems to be a predictor of inclusive assessment across countries, especially when countries declare a policy of Assessment for All. However, few countries have been able to realise this outcome.
7. Western countries are more likely to have policies and practices related to inclusive practices. While European countries have their own Agency to drive educational agendas such as inclusive assessment, the United States, Australia, and the United Kingdom have strong cultural ties that influence one another in the development of policy and practices, despite their own unique educational cultures.

Culture seems to be an intervening factor in the rollout of inclusive assessment, as indicated by the philosophical complexities experienced in Mainland China. Collectivist cultures, compared with individualistic cultures, are therefore less likely to acknowledge the needs of individuals and make adjustments to meet inclusive assessment needs.

Future Directions for International Policies and Practices

Acknowledgement of the above issues can provide some directions to improve inclusive assessment policies and practices across international settings. A number of suggestions and recommendations follow.

The UN declaration is an often quoted world policy initiative in relation to inclusive education, and signatories are more likely to drive the agenda of equity. However, while many countries produce the rhetoric of inclusive beliefs and practices, without legislative enactments or policy directives, practices are not likely to be forthcoming. Through such bodies as UNESCO, a more comprehensive review of inclusive assessment policies and practices across all international settings could be undertaken, to provide impetus for change. When countries are compared with one another in the international sphere (such as with PISA), and a ranking of countries is provided in international reports, with ensuing media interest, governments are more likely to move to action.

Inclusive and equitable assessment drives inclusive instruction and appropriate curriculum, and so within legislation, policy, and practices, the three concepts should be regarded as a composite. The Intended Curriculum Model proposed by Kurz (2011, Chap. 9 in the current volume) and adapted into Australian research (Davies et al., 2016) is an example of how these components need to be considered.

This review recognises that many countries will resist the legal requirements for inclusive assessments, so the question is how do we help countries to ensure that they apply inclusive assessment practices without this legal pressure? It is apparent that many of the policies and practices developed and applied in the United States need to be put into practice in international settings. While it is less likely that US policies will drive other countries to adopt the same policies, it is more likely that through research endeavours, the impact of these inclusive practices in other international settings can be trialled and demonstrated. Attempts have been made in Australia to position the benefits of US practices (see Davies, Elliott, & Kettler, 2012), but receiving funding to support research to demonstrate the transferability of these practices is yet to be realised.

There is a need to review and trial accountability systems such as OTL evaluative tools (*MyiLOGS – My instructional Learning Opportunities Guidance System;* Kurz & Elliott, 2009) and test item accessibility tools (*Test Accessibility and Modification Inventory*; Beddow, Kettler, & Elliott, 2008) and to consider how they can be more easily applied to other countries. The uptake internationally has been limited, and more active strategies that increase advancement need to be developed.

Additionally, there needs to be some encouragement for university researchers worldwide in inclusive education to evaluate their national inclusive assessment practices and to identify areas needing improvement. Those researchers in collectivist culture countries need to reflect on how they manage the complexities surrounding opposing belief systems and how to meet the needs of unique individuals with additional learning needs across inclusive and special education settings.

References

American Educational Research Association (AERA), American Psychological Association (APA), and the National Council on Measurement in Education (NCME) (2014). *Standards for Educational and Psychological Testing*. Washington DC; AERA.

Ainscow, M., & Miles, S. (2012). Making education for all inclusive: Where next? *Prospect: Quarterly: Review of Comparative Education*, 38(1), 15–34.

Altman, J. R., Lazarus, S. S., Quenemoen, R. F., Kearns, J., Quenemoen, M., & Thurlow, M. L. (2010). *2009 survey of states: Accomplishments and new issues at the end of a decade of change*. Minneapolis, MN: University of Minnesota, National Center on Educational Outcomes. Retrieved from www.cehd.umn.edu/NCEO/OnlinePubs/2009StateSurvey.pdf

American Educational Research Association (AERA), American Psychological Association (APA), and the National Council on Measurement in Education (NCME) (2014). Standards for Educational and Psychological Testing. Washington DC; AERA.

Australian Government Attorney-General's Department. (2005). *Disability standards for education*. Retrieved on December 4, 2009 from the World Wide Web: http://www.ag.gov.au/www/agd/agd.nsf/Page/Humanrightsandantidiscrimination_DisabilityStandardsforEducation

Australasian Legal Information Institute. (2009). *Disability discrimination act 1992*. Retrieved on December 3, 2009 from the World Wide Web: http://www.austlii.edu.au/

Australian Curriculum Assessment and Reporting Authority (ACARA). (2011). *National Assessment Program Literacy and numeracy handbook for principals 2011*. Brisbane, Australia: Queensland Studies Authority.

Australian Government (AG). (2013). *Budget overview*. . http://budget.gov.au/2013-14/content/overview/html/index.htm

Beddow, P. A., Kettler, R. J., & Elliott, S. N. (2008). *Test accessibility and modification inventory (TAMI)*. Nashville, TN: Vanderbilt University.

Bolt, S. E., & Roach, A. T. (2009). *Inclusive assessment and accountability: A guide to accommodations for students with diverse needs*. New York, NY: Guilford Press.

Cameto, R., Knokey, A.-M., Nagle, K., Sanford, C., Blackorby, J., Sinclair, B., & Lauer, K. (2009). *State profiles on alternate assessments based on alternate achievement standards: A report from the National Study on Alternate Assessments, NCSER 2009–3013*. National Center for Special Education Research. Retrieved from http://ies.ed.gov/ncser/

Cameto, R., & Nagle, K. (2007). *Orientation and mobility skills of secondary school students with visual impairments. Facts from NLTS2. (NCSER 2008–3007)*. Menlo Park, CA: SRI International.

Center on International Education Benchmarking. (2016). Education for all. Retrieved from http://www.ncee.org/programs-affiliates/center-on-international-education-benchmarking/top-performingcountries/shanghai-china/shanghai-china-education-for-all/

Cumming. (2012). *Valuing students with impairments: International comparisons of practice in educational accountability*. Dordrecht, The Netherlands: Springer.

D'Alessio, S., & Cowan, S. (2013). Cross-cultural approaches to the study of "inclusive" and "special needs" education. *Annual Review of Comparative and International Education*, 20, 227–261. https://doi.org/10.1108/S1479-3679(2013)0000020021

D'Alessio, S., & Watkins, A. (2009). International comparisons of inclusive policy and practice: Are we all talking about the same thing? *Research in Comparative and International Education Journal*, 4(3), 233–249.

D'Alessio, S., Watkins, A., & Donnelly, V. (2010). Inclusive education across Europe: The move in thinking from integration to inclusion. *Revista de Psicologı'a y Educacio'n Madrid*, 1(5), 109–127.

Davies, M. (2012). Accessibility to NAPLAN assessments for students with disabilities: A 'fair go'. *Australasian Journal of Special Education*, 36(1), 62–78.

Davies, M., & Dempsey, I. (2011). Ch. 5. Australian policies to support inclusive assessments. In S. N. Elliott, R. J. Kettler, P. A. Beddow, & A. Kurz (Eds.), *Handbook of accessible achievement tests for all students* (pp. 83–98). New York, NY: Springer.

Davies, M., Elliott, S. N., & Cumming, J. (2016). Documenting support needs and adjustment gaps for students with disabilities: Teacher practices in Australian classrooms and on national tests. *International Journal of Inclusive Education*, 1–18. https://doi.org/10.1080/13603116.2016.1159256

Davies, M., Elliott, S. N., & Kettler, R. J. (2012). Australian students with disabilities accessing NAPLAN: Lessons from a decade of inclusive assessment in the United States. *International Journal of Disability, Development and Education*, 59(1), 7–19.

Davies, M., Elliott, S. N., Sin, K. F., Yan, Z., & Yel, N. (2017). Using adjustments to support the learning and assessment needs of students with disabilities: Macao and Mainland China teachers' reports. *International Journal of Disability, Development and Education*. https://doi.org/10.1080/1034912X.2017.1346238

Dempsey, I., & Davies, M. (2013). National test performance of young Australian children with additional educational needs. *Australian Journal of Education*, 57(1), 5–18. First published in 2013. https://doi.org/10.1177/0004944112468700

Deng, M., & Pei, M. (2009). Instructions for students with special educational needs in Chinese mainstream classrooms: modifications and barriers. *Asia-Pacific Education Review, 10*, 317–325. https://doi.org/10.1007/s12564-009-9032-1

Deng, M., & Harris, K. (2008). Meeting the needs of students with disabilities in general education classrooms in China. *Teacher Education and Special Education, 31*, 195–207.

Deng, M., & Poon-McBrayer, K. F. (2004). Inclusive education in China: Conceptualisation and realization. *Asia-Pacific Journal of Education, 24*, 143–157.

Douglas, G., McLinden, M., Robertson, C., Travers, J., & Smith, E. (2016). Including pupils with special educational needs and disability: Comparison of three country case studies through and inclusive assessment framework. *International Journal of Disability, Development and Education, 63*(1), 98–121. https://doi.org/10.1080/1034912X.2015.1111306

Education Standards (2005)- DDA Education Standards. (2009). *Your right to an education: A guide for students with a disability, their associates, and education providers*. Retrieved January 19, 2010 from the World Wide Web: www.ddaedustandards.info

Education For All Global Monitoring Report. (2015). *Education for all 2000–2015: Achievements and challenges*. Paris, France: United Nations Educational Scientific and Cultural Organisation. Downloaded on Sept 1 2016 at en.unesco.org/gem.../2015/education-all-2000-2015-achievements-and-challenges

European Agency for Development in Special Needs Education. (2016). *Assessment in inclusive settings: Key policy messages*. Retrieved on Sept 1 2016 from https://www.european-agency.org/sites/default/files/assessment-key-policy-messages_Assessment-policypaper-EN.pdf

Geenen, K., & Ysseldyke, J. (1997). Educational standards and students with disabilities. *The Educational Forum, 61*, 220–229.

Geisinger, K. F., & McCormick, C. (2016). Chapter 18. Testing individuals with disabilities: An international perspective. In F. T. Leong, D. Bartram, F. M. Cheung, K. F. Geisinger, & D. Iliescu (Eds.), *The ITC international handbook of testing and assessment* (pp. 260–273). New York, NY: Oxford University Press.

Gu, D. Q. (1993). The changes of legislation on special education in China. *Research on Special Education, 1*, 1–9. (in Chinese).

Hornby, G. (2015). Inclusive special education: Development of a new theory for the education of children with special educational needs and disabilities. *British Journal of Special Education, 42*(3), 234–256. https://doi.org/10.1111/1467-8578.12101

Hernandez, V. T. (2008). Making good on the promise of international law: The convention on the rights of persons with disabilities and inclusive education in China and India. *Pacific Rim Law and Policy Journal, 17*, 497–526.

IDEA. (1997). *The individuals with disabilities education act*. Washington DC.

Kefallinou, A., & Donnelly, V. (2016). Inclusive assessment: Issues and challenges for policy and practice. In A. Watkins & C. Meijer (Eds.), *Implementing inclusive education: Issues in bridging the policy-practice gap (International perspectives on inclusive education, volume 8)* (pp. 209–227). Bradford, UK: Emerald Group Publishing Limited. https://doi.org/10.1108/S1479-363620160000008013

Ketterlin-Geller, L. R., & Jamgochian, E. M. (2011). Chapter 7. Instructional adaptations: Accommodations and modifications that support accessible instruction. In S. N. Elliott, R. J. Kettler, P. A. Beddow, & A. Kurz (Eds.), *Handbook of accessible achievement tests for all students* (pp. 131–146). New York, NY: Springer.

Kettler, R. (2012). Testing accommodations: Theory and research to inform practice. *International Journal of Disability, Development and Education, 59*, 53066. https://doi.org/10.1080/1034912X.2012.654952

Kurz, A. (2011). Access to what should be taught and will be tested: Students' opportunity to learn the intended curriculum. In S. N. Elliott, R. J. Kettler, P. A. Beddow, & A. Kurz (Eds.), *Handbook of accessible achievement tests for all students: Bridging the gaps between research, practice, and policy* (pp. 99–129). New York, NY: Springer.

Kurz, A., & Elliott, S. N. (2009). *My instructional Learning Opportunity Guidance System (MyiLOGS)*. Nashville, TN: Vanderbilt University.

Kyriazopoulou, M., & Weber, H. (2009). *Development of a set of indicators – For inclusive education in Europe*. Odense, Denmark: European Agency for Development in Special Needs Education. Retrieved from https://www.european-agency.org/sites/default/files/development-of-a-set-of-indicators-for-inclusive-education-in-europe_Indicators-EN-with-cover.pdf

Lazarus, S. S., Thurlow, M. L., Lail, K. E., & Christensen, L. (2009). A longitudinal analysis of state accommodations policies: Twelve years of change, 1993–2005. *The Journal of Special Education, 43*, 67–80.

Lazarus, S. S., Cormier, D. C., Crone, M., & Thurlow, M. L. (2010). *States' accommodations policies for alternate assessments based on modified achievement standards (AA-MAS) in 2008. (Synthesis Report 74)*. Minneapolis MN: University of Minnesota, National Center on Educational Outcomes.

Lazarus, S. S., Hodgson, J., & Thurlow, M. L. (2010). *States' participant guidelines for alternate assessments based on modifies academic achievement standards (AA-MAS) in 2008. (Synthesis Report 75)*. Minneapolis, MN: University of Minnesota, National Center on Educational Outcomes.

Lee, Y. H. (1995). *Reform of higher education in China (PRC) 1978–1989*. Ann Arbor, MI: U.M.I.

Leong, F. T., Bartram, D., Cheung, F. M., Geisinger, K. F., & Iliescu, D. (Eds.). (2016). *The ITC international handbook of testing and assessment*. New York, NY: Oxford University Press.

Lin, J. (1993). *Education in post-Mao China*. Westport, CT: Praeger.

Maxwell, L. A., & Shah, N. (2011). Often excluded, more special-needs students taking NAEP. *Education Week, 31*. Retrieved from http://www.edweek.org/ew/articles/2011/11/15/12exclusion.h31.html

Meijer, C., Soriano, V., & Watkins, A. (2007). Inclusive education across Europe: Reflections upon 10 years of work from the European Agency for Development in special needs education. *Childhood Education, 83*(6), 361–365. https://doi.org/10.1080/00094056.2007.10522951

Meijer, C., & Watkins, A. (2016). Changing conceptions of inclusion underpinning education policy. In A. Watkins & C. Meijer (Eds.), *Implementing inclusive education: Issues in bridging the policy-practice gap (International perspectives on inclusive education, volume 8)* (pp. 1–16). Emerald Group Publishing Limited. https://doi.org/10.1108/S1479-363620160000008001

Meijer, C. J. W. (Ed.). (2003a). *Inclusive education and classroom practices.* Middelfart, Denmark: European Agency for Development in Special Needs Education.

Meijer, C. J. W. (Ed.). (2003b). *Special education across Europe in 2003: Trends in provision in 18 European countries.* Middelfart, Denmark: European Agency for Development in Special Needs Education.

Ministerial Council for Education, Early Childhood Development and Youth Affairs (MCEECDYA). (2010). The Adelaide declaration on national goals for schooling in the twenty-first century. Retrieved from http://www.mceecdya.edu.au/mceecdya/

Ministry of Education of China. (2003). The major statistics of the national education development in 2003. (In Chinese). Retrieved from http://www.edu.cn/20040527/3106677.shtm

Mitchell, D. (2015). Inclusive education is a multi-faceted concept. *Center for Educational Policy Studies Journal, 5*(1), 9–30.

McLaughlin, M. J., & Thurlow, M. (2003). Educational accountability and students with disabilities: Issues and challenges. *Educational Policy, 17*(4), 431–451.

National People's Congress of People's Republic of China. (1986). Compulsory Education Law of People's Republic of China.

National People's Congress of People's Republic of China. (1990). Law on the Protection of Persons with Disabilities (LPPD) of People's Republic of China.

People's Republic of China. (2011). *People with disabilities education ordinance.* Issued by the State Council of the People's Republic of China (8 January 2011). Retrieved from http://www.gov.cn/gongbao/content/2011/content_1860775.htm

People's Republic of China. (2015). *Regulations on the national higher education entrance examination for people with disabilities.* State Council and China Disabled Persons' Federation. Retrieved from http://www.moe.edu.cn/publicfiles/business/htmlfiles/moe/B21_xxgk/201505/xxgk_187141.html

Programme for International Student Assessment (PISA). (2016). *PISA technical notes.* Downloaded on Oct 10, 2016 from https://www.oecd.org/pisa/aboutpisa/pisa-faq.htm

Schoonheim, J., & Ruebain, D. (2005). Reflections on inclusion and accommodation in childhood education. In A. Lawson & C. Gooding (Eds.), *Disability rights in Europe: From theory to practice* (pp. 163–186). Oxford, UK: Hart Publishing.

Smyth, F., Shevlin, M., Buchner, T., Biewer, G., Flynn, P., Latimer, C., … Ferreira, M. A. V. (2014). Inclusive education in progress: Policy evolution in four European countries. *European Journal of Special Needs Education, 29*(4), 433–445. https://doi.org/10.1080/08856257.2014.922797

Sanford, C., Newman, L., Wagner, M., Cameto, R., Knokey, A.-M., & Shaver, D. (2011). *The post-high school outcomes of young adults with disabilities up to 6 years after high school. Key findings from the National Longitudinal Transition Study-2 (NLTS2). (NCSER 2011–3004).* Menlo Park, CA: SRI International.

Technical Work Group. (2006). *Including students with disabilities in large scale assessment.* Washington DC: American Institute for Research.

US Department of Education. (2003). Standards and assessments non-regulatory guidance March 10, 2003.

United Nations. (2006). *Convention on the rights of persons with disabilities.* New York, NY: United Nations.

United Nations Educational, Scientific and Cultural Organization. (2009). *Policy Guidelines on Inclusion in Education.* Paris, France: Author.

United Nations Educational Scientific and Cultural Organisation. (2015). *Global education report. Education for all 2000–2015: Achievements and challenges.* Paris, France: United Nations Educational, Scientific and Cultural Organization.

United Nations Educational Scientific and Cultural Organisation. (2016). *Global education report. Education for people and the planet: Creating sustainable futures for all..* Downloaded 20th Sept 2016. http://en.unesco.org/gem-report/

UNESCO. (2011). *UNESCO and education: Everyone has a right to education.* Paris, France: Author.

Watkins, A. (Ed.). (2003). *Key principles in special needs education recommendations for policy makers.* Middelfart, Denmark: European Agency for Development in Special Needs Education.

Watkins, A. (Ed.). (2007). *Assessment in inclusive settings: Key issues for policy and practice.* Odense, Denmark: European Agency for Development in Special Needs Education.

Watkins, A., Ebersold, S., & Lenart, A. (2014). Data collection to inform international policy issues on inclusive education. In C. Forlin & T. Loreman (Eds.), *International perspectives on inclusive education: Measuring inclusive education* (Vol. 3, pp. 53–74). Bradford, UK: Emerald Group Publishing. https://doi.org/10.1108/S1479-363620140000003011

Wang, D. J., & Wang, H. L. (1994). *Foundation of Education.* Beijing, China: People's Education Press. (in Chinese).

Weng, M., & Feng, Y. (2014). Special education today in China. Special education international perspectives: Practices across the globe. *Advances in Special Education, 28,* 663–688.

Zhou, M. (2002). Continuation, transition, and challenge collectivism in China after 1949. Accessed January 17, 2007 from http://switch.sjsu.edu/nextswitch/switch_engine/front/front.php?artc=59.

Fair Testing and the Role of Accessibility

Elizabeth A. Stone and Linda L. Cook

Most discussions of fairness in educational and psychological testing begin with a disclaimer similar to the one presented in the Fairness in Testing Chapter of the Standards for Educational and Psychological Testing, "The term fairness has no single technical meaning and is used in many different ways in public discourse" (American Educational Research Association [AERA], American Psychological Association [APA], & National Council on Measurement in Education [NCME], 2014, p. 49). The authors of the Standards made the point that it is sometimes the case that psychometricians who agree that fairness is a desirable goal in testing will disagree regarding whether scores from a particular testing program provide the basis for fair inferences about individuals who participate in the program. Additionally, it is pointed out that one thing that most psychometricians do agree on is that fairness is a fundamental validity issue that should be addressed from the very conception of a new test or testing process.

In spite of differences in perspectives on fairness in testing, one commonly adopted position is that fair interpretations of test results are based on scores that have comparable meaning for all individuals in the intended population and that fair test score interpretations do not advantage or disadvantage some individuals because of characteristics they may have that are irrelevant to the construct the test is intended to measure. Tests that reflect this fairness perspective consider, to the degree possible, characteristics of all individuals in the intended test population throughout all stages of test development, administration, scoring, interpretation, and use so that barriers to fair assessment can be reduced (Thurlow et al., 2009).

An important concept associated with fairness in testing is the concept of an accessible assessment. In this chapter, we will elaborate on the definition of accessibility that has been used throughout this book. This definition describes accessibility as, "The extent to which a product, environment, or system eliminates barriers and permits equal access to all components and services for all individuals." This definition is fundamental to the notion just mentioned: fair test score interpretations are based on scores that have comparable meaning for individuals and groups in the intended population of test takers. The definition is also consistent with the discussion of "Fairness as Access to the Construct" that has been added to the 2014 revision of the Standards (AERA, APA, & NCME, 2014). According to the 2014 Standards, "Accessible testing situations are those that enable all test takers in the intended population, to the extent feasible, to show their status on the target

E. A. Stone (✉) · L. L. Cook
Educational Testing Services, Princeton, NJ, USA
e-mail: estone@ets.org

construct (s) without being unduly advantaged or disadvantaged by individual characteristics (e.g., characteristics related to age, disability, race/ethnicity, gender or language) that are irrelevant to the construct(s) the test is intended to measure" (p. 52).

It is important to note that the 2014 *Standards* view accessibility as a bias issue because if a test presents obstacles that prevent access to the construct a test is measuring for some groups and not others, the end result can be that it is invalid to make the same interpretations associated with the scores obtained for different groups of test takers. Concerns about differences in interpretations of scores being associated with different groups can be related directly to the notion that in order to provide valid interpretations of test scores, these interpretations must have comparable meaning across groups. Consequently, we contend that accessibility is a fundamental principle of testing that supports both fairness and the validity of test score interpretations.

In most cases, lack of comparability in inferences made from test scores obtained by different groups arises from construct-irrelevant variance that can be related to barriers created by a test or testing process that lacks accessibility. This lack of accessibility can be created by a number of factors. The 2014 *Standards* attribute the introduction of construct-irrelevant components in test scores to, "…inappropriate sampling of test content, aspects of the test context such as a lack of clarity in test instructions, item complexities that are unrelated to the construct being measured, and/or test response expectations or scoring criteria that may favor one group over another. In addition, opportunity to learn (i.e., the extent to which an examinee has been exposed to instruction or experiences assumed by the test developer and/or user) can influence the fair and valid interpretation of test scores for their intended uses" (p. 54).

Finding ways to improve the accessibility of an assessment can be quite complex. One reason is that improving accessibility for one group of test takers could possibly result in reducing the accessibility for another group. For example, in some cases, the use of graphics, animations, and videos in an assessment could improve the accessibility of an assessment for individuals who are hearing impaired; however, the use of a video in an assessment would be a barrier to the content of the assessment for examinees that have a visual impairment. Further, complex graphics may improve the ease and convenience of understanding content visually for students who can do so while decreasing that accessibility for students who require alternate text or a tactile graphic. In addition, some individuals may have multiple characteristics that interact with an assessment to create multiple barriers. Reducing construct-irrelevant variance in test scores for individuals with several—possibly conflicting—access issues can be quite challenging. Also, the test developer must always be concerned with representing the construct the test is designed to measure with the greatest degree of fidelity. For example, the use of a calculator on a math test may increase the accessibility of the test for some individuals but could possibly result in underrepresentation of the construct that the test is intended to measure. If the test construct includes the ability to carry out specific computations or mathematical operations, then the addition of a calculator might have an impact on the validity of the inferences made from the test scores.

In spite of the aforementioned complexities, important advances have been made over the past decade in the methods for increasing accessibility and fairness of assessments both through the careful design and development of the assessment and also through the use of accommodations and, in some cases, modifications[1] of the assessment (Thurlow et al., 2009). These test changes can improve access to part or all of the construct, better enabling test takers to demonstrate proficiency in situations that otherwise might be fraught with accessibility obstacles. However, it is important to note, as we discuss later in this chapter, that some test

---

[1]Accommodations are typically defined as adjustments to the test or testing process that do not alter the assessed construct; whereas, modifications are adjustments to the test or testing process that may affect the construct being measured and, consequently, result in scores that differ in meaning from scores on the unmodified test.

changes may mask measurement of components of the construct, a possibility that must be taken into account when defining accommodation policy. Currently, there is an emphasis on reducing the need for assessment accommodations or modifications by carefully considering the needs of all test takers at the earliest design stages. Universal design (Thompson, Johnstone, & Thurlow, 2002) provides a conceptual model that may be used to inform the design of accessible tests. Test developers using the principles of universal design begin the design process by focusing on the needs of all individuals who will eventually take the assessment. According to the 2014 *Standards*, universal design can be used to design and develop tests that are "… as usable as possible for all test takers in the intended test population, regardless of characteristics such as gender, age, language background, culture, socioeconomic status, or disability" (p. 57).

If the resulting inferences from an assessment are fair, they will fit the framework of having comparable meaning for all groups in the intended testing population. And comparable meaning of inferences can only result when barriers that result in construct-irrelevant variance in test scores have been removed by creating accessible assessments. The process of developing fair and accessible assessments begins with specification of the construct and focuses on test content, context, responses, and score reporting. If it is not possible to provide accessibility through design constraints, then accommodations and modifications to the testing process may be necessary.

In this chapter, we discuss (a) how to create accessible assessments with a focus on the design and development of the construct, content, format, response mode, and score reports, (b) how assistive technology can be used to increase accessibility and fairness for some groups of test takers, (c) what happens if assessments continue to present barriers to some groups of test takers in spite of efforts to make them accessible, and (d) the need for test accommodations and modifications including how to form policies for accommodations. Finally, we provide suggestions for how to evaluate the fairness and accessibility of an assessment.

Fairness and Accessible Tests

Creating Accessible Tests

To create tests that are accessible for all examinees while still maintaining validity and score interpretability, it is important for test specialists to first define several important properties of the test. These include the construct or constructs that the test seeks to measure, the content by which these constructs will be assessed, the format in which the test will be given, and the modes that test takers will be allowed to use to participate in the test. Additionally, there may be assistive technology to further support test takers in physically accessing the test content. The Individuals with Disabilities Education Act (IDEA, 2004) includes definitions of 13 disability subtypes or categories under which students with disabilities are eligible for special education. As specified by that law, these categories are autism, deaf-blindness, deafness, emotional disturbance, hearing impairment, mental retardation, orthopedic impairment, other health impairment, specific learning disability, speech or language impairment, traumatic brain injury, and visual impairment. This list gives some idea of the range of possible barriers that students in these categories may encounter related to testing, and we explore these with examples in this section of the chapter. Students who are English language learners (ELs) have accessibility challenges that overlap in some cases with those experienced by students with disabilities; however, there are additional challenges for ELs that we will also highlight as we discuss aspects of designing fair tests.

Constructs The *Standards for Educational and Psychological Testing* defines construct as the "concept or the characteristic that a test is designed to measure" (AERA, APA, & NCME, 2014, p. 11). A key focus of test validity is construct validity—that the test measures what it intends to measure and no more, nor less. Further, the test items should actually measure the construct(s) and not contain text or ancillary material (e.g., graphs, charts, figures) that either draw away from focus on the primary item content or that cue the test taker to the correct answer option. When test items do have features that are identified as possible impediments to test takers demonstrating their proficiency, this is referred to as construct-irrelevant variance. In other words, differences in performance on the item may be due to influences other than proficiency on the construct being measured. Because of the central role of the construct (or constructs) in test development and evaluation, we begin there.

How can test developers create an assessment that measures what it purports to measure? The first step is to define the construct(s). The construct for a particular assessment may be summarized as mathematics proficiency, for example, but to operationalize this description for test development, the definition must be expanded upon to include a conceptual framework that lists knowledge, skills, and abilities to be tested and that optimally does so in a way as to be distinct from other, similar, or related constructs. For example, reading proficiency in elementary school may include decoding as part of the definition of the construct, whereas in secondary school, the definition of reading proficiency may be focused on higher-order skills. Similarly, calculation may be a skill assessed on tests of mathematics proficiency in lower grades but may not be a focus in upper grades in which computational fluency is assumed. The definition of the construct is crucial to many of the aspects we discuss, and it plays a role in what steps we can and should take to remove barriers to accessibility.

Content The content included on the test is another area in which accessibility can be addressed from development forward. Universal Design for Learning (UDL; Center for Applied Special Technologies, 2011) consists of a set of principles designed to include accessibility from the start. UDL grew from the universal design paradigm introduced to architecture by Ron Mace, in which structural design was viewed as requiring an eye toward accessibility from the ground up rather than via retrofitting. Chapter 11 (Hall & Rosen) in this volume provides a detailed account of the role of UDL in the design of instruction and tests.

Application of the principles of UDL is one way that assessment specialists ensure that construct-irrelevant variance—differentiation in test scores due to aspects of the items not related to the construct being measured—does not impact the interpretation of test scores. For example, tests that require dexterity and speed due to the type or number and complexity of items may have construct-irrelevant variance (if dexterity and speed are not part of the intended construct), particularly for test takers with fine motor impairments or other characteristics that may negatively affect demonstration of those skills. Characteristics of the language in which the test is written may also contribute construct-irrelevant variance, and this can happen in several ways. The test should not include language to which students may be sensitive, unless required by the test. For example, person-first language is typically recommended for use when describing individuals with disabilities (e.g., "student who is blind" versus "blind student") (Snow, 2007); however, this perspective is not universal (Peers, Spencer-Cavaliere, & Eales, 2014). Fairness guidelines should be developed or adopted that define sensitive and insensitive language for groups of interest,[2] and test materials can then be reviewed to be sure that they adhere to these principles before being administered to test takers.

Language can also be problematic if it presents an extraneous obstacle to comprehending the content. The language should not be more advanced than required to measure the target construct. In some cases, students who are ELs may benefit from language modification, in which negative constructions, words with multiple meanings, and other potentially complex and idiomatic language features are avoided in favor

---

[2] See, for example, the fairness guidelines developed by Educational Testing Service: https://www.ets.org/Media/About_ETS/pdf/overview.pdf.

of simplified language and structure (Abedi & Sato, 2007). These changes are not intended to reduce the cognitive demand of the items but are designed to improve access to grade-level content by presenting the content in a more commonly used, accessible language and syntax.

Another potential concern arises when test forms must contain different items because some of the items cannot be rendered in all required formats. For example, some mathematics items may be infeasible to produce in braille, such as complex equations or figures with many colors or shading to indicate three dimensions, even with the use of braille systems developed for mathematical content (e.g., Nemeth code). Because these items cannot be administered to students who are blind and require a braille transcription, it is critical to evaluate the comparability of the items that take their place on the braille form and to ensure that content and construct representation are still present.

According to Sireci and Pitoniak (2007), construct-irrelevant variance can also arise from a number of sources including inappropriate use of testing accommodations or modifications. These authors point out that "Construct representation can also suffer when a change to a test administration completely alters what is being measured. For example, some reading specialists claim when a reading test is read aloud to students, the construct being measured changes from reading comprehension to listening comprehension" (p. 54).

Format A great many of the tests with which consumers are familiar are of the paper-and-pencil variety. In that scenario, test items are delivered linearly and conventionally. However, many testing programs have now moved to a computer-based setting, enabling the provision of tests tailored more to the individual in terms of content, difficulty, and accessibility features. By accessibility features, we refer to adjustments to the way the test is delivered or interacted with that allow test takers to better demonstrate their proficiency by removing barriers such as those due to disability or language minority status. However, while such contexts were some of the main drivers of the development of many accessibility features, large testing programs and consortia such as the Partnership for Assessment of Readiness for College and Careers (PARCC) and the Smarter Balanced Assessment Consortium (Smarter Balanced) have recognized that it is beneficial to provide varying levels of accessibility features to all test takers. Because some students may have barriers to their access to test content, Smarter Balanced has three tiers of test changes (from least to most restricted) that may or may not be embedded in the testing platform: universal tools, designated supports, and accommodations (Smarter Balanced, 2013). Universal tools such as highlighter and zoom are available to all students on all tasks, while English dictionaries are available only on particular components. In particular, calculators may be used only on calculator-allowed items. Designated supports are available to students with a documented need, with examples such as masking (e.g., covering parts of the screen to enhance focus on specific material) and a scribe. Accommodations are allowed only for students with individualized education programs (IEPs) or 504 plans that require them. (Chapter 5 by Chia and Kachchaf in the current volume provides additional information on Smarter Balanced's accessibility plan.) PARCC administers assessments with three tiers of test changes: accessibility features that are available for all students, accessibility features that are only available if identified in advance, and accommodations (Partnership for Assessment of Readiness for College and Careers [PARCC], 2016). In the first category are features that students can turn on or off individually in the testing platform. These include magnification and text-to-speech (TTS) rendering of mathematics content. In the second category are administrative conditions such as timing and setting changes that describe when and where a student takes the assessments. These changes must be enabled by the principal or test coordinator. In the final tier are accommodations that are limited to some students with disabilities and students who are ELs. Accommodations include the use of TTS for the English language arts (ELA)/literacy assessments and large print or braille formats. Note that the use of the term accommodations by the consortia differs from that in the Standards, in that the consortia refer to accommodations as the most drastic test changes, whereas many of these changes would be denoted as modifications in the taxonomy presented in the Standards. We further discuss accommodations and modifications in the section *Barriers to Accessible Testing*.

An additional method by which tests can be made more accessible through their formats is through the use of tablets which can often display more innovative item types and allow test takers to interact with the test in a more tactile sense, as well as allowing for delivery of more tailored accommodations and accessibility features that are specific to each test taker in a bring-your-own-device approach. Such an approach requires additional attention to test security because of the required integration of test material and platform with the test taker's own hardware. Further, it is crucial to consider and evaluate what effect fully individualized testing sessions has on score comparability. Note that delivery on a digital platform may actually lessen accessibility in some cases. For example, consider a mathematics assessment for students who are blind. A paper-and-pencil test easily allows for tactile representations of graphics and other figures. However, the computer screen is smooth and unchanging. How can this accessibility gap be bridged? Some options are through pre-printing of tactile graphics to accompany a test, on-demand embossed graphics printing, or on-demand printing of three-dimensional models where applicable. The use of the tablet allows for the incorporation of haptic technologies to provide tactile representations on a digital platform; however, these newer types of test material delivery require research to support the psychometric properties of the tests being administered (Hakkinen, 2015).

With states and state consortia now allowing the use of tablets in large-scale assessment, several empirical studies have investigated user experience and comparability of scores when tablet devices are employed (see, e.g., Davis, Kong, McBride, & Morrison, 2015; Steedle, McBride, Johnson, & Keng, 2015). While these studies mostly found a large degree of comparability between devices, there were some areas of discrepancy. For example, some mathematics tasks displayed significant differences in student performance without any identifiable pattern as to what caused those differences (Steedle et al., 2015). Screen size is also a concern when the smaller tablet display requires scrolling (e.g., for a reading passage). Device input has also been raised as an issue, particularly for writing tasks, as students tend *not* to prefer using a tablet for constructing longer written responses. It is important to note that although students with disabilities were included in some of these studies, the analyses did not focus on effects for those students—a group that possibly has the most potential to capitalize on flexible device usage—nor did it disaggregate by disability subtype. Students with different accessibility barriers may experience different benefits or disadvantages when using different types of technology. As with all technology, familiarity with the device is very important.

A report commissioned by the Council of Chief State School Officers (DePascale, Dadey, & Lyons, 2016) reviewed the literature to date on device comparability and provided a list of features and aspects that should be evaluated when considering the use of tablets in assessment. Overall, a computer- or tablet-based test format can enhance the flexibility by which the test taker can interact with the test items. For example, technologically enhanced items have been integrated into large-scale assessments in greater numbers. These new item types may be more amenable to students efficiently selecting or highlighting text, dragging and dropping elements, or working directly with elements that display data such as bar graphs, on a touchscreen than with a keyboard or mouse. However, it is clear that there is still much research to be done to examine device effects in varying testing scenarios. The report commissioned by CCSSO provided four aspects to consider when examining device comparability: (a) identify the comparability concern(s) being addressed; (b) determine the desired level of comparability; (c) clearly convey the comparability question or claim; and

(d) focus on the device. The report illustrates each of these aspects in detail, outlining a path for states to consider when designing comparability studies involving device effects. It is particularly important that these aspects be examined specifically for students with disabilities or who are ELs in order to identify how results differ for those students.

Response mode One particular type of test variation that can affect accessibility is the set of ways in which test takers can respond to items. Consider test takers with motor skill deficits who have trouble navigating using a mouse. For these test takers, and for test takers with visual impairments, keyboard navigation may be a viable alternative. However, more complex testing scenarios (e.g., simulations such as those used for some natural science classes) may be too complicated and may prohibit that use. Innovative item types, such as drag-and-drop or plotting elements on a graph (versus identifying coordinates of plotted elements), are less likely to be navigable using the keyboard. Further, some students may have typing issues that affect their ability to demonstrate their writing proficiency; in that case, allowing students to dictate responses to a scribe, submit handwritten responses on a piece of paper for optical character recognition (OCR) scanning or intelligent word recognition, use a pen that captures movements on a pen-based device screen surface, or read their responses into speech recognition software may ameliorate that problem to some extent. However, the resulting responses may need to be transcribed if produced via a method that does not deliver transcriptions automatically; in any case, an accurate transcription is critical. This need for a correct transcription adds an additional quality control step to the test scoring process. See Appendix C of PARCC (2016) for one example of procedure and policy related to these alternate response options. Human and automated scoring can both be problematic if rubrics are not clearly aligned to the construct of interest. For example, if raters prize response length or clarity of speech as proxies for proficiency when these aspects are not part of the construct, they may disadvantage test takers focused on providing the best response that they can within the confines of the technology they must use. This is true for all test takers, but in particular for students who struggle with barriers to accessibility.

Even in paper-and-pencil situations, response mode can influence test accessibility. For example, difficulties with the act of having to transfer answers to an answer sheet can be addressed by allowing test takers to respond in their test booklets (Stone, King, & Laitusis, 2011; Tindal, Heath, Hollenbeck, Almond, & Harniss, 1998). Test takers could also be allowed to read their answers aloud in an individual or carefully structured group setting.

Regardless of which decisions are made in developing and delivering assessments, states and testing agencies can improve fairness and validity by ensuring that test takers are provided with appropriate and accessible practice materials and are as familiar as possible with the testing platform and any accessibility features that are made available for their use.

Barriers to Accessible Testing

The need for test adaptations and modifications Despite the intention to produce tests that are accessible to all examinees, some test takers will not be able to access the test content fully and appropriately without changes to the test format or other administration aspects. There are both physical and cognitive barriers that may prevent the access required for students to show what they know and can do. The *Standards* define adaptations as a general class of changes to the standard testing form intended to make the test accessible for individuals who have characteristics that would impede that accessibility. Falling under that umbrella are a range of test changes that may be differentiated by their impacts on the construct being measured and the resulting comparability of test scores. Testing accommodations are typically defined as not changing the construct of interest, while testing modifications may change the construct. These different classes of changes are generally referred to as accommodations in the literature and are distinguished from one another most often when considering whether and how to report or aggregate scores. For example, under the No Child Left Behind Act of 2001, school systems were required to test 95% of students via a general assessment (i.e., as opposed to with an alternate assessment that measures alternate achievement standards, which is typically meant for only students with significant cognitive disabilities). To do this, states had developed policies, often very different policies, that dictated on which parts of tests students could use various test changes. Students may be allowed to use a calculator on a science test but may be restricted from using it on a mathematics test. Finer-grained policies might allow students to use calculators on mathematics tests that do not focus on the subconstruct of calculation, whereas students may not be allowed to use calculators on mathematics assessments, or portions thereof, that are focused on measuring calculation. In our earlier description of PARCC's accessibility and accommodation policy, we noted that audio delivery of content (TTS) is available to all students for mathematics but is considered an accommodation for ELA/literacy. This is because of the impact on the construct being measured. Decoding is not considered part of the mathematics construct, whereas it is being measured for ELA/literacy. Another example from that policy is the allowance of a calculator for all students on some mathematics sections and only as an accommodation on other mathematics sections. This dichotomy, again, depends on the specific mathematics content and the goals of the assessment.

Even when a test has been built from the ground up to be as accessible as possible through the application of universal design, further test changes may be needed for some test takers to access test content appropriately. For example, no matter how well designed a test, test takers who are blind will require some mode of accessing the content that they cannot see. There is some question of how to accommodate or modify tests that will provide accessibility to test takers with disabilities or who are ELs while resulting in comparable scores for all candidates taking the test. Why is comparability important? While tests may be designed to measure individual proficiency and growth, this outcome is typically evaluated with respect to one particular criterion (i.e., the tests are criterion-referenced), in which case the score must be comparable to that criterion. Or, tests may be norm-referenced, in which case all tests combined to form the norming distribution and those compared to that distribution must be comparable.

How to support comparable interpretations of test scores It is imperative that testing programs capture information that allows them to evaluate the validity of interpretations of scores when accommodations are provided to test takers. Often, testing programs must develop a testing accommodation policy in the absence of empirical evidence about the accommodation in the context of that specific test. This is because the test content, the item types, the test delivery format, or the way the accommodation is implemented may be new, among other reasons. Therefore, the combination of the test material, format, accommodated group, and accommodation may not have been researched adequately or at all. If this is the case, testing programs should have a plan in place during test development to explicitly list the steps that they plan to take to evaluate this new testing condition. This would include validity research as a portion of the overall research agenda, and the *Standards* provide statements about specific areas of focus in the validity and fairness chapters (AERA, APA, & NCME, 2014).

A preferred approach for evaluating comparability is to do an experimental study in which only the accommodation status differs across groups. However, this is challenging for a number of reasons. One reason is that it is challenging to form coherent groups to compare. It is very important to clearly define who the accommodation is meant for and to try to match the makeup of that group when performing the study. The resulting report should then clearly describe the intended and actual group representativeness. A second challenge is that it is often very difficult to recruit enough test takers in some disability groups (particularly low-incidence groups, such as students who are blind) to form subgroups of adequate size for typical fairness analyses, such as those using a differential boost approach (e.g., using analysis of variance methods to identify the interaction of disability status and accommodation usage when examining group performance differences), differential item functioning (DIF), or factor analysis. However, when tests are administered on digital platforms such as computers or tablets, there is an additional opportunity to capture characteristics about the test session. Process data, which typically refers to navigation (keyboard arrowing or movement with a mouse) or selection (e.g., mouse click) options, can indicate how many times a student changes answers and can store what the responses are, can track when and how often a student accesses help features, can show when there may be confusing aspects of the platform or assessment (e.g., if a student tries to click in an inactive spot on the screen or tries to click to select when the item requires the student to drag and drop), and can provide rich information about accessibility feature and accommodation usage. While process data can enhance our understanding of how test takers interact with their tests, there are practical and ethical caveats that should be taken into account, such as the feasibility of storing, analyzing, and interpreting the massive volume of data obtained and test-taker privacy issues (Stone, 2016).

Some alternatives are the following. First, an embedded research section could be added to an operational test, allowing test specialists to evaluate the testing condition with test takers who will already be participating in testing. There are pros and cons to this approach. One positive aspect is that there is a greater chance that students will be motivated to perform well *if* it is the case that they cannot tell the research section from the operational sections. This conditional is not a given. Further, the resulting sample is a convenience sample and may not be representative of the overall population who would typically take the test. It would then be important to consider sampling down some of the subgroups if the overall sample size is large enough, when it is important that sample sizes be proportional to those found in the overall population. One negative aspect is that including an extra section puts additional burden on the test takers, which they may perceive as less palatable compared to the extra section used for operational purposes, such as field testing items or administering an equating set of items that can be used to link test scores across operational forms.

A less optimal approach is to analyze extant data (i.e., data from operational testing). Again, there are benefits to using existing test data. One major benefit is that there is typically a great deal of existing test data available. One downside is that unless a researcher works for a vendor associated with the test, it may be very challenging to obtain access to the data. Even with data in hand, there is a risk that an external researcher not directly involved with the operational development or scoring of the test (even external to the testing program but experienced with operational testing) will not understand all of the details concerning the data and the way they were captured, making it difficult to produce accurate inferences. A bigger downside with respect to examining comparability of test scores is that, while test takers should have been tested under conditions for which they are eligible, these conditions are not randomly assigned. Therefore, inferences about performance on the test under the different testing conditions are confounded with performance on the test for students with different disability statuses. Additionally, test takers using accommodations often use bundled accommodations (e.g., an audio accommodation and extended time), and therefore it is important to take these bundled conditions into account when evaluating subgroup performance.

When are modifications needed? How do modifications impact the fairness and validity of test score interpretations? In some situations, it may be the case that empirical research demonstrates that scores resulting from a particular test change for a particular group are not comparable to those from students taking the standard form of the test in light of the fact that the test may measure different constructs under the different conditions.

The test change would then be considered a modification. While it may not be considered optimal to change the construct being measured, modifications are not rejected outright. Some test takers will not be able to access any test content without some modification. For example, the read-aloud/audio accommodation may be considered a modification when it is provided on a test in which the construct being measured includes decoding, a component skill in many definitions of reading (Laitusis & Cook, 2008). However, when the decoding is done by the audio assist, a test taker may be able to demonstrate higher-order skills such as reading comprehension. Therefore, those making the test must consider the balance of fairness and accessibility versus the value in the resulting test scores and the validity of interpretations that can be made based on them. Scores resulting from modifications are sometimes flagged (a notation is added to the score report indicating that the test was taken under nonstandard conditions) to convey to score users that the test score should not be interpreted in the same way as those resulting from the standard form or taken with accommodations. However, flagging has also been a controversial topic because it discloses information about the test taker to the score user (e.g., that the test taker took the test with the modification, typically indicating that the test taker has a disability that makes him eligible to have the test modified); the Americans with Disabilities Act requires the provision of accommodations when need is documented and prohibits the flagging of scores. An additional fairness issue concerns the opportunity to participate in testing and to have the resulting scores count. This is sometimes the case for students who require certain types of modifications to access the test content (e.g., by having reading test passages read aloud). Without this access, some students may not be able to demonstrate their proficiency, although the use of modifications may prevent the measurement of part or all of the construct, as noted previously. This issue, the balance of improving access and inclusion while trying to maintain score comparability, is clearly at the heart of any discussion of making changes to tests that affect only some students.

While there are many students who might gladly be deemed ineligible to take particular tests, some students or their parents may consider it a civil rights issue not to be able to take a test with modifications or not to have their scores resulting from the modified test counted. Gatekeeper exams, which may be thought of as assessments that an individual must take (e.g., for college admissions, for promotion or graduation within school or professional contexts, for certification to practice a trade), present challenging issues because not allowing those tests to be taken with modifications may prevent the candidate test takers from being able to pursue a particular life path. However, there are practical issues regarding inferences made from tests taken with modifications, particularly in the area of certification. For example, when real-life situations in a field will not allow for that modification to be in place, it is uncertain that proficiency on the test taken with the modification accurately reflects how the student will perform in the field. Medical licensing tests are one area in which modifying the test in a way not replicable in practice has been challenged; however, legislation and legal action have supported the use of accommodations by these test takers without notations on score reports reflecting these changes to the test conditions. Cases such as *Department of Fair Employment & Housing v. Law School Admission Council Inc.*, Case No. 3:12-cv-1830 (US District Court for the Northern District of California) and the settlement agreed to by the National Board of Medical Examiners have forced licensing agencies to reexamine and revise their policies toward providing test accommodations and flagging resulting scores.

How to form a testing accommodation policy Every set of testing conditions is different, so that setting an accommodation policy often requires doing so without empirical support. A first step in developing such a policy is to consider the test construct(s) and the intended use(s) of test scores. The test items should then be examined to identify possible barriers that test takers may come up against. Once the target test-taking population has been identified, states and testing agencies may assemble an advisory group consisting of experts in various aspects of accommodated assessments: psychometricians, test content developers, special education researchers, and researchers who specialize in validity. Additional useful sources of input are test coordinators and general education, special education, and EL practitioners. It may be helpful to review testing policies in place for similar tests (see, e.g., Christensen, Albus, Liu, Thurlow, & Kincaid, 2013; Lazarus, Kincaid, Thurlow, Rieke, & Dominguez, 2014; Thurlow & Larson, 2011; Young & King, 2008); however, it cannot be assumed that accommodation effects generalize across contexts. The National Center on Educational Outcomes (NCEO) at the University of Minnesota has many resources available to support the formation of an initial policy. The state policies section includes accessibility and accommodations for students with disabilities by state,[3] providing a source for comparison with other similar assessments. NCEO has also put together a comprehensive database of studies related to accommodations[4] that can be used to examine the research bases underpinning some of the existing testing policies and to determine whether particular accommodations might or might not be appropriate for the test under development. The database can be searched by keywords related to accommodation type, test content, grade level, and disability, among others. Similarly, researchers and practitioners have developed guidelines for the assessment of ELs that include a focus on test development, testing conditions, and accommodations (Young, 2009). These guidelines, and guidelines describing the standardization of implementation of supports, are critical to fair assessment but are outside the scope of this chapter.

Once an initial accommodation policy has been set, a plan should be put into place to collect and analyze data on accommodation usage and subgroup performance.

Other test changes Throughout this chapter, we have focused on the development and delivery of standard test forms, perhaps with accommodations or modifications. In this section, we briefly consider two other types of changes that are largely outside the scope of this chapter but that are part of the pantheon of accessibility.

Some students with disabilities may require more support than is available through the changes discussed previously. Alternate academic achievement standards and modified academic achievement standards are variations in the regulations that have been intended to improve the testing experience and resulting measurement of students who are disadvantaged by taking the general accountability assessment. Alternate assessments of alternate achievement standards (AA-AAS) are typically administered only to students with significant cognitive disabilities, which is why they are referred to as "1% tests." These tests are usually administered in a one-on-one setting, between the student and the teacher or a proctor who is familiar with the student, and include out-of-level material (Albus & Thurlow, 2013). Regulations for the development and administration of alternate assessments using modified academic achievement standards (AA-MAS) were introduced in 2007 in an attempt to better measure the proficiency of students who did not have significant cognitive disabilities, and who would not be eligible for the alternate assessment, but who were not expected to be able to demonstrate grade-level proficiency on track with their peers. Unlike the AA-AAS tests, AA-MAS tests were aligned to grade-level content standards; however, they included changes such as a reduced number of distractors per item, more white space on the page, and simplified language that were geared toward increasing accessibility. These tests were referred to as "2% tests"; however, as of 2015, this testing option is no longer allowed for accountability purposes.[5]

Aside from changes such as accommodations and modifications, tests to be administered to examinees who are not native speakers of the

---

[3] https://nceo.info/state_policies/accommodationsswd.
[4] https://nceo.info/Resources/bibliographies/accommodations/bibliography.

[5] http://www2.ed.gov/policy/speced/guid/modachieve-summary.html.

language in which the test is usually administered may be adapted by translating the tests into other languages. Adapting tests in this way may be appealing because doing so involves a linguistic translation of the original content. However, translation does not necessarily result in an exact and accurate representation of that content. Comparability of scores depends on the psychometric properties of the test and validity of score interpretations for the different populations being tested to be preserved (Hambleton & Patsula, 1999). Additional challenges to developing and administering a translated test involve forming an effective test translation team and the interaction of home language proficiency and the target language of the translated test version. An alternative to translation is concurrent development of the various language versions of the test (Solano-Flores & Trumbull, 2003).

A final point is that all underserved subgroups are heterogeneous; therefore, while policies need to define feasible approaches to balancing validity, fairness, and accessibility, no policy will fit all test takers perfectly. There will also be test takers who are in multiple categories, such as students with disabilities who are also ELs. Therefore, assessment programs should be flexible enough to adapt their accessibility and accommodation policies in concert with governing policies, empirical evidence, and new research and should continually reevaluate and document decisions and implications. However, changes to these policies over time will preclude some longitudinal research, growth modeling, and even performance comparability for each student over years under differing policies, so these changes must be made carefully and with those consequences in mind.

Evaluating and Reviewing the Accessibility of Assessments

Evidence of fairness and accessibility should begin to accrue at the very earliest stages of the assessment design (e.g., documentation of how the characteristics of all individuals and subgroups in the test population were taken into consideration in the choice of constructs). Evidence to support claims of fairness should be obtained through documentation of the types of reviews that were carried out by expert panels. These reviews include content, item, and test reviews, as well as sensitivity reviews. Documentation of the statistical analyses of pretest and field trial items should include the results of item analysis and DIF analyses carried out for all relevant subgroups where subgroup sizes permit. The results of studies carried out to investigate fairness and validity using techniques appropriate for small sample sizes such as cognitive labs should be included in the documentation. Cognitive labs, including think-aloud studies, allow researchers and practitioners to identify misconceptions that test takers have as well as problematic item features that are preventing test takers from demonstrating proficiency.

Documentation of the results of any field trial studies that were carried out should provide particularly important evidence of comparable validity for relevant subgroups. The analyses should be carried out for accommodated and non-accommodated items and tests. These types of analyses should demonstrate, for example, that within reason, the assessments are comparable in reliability, display minimal amounts of DIF, and so forth for all relevant subgroups. Comparability of the underlying constructs that the assessments are measuring for relevant subgroups can be evaluated through the use of confirmatory factor analysis at the field trial stage. Factor analysis studies should be carried out for each relevant subgroup (where adequate sample sizes exist) and for assessments given with and without accommodations to determine whether or not the accommodations have any effect on the construct(s) that the test is measuring. See Hancock, Mueller, and Stapleton (2010) for specific steps involved in planning, carrying out, and documenting these types of analyses.

As mentioned previously, differential boost studies or, relatedly, studies of the interaction hypothesis (Sireci, Scarpati, & Li, 2005) can be carried out during field trials to evaluate the effects of accommodations on the validity of inferences made from the test scores. According to Sireci et al., "The interaction hypothesis states that (a) when test accommodations are given to [SWD] who need them, their test scores will improve, relative to the scores they would attain when taking the test under standard conditions; and (b) students without disabilities will not exhibit higher scores when taking the test with those accommodations" (p. 458). The logic of the differential boost study is based on the premise that if everyone benefits from an accommodation, then the scores from the accommodated examination may be artificially inflated. And, this inflation is most likely caused by construct-irrelevant variance. There are many different designs that can be used to carry out a study of differential boost, but studies that are most effective in detecting differential boost typically use random assignment to the accommodated and non-accommodated assessments and reasonably large samples.

Additional evidence that individuals and groups in the testing population are being treated fairly can be obtained through the documentation of test administration procedures, including documentation of participation rules, accommodations procedures, and test security procedures. If the assessment is administered in different modes (e.g., paper and pencil and computer or tablet), it is important to look for documentation of the comparability of scores obtained from these different modes for all groups of examinees.

In addition, studies that indicate that the human scoring and the automated scoring procedures used for the assessments provide results that are of comparable quality for all groups of examinees should be documented.

Finally, it is clear that the amount and the quality of instruction that students receive on the constructs assessed may vary considerably. No matter how carefully an assessment is designed, developed, and administered, students who have not received adequate instruction will likely do poorly on the assessments. Opportunity to learn can arise as a consequence of several different issues when considered for students with disabilities. One is known as the Matthew Effect, which has been applied both to a cumulative effect of lack of resources and specifically to a cumulative effect of a reading deficit that creates and widens gaps between students in what is learned in other subjects. A second type of cause occurs when an inability to see the blackboard leads to an inability to visually access the material, causing a gap in learning. A more pernicious cause of a gap in learning occurs when there are low expectations for student achievement or insufficient resources and infrastructure to provide appropriate instruction to underserved populations. See Scarborough and Parker (2003) for a discussion of some of these issues. Opportunity to learn is an important consideration in the interpretation of test scores and should be included in the evaluation of any assessment. Chapter 9 (Kurz) in this volume provides more information on opportunity to learn.

Concluding Remarks

This chapter focused on a discussion of the creation and evaluation of fair and accessible assessments. We began by setting a general framework for considering what fairness and accessibility mean for assessments. We continued with a discussion of the creation of accessible tests that includes a focus on the design, particularly the content and constructs measured by the test. A good deal of the discussion focused on barriers to accessible assessments including opportunity to learn. The use of accommodations and modifications and their effects on test validity were explored. In addition, we addressed the development and use of policies for administering tests with accommodations and modifications. We have been working in the area of test fairness and accessibility with a focus on individuals with disabilities for more than a decade. We are heartened by the gains that have been made in the awareness of the importance of administering fair and accessible tests to all individuals, particularly those with disabilities recently. Many of the issues that were considered intractable only a short while ago have been tackled successfully. Although there are still many barriers to overcome, we are cautiously optimistic that we will see increased educational and life opportunities for a diverse population due to increases in the fairness and accessibility of educational assessments.

References

Abedi, J., & Sato, E. (2007). Linguistic modification. *A report prepared for the US Department of Education LEP Partnership*. Washington, DC: US Department of Education. Retrieved from http://www.ncela.us/files/rcd/BE024210/Linguistic_Modification.pdf

Albus, D., & Thurlow, M. L. (2013). *Accommodation policies for states' alternate assessments based on alternate achievement standards* (AA-AAS) (Synthesis Report 90). Minneapolis, MN: University of Minnesota, National Center on Educational Outcomes.

American Educational Research Association, American Psychological Association, & National Council on Measurement in Education. (2014). *Standards for educational and psychological testing*. Washington, DC: American Educational Research Association.

CAST (2011). Universal Design for Learning Guidelines version 2.0. Wakefield, MA: Author.

Christensen, L. L., Albus, D. A., Liu, K. K., Thurlow, M. L., & Kincaid, A. (2013). *Accommodations for students with disabilities on state English language proficiency assessments: A review of 2011 state policies*. Minneapolis, MN: University of Minnesota, Improving the Validity of Assessment Results for English Language Learners with Disabilities (IVARED).

Davis, L. L., Kong, X., McBride, Y., & Morrison, K. M. (2015). *Device comparability of tablets and computers for assessment purposes*. Retrieved from http://www.acara.edu.au/_resources/20150409_NCME_DeviceComparabilityofTablesComputers.pdf

DePascale, C., Dadey, N., & Lyons, S. (2016). *Score comparability across computerized delivery devices*. Retrieved from http://www.ccsso.org/Documents/CCSSO%20TILSA%20Score%20Comparability%20Across%20Devices.pdf

Hakkinen, M. (2015). Assistive technologies for computer-based assessments. *R&D Connections, 24*, 1–9.

Hambleton, R. K., & Patsula, L. (1999). Increasing the validity of adapted tests: Myths to be avoided and guidelines for improving test adaptation practices. *Journal of Applied Testing Technology, 1*(1), 1–13.

Hancock, G. R., Mueller, R. O., & Stapleton, L. M. (2010). *The reviewer's guide to quantitative methods in the social sciences*. New York, NY: Taylor and Francis.

Individuals with Disabilities Education Act of 2004, 20 U.S.C. § 1400.

Laitusis, C. C., & Cook, L. L. (2008). *Reading aloud as an accommodation for a test of reading comprehension*. Research Spotlight, 15. Retrieved from https://www.ets.org/Media/Research/pdf/SPOTLIGHT1.pdf#page=16

Lazarus, S. S., Kincaid, A., Thurlow, M. L., Rieke, R. L., & Dominguez, L. M. (2014). *2013 state policies for selected response accommodations on statewide assessments* (Synthesis Report 93). Minneapolis, MN: University of Minnesota, National Center on Educational Outcomes.

Partnership for Assessment of Readiness for College and Careers. (2016). *PARCC accessibility features and accommodations manual 2016–2017* (5th ed.). Washington, DC: PARCC Assessment Consortium.

Peers, D., Spencer-Cavaliere, N., & Eales, L. (2014). Say what you mean: Rethinking disability language in Adapted Physical Activity Quarterly. *Adapted Physical Activity Quarterly, 31*(3), 265–282.

Scarborough, H. S., & Parker, J. D. (2003). Matthew effects in children with learning disabilities: Development of reading, IQ, and psychosocial problems from grade 2 to grade 8. *Annals of Dyslexia, 53*(1), 47–71.

Sireci, S. G., Scarpati, S. E., & Li, S. (2005). Test accommodations for students with disabilities: An analysis of the interaction hypothesis. *Review of Educational Research, 75*(4), 457–490.

Sireci, S. G., & Pitoniak, M. J. (2007). Assessment accommodations: What have we learned from research. In C. C. Laitusis & L. L. Cook (Eds.), *Large-scale assessments and accommodations: What works* (pp. 53–65). Arlington, VA: Council for Exceptional Children.

Smarter Balanced Assessment Consortium. (2013). *Smarter Balanced Assessment Consortium: Usability, accessibility, and accommodations guidelines*. Retrieved from http://www.smarterbalanced.org/wordpress/wp-content/uploads/2013/09/SmarterBalanced_Guidelines_091113.pdf

Snow, K. (2007). People first language. *Disability is natural*. http://www.disabilityisnatural.com

Solano-Flores, G., & Trumbull, E. (2003). Examining language in context: The need for new research and practice paradigms in the testing of English-language learners. *Educational Researcher, 32*(2), 3–13.

Steedle, J., McBride, M., Johnson, M., & Keng, L. (2015). *Spring 2015 device comparability study*. Retrieved from http://blogs.edweek.org/edweek/DigitalEducation/PARCC%20Device%20Comparability%202015%20%28first%20operational%20year%29_FINAL.PDF

Stone, E. (2016, April). *Integrating digital assessment meta-data for psychometric and validity analysis*. Paper presented at the annual meeting of the National Council on Measurement in Education, Washington, D.C.

Stone, E., King, T. C., & Laitusis, C. C. (2011). *Examining the comparability of paper-based and computer-based administrations of novel item types: Verbal text completion and Quantitative numeric entry items*. ETS Research Memorandum RM 11–03.

Thompson, S. J., Johnstone, C. J., & Thurlow, M. L. (2002). *Universal design applied to large scale assessments* (Synthesis Report 44). Minneapolis, MN: University of Minnesota, National Center on Educational Outcomes. Retrieved from http://education.umn.edu/NCEO/Online Pubs/Synthesis14.html

Thurlow, M., Laitusis, C. C., Dillon, D. R., Cook, L. L., Moen, R. E., Abedi, J., & O'Brien, D. G. (2009). *Accessibility principles for reading assessments*. Minneapolis, MN: National Accessible Reading Assessments Projects.

Thurlow, M. L., & Larson, J. (2011). *Accommodations for state reading assessments: Policies across the nation*. Minneapolis, MN: University of Minnesota, Partnership for Accessible Reading Assessment.

Tindal, G., Heath, B., Hollenbeck, K., Almond, P., & Harniss, M. (1998). Accommodating students with disabilities on large-scale tests: An experimental study. *Exceptional Children, 64*(4), 439–450.

Young, J. W. (2009). A framework for test validity research on content assessments taken by English language learners. *Educational Assessment, 14*(3–4), 122–138.

Young, J. W., & King, T. C. (2008). Testing accommodations for English language learners: A review of state and district policies. *ETS Research Report Series, 2008*(2), i–13.

Designing, Developing, and Implementing an Accessible Computer-Based National Assessment System

Magda Chia and Rachel Kachchaf

Introduction

The first 15 years of the twenty-first century generated a number of revolutionary changes in educational policies and practices. In 2001, with No Child Left Behind (NCLB), the federal government reauthorized the Elementary and Secondary Education Act (ESEA) and increased state accountability for students who are English learners (ELs) and students with disabilities (Duran, 2008; Yell & Katsiyannas, 2006). Prior to NCLB, ELs and students with disabilities were often excluded from participation in state assessments, preventing the monitoring of these student groups' academic performance and progress (Abedi, Hofstetter, & Lord, 2004).

In parallel, legislators and other stakeholders called for academic standards that would better prepare US students for the college demands of the twenty-first century. In 2009, the National Governors Association (NGA) supported efforts by a group of content experts, teachers, and other stakeholders in a large effort to create internationally benchmarked Common Core State Standards (CCSS) for English language arts/literacy (ELA) and mathematics (Common Core State Standards Initiative (CCSS), 2016a). The NGA and Council of Chief State School Officers (CCSSO) published and licensed the standards (Common Core State Standards Initiative (CCSS), 2016b), and the District of Columbia along with 42 states adopted them (CCSS, 2016b). As organized by the Smarter Balanced Assessment Consortium (Smarter), the ELA CCSS include four claims: reading, writing, speaking/listening, and research; the mathematics CCSS include four claims: concepts and procedures, problem solving, communicating reasoning, and modeling and data analysis (see Table 5.1) (Smarter Balanced Assessment Consortium (Smarter), 2015a, 2015b, 2015c).

Most recently, the federal government passed the Every Student Succeeds Act (ESSA) in December of 2015. ESSA increased state autonomy and flexibility regarding achievement goals, timelines for progress, and improvement strategies (Alliance for Excellence, 2015). Similar to previous legislation, however, ESSA calls for each state to implement high-quality assessments in mathematics and reading or language arts in grades 3–8 and once in high school; it also requires a science assessment in grades 3–5, 6–8, and once in high school (United States Department of Education, 2015). In addition, ESSA stipulates that states create goals and interim measures for English language

M. Chia (✉)
Stanford University, Understanding Language/
Stanford Center for Assessment, Learning,
and Equity, Stanford, CA, USA
e-mail: chiam@stanford.edu

R. Kachchaf
University of California Los Angeles,
Smarter Balanced Assessment Consortium,
Los Angeles, CA, USA

Table 5.1 Smarter claims 1–4 by English language arts/literacy (ELA) and mathematics

Content area	Claim 1	Claim 2	Claim 3	Claim 4
ELA	Reading	Writing	Speaking and listening	Research/inquiry
Mathematics	Concepts and procedures	Problem solving	Communicating reasoning	Modeling and data analysis

proficiency (United States Department of Education, 2015). Finally, ESSA allows states to plan and implement creative testing solutions via innovative assessment systems (IAS) that up to seven states can pilot within 3 years. As a result of the flexibility contained within ESSA, states will need to create long-term goals for all students and all student subgroups, including ELs and students with disabilities. States will need to plan their instructional and assessment practices so that they attend to ELs and students with disabilities, acknowledging the group's heterogeneity, as well as how they will support staff for plan implementation.

As a result of the demand to increase participation by diverse students and subgroups, it is necessary for assessment development processes to rely heavily on universal design (UD) principals and offer greater accessibility resources as needed[1]. In 2010, two state-led assessment consortia won federal Race to the Top (RTT) grant funds to create assessment systems based on UD principles that would allow states to assess student progress on learning the new ELA and mathematics CCSS: Smarter Balanced Assessment Consortium (Smarter) and Partnership for Assessment of Readiness for College and Careers (PARCC) (Department of Education, 2014). Smarter currently consists of 19 members; PARCC includes 9. Smarter projected participation of over 5.3 million students for their spring 2016 summative assessment (Smarter Balanced Assessment Consortium (Smarter), 2016a, 2016b, 2016c, 2016d, 2016e). Both consortia support their members in validly assessing all students with the exception of those students participating in the 1% percent/alternate assessments based on alternate achievement standards. Although both consortia provide assessment systems, they vary in implementation practices and what they offer. Smarter includes a computer adaptive summative assessment, interim assessments, and formative assessment tools (SmarterBalanced.org). PARCC includes annual year-end computer-based summative assessments and instructional tools (Partnership for Assessment of Readiness for College and Careers PARCC, 2016).

To support the application of UD principals in assessment development, Smarter developed a conceptual framework. The Smarter Accessibility and Accommodations Framework details ways in which next-generation assessments can support increased accessibility (Smarter Balanced Assessment Consortium (Smarter), 2014). First, Smarter requires a paradigm shift from focusing on group needs to individual student needs. Second, there is a focus on ways in which computer-based testing can provide increased access and flexibility to assessments for the greatest number of students. Third, Smarter emphasizes the use of evidence-based design, grounded in making design decisions based on research. This includes research from multiple fields of study that focus on accessibility, equity, and assessment validity (see Fig. 5.1).

By utilizing this approach, Smarter established a system of accessibility resources that is customizable for individual student need(s), a critical feature given the extreme heterogeneity in the student population participating in Smarter assessments. This chapter further explains each component of the process of development and provides details for implementation.

---

[1] We use the term accessibility resources as a broad categorical term referring to any support offered to students as part of the test materials or the test administration procedures.

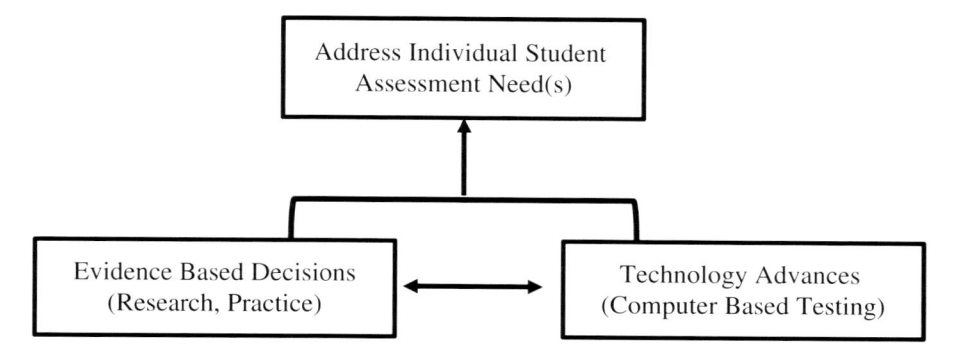

Fig 5.1 Conceptual model underlying the Smarter Balanced Assessment Consortium work to increase assessment accessibility

Heterogeneity: From Student Subgroups to Individual Students

Reflecting the country's diversity, students who participated in the 2016 Smarter mathematics online summative assessment show a high degree of heterogeneity, particularly by ethnicity, socioeconomic background, disability, and home language.

The almost even split by gender is representative of the national numbers for students in k-12 public schools (see Table 5.2).

A total of 5,112,555 students participated in the online Smarter mathematics summative assessment. Of those over five million students, 49 percent identified as female, and 51 percent identified as male. Student demographics in additional categories mirror national figures as well.

We observe much diversity by ethnicity (see Table 5.3). Of the students who participated in the online Smarter mathematics summative assessment, 98 percent identified with one of the ethnic group categories used by the federal government.

Of the almost five million students reporting ethnicity, the greatest number of students identified as white (41 percent). However, there were almost as many students who identified as Hispanic or Latino (36 percent). The remaining 24 percent of students reported identifying with five other ethnic categories: American Indian/Alaska Native (1 percent), Asian (8 percent), Black/African-American (6 percent), Native Hawaiian/Pacific Islander (1 percent), and two or more (8 percent).

Table 5.2 Participants in the 2016 online smarter mathematics summative assessments by gender

Gender	Number of students	Percent of students
Female	2,502,731	49
Male	2,609,824	51
Total	5,112,555	100

Table 5.3 Participants in the 2016 online smarter mathematics summative assessments by reported ethnicity

Ethnic group	Number of students	Percentage of students
Am. Indian/Alaska Native	61,787	1.24
Asian	394,132	7.89
Black/African American	297,486	5.95
Native Hawaiian/Pacific Islander	53,902	1.08
Hispanic/Latino	1,781,740	35.65
White	2,031,734	40.65
Two or more	377,053	7.54
Total	4,997,834	100.00

Even within ethnic groups, we find diversity if we further disaggregate by additional student characteristics. More specifically, Smarter has information regarding student English language proficiency status (LEP), students with disabilities as addressed in the Individuals with Disabilities Education Act (IDEA) and captured in a student's Individualized Education Plan (IEP), 504 status, or economically disadvantaged (see Table 5.4).

Table 5.4 Participants in the 2016 online smarter mathematics summative assessments by LEP, IDEA, 504, or low SES

	Number of students	Percent of students
LEP	755,387	19.00
IDEA/IEP	502,361	.64
504 Status	60,791	1.53
Economically disadvantaged	2,656,821	66.83
Total	3,975,360	100.00

Of the 5,112,555 students who participated in the online Smarter mathematics summative assessment, 3,975,360 students identified as belonging to at least one of four special populations, which are traditionally underserved. Of these students, over two-thirds— (67 percent)— qualified as economically disadvantaged. Almost 15% of students identified as having special needs: 13 percent as IDEA and 2 percent as having a 504 plan. Finally, 19 percent of the 3,975,360 students are categorized as limited English proficient. There are most likely overlaps between the four categories; for example, a student may be limited English proficient, have an IEP or 504 plan, and be economically disadvantaged. In addition, a student may have multiple disabilities. This results in individual students who have very specific needs or combinations of needs during testing.

Student heterogeneity is also detected in the type of assessment resources that individual students require. Smarter member data details the number of students participating in the mathematics summative assessment who were provided with an accessibility resource (see Table 5.5). Here, we focus on four accessibility resources considered new and unique due to the way in which Smarter created and offered them on a next-generation assessment system: American Sign Language (ASL), online Braille, stacked Spanish translation, and translated glossaries. Of the 94,196 students who—as determined by an IEP, 504, or educator—were provided with at least one of these four accessibility resources, only 0.03 percent of students had access to online Braille. This number reflects the low-instance population numbers members have seen prior to Smarter assessments. Similarly, reflecting another low-instance population, only 2 percent of the 94,196 students had access to ASL videos.

Some accessibility resources are specifically geared toward students who are developing their English language proficiency, including English learners (ELs). For students learning in dual language immersion programs (Spanish-English), Smarter offers stacked Spanish translations in which students can view all text in Spanish and scroll downward to access the English version.[2] For other ELs, Smarter offers translated glossaries in over ten languages plus dialects (see Table 5.6).

To select languages to support students through the translated glossaries, Smarter administered a survey to membership asking for information about language usage among ELs. The languages supported via the translated language glossaries represent home language use of over 97 percent of students participating in the consortium in 2014.

The availability of accessibility resources varies by content area to ensure construct validity and valid inferences from test score results. ASL and Braille are two accessibility resources available for the ELA summative assessment that are of particular interest due to their application in a computer adaptive next-generation assessment system (see Table 5.7).

Contracted and uncontracted literary Braille[3] is available on all ELA items across all grades and claims. For the ELA assessment, ASL videos are available only on Claim 3 (listening) across all grades. For Claim 3, hearing students access the test information via a one-minute audio recording of a human voice and text items. For students who are deaf/hard of hearing, access is gained through the ASL videos of human native signers who interpret the audio information as well as the text included in the associated items. Given the intended construct of the *English language arts/literacy standards*, spoken language translations are not available on the Smarter ELA

---

[2] A Smarter-administered survey showed that, across its membership, dual language immersion programs offered to ELs included instruction in Spanish-English.

[3] In the 2015–2016 school year, Smarter supported English Braille, American Edition (EBAE) literary code, and Nemeth math code, with formal plans to support EBAE literary, Nemeth math, and Unified English Braille (UEB) math and literary codes.

Table 5.5 Number of students who were provided with several accessibility resources on the 2016 online smarter mathematics summative assessments

	Number of students	Percent of students
ASL	1767	1.88
Braille	31	0.03
Stacked Spanish	17,534	18.61
Translated glossaries	74,864	79.48
Total	94,196	100.00

Table 5.6 Languages and dialects of translated glossaries offered on all grades of the 2016 online smarter mathematics summative assessments

Language	Dialect(s)
Spanish	Mexican, El Salvadorian, Puerto Rican
Arabic	Saudi Arabian, Egyptian
Filipino	Ilokano, Tagalog
Mandarin	Standard, simplified
Russian	Standard
Punjabi	Eastern, Western
Vietnamese	North and South
Cantonese	Standard, simplified
Ukrainian	Standard
Korean	Standard

Table 5.7 Number of students with access to several accessibility resources on the 2016 online smarter English language arts/literacy summative assessments

	Number of students	Percent of students
ASL	1765	94
Braille	112	6
Total	1877	100

assessments. Likewise, given advice that Smarter treat ASL the way that spoken languages are treated, ASL is not available on Claims 1, 2, or 4 ELA Smarter items.

Flexibility: Computer-Based Assessments

Smarter integrates a high degree of flexibility into the accessibility system and provides support for educators, parents, students, and others involved. To assist states with the paradigm shift to focus on individual student needs as opposed to general student subgroups, Smarter created the *Usability, Accessibility, and Accommodations Guidelines* (Smarter, 2016b), which list the available accessibility resources by level of adult involvement in selecting accessibility resources that meet individual student need(s) and reflect the consortia's *Accessibility Framework* (see Fig. 5.2).

The UAAG's three-tier system reflects a limited amount of needed adult involvement and increased independent access to various accessibility resources for more students.

Universal tools are accessibility resources that are by default available to all students. Universal tools do not require any adult involvement; they are available automatically. Students are often already familiar with these tools: highlighter, calculator, digital notepad, zoom, and English glossaries. Some universal tools have been considered accommodations in the past but can now be available to *all* students because of the computer administration aspect of next-generation assessments. For example, English glossaries have often been considered an accommodation offered only to English language learners (Abedi & Ewers, 2013). However, Smarter views English glossaries as a tool that can benefit all students as glossaries provide content-specific information for construct-irrelevant terms. Computer-administered assessments allow for high-quality accessibility resources without increasing cost per student making English glossaries affordable. For example, making English glossaries available to all students does not increase printing cost as they are available digitally via the computer administration system.

Designated supports are those accessibility resources that are available for use by any student for whom the need has been indicated by an educator or team of educators (with parent/guardian and student input as appropriate). These supports include color contrast, masking, and text-to-speech for certain grades depending on content area. Given the legal and historical connotation of the term *accommodations*—and their association with disabilities—Smarter categorizes language supports as designated supports and not accommodations. Categorizing language supports in this way acknowledges the fundamental principle that emerging biliterate students should be able to use the full set of knowledge and skills

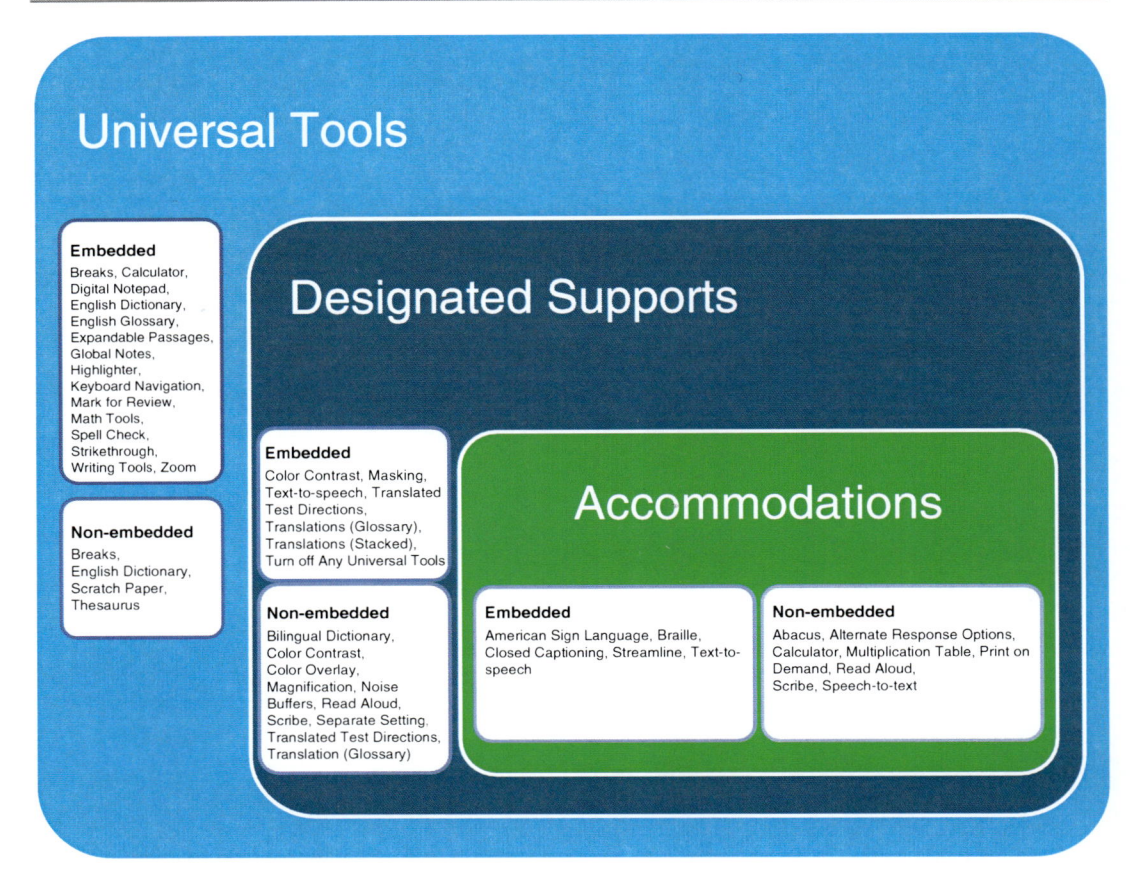

Fig. 5.2 Conceptual model underlying the Smarter Usability, Accessibility, and Accommodations Guidelines (UAAG) (Reprinted with permission from the Smarter Balanced Assessment Consortium)

they possess rather than consider language skills in a home language a type of disability. Color contrast is another example of a designated support. Color contrast enables students to adjust screen background or font color, based on student needs and preferences. This may include reversing the colors for the entire interface or choosing the color of font and background (Smarter, 2016b). Color contrast can help students with attention difficulties, visual impairments, or other print disabilities (including learning disabilities).

Accommodations are changes in procedures or materials that increase equitable access during the Smarter assessments by generating valid assessment results for students who need them, allowing these students to show what they know and can do. Accommodations require documentation of need via an Individualized Education Program (IEP) or 504 plan, making this category the one for which there is greatest formal adult involvement. Accommodations include ASL, Braille, closed captioning, streamline, text to speech, and others. These accessibility resources can be harmful to students if they do not have experience with them. Accommodations often support what are considered to be low-instance disabilities.

As shown in the conceptual model in Fig. 5.2, the vast majority of accessibility resources can be part of the universal tools with fewer being included as designated supports and even fewer as accommodations. As a result, the majority of accessibility resources are available to students automatically or with minimal adult intervention.

The Smarter UAAG further divides each of the three main categories of accessibility resources (universal tools, designated supports, and accommodations) into two subcategories: embedded and non-embedded. Embedded accessibility resources are automatically available to students via the test administration platform. Non-embedded resources are provided externally from the technology platform. Adding a specific resource as either embedded or non-embedded depends on the test administration platform's technology, the amount of student experience required to interact with the resources successfully, assistive technology available, and whether it allows a student greater independence during testing while maintaining validity.

When designing a computer-based assessment system, a key step is to examine the assistive technology (AT) available to and used by students. Assistive Technology Partners at the University of Colorado worked closely with Smarter staff to produce a detailed list of the most common AT devices—hardware and software—that students use nationally (Smarter, 2015a). AT hardware and/or software can address student needs with regard to assessment presentation and student methods of responding as well as testing setting and timing. AT examples include adjustment of text and graphics size (presentation), word prediction (response), noise buffers (setting), and ability to pause computer-based testing (timing). Important factors were taken into account when creating the typology. First, the authors identified the AT most commonly used in classrooms and during testing. Second, the typology includes the descriptions of features each AT product contains. Third, the typology makes explicit the connections between the AT device features and the student needs that benefit most from each feature. Fourth, it makes explicit which, if any, of the AT device features may pose a threat to construct validity for particular assessments. Fifth, the typology examines the compatibility between the AT device and the test administration platform.

If a particular AT is widely used, does not contain features that could invalidate student test scores due to violation of construct validity, has a history of helping students during testing through research on differential boost, and works well with the test administration system, it is advisable to allow the use of the AT device as an embedded accessibility resource. Text to speech meets all criteria and as such is available as an embedded resource on the Smarter assessments. However, if an AT device does not meet any of the criteria, student needs may best be met via a non-embedded accessibility resource. For example, speech-to-text does not invalidate the Smarter math assessment and has shown to help students in testing (Abedi & Ewers, 2013). Yet, it does not work well for students as an embedded accessibility resource because of the amount of student and device training required to make it work properly. Therefore, although Smarter allows speech-to-text as an accommodation, it is non-embedded.

Regardless of whether an accessibility resource is embedded or non-embedded, the adults making decisions about an individual student's testing arrangements need guidance on how to make these decisions. Furthermore, Smarter's approach to accessibility requires educators, parents/guardians, and school administrators to undergo a paradigm shift from focusing on student-group need(s) to focusing on individual student need(s) and understanding a shift in constructs measured under the new CCSS.

In response to this shift, the consortium produced the *Individual Student Assessment Accessibility Profile* (ISAAP) process (see Fig. 5.3) and the ISAAP tool (see Fig. 5.4) (Smarter Balanced Assessment Consortium (Smarter), n.d.-a, n.d.-b). The ISAAP process represents a thoughtful, systematic, and inclusive approach to addressing student access needs for the Smarter assessments. The ISAAP process includes preparatory steps that involve parents/guardians, educators, and, when appropriate, the student. The critical first step is to select key staff members and define their roles throughout the ISAAP process. These individuals should be knowledgeable of an individual student's need, background, and experience with accessibility resources, testing policies, and available accessibility resources. Once staff is selected,

Select key staff → Train staff, parents, student → Identify student needing resource → Select resource(s) → Enter into test → Pre-admin check → Check test delivery system

Fig. 5.3 The Individual Student Assessment Accessibility Profile (ISAAP) Process

Enter Student One Data

Print

☐ Thesaurus:

Student Need(s)

☐ Support for executive functioning: attention, cognition control, and processing
☐ Support for persistent calculation disability, dyscalculia
☐ Support for reading-related disabilities, print disabilities, struggling readers
☐ Support for students needing access in language(s) of translation
☐ Support for significant motor difficulties and recent injury
☐ Support for vision impairments/blindness
☐ Support for hard-of-hearing/deafness

Identification of Student Need

☐ Individualized Education Program
☐ 504 Plan
☐ Educator(s) Recommendation

Designated Supports

*Use of this support will likely also require a separate setting or extra time

Accommodations IEP or 504 Plan Documentation

*Use of this support will likely also require a separate setting or extra time

OK   Cancel

Fig. 5.4 Individual Student Assessment Accessibility Profile (ISAAP) Tool (Reprinted with permission from the Smarter Balanced Assessment Consortium)

schools must provide their staff with training and information about the assessment and the ISAAP process. The training can extend to students and parents/guardians. Once trained, staff should identify students who will benefit from designated supports, accommodations, or both. For each student identified, school staff, parents, and, when appropriate, the student should then select the suitable designated supports and accommodations.

The ISAAP tool is designed to facilitate the fourth step in the ISAAP process: selection of designated supports and accommodations that match student access needs for the Smarter assessments, as supported by the UAAG. This web-based tool also allows for the de-selection of universal tools for a student's testing experience. When using the ISAAP tool to select designated supports and/or accommodations, the team begins by entering basic information—such as student name, teacher name, grade, and school ID. The team can also enter comments for various purposes as determined by the school site (e.g., directions to test administrator or other school procedure). Then, the team can click on the appropriate "student need(s)," and select all values that apply. For each box (student need) selected, a specific set of recommended designated supports and/or accommodations will be automatically populated (see Fig. 5.4). Based on student experience, the team selects those supports and accommodations most beneficial and recommended for the student need selected. To select a recommended designated support or accommodation, the team simply clicks on the box to the left of the resource.

Once the group is in agreement about the most appropriate resource(s) for the student, staff should enter the selected designated supports and/or accommodations into the test engine. Staff should perform a pre-administration check of selected accessibility resources prior to student testing. Likewise, staff should verify that the designated supports and/or accommodations are present at the time of test administration.

The overall goal of using the ISAAP process and ISAAP tool is to provide students with a testing experience that allows them to demonstrate what they know and can do by decreasing the barriers to do so. However, the way in which students interact with each accessibility resource is important. During accessibility resource design and development Smarter took four dimensions of validity and fairness into account (Solano-Flores, 2012): First, students who do not need the accessibility resource and yet get access to it during testing are not harmed by it. Second, the accessibility resource is optional, available for students based on specific need. Third, it is likely that the accessibility resource can be used as intended and in a standard form across all students with access to it. Fourth, the accessibility resource should be easy for the student to use. It should require little, if any, additional effort, learning, attention, or cognitive demand.

The ASL resource serves as a prime example of successfully implementing these dimensions during design and development. Students who are deaf/hard of hearing participating in Smarter assessments have access to videos of humans using ASL to interpret all text on the screen. Students have the ability to access videos at any point as they interact with items. If a student does not need the videos, they do not need to access them. Once a student opts to access a video, she can pause, stop, rewind, and fast-forward the video as needed. To ensure high-quality standardized videos, signers are certified natural users of ASL who follow strict guidelines for interpretation, dress, and general appearance (e.g., Higgins, Famularo, Bowman, & Hall, 2015).

Another example of successful implementation is the translated glossaries. In mathematics, students should be able to access features in and use knowledge of their home language in addition to English. Given the heterogeneity of this student subgroup, the language supports included in the Smarter assessments cater to individual student need. Students can access the translated glossaries, a designated support, if the need is determined via the ISAAP process. If the student does not need the support to understand a glossed word, he simply continues to solve the item without interacting with any glossary. If a student needs support with a glossed term, the student clicks on the term, and the glossary content appears. For translated glossaries, students have access to both text and an audio component due to ELs' varying abilities to read in their home language. As a student selects a glossed term, she can read the text and, if no further support is needed, can close the glossary and continue to solve the item. If the student wants further support, she can access the audio recording for each translated term. As a result, the student has control over the type and level of support best suited for her needs and experience.

Smarter's approach to categorizing accessibility resources to maximize student independence and control takes advantage of just how flexible computer testing can be. A student can simultaneously access universal tools, designated supports, and/or accommodations according to her specific assessment need(s). To support adults in understanding and utilizing these new resources and accessibility structures, Smarter created the ISAAP process and ISAAP tool. These efforts all involved a multidisciplinary approach grounded in research and by discussions with national and international experts from the field and from academia.

Experts and Research

From its inception, the RTT grant urged the local government officials and departments of education to bring together the top experts in their respective fields who contribute to and help improve national public education. Upon awarding grants, the federal government hailed examples of states that brought together stakeholders to change practice and policy (Department of Education, 2014). Smarter also believed in the power of multidisciplinary teams of national and international experts to contribute to their assessment system's design and development.

As an initial step, Smarter sought experts from within states who could contribute to work in content, psychometrics, accessibility, reporting, technology, and research. Membership nominated k-12 and university staff with expertise in specific areas to fill positions on ten work groups (Smarter, 2016c). Each work group had at least ten participants with representation from various states (see Table 5.8). In addition to other participants, each work group had two co-chairs, an executive committee liaison, and at least one staff member as advisors and liaisons between the work group and the rest of membership and staff. Also, each group had one project management coordinator and one project management liaison.

Every work group benefitted by having expertise from across states. Of the ten work groups, five had as many states represented as they had members; the rest of the work groups were very close. States varied by geographic location, size, diversity of students, and diversity of previous assessment practices and policies.

The Usability, Accessibility, and Accommodations Committee (UAAC) provides an example of a way through which Smarter benefitted from the diversity of expertise across disciplines (see Table 5.9). The UAAC includes two Smarter staff members and ten state members. Staff members of the UAAC have working knowledge across content, English language acquisition, disabilities, and technology.

Smarter focused on finding member representatives that were each strong in two areas of study cutting across content and accessibility, including assistive technology and how it could interact with the test registration system and the test administration platform.

The consortium also benefited from external expertise across various disciplines. Table 5.10 shows an example of a way to implement multidisciplinary discussions and decision-making practices systematically via advisory committees. Smarter created three advisory committees that include nationally and internationally respected experts: the Technical Advisory Committee (TAC), English Language Learner Advisory Committee (ELLAC), and Students with Disabilities Advisory Committee (SWDAC) (Appendix A). Although specific members of each advisory committee might change on occasion, the general makeup and areas of expertise remain fairly consistent (Smarter, 2016d).

For each committee, the consortium wanted expertise across five main disciplines: psychometrics, content, accessibility, policy, and instruc-

Table 5.8 2012 Smarter work group membership numbers by K-12, higher education, and states/territories

Work group	K-12 members	Higher ed. members	Total state members	States
Accessibility and accommodations	9	2	11	11
Assessment design: item development	10	2	12	10
Assessment design: performance tasks	7	3	10	8
Assessment design: test administration	9	2	11	11
Assessment design: test design	9	2	11	9
Formative assessment practices and professional learning	10	2	12	10
Reporting	11	2	13	13
Technology approach	8	2	10	9
Transition to common core	8	2	10	10
Validation and psychometrics	8	2	10	10

Table 5.9 2015 smarter UAAC multidisciplinary representation

Member number	State	Primary area of expertise	Secondary area of expertise
1.	Hawaii	ELA	SWD
2.	California	ELA	ELL
3.	Oregon	Math	SWD
4.	Nevada	Math	General access
5.	Delaware	ELL	Math
6.	Michigan	ELL	ELA
7.	North Dakota	SWD	ELA
8.	Oregon	SWD	ELA
9.	Connecticut	Assistive technology	SWD
10.	California	Assistive technology	ELA

Note. ELA English/language arts, *ELL* English language learner, *SWD* student with a disability

Table 5.10 2015 smarter advisory committees, multidisciplinary representation

Advisory committee	Psychometrics expertise	Content expertise	Accessibility expertise	Policy	Instruction
Technical advisory committee	H	H	H	M	H
ELL advisory committee	H	M	H	H	H
SWD advisory committee	H	M	H	H	H

Note. H highest level of expertise, *M* middle level of expertise, *L* low level of expertise

tion. Each committee includes the highest level of expertise across at least four disciplines and only one area of middle level of expertise.

Another way to engage experts and stakeholders is through gathering feedback. Smarter included diverse groups via online presentations, discussions, document sharing, surveys, and one-on-one communication. In particular, accessibility staff included and continues to include a number of advocacy groups during development and maintenance of the UAAG (Appendix B (Smarter, 2015c)). In addition to members of the advisory committees, advocacy groups were included in conversations addressing translation, text-to-speech, ASL, dyscalculia, Braille, and the UAAG categories and format.

As a result of bringing together internal and external experts, Smarter produced vast materials geared toward various stakeholders. These documents and tools can help support the transition to a new assessment—and new standards (Smarter, 2016a, 2016b, 2016c, 2016d, 2016e).

Some documents support stakeholders (e.g., districts, teachers, and parents) in preparation for testing: UAAG, Implementation Guide, Guidelines for Choosing TTS, or Read Aloud in Grades 3–5. Other tools are meant for test preparation *and* administration: Scribing Protocol, Instructions for Using Embedded Glossaries, and the Smarter Balanced Resources and Practices Comparison Crosswalk. Using a multidisciplinary approach that includes internal and external experts results in rich discussions, intelligent decisions, and materials that support all levels of stakeholders.

Implementation Examples Throughout Development

As Smarter worked with experts from multiple disciplines to inform the assessment system's development, it was clear that it was critical to include and consider the needs of *all* students at each step. That is, from the very beginning of development, assessment systems must incorporate aspects of universal design as well as explicitly examine ways in which the process of development considers diverse student needs.

From the very early stages, starting with the development of the content specifications in ELA and mathematics, Smarter addressed diverse student needs. These specifications identify claims and targets to cover the range of knowledge and skills in the CCSS (Smarter, 2015b, 2015c). In addition to content specifications, item specifications were created to guide item development (Smarter, 2015b, 2015c). Numerous organizations and individuals provided feedback on the development of these specifications, including Smarter work groups consisting of experts in assessing ELs, students with disabilities, and aspects of bias and sensitivity. By ensuring that content and item specifications underwent thorough reviews that included experts in accessibility, diverse student needs were considered from the very first stages of development.

Throughout development, items go through multiple rounds of review, including for language use, accessibility, bias, and sensitivity. In addition, during initial item development, Smarter conducted cognitive labs. Cognitive labs are used to understand the thought process of an individual in a specific situation (Ericsson & Simon, 1993). Including a diverse sample of students in cognitive labs provides in-depth insight into the ways in which all students interact with the items and the test. As a result, Smarter reevaluated technology-enhanced items for accessibility needs and modified language included in items. As previous research notes (e.g., Kopriva, 2001), in early stages of development, this information ensures that items and tests function as intended for all students.

In addition to including a diverse sample of students in item development, Smarter implemented rigorous procedures to develop high-quality accessibility resources. For example, Smarter's translation framework, for spoken languages and ASL, describes the most rigorous translation process used in assessment to date (Solano-Flores, 2012). A key component of the framework is conducting internal and external reviews utilizing a research-proven approach that improves quality of individual item translations and system-wide components (Solano-Flores, Backhoff, & Contreras-Niño, 2009). Reviewers examine test translations with a *disconfirming* lens, to identify translation error. Smarter systematically collected external reviewer feedback for a percentage of items to ensure quality of individual translations and to identify patterns in the errors across items that could inform system-wide changes. Figure 5.5 provides the error categories analyzed for the ASL external reviews. Reviewers completed a table for each item.

After accessibility resources go through rigorous development processes, items with these resources are included in the pilot and field testing, which provides performance data from large numbers of students. Once items are piloted or field tested, student performance is reviewed. During range finding, reviewers examine diverse student responses to constructed response items to identify model responses for each score point of an item. For example, for mathematics, ELL responses are included and reviewed to focus on

| Item: _____ Item Type: _____ Content Area: _____ Grade: _____ |
| Participant: _____ Date: _____ |

Type of Error	Code and Justification
1a. Grammar and Syntax	
1b. Semantics	
2a. Construct	
2b. Origin	
2c. Quality of the Sign	
3a. Computer Administration	
3b. Quality of the Video	
4a. Standardization of Signs	
4b. Diversity of Signers	

Fig. 5.5 Translation error dimensions for external review of ASL videos

the student response regarding the mathematics content assessed rather than grammatical correctness. Similarly, for students taking the mathematics items in Braille, scoring rubrics are created for individual items to adequately describe the variety of ways in which these students may respond. For example, scoring rubrics include all variations a student may enter as a response, including "1 + 2 = 3" and "one plus two equals three."

Maximizing student access does not stop with item development and resource creation. It was also essential that Smarter create accessibility resources at the test level, including supplemental materials. For example, Smarter currently provides translated test directions in 18 languages plus dialects that students can use as they navigate the online assessment (Smarter, 2016b).

Fulfilling the need for a fully accessible *system*, Smarter ensures that these accessible materials and items are available for both the summative and interim assessments. Smarter also offers fully accessible practice tests on which students, teachers, and parents can access and become familiar with the tests, items, and accessibility resources in preparation for participating in any of the Smarter assessments.

Considering the needs of all students throughout the entire process of development is critical for assessment systems. Assessment systems must explicitly identify how diversity can be addressed at each step to create a comprehensive system that accurately assesses student knowledge. This includes, but is not limited to, item development, rigorous processes for creating accessibility resources, and ensuring all components of the system are fully accessible.

Throughout the creation of the Smarter assessment system, staff learned a number of key lessons that can help others who are a part of assessment development. First, any assessment development effort—whether for summative high stakes or formative or interim purpose—needs to include at least one leadership team person with deep knowledge of language development and disabilities fields. This specific staff must be involved in all aspects of the design and development of items, test(s), and computer delivery platform. Second, throughout the design and development work, it is important to include a diverse group of stakeholders. Advocates, researchers, practitioners, parents/guardians, unions, and communications experts each provide important feedback and guidance as well as support for implementation. Third, providing accessibility experts with opportunities to have candid and informational conversations with traditional technologists working on computer-based testing design and development will help technologists understand the impact of decisions on a diverse population of end-users, including students with disabilities, ELs, and ELs with disabilities. Finally, design and development efforts are not enough to ensure appropriate assessment practices. Creating ongoing and multilevel professional development materials, plans, and supports is essential to successful implementation. Guardians/parents, educators, students, counselors, district-level staff, and state-level staff need ongoing support. Ongoing professional development will ensure that all involved understand the UAAG, the ISAAP tool and process, and the evidence-based decision-making process.

Conclusion

For over 20 years, policy makers, advocates, researchers, and other stakeholders have helped increase attention and implement strategies that result in greater inclusion of all students in public education. If designed and developed appropriately, next-generation assessment systems can provide ample examples on ways to improve equity and increase accessibility for all students in all aspects of education.

A pivotal initial step geared toward increased student involvement is shifting attention from general student subgroups to focusing on individual students. The group "English language learners" actually encompasses a deep and vast group of individual students, each with their own specific needs. These students vary in the home language they use, their English language development, and the level of familiarity in their home language across modalities (speaking, listening, reading, and writing). Similarly, students within the grouping of "students with disabilities" are equally as rich and diverse. The special needs for each student vary depending on what they require in order to access and share information. Often, students have multiple needs. Students may have more than one disability or still be developing their English language skills. In addition, all of these students vary in their development of specific content-area knowledge and skills—in either their home language or English. As a result, educators and parents should consider accessibility needs for instruction and assessment at the individual student level. We should no longer categorize accessibility resources within the scope of vastly complex groups such as students with disabilities or English language learners. To assist people in this paradigm shift, we need to produce easy to access materials that guide and prepare for these rapidly occurring changes. In addition, schools, districts, and states must provide professional development and improve communication and outreach to the general public that explains how systems are changing, how the changes help students, and how to implement those changes in a systematic and efficient way.

This necessary shift can be facilitated if researchers, curriculum developers, assessment developers, and technologists examine the ways in which technology can help. For example, there are ways through which computer-based testing can increase access and independence for students while decreasing overall development costs. English and translated glossaries can include context-specific information, and text as well as audio support, in such a way that is not intrusive to students—without the cost of reproducing a hard copy for every single student needing the support. Computer available accessibility resources reduce the production and administration costs while increasing test security; the support appears only via the computer administration platform.

Despite all of the progress made so far, there are still areas requiring additional work. One field that requires perhaps greatest attention is the assistive technology field. Working with AT professionals and clinicians can help with item, test, and platform design and development. AT professionals often understand the technology demands of UD-based platforms. This collaboration can help the general test delivery usability as well as improve compatibility between AT devices and the test delivery platform. In addition, assistive technology often addresses the needs of students with the lowest-instance disabilities. This causes a number of AT devices and software to be quite expensive. Leveraging appropriate AT by all online educational development efforts may help keep technology costs down. Though not an easy task, often due to the size of the design and manufacturing teams involved in AT as well as the varied AT available to students, it can be done using a multidisciplinary research-based inclusive approach.

Given the new conceptual and technological underpinnings of a well-designed and well-developed system, progress should be steady but also cautious, purposeful, and informed. It is imperative that design and development be guided by the use of evidence-based design grounded in research. This includes research from multiple fields of study that focus on accessibility, equity, and assessment validity.

Too often, adults with the best of intentions advocate for "more"—more features, more design, and more variety in items. We must keep in mind that results of including additional features and resources is not binary: helpful additions or benign conditions. In fact, ill-conceived designed or developed features can result in harm to students. Students may be confused by a feature's function and layout, experience a significant increase in cognitive demand, or encounter low-quality resources. Relying on existing research, currently in progress research projects, and general knowledge from experts can help mitigate potential negative results. In addition, reaching out to state staff, district staff, school staff, diverse groups of students, advocacy groups, parents/guardians, and others will help guide important components of a system's usability and feasibility of implementation.

Of course, as technology, computer adaptive testing, and accessibility resources evolve, so does the need for more research. There is an urgent need for quasi-experimental, qualitative, and mixed methods research in the field of computer-based administration of instruction, professional development, and assessment. More specifically, all fields need researchers to continue their work in these areas with a focus on all students but particularly with low-instance populations. Gathering sufficient numbers of students can be particularly challenging, but a call for participation from all states and territories, particularly with help from advocacy groups, can prove fruitful.

This chapter shared conceptual underpinnings for improved assessment practices as well as concrete examples for operationalizing each. Both the conceptual framework and implementation practices can be applied to all aspects of education. Like assessments, teacher and administrator professional development, curriculum and instructional programs, and technology practices can all benefit from improving accessibility, making research-based decisions, and leveraging the talent, knowledge, and expertise of those committed to improving education from various areas of study and work.

Appendix A

Members for of the Three Smarter Balanced Assessment Consortium in 2016
   Technical Advisory Committee Members

- Randy Bennett, Ph.D.
- Derek Briggs, Ph.D.
- Gregory J. Cizek, Ph.D.
- David Conley, Ph.D.
- Brian Gong, Ph.D.
- Edward Haertel, Ph.D.
- Gerunda Hughes, Ph.D.
- G. Gage Kingsbury, Ph.D.
- Joseph Martineau, Ph.D.
- William McCallum, Ph.D.
- James W. Pellegrino, Ph.D.
- Jim Popham, Ph.D.
- Joseph Ryan, Ph.D.
- Guillermo Solano-Flores, Ph.D.
- Martha Thurlow, Ph.D.
- Sheila Valencia, Ph.D.
- Joe Willhoft, Ph.D.

English Language Learners Advisory Committee Members

- Stephanie Cawthon, Ph.D.
- Magda Chia, Ph.D.
- Donna Christian, Ph.D.
- Gary Cook, Ph.D.
- Kathy Escamilla, Ph.D.
- James Green, Ph.D.
- Kenji Hakuta, Ph.D.
- Robert Linquanti
- Guillermo Solano-Flores, Ph.D.
- Guadalupe Valdés, Ph.D.

   Students with Disabilities Advisory Committee Members

- Magda Chia, Ph.D.
- Donald D. Deshler, Ph.D.
- Barbara Ehren, Ed.D.
- Cheryl Kamei-Hannan, Ph.D.
- Jacqueline F. Kearns, Ed.D.
- Susan Rose, Ph.D.
- Jim Sandstrum
- Ann C. Schulte, Ph.D.
- Richard Simpson, Ed.D.
- Stephen W. Smith, Ph.D.
- Martha L. Thurlow, Ph.D.

Appendix B

Advocacy Groups with which the Smarter Balanced Assessment Consortium Collaborates

- American Federation of Teachers
- California School for the Blind
- California School for the Deaf
- Californians Together
- California State Teach
- Center for Applied Special Technology
- Center for Law and Education
- Conference of Educational Administrators of Schools and Programs for the Deaf
- Council for Exceptional Children
- Council of the Great City Schools
- Council of Parent Attorneys and Advocates
- Learning Disabilities Association of Maryland
- Mexican American Legal Defense and Education Fund
- Missouri School Boards' Association
- Missouri Council of Administrators of Special Education
- National Center for Learning Disabilities
- National Association of Latino Elected and Appointed Officials
- The Advocacy Institute
- The National Hispanic University

References

Abedi, J., & Ewers, N. (2013). *Accommodations for English language learners and students with disabilities: A research based algorithm*. Retrieved from http://www.smarterbalanced.org/wordpress/wp-content/uploads/2012/08/Accomodations-for-underrepresented-students.pdf

Abedi, J., Hofstetter, C., & Lord, C. (2004). Assessment accommodations for English language learners: Implications for policy-based empirical research. *Review of Educational Research, 74*(1), 1–28.

Alliance for Excellence. (2015). *Every student succeeds act: Accountability provisions*. Retrieved from: https://www.sifassociation.org/NewsRoom/Documents/ESSA_accountability_chart.pdf

Common Core State Standards Initiative (CCSS). (2016a). *About the standards*. Retrieved from http://www.corestandards.org/about-the-standards/

Common Core State Standards Initiative (CCSS). (2016b). *Public license*. Retrieved from http://www.corestandards.org/public-license/

Department of Education. (2014). *Setting the pace: Expanding opportunity for America's Students Under Race to the Top*. Retrieved from https://www.whitehouse.gov/sites/default/files/docs/settingthepacerttreport_3-2414_b.pdf

Duran, R. (2008). Assessing English-language learners' achievement. *Review of Research in Education, 32*, 292–327.

Ericsson, K. A., & Simon, H. A. (1993). *Protocol analysis: Verbal reports as data*. Cambridge, MA: MITE Press.

Higgins, J., Famularo, L., Bowman, T., & Hall, R. (2015). *Research and development of audio and American Sign Language guidelines for creating accessible computer-based assessments*. Retrieved from http://gaap.measuredprogress.org/gaap/docs/GAAP_Research_White_Paper_Final.pdf

Kopriva, R. (2001, June). *ELL validity research designs for state academic assessments: An outline of five research designs evaluation the validity of large-scale assessments for English language learners and other test takers*. Paper presented at the Council of State School Officers Meeting, Houston, TX.

Partnership for Assessment of Readiness for College and Careers (PARCC). (2016). *The PARCC tests: Modern, high-quality assessments*. Retrieved from http://www.parcconline.org/about/the-parcc-tests

Smarter Balanced Assessment Consortium (Smarter). (n.d.-a). *The individual student assessment accessibility profiles (ISAAP) process*. Retrieved from http://www.smarterbalanced.org/assessments/accessibility-and-accommodations/

Smarter Balanced Assessment Consortium (Smarter). (n.d.-b). *Interim assessment statement of purpose*. Retrieved from www.smarterbalanced.org/wp-content/uploads/2015/09/Interim-Assessment-Statement-Purpose-FINALmerged.pdf

Smarter Balanced Assessment Consortium (Smarter). (2014). *Smarter balanced assessment consortium: Accessibility and accommodations framework*. Retrieved from https://www.smarterbalanced.org/wp-content/uploads/2015/09/Accessibility-and-Accommodations-Framework.pdf

Smarter Balanced Assessment Consortium (Smarter). (2015a). *Smarter balanced assistive technology typology*. Retrieved from http://www.smarterbalanced.org/assessments/accessibility-and-accommodations/

Smarter Balanced Assessment Consortium (Smarter). (2015b). *Content specifications for the summative assessment of the Common Core State Standards for Mathematics*. Retrieved from http://www.smarterbalanced.org/wp-content/uploads/2015/08/Mathematics-Content-Specifications.pdf

Smarter Balanced Assessment Consortium (Smarter). (2015c). *Content specifications for the summative assessment of the Common Core State Standards for English language arts and literacy in history/social studies, science, and technical subjects*. Retrieved from www.smarterbalanced.org/wp-content/uploads/2015/08/ELA_Content_Specs.pdf

Smarter Balanced Assessment Consortium (Smarter). (2016a). *Projected and actual student counts*. Unpublished internal document.

Smarter Balanced Assessment Consortium (Smarter). (2016b). *Smarter balanced assessment consortium usability, accessibility, and accommodations guidelines (UAAG)*. Retrieved from http://www.smarterbalanced.org/wp-content/uploads/2015/09/Usability-Accessibility-Accomodations-Guidelines.pdf

Smarter Balanced Assessment Consortium (Smarter). (2016c). *Smarter balanced assessment consortium: 2013–14 technical report*. Retrieved from www.smarterbalanced.org/wp-content/uploads/2015/08/2013-14_Technical_Report.pdf

Smarter Balanced Assessment Consortium (Smarter). (2016d). *Smarter balanced assessment consortium advisory committees*. Retrieved from http://www.smarterbalanced.org/about/advisory-committees/

Smarter Balanced Assessment Consortium (Smarter). (2016e). *Accessibility and accommodations*. Retrieved from http://www.smarterbalanced.org/assessments/accessibility-and-accommodations/

Solano-Flores, G. (2012). *Smarter balanced assessment consortium: Translation accommodations framework for testing English language learners in mathematics*. Retrieved from http://www.smarterbalanced.org/wp-content/uploads/2015/08/Translation-Accommodations-Framework-for-Testing-ELL-Math.pdf

United States Department of Education (2015). *Every Student Succeeds Act*. Retrieved from https://www.ed.gov/essa?src=rn

Solano-Flores, G., Backhoff, E., & Contreras-Niño, L. A. (2009). Theory of test translation error. *International Journal of Testing, 9*(2), 78–91.

Yell, M. L., & Katsiyannas, A. (2006). *Adequate yearly progress, and students with disabilities*. Retrieved from http://www.redorbit.com/news/education/424129/the_no_child_left_behind_act_adequate_yearly_progress_and/

The Accessibility Needs of Students with Disabilities: Special Considerations for Instruction and Assessment

Jennifer R. Frey and Carrie M. Gillispie

Over 6 million American students between the ages of 3 and 21 years receive special education services (National Center for Education Statistics [NCES], 2016). Each of these students is entitled to a free and appropriate public education in the least restrictive environment (Individuals with Disabilities Education Improvement Act [IDEA], 2004), which means, to the extent possible, students with disabilities should be educated in general education classrooms with peers who do not have disabilities. These students present a unique set of considerations for ensuring access to high-quality instruction and assessing their learning and growth. In this chapter, we will discuss the distinct needs of students with learning differences and strategies to increase their access to effective instruction and testing.

The Educational Landscape of Students with Disabilities

The percentage of students with disabilities (SWDs) enrolled in regular schools and spending the majority of their days in general education settings has nearly doubled in the last 25 years. In 2013–2014, about 95% of students between 6 and 21 years old receiving special education services attended nonspecialized public schools, and about 62% of these students spent the majority of their days (at least 80% of the school day) in general education classrooms (NCES, 2016). Most of these students (87%) were identified as having speech or language impairment. The majority of students with specific learning disabilities (68%), visual impairments (64%), and developmental delays (63%) spent 40–79% of their school day in general education settings (NCES, 2016). Meaningful inclusion in high-quality educational programs provides equal opportunity to all students and supports SWD in achieving their full potential, thus providing the foundation for them to be more successful and productive adults. This improved access to education for SWD has been the result of federal legislation designed to support equal opportunities (Americans with Disabilities Act, 1990; IDEA, 2004; Section 504 of the Rehabilitation Act, 1973) and a growing body of empirical evidence supporting the use of inclusive practices.

Through improved access, SWDs have shown growth in academic achievement during elementary and middle school years (Schulte, Stevens, Elliott, Tindal, & Nese, 2016; Stevens, Schulte, Elliott, Nese, & Tindal, 2015). The rate of achievement growth for SWD was actually very similar to that of students without disabilities; however, this growth varied significantly among students according to disability type, with students with intellectual disability having the

J. R. Frey (✉) · C. M. Gillispie
The George Washington University,
Washington, DC, USA
e-mail: jrfrey@gwu.edu

lowest performance and students with speech/language impairment having the highest performance throughout grades 3 through 7, and the overall achievement gap between SWD and students in general education has remained relatively stable (Schulte et al., 2016). Compared to peers in general education, SWDs have significantly lower reading comprehension and mathematic achievement in third grade, with the exception of students with learning disabilities related to reading, who showed more rapid growth and somewhat narrowed this achievement gap on tests of reading comprehension in the early grades. For this group, it is possible that general and special educators emphasized word recognition skills during early grades, which supported these students in making gains during early reading assessments. However, as reading comprehension demands grew during later grades, such word recognition interventions did not adequately support optimal reading comprehension acquisition, and without support targeting skills related to comprehension, reading achievement scores showed a decelerating trend. These patterns highlight the effects of and need for specialized support and accessibility considerations for some SWD to improve academic achievement in general education settings.

Inclusion

In 2015, the US Department of Health and Human Services (HHS) and Department of Education (ED) issued a policy statement on the inclusion of children with disabilities in early childhood programs. While this statement was related to early childhood specifically, the Departments also emphasized the need for meaningful inclusion for all children and adults, beginning in early childhood, continuing into school, and extending to community placements and the workforce.

Inclusion describes the practice of teaching students with and without disabilities in the same settings, establishing high expectations for performance and learning for SWD, creating opportunities for SWD to participate in all learning and social programming, and using evidence-based practices to support the learning and growth of SWD (US Department of Health and Human Services & US Department of Education [HHS & ED], 2015). Research evidence has documented that SWD can be successful in inclusive settings, inclusion can benefit both students with and without disabilities, and SWD educated in inclusive settings can make greater academic gains than SWD educated in self-contained settings (HHS & ED, 2015; Rafferty, Piscitelli, & Boettcher, 2003). Furthermore, SWDs who spend more time in general education classrooms often perform better on reading and math tests compared to SWD who spend less time in general education settings (Blackorby et al., 2004; McLaughlin & Walther-Thomas, 2002).

Successful inclusion often requires teachers to adapt instruction and assessment to accommodate the needs of SWD. Using the framework provided in the *Standards for Educational and Psychological Testing* (American Educational Research Association [AERA], American Psychological Association [APA], & the National Council on Measurement in Education [NCME], 2014), adaptations are changes that enhance the accessibility of instruction or testing and may include accommodations or modifications. Accommodations are supports used to help students access the curriculum and demonstrate their learning on a test. These supports are not intended to change the curricular standards of instruction or the constructs measured on a test. Rather, these supports provide a means for the student to learn what he/she is able to learn and to show what he/she has learned. Modifications, on the other hand, change either the curriculum (e.g., change program goals or performance standards or instructional content) or the test (e.g., test content, format, or administration conditions) in such a way that the construct measured is likely different from the construct measured in an unmodified test. With appropriate accommodations, SWD can have increased access to both instruction and assessment. Evidence-based, specialized instructional strategies should be used to meet the learning needs of SWD across educational settings (Odom, Buysse, & Soukakou, 2011).

Common Barriers to Instruction and Assessment for Students with Disabilities

Despite efforts made to create meaningful inclusive educational opportunities for SWD, many barriers continue to limit students' access to high-quality inclusive programs. A significant challenge is teachers' and parents' attitudes and beliefs about inclusion (HHS & ED, 2015). Children who are meaningfully included in early childhood are more likely to be meaningfully included in elementary school and more likely to be successful in secondary school years and beyond, but even in early childhood, attitudes toward inclusion are preventing young children from accessing high-quality inclusive programming (Barton & Smith, 2015; HHS & ED, 2015). Some educators, administrators, and parents are resistant to adopting inclusive practices because they feel inclusion is not feasible, and they may have concerns that individualized support for SWD will reduce instructional time and attention provided to students without disabilities (Barton & Smith, 2015). Professional development for educators and administrators, along with parent education and support, is needed to change the attitudes and beliefs that prevent SWD's access to inclusion.

Once inclusion is embraced, instructors should continually assess the need for providing individualized accommodations to support student learning. Without these supports, some students may face challenges accessing instruction and content and demonstrating what they know on tests. It should be noted that such supports are not unique to a specific disability category. Moreover, services may vary for students with the same diagnosis (e.g., specific learning disability) because needs within disability categories vary. Common barriers to optimal learning of SWD include insufficient time or opportunity to learn content, use of instructional materials or strategies that are not aligned with a student's learning needs, insufficient opportunities to respond, and testing conditions that interfere with a student's opportunity to demonstrate academic achievement (Elliott, Kurz, & Schulte, 2015). To address these barriers, instructors can provide an array of individualized accommodations for instruction, and examples are provided in Table 6.1.

Moving Beyond Disability Status

Acquisition of specific academic skills (e.g., reading fluency, algebra) requires that a student have all the necessary *access skills* to learn and then demonstrate the academic content. To better understand the individualized support a student with a disability may need to successfully learn and demonstrate knowledge, an educator first must be aware of the access skills needed to acquire and perform a targeted academic skill. Then, the educator must determine whether a student has any deficits in any of the required skills needed to achieve the targeted skill. For example, reading comprehension (a *target skill*) requires a student be able to attend to the written material, remember what he/she has read, read fluently, and have the receptive vocabulary to understand the text. If a student has a relative weakness within any of these domains, he/she may struggle to comprehend what he/she is reading and also perform poorly on tests of reading comprehension. Thus, a teacher should take into account not only the student's disability status but also the student's repertoire of access skills when making decisions about instructional content, teaching strategies, tests, and testing conditions. While challenges with some access skills (e.g., attention) may be associated with a specific disability (e.g., attention-deficit hyperactivity disorder, fetal alcohol spectrum disorder), the access skills should be understood in relation to the identified target skills to provide optimal testing of a student's target skills and to inform teachers' instructional methods and strategies.

Access to Instruction

An underlying assumption in the move toward inclusion is that all students should have the opportunity to access the general education curriculum in a general education setting and be held

Table 6.1 Universal Design for Learning (UDL) principles and guidelines with corresponding examples of accommodations for students with disabilities based on Rose and Gravel (2010)

UDL principle/guideline	Examples of possible accommodations
Principle: providing multiple means of representation	
Guidelines:	
(1) Provide options for perception	Large print
	Auditory support of text
	Specialized lighting
	Visual support of content
	Proximity to teacher
	Assistive technology
	Altered sensory input levels (e.g., lower audio volume)
	Use of manipulatives
(2) Provide options for language and symbols	Text-to-speech
	Large print
	Braille
	Designated reader
(3) Provide options for comprehension	Audiobooks or graphic organizers
	Use of manipulatives, instructional pacing, explicit instruction, or repetition
Principle: providing multiple means of action and expression	
Guidelines:	
(4) Provide options for physical action	Multiple means of activity participation
	Typing rather than writing responses
(5) Provide options for expressive skills and fluency	Assistive technology
	Calculator or number line
	Dictate to scribe or audio recorder instead of writing responses
	Supplemental time on assignments
(6) Provide options for executive functions	Test taking in separate room or small group (distraction-free environment)
	Supplemental time
	Frequent breaks
	Standing at desk
	Use of timer
	Color-coded materials
Principle: providing multiple means of engagement	
Guidelines:	
(7) Provide options for recruiting interest	Assigning a classroom job as a motivational strategy
	Using a topic of personal interest as lesson content
(8) Provide options for sustaining effort and persistence	Immediate feedback
	Shortened instructional periods or test taking in segments
	Visual and verbal cues of behavioral expectations
	Visual schedules
	Token economy
(9) Provide options for self-regulation	Proximity to teacher
	Frequent breaks
	Self-monitoring system
	Quiet area

to the same academic content standards as their grade-level peers (Jorgensen, McSheehan, & Sonnenmeier, 2007; Morningstar, Shogren, Lee, & Born, 2015; US Department of Education [ED], 2016). To optimize such access, and to comply with IDEA (2004), school specialists must conduct regular evaluations and develop individualized education programs (IEPs) for all SWD who are eligible for special education services. In conducting an evaluation, school specialists, such as a school psychologist, speech language pathologist, and/or reading specialist, administer a series of assessments from which they document a student's relative strengths and weaknesses and other data pertinent to how the student learns and performs. Based on these evaluations and other team members' input, student IEP teams (comprised of general and special educators, parents, and specialists) meet regularly to develop and update individualized strategies and goals for each student in special education. Teachers use the strategies outlined in IEPs, along with student data, to enhance the accessibility of their instruction.

Increasing Access to Instruction

Evidence-based strategies to increase access to instruction include increasing students' opportunity to learn content objectives within the intended curriculum, applying principles of universal design to instructional and test materials, and employing appropriate accommodations to optimize student success (Elliott et al., 2015).

Opportunity to learn (OTL) Fundamental to increasing access to instruction is increasing students' opportunity to learn (OTL). Importantly, OTL can vary by student within a class. Differences in OTL are of particular concern for SWD because, with insufficient supports, they may experience fewer opportunities to actually engage in learning within a general education setting (Kurz et al., 2014). Teachers can support students' OTL by examining their content of instruction, time on instruction, and quality of instruction (Kurz et al., 2014). Doing so requires effective monitoring of these variables and data-driven decision-making. In addition to monitoring their own teaching, teachers can collaboratively analyze OTL data within a curricular or instructional coaching context. These activities supplement longer-term OTL assessment strategies, such as end-of-year OTL feedback (Kurz et al., 2014; Kurz, Talapatra, & Roach, 2012). Technological innovations can support and facilitate such self-monitoring (e.g., Kurz, Elliott, & Shrago, 2009), and administrators and school specialists can use teachers' OTL data to provide feedback to teachers (Roach, Kurz, & Elliott, 2015). The OTL data collection, feedback, and monitoring process should increase teachers' awareness of their own teaching and support them in identifying barriers to students' OTL and employing strategies to increase OTL for all students in the classroom.

Universal Design for Learning (UDL) A useful framework in supporting access to instruction for SWD is Universal Design for Learning (UDL), which is further detailed in Chap. 10 (Hall & Rose) of this text. UDL promotes three core principles: (a) provide multiple means of representation, (b) provide multiple means of action and expression, and (c) provide multiple means of engagement (Rose & Gravel, 2010). Means of representation include providing options for how students perceive information, how information is represented through language and symbols, and how students might comprehend content in a meaningful way. Means of action and expression include providing options for physical action, expressing one's self, and being mindful and supportive of executive functions, and means of engagement include recruiting initial interest in information, sustaining student effort and persistence, and supporting self-regulation (Rose & Gravel, 2010). Within each of these principles (providing multiple means of representation, action and expression, and engagement), there are three UDL guidelines, for a total of nine UDL guidelines. Table 6.1 provides examples of the many ways in which special educators might use instructional supports that align with UDL guidelines to enhance SWD's access to instruction.

Many of the goals of UDL pertain directly to SWD, including reducing barriers to instruction, offering accommodations and supports, and holding students to high achievement standards (Elliott et al., 2015). UDL principles are particularly relevant to SWD, as educators often use the accommodations recommended in the guidelines as part of special education instructional programming. No strategy is limited to use for just one disability type, and special educators use many of the same strategies to support a range of disabilities. For instance, special educators may use visual supports (e.g., diagrams, photographs) to support the delivery of instructional content for students with a variety of disabilities, including those with auditory processing disorder, specific learning disability, speech/language impairment, traumatic brain injury, and autism. By contrast, teachers may use different accommodations to support students with the same disability identification. For example, one student with autism who has limited spoken language skills and who exhibits challenging behaviors may require a text-to-speech device and frequent breaks with access to a quiet area. A second student, who also has autism, may not benefit from text-to-speech but may require supplemental time on tests and support for organizing study materials.

Accommodations in the inclusive classroom Special and general educators in inclusion settings differentiate instruction within the context of a universal approach to behavioral and curricular supports (Morningstar et al., 2015). Teachers may increase student access to instruction by employing adaptations, such as conveying information through multiple modalities, allowing students to demonstrate mastery in meaningful ways, and adjusting instructional explicitness, pacing, duration, complexity, response feedback, and frequency and type of reinforcement (Morningstar et al., 2015; Shepherd, Fowler, McCormick, Wilson, & Morgan, 2016). Identifying appropriate accommodations for supporting access to instruction for all students in an inclusion classroom requires collaboration among general and special educators and support staff in the design and implementation of instruction, and in the evaluation of its outcomes, for an array of student needs across tiered systems of support (Fuchs, Fuchs, & Stecker, 2010; Shepherd et al., 2016).

Accommodations can be conceptualized in four categories, which Harrison, Bunford, Evans, and Owens (2013) described as:

1. *Presentation accommodations*: changes in the way that instruction, assignments, or assessments are presented or delivered
2. *Response accommodations*: changes in the way that students are permitted to respond to instruction (on assignments or assessments) or use organizational devices as an aid to formulate a response
3. *Timing/scheduling accommodations:* changes in the (a) organization of time allotted for an activity or test, (b) amount of time allocated for the presentation of a lesson or test, or (c) time allowed to complete a lesson or test
4. *Setting accommodations:* changes to the location (i.e., physical placement) in which students complete assignments or assessments and/or the instructors present at that location

An often overlooked but critical piece of inclusive instruction is the provision of behavioral and social-emotional supports, as behavioral and social-emotional challenges often coexist with learning differences and interfere with academic engagement and performance (Kuchle, Edmonds, Danielson, Peterson, & Riley-Tillman, 2015). For instance, students with emotional and behavioral disorders (EBD) and/or attention-deficit hyperactivity disorder (ADHD) often require support specific to engaging in desired classroom and social behaviors. By providing behavioral and social-emotional supports for these students in conjunction with academically focused accommodations, teachers may increase students' OTL.

Common accommodations for students with disabilities By adjusting their instruction and utilizing accommodations, teachers can minimize the risk that a lack of access skill(s) is impeding student acquisition of a target skill. Common instructional accommodations that enhance access for SWD include extended time to complete assignments, more breaks, assistance with reading, use of calculators or other technology, reduced or modified assignments, and access to distraction-reduced settings (Elliott et al., 2015). Educators should strive to increase academic engaged time, as increasing engaged time is more effective than adding time alone. School psychologists and special educators can support educators in differentiating instructional time (e.g., during centers or small group activities) to meet students' needs, increasing proportion of time students are engaged in instruction, and making more effective use of existing, designated instructional time (Gettinger & Miller, 2014). Educators also should frequently monitor student progress and adjust their instruction as needed (Shepherd et al., 2016). Ideally, the effective use of universal strategies, both academic and social-emotional, decreases the need for specialized adaptations (Morningstar et al., 2015).

Response to Intervention (RTI)

While many students have an IEP in place and receive special education services, other students are at risk for requiring services and, thus, benefit from careful assessment and progress monitoring. As described in Chap. 9 (Glover) of this text, RTI frameworks comprise progressively intensive intervention tiers through which students progress according to their response to evidence-based instruction (Vaughn & Swanson, 2015). In Tier 1, assessment takes place in the general education setting to determine for whom the universal strategies are effective. At the same time, effective progress monitoring identifies students for whom more targeted instruction is needed. Students who require special education services may receive such services while transitioning through these tiers (Vaughn & Swanson, 2015). Ideally, educators will implement high-quality, research-based interventions, thereby eliminating the possibility that a student's lack of progress is due to inadequate instruction (Vaughn & Swanson, 2015). Through a careful and thorough assessment and intervention process, teachers can focus specialized instruction on students with exceptional learning needs.

Professional Development to Increase Access to Instruction for Students with Disabilities

In a review of professional development strategies for improving teachers' accommodation decisions, Hodgson, Lazarus, and Thurlow (2011) outlined key knowledge and skills that teachers need. They recommended that teachers should have:

1. A basic understanding of relevant federal and state laws (e.g., IDEA), including the expectation that SWD will achieve grade-level academic standards
2. An understanding of the relationship between accommodations for instruction and accommodations for assessment and how to use the IEP to inform use of accommodations for each
3. Skills to provide consistency in accommodation provision among instructional and assessment settings
4. An understanding that accommodation decisions must be individualized per student according to their unique needs
5. The knowledge and skills to evaluate accommodation efficacy for each student

Hodgson and colleagues (2011) promoted project-based learning, case-based instruction, and communities of practices as potential strategies for supporting teachers in acquiring and using these skills. Project-based learning entails teachers solving a real-world problem in an applied setting and, in doing so, producing artifacts to demonstrate the problem-solving process (Blumenfeld et al., 1991; Hodgson et al., 2011). Case-based instruction also involves solving a real-world problem but provides more scaffolding and support through small group discussions of the case, wherein teachers from different educational settings share perspectives (Hodgson et al., 2011; Kagan, 1993). Communities of practice can enhance the efficacy of case-based instruction and require educators to join a group with predefined roles, shared objectives and goals, and artifacts or products of collaboration, such as publications, routines, or shared vocabulary (Hodgson et al., 2011; Mott, 2000). Hodgson and colleagues (2011) further recommended online forms of these professional development methods be used to minimize logistical challenges and maximize participation.

The joint policy statement on the inclusion of children with disabilities in early childhood programs (HHS & ED, 2015) called for resources for professional development at the systems level, continued coaching and collaboration, and built-in time for planning and communication to ensure sufficient support for individual student needs. Ongoing systems support for professional development strategies, such as project-based learning, case-based instruction, and communities of practice, likely would be effective in increasing educators' mastery of desired knowledge and skills.

Access to Testing

While more students are receiving special education services and are being educated in general education settings, challenges remain in over- and under-identification of subgroups of students for special education, delays in identifying and serving SWD, and use of appropriate assessments for eligibility determination and academic progress monitoring for educational and accountability purposes (Aron & Loprest, 2012). Some of these challenges lie in students' limited access to assessments and testing conditions that yield valid and reliable results. The testing conditions or methods used to assess achievement may unnecessarily interfere with students' performance and result in an underestimation of learning (Elliott et al., 2015).

Improving Accessibility

When a student's disability interacts with the testing format or conditions, a student's performance on that test may reflect his/her disability and not what has been learned (or what the test was designed to measure). In these instances, testing barriers need to be reduced so that students have the opportunity to demonstrate their academic growth. These barriers can be overcome through the sound application of universal design principles and testing accommodations. Testing accommodations are defined as:

> Adjustments that do not alter the assessed construct that are applied to test presentation, environment, content, format (including response format), or administration conditions for particular test takers, and that are embedded within assessments or applied after the assessment is designed. (AERA et al., 2014, p. 215)

Such accommodations should be grounded in effective instructional support practices and directly linked to an individual student's needs (Elliott et al., 2015). Specifically, when selecting accommodations, educators should ask themselves if a student has challenges with an access skill for the test being considered. If so, are there any accommodations available to address the impairment and will the accommodation(s) change the construct being measured by the test (Kettler, 2012)?

When students receive appropriate test accommodations, the validity of the inferences made from their test scores is increased. Common testing accommodations include changes in presentation of a test (e.g., oral delivery), timing of the test (e.g., extended time, delivery across multiple days or testing sessions), response format (e.g., responding in the test booklet instead of on an answer sheet), or to the testing environment (e.g., testing in a separate, distraction-free room; Elliott et al., 2015). In a review of testing accommodations, the two most frequently utilized testing accommodations were reading support and extended time (Sireci, Scarpati, & Li, 2005). However, these common accommodations may not be appropriate for all SWD or across all tests.

After accommodations have been identified, there remain challenges in implementing these accommodations, as often they require additional time, personnel, and costs to implement (Elliott et al., 2015). Thus, education personnel must work together to support each other in learning about the importance of accommodations and planning how to utilize accommodations in their own schools.

Special Considerations for Students with Significant Disabilities

Despite research evidence that suggests inclusion benefits students across a range of disabilities, including students with significant disabilities (HHS & ED, 2015), the majority of students with intellectual disabilities and multiple disabilities spend less than 40% of their school days in general education settings (NCES, 2016). Almost all SWDs (99%), however, are held to the same academic achievement standards as their grade-level peers and participate in large-scale, state assessments, regardless of their classroom placements (Every Student Succeeds Act [ESSA], 2015). This federal legislation has resulted in greater OTL in academic areas for SWDs but also requires innovative and differentiated instructional approaches to support meaningful academic progress. Students with the most significant cognitive disabilities (no more than 10% of SWD or 1% of all students) are entitled to alternate academic achievement standards and participate in alternate assessments to measure their performance against these alternate standards (ESSA, 2015). These alternate standards for 1% of students may only be used if they are aligned with the state's academic content standards, promote access to the general education curriculum (a requirement of IDEA), reflect high and achievable learning standards, support students' preparation for postsecondary education or employment, and are noted in a student's IEP (ED, 2016). Access to testing that accurately measures learning and progress of students with significant disabilities has been a challenge, as test developers have had to move beyond traditional paper and pencil tests to document and evaluate student performance. This work has led to the development of alternate assessments, which may include performance data collected through portfolios, rating scales, item-based tests, and instructionally embedded tasks (National Center on Educational Outcomes [NCEO], 2016).

Instruction for Students with Significant Disabilities

Students with significant disabilities can learn academic, social, communication, and self-determination skills in inclusive settings (Kurth, Lyon, & Shogren, 2015). In more recent years, learning goals for students with significant cognitive disabilities have shifted from being focused on functional or life skills to a more comprehensive curriculum including general academic goals (Petersen, 2016). Students with significant disabilities acquire knowledge and skills at a slower rate and require methodical and systematic instruction with repeated practice opportunities to acquire, maintain, and generalize new skills (Kleinert, Browder, & Towles-Reeves, 2009). To support overall learning and development, students with significant disabilities often work with an interdisciplinary team of educators and specialists, such as general educators, special educators, speech language pathologists, and physical and occupational therapists (Petersen, 2016). In addition, this team can provide direct support to educators to strategize how to integrate accommodations and supports in the classroom to maximize students' opportunities to practice target skills (Kearns, Kleinert, Thurlow, Brian, & Quenemoen, 2015). An instructional assistant also may be assigned to work directly with a student with a significant disability within the classroom setting to implement accommodations and provide support (e.g., prompting and coaching) during classroom instruction (Kurth et al., 2015).

In addition to working with specialists and having an instructional assistant to support their learning, students with significant disabilities may benefit from having a peer-partner in the classroom (Carter et al., 2016). Peer support arrangements pair students without disabilities with students with significant disabilities to collaborate on teacher-designed academic and/or social activities throughout the school year (Carter et al., 2016). These arrangements can increase opportunities for students with significant disabilities to practice social and communication skills with their peers while learning academic content in a general education environment and also have been shown to improve the academic achievement of students without disabilities and to advance peers' attitudes toward individuals with disabilities (Carter et al., 2016).

Considerations for Assessment

Students with significant disabilities may be unable to demonstrate their knowledge and learning through traditional tests. Alternate assessment methods are needed to collect data on students' performance. These methods may include portfolios of student work that include tasks teachers designed or modified to measure learning benchmarks or objectives, teacher rating scale and observational data of student performance, or assessments embedded within instruction. For students with significant disabilities, the cognitive demand placed on the student during the assessment must be considered (Kleinert et al., 2009). It is important to attempt to minimize the demands on working memory during an assessment, unless the measured construct is in fact working memory (Kleinert et al., 2009). In addition, it is essential that students with significant disabilities have a mode of communication that is both dependable and understandable so that they can communicate what they have learned (Kearns et al., 2015). Communication skills are highly variable within the population of students with significant disabilities. Some students communicate orally, while others require augmentative alternative communication, such as picture or symbol boards or speech-generating devices (Kleinert et al., 2009). By considering cognitive demands, communication skills, and assessment format, results from alternate assessments may more accurately reflect what students with significant disabilities know and can do.

From School Access to Community Inclusion

As a student with a disability ages, the concept of accessibility can no longer be limited to the classroom, and instead, skills, including how to independently use accommodations outside of the school building, must be taught in the context of postsecondary life. Postsecondary outcomes, including higher education, independent living, and employment, are poorer for SWD (Newman et al., 2011). Youth with disabilities who are preparing to transition out of secondary school can do so more successfully by understanding their disability and how it will affect their ability to independently learn and live (Asselin, 2014). IDEA (2004) mandates secondary transition requirements for IEPs beginning no later than students' 16th birthdays. The law also requires the IEP to include appropriate and measurable transition goals based on age-appropriate transition assessments. These assessments must evaluate training, education, employment, and independent living skills, as appropriate for each individual student. The IEP must also outline instructional strategies to support the student in achieving these goals. Schools must provide the student with a Summary of Performance upon exiting secondary school, which may include assessment data regarding academic achievement and functional performance and recommendations for pursuing postsecondary goals, such as anticipated accessibility needs for college or career (IDEA, 2004). Secondary special educators need to integrate transition goals into their curricula and consider how doing so will affect instructional and assessment practices. Furthermore, educators should guide students to be active members of their own transition planning team. Students who meaningfully participate in the process of creating the Summary of Performance will likely be better equipped in postsecondary life to self-advocate for accommodations, assistive technology, and accessible information technology (Asselin, 2014). Designating the student as the central participant in transition planning builds self-determination skills, which are central target skills of transition special education (Seong, Wehmeyer, Palmer, & Little, 2015).

In addition to the required components, transition research has identified key components associated with successful postsecondary transition outcomes. Secondary transition programs often focus on traditional academics and college admission. However, SWD can achieve access to more postsecondary options if they are assessed on and instructed in functional life areas, such as social skills, time management, self-advocacy, problem-solving, decision-making, independent living skills, recreation and leisure skills, transportation, and understanding of assistive technology (Asselin, 2014).

Graduation and College Entrance Exams

Nearly 80% of secondary SWD cite postsecondary education as a primary goal (Newman, Wagner, Cameto, & Knokey, 2009). Many SWD who plan to enter college face challenges taking graduation and college entrance exams (Gregg & Nelson, 2012). In a meta-analysis of accommodations in high-stakes tests for transition-age adolescents with learning disabilities, the most common accommodation used was extended time, and transitioning students with learning disabilities performed significantly better on these standardized tests when using the accommodation (Gregg & Nelson, 2012). However, results of this meta-analysis also revealed a dearth of research on this topic. Effective methods for improving access to graduation and college entrance exams for SWD are an area for future research.

Inclusion and Postsecondary Outcomes

There is growing evidence that secondary SWDs who are taught the general curriculum in inclusive settings have more positive postsecondary education and employment outcomes in adulthood (Carter, Austin, & Trainor, 2012; Rojewski, Lee, & Gregg, 2013; Test et al., 2009). It is likely that an inclusive environment that provides strong academic and social-emotional supports over a long-term, consistent basis will only strengthen these outcomes. By proactively incorporating transition concepts and skills into everyday instruction, teachers can more fluidly build toward centralized, transition-focused target skills during students' last years of secondary school.

Conclusion

Despite increased numbers of SWD participating in general education settings for greater portions of the school day, many of these students continue to face barriers that obstruct their access to effective instruction and testing. To meet the needs of these students, educators should maintain high learning standards for all students, identify the access and target skills that need to be addressed within the curriculum, utilize principles of universal design in the education and testing of all students to reduce the number of accommodation needs of individual students, and design and implement appropriate instructional and testing accommodations to enhance access for SWD. In addition, specifically for SWD, teachers should consider (a) increasing the amount of academic engaged time to increase students' opportunities to learn the academic content associated with their grade-level content standards, (b) aligning instructional and testing supports to improve accommodation integrity and enhance access to both instruction and testing, and (c) removing inessential instructional and testing content to focus on identified target and access skills linked to the educational content standards (Elliott et al., 2015; Gettinger & Miller, 2014). These steps can be taken through increased resources and training provided to educators and administrators, which in turn can support these students in building critical self-determination skills that will benefit them across their life span.

References

American Educational Research Association, American Psychological Association, & National Council on Measurement in Education. (2014). *Standards for educational and psychological testing*. Washington, DC: American Educational Research Association.

Americans With Disabilities Act of 1990, Pub. L. No. 101-336, 104 Stat. 328. (1990).

Aron, L., & Loprest, P. (2012). Disability and the education system. *The Future of Children, 22*, 97–122.

Asselin, S. B. (2014). Learning and assistive technologies for college transition. *Journal of Vocational Rehabilitation, 40*, 223–230. https://doi.org/10.3233/JVR-140687

Barton, E. E., & Smith, B. J. (2015). Advancing high quality preschool inclusion: A discussion and recommendations for the field. *Topics in Early Childhood Special Education, 35*, 65–78.

Blackorby, J., Wagner, M., Cameto, R., Davies, E., Levine, P., Lunn, N., … Sumi, C. (2004). *SEELS: Engagement, academics, social adjustment, and independence: The achievements of elementary and middle school students with disabilities*. Menlo Park, CA: SRI International.

Blumenfeld, P. C., Soloway, E., Marx, R. W., Krajcik, J. S., Guzdial, M., & Palincsar, A. (1991). Motivating project-based learning: Sustaining the doing, supporting the learning. *Educational Psychologist, 26*, 369–398.

Carter, E. W., Asmus, J., Moss, C. K., Biggs, E. E., Bolt, D. M., Born, T. L., … Weir, K. (2016). Randomized evaluation of peer support arrangements to support the inclusion of high school students with severe disabilities. *Exceptional Children, 82*, 209–233. https://doi.org/10.1177/0014402915598780

Carter, E. W., Austin, D., & Trainor, A. A. (2012). Predictors of postschool employment outcomes for young adults with severe disabilities. *Journal of Disability Policy Studies, 23*, 50–63. https://doi.org/10.1177/1044207311414680

Elliott, S. N., Kurz, A., & Schulte, A. (2015). *Maximizing access to instruction and testing for students with disabilities: What we know and can do to improve achievement*. Smarter Balanced Assessment Consortium. UCLA: McGraw Hill.

Every Student Succeeds Act (ESSA) of 2015, Pub. L. No. 114-95. (2015).

Fuchs, D., Fuchs, L. S., & Stecker, P. M. (2010). The "blurring" of special education in a new continuum of general education placements and services. *Exceptional Children, 76*, 301–323.

Gettinger, M. & Miller, K. (2014). Best practices in increased academic engaged time. In A. Thomas & P. Harrison (Eds.), *Best Practices in School Psychology - Student Level Services* (6th ed.), 19–36. Bethesda, MD: National Association of School Psychologists.

Gregg, N., & Nelson, J. M. (2012). Meta-analysis on the effectiveness of extra time as a test accommodation for transitioning adolescents with learning disabilities: More questions than answers. *Journal of Learning Disabilities, 45*, 128–138. https://doi.org/10.1177/0022219409355484

Harrison, J. R., Bunford, N., Evans, S. W., & Owens, J. S. (2013). Educational accommodations for students with behavioral challenges: A systematic review of the literature. *Review of Educational Research, 83*, 551–597. https://doi.org/10.3102/0034654313497517

Hodgson, J. R., Lazarus, S. S., & Thurlow, M. L. (2011). *Professional development to improve accommodations decisions—A review of the literature (Synthesis Report 84)*. Minneapolis, MN: University of Minnesota, National Center on Educational Outcomes. Retrieved from: https://nceo.umn.edu/docs/OnlinePubs/Synthesis84/SynthesisReport84.pdf

Individuals with Disabilities Education Improvement Act, 20 U.S.C. § 1400. (2004).

Jorgensen, C. M., McSheehan, M., & Sonnenmeier, R. M. (2007). Presumed competence reflected in the educational programs of students with IDD before and after the beyond access professional development intervention. *Journal of Intellectual & Developmental Disability, 32*, 248–262. https://doi.org/10.1080/13668250701704238

Kagan, D. M. (1993). Contexts for the use of classroom cases. *American Educational Research Journal, 30*, 703.

Kearns, J. J., Kleinert, H. L., Thurlow, M. L., Brian, G., & Quenemoen, R. (2015). Alternate assessments as one measure of teacher effectiveness: Implications for our field. *Research & Practice for Persons with Severe Disabilities, 40*, 20–35.

Kettler, R. J. (2012). Testing accommodations: Theory and research to inform practice. *International Journal of Disability, Development and Education, 59*, 53–66.

Kleinert, H., Browder, D., & Towles-Reeves, E. (2009). Models of cognition for students with significant cognitive disabilities: Implications for assessment. *Review of Educational Research, 79*, 301–326.

Kuchle, L. B., Edmonds, R. Z., Danielson, L. C., Peterson, A., & Riley-Tillman, T. C. (2015). The next big idea: A framework for integrated academic and behavioral intensive intervention. *Learning Disabilities Research & Practice, 30*, 150–158. https://doi.org/10.1111/ldrp.12084

Kurth, J. A., Lyon, K. J., & Shogren, K. A. (2015). Supporting students with severe disabilities in inclusive schools: A descriptive account from schools implementing inclusive practices. *Research and Practice for Persons with Severe Disabilities, 40*, 261–274.

Kurz, A., Elliott, S. N., Lemons, C. J., Zigmond, N., Kloo, A., & Kettler, R. J. (2014). Opportunity to Learn: A differentiated opportunity structure for students with disabilities in general education classrooms. *Assessment for Effective Intervention, 40*, 24–39.

Kurz, A., Elliott, S. N., & Shrago, J. S. (2009). *MyiLOGS: My instructional learning opportunities guidance system*. Nashville, TN: Vanderbilt University.

Kurz, A., Talapatra, D., & Roach, A. T. (2012). Meeting the curriculuar challenges of inclusive assessment: The role of alignment, oppportunity to learn, and student engagement. *International Journal of Disability, Development and Education, 59*, 37–52.

McLaughlin, R., & Walther-Thomas, C. (2002). Outcomes for students with disabilities in inclusive and pullout programs. *Exceptional Children, 68*, 203–222.

Morningstar, M. E., Shogren, K. A., Lee, H., & Born, K. (2015). Preliminary lessons about supporting participation and learning in inclusive classrooms. *Research and Practice for Persons with Severe Disabilities, 40*, 192–210. https://doi.org/10.1177/1540796915594158

Mott, V. W. (2000). The development of professional expertise in the workplace. *New Directions for Adult and Continuing Education, 86*, 23–31.

National Center for Education Statistics. (2016). *Children and youth with disabilities.* Retrieved from http://nces.ed.gov/programs/coe/indicator_cgg.asp

National Center on Educational Outcomes. (2016). *Alternate assessments for students with disabilities.* Retrieved from https://nceo.info/Resources/publications/TopicAreas/AlternateAssessments/altAssessFAQ.htm

Newman, L., Wagner, M., Cameto, R., & Knokey, A. M. (2009). *The post-high school outcomes youth with disabilities up to 4 years after high school. A report from the National Longitudinal Transition Study-2 (NLTS2).* Menlo Park, CA: SRI International.

Newman, L., Wagner, M., Knokey, A. M., Marder, C., Nagle, K., Shaver, D., … Schwarting, M. (2011). *The post-high school outcomes of young adults with disabilities up to 8 years after high school. A report from the National Longitudinal Transition Study-2 (NLTS2).* Menlo Park, CA: SRI International. Retrieved from http://www.nlts2.org/reports/2011_09_02/index.html

Odom, S. L., Buysse, V., & Soukakou, E. (2011). Inclusion for young children with disabilities: A quarter center of research perspectives. *Journal of Early Intervention, 33*, 344–356.

Petersen, A. (2016). Perspectives of special education teachers on general education curriculum access. *Research and Practice for Persons with Severe Disabilities, 41*, 19–35.

Rafferty, Y., Piscitelli, V., & Boettcher, C. (2003). The impact of inclusion on language development and social competence among preschoolers with disabilities. *Exceptional Children, 69*, 467–479.

Roach, A. T., Kurz, A., & Elliott, S. N. (2015). Using personalized instructional feedback data to facilitate opportunity to learn for students with disabilities. *Prevening School Failure.* doi: 10.1080/1045988X.2014.901288.

Rojewski, J. W., Lee, I. H., & Gregg, N. (2013). Causal effects of inclusion on postsecondary education outcomes of individuals with high-incidence disabilities. *Journal of Disability Policy Studies, 25*, 210–219.

Rose, D. H., & Gravel, J. W. (2010). Universal design for learning. In P. Peterson, E. Baker, & B. McGaw (Eds.), *International encyclopedia of education* (3rd ed., pp. 119–124). Oxford, UK: Elsevier.

Schulte, A. C., Stevens, J. J., Elliott, S. N., Tindal, G., & Nese, J. F. T. (2016). Achievement gaps for students with disabilities: Stable, widening, or narrowing on a state-wide reading comprehension test? *Journal of Educational Psychology, 108*, 925–942.

Section 504 of the Rehabilitation Act of 1973, 34 C.F.R. Part 104. (1973).

Seong, Y., Wehmeyer, M. L., Palmer, S. B., & Little, T. D. (2015). Effects of the self-directed individualized education program on self-determination and transition of adolescents with disabilities. *Career Development and Transition for Exceptional Individuals, 38*, 132–141.

Shepherd, K. G., Fowler, S., McCormick, J., Wilson, C. L., & Morgan, D. (2016). The search for role clarity: Challenges and implications for special education teacher preparation. *Teacher Education and Special Education, 39*, 83–97. https://doi.org/10.1177/0888406416637904

Sireci, S. G., Scarpati, S. E., & Li, S. (2005). Test accommodations for students with disabilities: An analysis of the interaction hypothesis. *Review of Educational Research, 75*, 457–490.

Stevens, J. J., Schulte, A. C., Elliott, S. N., Nese, J. F. T., & Tindal, G. (2015). Growth and gaps in mathematics achievement of students with and without disabilities on a statewide achievement test. *Journal of School Psychology, 53*, 45–62.

Test, D. W., Mazzotti, V. L., Mustian, A. L., Fowler, C. H., Kortering, L., & Kohler, P. (2009). Evidence-based secondary transition predictors for improving postschool outcomes for students with disabilities. *Career Development for Exceptional Individuals, 32*, 160–181. https://doi.org/10.1177/0885728809346960

U.S. Department of Education. (2016). *Elementary and Secondary Education Act of 1965, as amended by the Every Student Succeeds Act, negotiated rulemaking committee issue paper #4b.* Retrieved from http://www2.ed.gov/policy/elsec/leg/essa/session/nrmissuepaper4b32016.pdf

U.S. Department of Health and Human Services, & U.S. Department of Education. (2015, September). *Policy statement on inclusion of children with disabilities in early childhood programs.* Retrieved from http://www2.ed.gov/policy/speced/guid/earlylearning/joint-statement-full-text.pdf

Vaughn, S., & Swanson, E. A. (2015). Special education research advances knowledge in education. *Exceptional Children, 82*, 11–24. https://doi.org/10.1177/0014402915598781

Assessing Students with Autism: Considerations and Recommendations

Peter A. Beddow

Inclusive assessment practices in the United States require states to test 95% of students in reading and math in grades 3 through 8 and in one grade in high school, as well as in science at three points across the grade span (Every Student Succeeds Act, 2017). Under ESSA, states must report disaggregated results by subgroups including students receiving special education services, racial minorities, and students in poverty. ESSA allows states to create their own opt-out laws for assessments and to determine consequences for schools that miss participation targets. Although states must use the same statewide assessment for all elementary students, ESSA permits the use of nationally recognized assessments at the high school level and allows states to set an upper limit on the total time students participate in assessments for each grade.

Of critical importance for this chapter, ESSA (2016) rescinded the "2 percent" alternate assessments based on modified academic achievement standards (AA-MAAS), leaving only the "1 percent" alternate assessment, which is intended for students with significant cognitive disabilities who, under most states' participation criteria, exhibit severe and pervasive delays in both academics and adaptive behavior. Presumably, this major change was made in part with the objective of encouraging states to focus on increasing test accessibility for the students who previously qualified for the AA-MAAS (i.e., at least 2% of the student population of a given state).

There currently are 13 disability categories recognized in federal policy. Approximately 9% of these students receiving special education services in the United States are identified with autism. Given the increasing prevalence of autism spectrum disorder (ASD; see below) and the emphasis in the 2014 *Standards* (AERA, APA, NCME) for evaluating fairness, attending to universal design, and ensuring accessibility of tests for all groups, it is imperative test developers ensure standardized achievement tests yield results that are valid for these students. Test validity is of critical importance because the alternate assessment, while designed for students with disabilities, cannot be used to assess the majority of students with ASD. In fact, the plurality of students with ASD will not be eligible for, or participate in, 1% of alternate assessments. Not only will most students with ASD be excluded under many states' participation criteria (e.g., if they participate in common core instruction), but also, current estimates indicate 35% of individuals with ASD score above the IQ cutoff for intellectual disability (Dykens & Lense, 2011). Test developers, therefore, should examine how assessment events might be designed so that inferences from test results are valid for all students, including students with ASD.

P. A. Beddow (✉)
Accessible Hope, LLC, Nashville, TN, USA

Since the first descriptions of "classic autism" by Leo Kanner in 1943, and Hans Asperger in 1944, estimates of the global prevalence of ASD have markedly increased, from 4 to 5 in 10,000 prior to 1985 to the most recent Centers for Disease Control and Prevention (CDC) statistics indicating 1 in 68 children has ASD (Christensen et al., 2016). It should be noted the reported increases in the prevalence of ASD may be explained, at least in part, methodologically, and a degree of skepticism is warranted before they are assumed to be illuminative of a pandemic. Lenoir et al. (2009) argued increased knowledge of ASD compared to 30–40 years ago, changing diagnostic criteria (the expansion of autism to encompass a spectrum represented a major shift), and increased frequency of diagnosis at a younger age have caused "artificial" increases in the number of cases identified.

Regardless of the reasons for the consistent rise in ASD prevalence estimates, the importance of addressing the educational needs of students with ASD is inarguably critical. In addition to the Individuals with Disabilities Education Act (IDEA) provision that all students have the right to a free and appropriate public education, additional services have been increasingly highlighted as necessary for meeting the needs of individuals with ASD. As recently as 2008, only one state had an insurance mandate for children with ASD; as of October, 2016, 49 states have passed legislation mandating insurance coverage for ASD-related services such as applied behavior analysis (ABA) and speech therapy. Some insurers even cover education-related behavior services, which is in sharp contrast to the previously accepted notion that payers should cover treatment to reduce the most severe behaviors of individuals with ASD, such as self-injury or aggression.

Assessment is required for data-based decision-making to inform effective instruction and learning. The accuracy of assessment result is required for decisions based on test results to be valid and useful. Given the substantial population of students with ASD, it is incumbent upon assessment professionals to consider whether there are characteristics of these groups that may confound their ability to demonstrate what they know and can do on achievement tests (i.e., reduce the accuracy of results) and to examine how achievement tests might be designed to ameliorate any putative deleterious effects of these characteristics on test performance.

This chapter begins with a discussion of the characteristics of ASD with a focus on strategies to reduce the effects of test anxiety for this population. Next, I provide an overview of applied behavior analysis and the relevance of behaviorism to the treatment of ASD. I then discuss several behavioral strategies that may warrant consideration for testing and recommend ways to implement these strategies in the assessment milieu. Finally, I propose several guidelines for approaching test design and implementation for individuals with ASD to ensure the validity of inferences from their test results.

Characteristics of Autism Spectrum Disorder

The criteria in the 2013 update to the *Diagnostic and Statistical Manual of Mental Disorders* (DSM-V; American Psychiatric Association) define ASD as a neurodevelopmental disorder that is characterized by (a) deficits in social-emotional reciprocity and communication, (b) stereotyped motor movements and speech patterns, (c) insistence on sameness, (d) restricted or hyper-focused interests, and (e) hyper- or hypo-reactivity to sensory input (temperature, sound, texture, visual stimuli). Oliver, Berg, Burbidge, Arron, and Moss (2011) reported when compared with the general population, individuals with ASD commonly demonstrate deficits in social interaction, responsiveness to social cues and modeling, and expressive and receptive communication. They reported many children with ASD engage in repetitive behaviors, demonstrate fixated interests, have broad and frequent changes in mood, and are comparatively overactive and impulsive to a degree that is significantly greater than the general population. Anxiety is more prevalent among individuals with ASD compared to the general population (White, Oswald, Ollendick, & Scahill, 2009).

Anxiety and Individuals with ASD: Implications for Testing

Anxiety-related issues are common among individuals with ASD (Gillott, Furniss, & Walter, 2001; Kim, Szatmari, Bryson, Streiner, & Wilson, 2000); not every child with ASD, however, demonstrates clinical indications of anxiety (e.g., Lovaas, 1977). According to White, Oswald, Ollendick, and Scahill (2009), it is often assumed individuals with ASD simply prefer social isolation and avoid contact with others as a result; however, it may be that social communication deficits and sensory integration issues make certain situations exceeding challenging, which causes anxiety. As mentioned previously, among the common characteristics of individuals with ASD is an insistence on sameness (sometimes perceived as rigidity), a condition that cannot be easily satisfied apart from highly controlled environments with few people. Anxiety, therefore, may merely represent an emotional response to the inability to control environmental variables.

As well, children with ASD often require discrete, task-analyzed instruction to teach complex behavior chains, such as those needed during many facets of the school day, from entering a classroom, to transitioning from one activity, location, or teacher to another, to completing a multipart academic task. Given the many competing objectives and contingencies during the school day, it is conceivable that students with ASD often are not provided the type of instruction, or specificity of instruction, in some of the many skills that are needed to be successful throughout the educational milieu.

A large body of research indicates anxiety has a deleterious impact on test performance (Hembree, 1988.) Two primary models have been proposed to explain the putative mechanism by which test anxiety might affect scores. The first model assumes anxiety interferes with recall of prior learning (i.e., the interference model; the test-taker "goes blank" upon entering the testing room), but there is evidence anxiety also affects test-takers' ability to encode, organize, and store information effectively (i.e., the process model; Benjamin, McKeachie, Lin, & Holinger, 1981).

Another consideration is lower test scores may be caused, in part, by poor test-taking skills (i.e., the deficit model.) Research indicates not only do high- and low-anxiety test-takers differ in their knowledge of test-taking skills (Bruch, 1981), but also training in test-taking skills may improve the scores of individuals with high anxiety to a greater degree than training in anxiety-reduction techniques (Kirkland & Hollandsworth, 1980).

Of course, it is likely that test anxiety is correlated with perceived evaluative pressure – the "high-stake" element of testing in schools and elsewhere certainly lends credence to this possibility. To reduce perceived evaluative pressure, test administrators should emphasize, whenever possible, the role of testing as a tool for discovering what students have learned and de-emphasize the role of testing as a means of determining performance-based rewards and consequences and of evaluating students' value.

As well, the mere gravity of the examination environment may lend itself to anxiety or fear: comparatively reduced noise and activity, different materials, novel task demands, the serious tenor of instructional staff and students, and so forth. Cassidy (2004) found evidence that test anxiety may be reduced when evaluative pressure is removed, but overall, the author indicated the data supported models of test anxiety that address not only situational factors but also stable factors. It should be noted the interference, process, and deficit models may be complementary; indeed, concerns about failure, panic, apprehension, etc. may be exacerbated by inadequate knowledge or fluency of skills necessary for successful testing, which not only may impact the test-taker's ability to recall information but also may hinder his or her capacity to store, encode, and process it for the purpose of responding to test items.

Notwithstanding cognitive load theory's primary focus on effective instruction, the similarities between instructional events and test events suggest test developers should consult the theory to inform the design of accessible tests (Beddow, Ch.13). Indeed, to the degree a test requires cognitive resources that are extraneous to the tested content, the results may underrepresent the target construct and may represent a measure of working memory capacity. Test developers should consider utilizing principles of cognitive load theory (CLT), therefore, to inform the development of accessible tests and test items, not only for individuals with ASD but also for the general population. There is strong evidence that anxiety decreases working memory capacity (Ashcraft & Kirk, 2001; Shackman et al., 2006; Sorg & Whitney, 1992). Chadwick, Tindall-Ford, Agostinho, and Paas (2015) recommended the use of cognitive load strategies for anxious students to facilitate the availability of their working memory resources during instruction.

I also offered recommendations for the integration of cognitive load strategies to enhance the accessibility of assessments by reducing extraneous cognitive load (Chap. 13). These include reducing language load, integrating audio- and visual information carefully to avoid redundancy, and removing distracting elements. While these design features likely will ameliorate some of the putative effects of anxiety for test-takers, they do not address the other characteristics of test anxiety, namely, ruminating concerns about failure, panic, and apprehension related to the test event. While they arguably are separate from the test event, test administrators and teachers should be encouraged to attend to these characteristics prior to, and during, test events, with the purpose of helping these students show what they know and can do and ensure inferences from test results are as valid as possible.

Applied Behavior Analysis for Individuals with ASD

Results of early research conducted by Lovaas and colleagues (e.g., Lovaas, Koegel, Simmons, & Long, 1973) suggested children with ASD may benefit from intensive treatment using principles of operant behavior to ameliorate skill deficits (particularly in the domain of communication and language). In the four-plus decades since this work, the field of applied behavior analysis (ABA) has developed to a degree that it is widely considered the standard of treatment methods for individuals with ASD (Kazdin & Weisz, 1998). The technology of ABA has evolved significantly over time, and Lovaas' behavior modification strategies, as well as those of others, have morphed into a broad range of tools and techniques used by behavior analysts across the globe (Wong et al., 2014).

As a field of study, applied behavior analysis began with Skinner's (1953, 1974) work on human behavior. Skinner's discoveries rested largely on the concept of operant conditioning, which describes how behavior is shaped by its consequences (typically, reinforcement or punishment). Manipulation of consequences is coupled with the use of antecedent stimuli to signal the availability of reinforcement, or likelihood of punishment, contingent on a particular behavior or set of behaviors. When antecedents are used to signal contingencies such as reinforcement or punishment, they are referred to as *discriminative stimuli*, and the delivery of rewards contingent on the emittance of target behaviors is called *differential reinforcement*. Additionally, for a reinforcer to be effective, some state of deprivation is needed (deprivation and satiation are referred to as *motivating operations;* Laraway, Snycerski, Michael, & Poling, 2003.) Behavior analysts use some combination of these principles – namely, controlling motivating operations, establishing discriminative stimuli, and using differential reinforcement – to teach individuals to engage in specific behaviors dependent on environmental cues. Useful changes in behavior (sometimes called *learning*[1]) can be maintained provided reinforcement is delivered periodically contingent on the target behavior or behaviors. Indeed, even the rate and consistency of responding can be shaped simply by varying factors such as the timing and frequency of reinforcers (interval schedules of reinforcement, e.g., elicit different patterns of responding compared to ratio schedules; Cooper, Heron, & Heward, 2007.)

---

[1] This behavioral definition of learning may be distinguished from that of Sweller's (2010) cognitive load theory, in which learning can be defined as useful changes in long-term memory.

While sharing some theoretical and pragmatic forebears, the underlying philosophy of the field of behaviorism is largely distinct from that of modern psychology. The contrast between the fields is perhaps most evident in behaviorism's assertion that cognitive processes need not be considered in treatment, with radical behaviorists insisting that behavior change procedures can effectively address many psychiatric diagnoses, including those specified in the DSM-V (APA, 2013). With regard to the current discussion, ABA procedures have been used with individuals with ASD for over 40 years (e.g., Wolf, Risley, & Mees, 1963).

Considerations for Testing

Among the myriad behavioral strategies that commonly are used by ABA therapists in the treatment of individuals with ASD, several warrant consideration by test developers, test administrators, and even teachers who use assessments, with the purpose of ensuring test events permit this population to show what they know and can do on a test (i.e., that the test is accessible). Drawing broadly from the field of behavior analysis and with attention to the characteristics described previously, this section will consist of a selective set of recommendations for facilitating the accessibility of test events for students with ASD.

Remember that Test Events May Represent Deprivation Conditions

Reinforcing stimuli that typically are present in the instructional environment, such as attention, peer interaction, or even the opportunity to stand and move about the room, may be diminished during assessment. Therefore, the test event may represent, for many test-takers, an experience tantamount to an extinction condition (i.e., withholding reinforcement, especially once a contingency has been established). Research indicates extinction often is associated with higher rates of problem behavior and even extinction-induced aggression (Lerman, Iwata, & Wallace, 1999). Problem behaviors may range from mild, such as disruptive vocalization, fidgeting, tapping, or calling-out, to more severe, such as aggression, elopement (i.e., getting out of an assigned seat or leaving the assigned area, or running away), or self-injury (Allen & Wallace, 2013).

The primary assessment tool used in the development of treatment plans for children with problem behaviors, including those with ASD, is functional analysis (Hanley, Iwata, & McCord, 2003). Proponents of functional analysis suggest behavioral treatment plans to reduce the occurrence of a target (e.g., problem) behavior should include two components. First, the *function* of the behavior targeted for reduction should be specified; in other words, the plan must address the putative contingency maintaining the behavior (e.g., reinforcement), not only in terms of the presentation or delivery of preferred stimuli or avoidance of aversive stimuli but also in terms of the stimuli that are involved. For instance, if data indicate a child's self-injurious behavior is maintained by negative reinforcement, it is important to specify the reinforcer as clearly as possible. If the self-injury is maintained by escape from task demands, for example, it may be important to specify that the task demand preceding the behavior typically consists of mathematics word problems. Second, a replacement behavior should be designated as a target for increase; this behavior should be maintained by a similar contingency (i.e., have the same function) as the problem behavior. In the case of the child who engages in self-injurious behavior, a replacement behavior may be to signal a request for a break by presenting a colored card to the assistant teacher. In this scenario, it also may be important to ensure there are preferred activities available to the child during break time, so the replacement behavior is sufficiently reinforced.

Often, when behaviors are targeted for decrease, differential reinforcement is used to ensure, while the behavior that is reduced is placed on extinction (e.g., reinforcers are withheld contingent on its occurrence), reinforcement is provided contingent on the replacement behavior. As discussed previously, however, extinction procedures can yield undesirable results. While research indicates most behaviors decrease significantly when reinforcement is withheld consistently, the response typically is not immediate. Before the extinction procedures "take hold," it is common for individuals to engage in higher rates of the problem behavior(s) and even to engage in other problem behaviors. Allen and Wallace (2013) found that noncontingent reinforcement – delivering reinforcers without requiring a particular response by the individual – can reduce the "extinction burst" and help to ameliorate these challenges. The reason for the effect is unclear, but there are a number of plausible theories. The first is that an individual who is accustomed to accessing preferred stimuli at a certain rate experiences deprivation when the rate of reinforcement decreases following the implementation of extinction conditions. As well, as the schedule of reinforcement may be thin as the replacement behavior is trained and assimilated, so deprivation of the reinforcer may persist. Delivering the reinforcer – or preferred stimulus – independent of a particular response can serve to alleviate some of this deprivation as the individual adjusts to the new schedule of reinforcement (Bullock & Normand, 2006). Put simply, let us make the training scenario as positive as possible, because learning is sometimes difficult!

To reduce the impact of the perceived deprivation that may be experienced by students with ASD, test administrators should consider allowing ample opportunity before, after, and even during test events to access preferred stimuli. Providing said stimuli do not interfere with the assessment of the target construct(s) of the test – for the individual or for his or her peers – administrators may permit him or her to take a break in a designated area of the room from time to time, either independent of responding (e.g., on a schedule) or upon request (Allen & Wallace, 2013). Teachers may provide items to fidget during the test. Between test sections, students may be permitted to engage in preferred, test-irrelevant activities. Decisions regarding access to stimuli should be based, whenever possible, on an understanding of stimuli that are known to be rewarding to the individual; this can be ascertained through the use of formal or informal preference assessments (Cooper et al., 2007; Gottschalk, Libby, & Graff, 2000).

Teach All of the Requisite Skills that Will Enable Students with ASD to Successfully Participate in the Test Event

It is critical test developers and test administrators (in schools, this likely includes teachers) ensure students with ASD have achieved mastery of the range of skills needed to engage in the test-taking process. In many cases, this will require suspending assumptions or expectations about what students should already know how to do.

Broadly, many students with ASD may benefit from intensive training to mastery for navigating the user interface of a digitally delivered test system including using a pointer device, logging into the system, selecting the correct test, selecting test items, and using standard accessibility features (or those that may be included in their personal needs profiles; Russell, Chap. 16),

Discrete trial training (DTT; Cooper et al., 2007; Smith, 2001) is a behavioral instruction process that involves the presentation of a discriminative stimulus (a signal indicating availability of a reward for engaging in a particular behavior or demonstrating a skill), followed by the expectation of a response. To facilitate responding, the instructor may provide graduated prompts following a brief delay. If the subject responds correctly, the behavior is reinforced. This simple, "discrete" procedure (referred to as a *trial*) is repeated numerous times to facilitate acquisition of the target response or skill. The procedure emphasizes focused, targeted skills for instruction, clear contingencies, frequent reinforcement, and repetition until mastery.

Implicit in the process of DTT is the understanding that instruction is most effective for students with ASD when objectives are taught explicitly (even singularly), by contrast to many pedagogical strategies that embed numerous objectives into instructional sessions. Whereas teachers may find traditional learners are able to "learn by osmosis," assimilating skills and knowledge from social cues or peer example, students with ASD may not benefit from such things. The difference can be frustrating for many teachers (Cassady, 2011), particularly those that feel instructional time should not be allocated to teaching discrete skills, even if those skills are requisite to learning target objectives. A paradigm shift may be necessary, therefore, for many teachers whose expertise is derived primarily from working with students without ASD.

It should be noted effective instruction for students with ASD – especially, but not limited to, DTT – typically includes clear, precise contingencies that are signaled with established discriminative stimuli. These signals may be presented in the form of directions, instructions, rules, or any number of visual cues that indicate a condition in which a certain behavior or set of behaviors is expected. A discriminative stimulus develops when it is paired repeatedly with a consequence (during differential reinforcement procedures, the consequence typically is the presentation of a positive stimulus or reward or the removal of an aversive one) until the individual associates the antecedent stimulus with a consequence contingent on engaging in a specific behavior. Strong contingencies that use valuable reinforcers are more likely to elicit the target behaviors than weak contingencies that use less valuable reinforcers.

Establish, Maintain, and Practice Requisite Routines, Procedures, and Skills

For many students with ASD, predictability is comfort. Schedules, routines, and procedures are among the essential aspects of evidence-based instructional programs for students with ASD. Within the boundaries of structure, students with ASD often find a sense of predictability and security. Schedules should be developed with a focus on maintaining a balance between consistency and variety while ensuring the students' specific needs are met from day to day and over the course of the school year. Since assessment is critical to effective instruction, testing should be integrated into the structure of the educational milieu to build familiarity with the test-taking process.

Given the insistence on sameness – or, if you will, resistance to change – which is characteristic of the population of individuals with ASD, there must be a deliberate emphasis on consistency of scheduling throughout the school year, across the instructional day, and even within each instructional period. Consistency and predictability facilitate positive responses to the unavoidable changes that come with instruction: new concepts, new materials, new environments, new instructors, new peers, etc. In essence, maintaining a structured schedule and holding fast to established routines acknowledge these students' tendencies to resist change but allow for the momentum and growth that is required by the instructional process. Deliberately integrating variation (i.e., programming change) ensures students learn to adapt over time.

From the perspective of test administrators and teachers, it is critical that the assessment process does *not* represent an imposition into the typical routine and schedule of the school day, but rather it should be integrated into the schedule frequently enough as to become normalized. For this reason, it would be helpful for test companies to consider adding features to current test-delivery systems that enable districts, schools, and even teachers to use the systems to generate and deliver their own test items. Even though some districts may have the resources to develop and use test-delivery systems that are similar to large-scale assessment systems with the purpose of establishing uniformity and consistency across the range of assessments, even moderate discrepancies likely will detract from their intent (e.g., differences in font families, sizes, and colors; composition of user interface elements; navigation structure). It bears repeating that students with ASD often become comfortable with the status quo: structure, routine, and established schedules and systems; to depart from them, therefore, may be aversive and portend suboptimal motivation, participation, and performance.

To establish the kind of structure that lends itself to the *expectation* of testing rather than a feeling that assessment is outside the norm, it may be necessary to increase the frequency of test events to build fluency – an admittedly unpalatable notion for teachers and students who may have felt the amount of testing required in schools is already both tiresome and excessive. Although this concern has validity, there is strong evidence suggesting once a skill is integrated into an individual's repertoire, the practice of that skill yields fluency. Indeed, research indicates not only does fluency increase retention of skills, but it also is associated with increased ability to remain on task, even in the face of distraction (Binder, 1996). Moreover, learners tend to prefer engaging in activities in which they are fluent, even choosing them over less difficult ones. With regard to test-taking skills, practice for fluency may prove essential to facilitate responding for some individuals, particularly those with ASD.

Further, many individuals with ASD have difficulty attending to, or assimilating information from, social cues. Teachers and test administrators, therefore, should not assume all students – particularly those with ASD – understand and can demonstrate proficiency with procedures. Teaching specifically, with detailed descriptions of expectations and contextual variables, is of paramount importance when working with individuals with ASD. Results of a comprehensive review of evidence-based practices (EBPs) by Wong and colleagues (2014) indicated scripting – verbal or written descriptions of specific skills and situations – is considered an EBP. Similarly, the authors indicated there is a substantial evidence base to support the use of social narratives, which involve highlighting relevant cues in social situations to teach appropriate responding.

Testing, therefore, is neither automatically *important* nor automatically *understood* by individuals with ASD. Even when teachers, administrators, and parents mention testing frequently, from the first day of school onward, even when its importance is touted repeatedly, not all students receive the message in such a way that they will integrate their skills and effort to perform well during a test event. Moreover, the ability to integrate skills during a high-stake test event – concentration, effective navigation of the test booklet or test-delivery system, comprehension of directions, proper engagement with various item formats across the range of subject areas, elimination of incorrect response options and selecting the best response from the balance of options, and so forth – may not "come naturally" to many students with ASD. Teaching test-taking skills and strategies in isolation is of course important, but many students will learn to generalize them and apply them in novel scenarios only after abundant repetition. In an era in which each instructional minute counts, this may be a challenging idea in many schools and classrooms, but it is one that may make a tremendous difference in the test performance of some students.

Harris et al. (2015) found, however, individuals with ASD may share a learner characteristic, whereby new skills can be learned quickly, but if the skill is drilled repeatedly without providing the opportunity to generalize it to a new context, performance diminishes. This characteristic, which Harris and colleagues referred to as *hyperspecificity*, warrants consideration for the teaching of test-taking skills and strategies. While repetition of opportunities to experience the test-taking environment and practice learned skills may be useful, it is also important to ensure students remain engaged in the learning process, by assessing mastery throughout the process and teaching new skills as soon as it is feasible to do so. In short, students with ASD may require different instructional strategies from learners who assimilate new knowledge in a more traditional way, but teachers should not assume they learn less efficiently than their typical peers.

Order is Important

There is evidence the order of instruction can influence its effectiveness. Proponents of a theory known as *behavioral momentum* have suggested compliance, motivation, engagement, and fluency can be increased through the careful ordering of task demands, whereby a sequence of high-probability instructions is presented immediately before a lower-probability instruction. Lee, Lylo, Vostal, and Hua (2012) found initiation of nonpreferred tasks increased when they were preceded by high-preference tasks. Mace and Belfiore (1990) found decreases in escape-motivated stereotypy (i.e., behavior that often is maintained by "the alleviation, attenuation, or postponement of engagement" with a task) when a high-probability instructional sequence was used. There are several putative explanations for these results, among them being attention control (building compliance by gaining the student's attention increases the likelihood the student will engage in subsequent task directives), functional incompatibility (engaging in a task momentarily eliminates the reinforcing value of escape), and access to reinforcing stimuli.

Simply put, behavioral momentum involves generating "inertia" by carefully ordering tasks in a manner that encourages continued responding. In coordination with manipulation of schedules of reinforcement to ensure sufficient access to preferred stimuli while preventing satiety, and monitoring the variety and value of rewards, behavioral momentum theorists suggest the "stacking" of schedules can facilitate engagement for individuals for whom some tasks may be aversive (Lee, Belfiore, Scheeler, Hua, & Smith, 2004). The use of behavior momentum may help foster participation for many students, including for those with a history of test failure or those for whom test events are inordinately aversive for other reasons.

If it is possible to do so without compromising the standardization of certain tests, to improve test accessibility, test developers and test administrators should consider adjusting not only the order of testing at the domain or subtest level but even the ordering of test items. While Laffitte (1984) found on classroom tests that item order is not only inconsequential, but also imperceptible, in a meta-analysis of item characteristics, Aamodt and McShane (1992) found standardized tests in which less difficult items were presented first were easier than those with more difficult items first or those in which item order was randomized. The authors also found tests in which items were ordered by content were easier. With respect to behavioral momentum theory, test developers may consider deliberately varying the difficulty of items such that sequences of easier items precede more difficult ones, with the notion that the reinforcing value of the easier items may promote increased effort for the more challenging ones (i.e., they may take less time, require fewer cognitive resources, etc.) Of course, there are the confounds of item difficulty being based on the historical test statistics (i.e., field test sample, prior administrations), leading to questions about whether the item order should be based on subgroup psychometrics, the overall sample, etc. There is also the problem of the influence of opportunity to learn (OTL) on item difficulty, considering OTL varies by individual, classroom, school, and other factors (Kurz, Chap. 8).

Plan, Teach, and Announce Transitions

Providing advance notice of transitions can help children with ASD to transition more easily, efficiently, and with fewer behavior problems (Tustin, 1995). Giving an anxious student notice before transitions occur can help him or her prepare for the change (let us reflect once again on the characteristic insistence on sameness that is common to this population). The importance of advance notice is not limited to transitions between a favorite activity, person, location, and object to a less preferred one. To the contrary, individuals with ASD, once engaged, often have little difficulty remaining engaged. It is the termination of the current situation combined with movement and change to another that causes frustration and anxiety, as opposed to merely "letting go" of something that is rewarding or satisfying. Thus, transitions should not be entered into lightly but should be initiated following careful deliberation and planning.

On a related note, disruptions in the test-taking process – connection issues, hardware problems, printing or mailing complications, or other glitches that may cause delays or affect the schedule or timing of a test event – may be more detrimental for students with ASD than for their typical peers. As uncommon as these issues may be, they do occur, and their impact should not be underestimated nor should it be ignored. Minor changes should be expected to have major impacts.

As well, it is important to note that the ease with which students with ASD transition depends largely on the degree of consistency in routines and schedules. As a student becomes accustomed to the routine or schedule, transitions tend to become easier because they are predictable (and, as a result, perhaps they are less discomforting or worrisome). To facilitate transitions, visual timers or verbal countdowns can help students to experience the passage of time and to understand that a transition is imminent. As well, behavioral momentum may play a role in facilitating transitions. Difficulties with transitions, such as those between test sessions and subtests, may be alleviated to some degree by placing preferred or high-probability tasks or activities in front of nonpreferred ones (Lee, 2006). Difficult sections of tests, for example, may be placed immediately after easier ones, followed by a break or alternate activity.

Conclusions and Next Steps

It is difficult to encapsulate precisely the population of students with ASD without perseverating on the common skill deficits of this population, which include communication, responding to social cues, and sensory regulation. Based on the considerations described in the current chapter, there are numerous implications for testing with a focus on enhancing accessibility for individuals with ASD. The following does not represent an exhaustive list:

1. Attend to cognitive load issues in the design of test events, particularly in terms of eliminating redundancy and other sources of extraneous load.
2. Familiarize the students to test procedures, including navigating the test-delivery system and/or using test materials.
3. Teach, reteach, and provide opportunities to practice strategies for engaging, processing, and responding to test items.
4. Build test-delivery systems that can be used not only for large-scale, standardized tests but also by teachers for classroom assessments – including permitting access to the range of accessibility tools.
5. Assume minor changes in the above will have major impacts.
6. Emphasize the role of testing as a tool for discovering what students have learned; and de-emphasize the role of testing as a means of determining performance-based rewards and consequences and of evaluating students' value.

Finally, little research has been done to draw inferences about how characteristics of ASD interact with test events, including, but not limited to, test-delivery systems, test materials, and test items. With the increasing population of these students and the need for accurate assessment of their skills and abilities, it is incumbent upon the assessment research field to consider this population for study. Specifically, research should address the degree to which these students have access to learn the tested content. Studies should include analysis of observational data of students with ASD participating in assessments, interview/focus group/think-aloud feedback, and analyses of test performance and psychometric indices for this population. Researchers should consider integrating the input of adults (or older students) with diagnoses of ASD into test development process (e.g., through interviews, focus groups, or think-aloud studies; Roach & Beddow, 2011). As our collective understanding of autism increases, so too should the accessibility of testing practices increase for individuals with ASD and with it our confidence in the validity of inferences based on test results for this population.

References

Aamodt, M. G., & McShane, T. (1992). A meta-analytic investigation of the effect of various test item characteristics on test scores and test completion times. *Public Personnel Management, 21*(2), 151–160.

Allen, K. D., & Wallace, D. P. (2013). Effectiveness of using noncontingent escape for general behavior management in a pediatric dental clinic. *Journal of Applied Behavior Analysis, 46*, 723–737.

American Psychiatric Association. (2013). *Diagnostic and statistical manual of mental disorders* (5th ed.). Arlington, VA: American Psychiatric Publishing.

Ashcraft, M. H., & Kirk, E. P. (2001). The relationships among working memory, math anxiety, and performance. *Journal of Experimental Psychology: General, 130*(2), 224.

Benjamin, M., McKeachie, W. J., Lin, Y., & Holinger, D. P. (1981). Test anxiety: deficits in information processing. *Journal of Educational Psychology, 73*, 816–824.

Binder, C. (1996). Behavioral fluency: Evolution of new paradigm. *The Behavior Analyst, 19*, 163–197.

Bruch, M. A. (1981). Relationship of test-taking strategies to test anxiety and performance: Toward a task analysis of examination behavior. *Cognitive Therapy and Research, 5*, 41–56.

Bullock, C., & Normand, M. P. (2006). The effects of a high-probability instruction sequence and response-independent reinforcer delivery on child compliance. *Journal of Applied Behavior Analysis, 39*, 495–499.

Cassady, J. M. (2011). Teachers' attitudes toward the inclusion of students with autism and emotional behavioral disorder. *Electronic Journal for Inclusive Education, 2*, 5.

Cassidy, J. G. (2004). The impact of cognitive test anxiety on text comprehension and recall in the absence of external evaluative pressure. *Applied Cognitive Psychology, 18*, 311–325.

Chadwick, D., Tindall-Ford, S. K., Agostinho, S., & Paas, F. (2015). *Using cognitive load compliant instructions to support working memory for anxious students*. 8th Cognitive Load Theory Conference (p. 32).

Christensen, D. L., Baio, J., Braun, K. V., et al. (2016). Prevalence and characteristics of autism spectrum disorder among children aged 8 years — Autism and developmental disabilities monitoring network, 11 Sites, United States, 2012. *Morbidity and Mortality Weekly Report Surveillance Summary, 65*, 1–23.

Cooper, J. O., Heron, T. E., & Heward, W. L. (2007). *Applied behavior analysis* (2nd ed.). Upper Saddle River, NJ: Pearson Education.

Dykens, E. M., & Lense, M. (2011). Intellectual disabilities and autism spectrum disorders: A cautionary note. In D. Amaral, G. Dawson, & D. Geschwind (Eds.), *Autism spectrum disorders* (pp. 261–269). New York, NY: Oxford University Press.

Every Student Succeeds Act. (2017). Pub. L. No. 115–64. Retrieved from https://legcounsel.house.gov/Comps/Elementary%20And%20Secondary%20Education%20Act%20Of%201965.pdf.

Gillott, A., Furniss, F., & Walter, A. (2001). Anxiety in high-functioning children with autism. *Autism, 5*(3), 277–286.

Gottschalk, J. M., Libby, M. E., & Graff, R. B. (2000). The effects of establishing operations on preference assessment outcomes. *Journal of Applied Behavior Analysis, 33*, 85–88.

Hanley, G. P., Iwata, B. A., & McCord, B. E. (2003). Functional analysis of problem behavior: A review. *Journal of Applied Behavior Analysis, 36*, 147–185.

Harris, H., Israeli, D., Minshew, N., Bonneh, Y., Heeger, D. J., Behrmann, M., & Sagi, D. (2015). Perceptual learning in autism: Over-specificity and possible remedies. *Nature Neuroscience, 18*, 1574–1576.

Hembree, R. (1988). Correlates, causes, effects, and treatment of test anxiety. *Review of Educational Research, 58*, 47–77.

Kazdin, A. E., & Weisz, J. R. (1998). Identifying and developing empirically supported child and adolescent treatments. *Journal of Consulting and Clinical Psychology, 66*(1), 19–36.

Kim, J. A., Szatmari, P., Bryson, S. E., Streiner, D. L., & Wilson, F. J. (2000). The prevalence of anxiety and mood problems among children with autism and asperger syndrome. *Autism, 4*(2), 117–132.

Kirkland, K., & Hollandsworth, J. (1980). Effective test-taking: Skills-acquisition versus anxiety-reduction techniques. *Journal of Counseling and Clinical Psychology, 48*, 431–439.

Laffitte, R. G. (1984). Effects of item order on achievement test scores and students' perception of test difficulty. *Teaching of Psychology, 11*, 212–214.

Laraway, S., Snycerski, S., Michael, J., & Poling, A. (2003). Motivating operations and terms to describe them: Some further refinements. *Journal of Applied Behavior Analysis, 36*(3), 407.

Lee, D. L. (2006). Facilitating transitions between and within academic tasks: An application of behavioral momentum. *Remedial and Special Education, 27*, 312–317.

Lee, D. L., Belfiore, P. J., Scheeler, M. C., Hua, Y., & Smith, R. (2004). Behavioral momentum in academics: Using embedded high-p sequences to increase academic productivity. *Psychology in the Schools, 41*, 789–801.

Lenoir, P., Bodier, C., Desombre, H., Malvy, J., Abert, B., Ould Taleb, M., & Sauvage, D. (2009). Prevalence of pervasive developmental disorders: A review. *L'Encéphale, 35*, 36–42.

Lerman, D. C., Iwata, B. A., & Wallace, M. D. (1999). Side effects of extinction: Prevalence of bursting and aggression during the treatment of self-injurious behavior. *Journal of Applied Behavior Analysis, 32*(1), 1–8.

Lovaas, O. I. (1977). *The autistic child*. New York, NY: Irvington.

Lovaas, O. I., Koegel, R. L., Simmons, J. Q., & Long, J. (1973). Some generalization and follow-up measures on autistic children in behavior therapy. *Journal of Applied Behavior Analysis, 6*, 131–166.

Lee, D. L., Lylo, B., Vostal, B., & Hua, Y. (2012). The effects of high-preference problems on the completion of nonpreferred mathematics problems. *Journal of Applied Behavior Analysis, 45,* 223–228. https://doi.org/10.1901/jaba.2012.45-223.

Mace, F. C., & Belfiore, P. (1990). Behavioral momentum in the treatment of escape-motivated stereotypy. *Journal of Applied Behavior Analysis, 23,* 507–514.

Oliver, C., Berg, K., Burbidge, C., Arron, K., & Moss, J. (2011). Delineation of behavioral phenotypes in genetic syndromes: Comparison of autism spectrum disorder, affect, and hyperactivity. *Journal of Autism and Developmental Disorder, 41,* 1019–1032.

Roach, A. T., & Beddow, P. A. (2011). Including student voices in the design of more inclusive assessments. In S. N. Elliott, R. J. Kettler, P. A. Beddow, & A. Kurz (Eds.), *Handbook of accessible achievement tests for all students* (pp. 243–254).

Shackman, A. J., Sarinopoulos, I., Maxwell, J. S., Pizzagalli, D. A., Lavric, A., & Davidson, R. J. (2006). Anxiety selectively disrupts visuospatial working memory. *Emotion, 6*(1), 40.

Skinner, B. F. (1953). *Science and human behavior.* New York, NY: Free Press.

Skinner, B. F. (1974). *About behaviorism.* New York, NY: Alfred A. Knopf.

Sorg, B. A., & Whitney, P. (1992). The effect of trait anxiety and situational stress on working memory capacity. *Journal of Research in Personality, 26*(3), 235–241.

Sweller, J. (2010). Cognitive load theory: Recent theoretical advances. In J. L. Plass, R. Moreno, & R. Brunken (Eds.), *Cognitive load theory* (pp. 29–47). New York, NY: Cambridge University Press.

Tustin, R. D. (1995). The effects of advance notice of activity transitions on stereotypic behavior. *Journal of Applied Behavior Analysis, 28,* 91–92.

Wong, C., Odom, S. L., Hume, K., Cox, A. W., Fettig, A., Kucharczyk, S., … Schultz, T. R. (2014). *Evidence-based practices for children, youth, and young adults with Autism Spectrum Disorder.* Chapel Hill, NC: The University of North Carolina/Frank Porter Graham Child Development Institute/Autism Evidence-Based Practice Review Group.

White, S. W., Oswald, D., Ollendick, T., & Scahill, L. (2009). Anxiety in children and adolescents with autismspectrum disorders. *Clinical Psychology Review, 29*(3), 216–229.

Wolf, M., Risley, T., & Mees, H. (1963). Application of operant conditioning procedures to the behaviour problems of an autistic child. *Behaviour Research and Therapy, 1,* 305–312.

Moving Beyond Assumptions of Cultural Neutrality to Improve Accessibility and Opportunity to Learn for English Language Learners

Tim Boals, Mariana Castro, and Lynn Shafer Willner

Rigorous, discipline-specific language development is an essential component of the achievement of access and equity for all students, but most especially English language learners (ELLs; NGA & CCSSO, 2010). To develop the language proficiency needed to engage in academic activities, ELLs need accessible instruction and assessment. Because current educational law and practices encourage inclusionary, rather than separate, instruction and assessment for ELLs, it is essential that general educational instructional and assessment practices work effectively with ELLs as well as with native-English-speaking students.

Yet, contrary to the common saying, "good teaching" is not always "good teaching." In other words, while highly effective instructional and assessment practices for native-English-speaking students may be relevant for ELLs in some ways, they may not sufficiently meet ELLs' unique linguistic and cultural needs (De Jong & Harper, 2005). Lack of relevancy for ELLs may occur because there is a tendency to perceive ELLs as if they were failed native speakers rather than as students who are emergent bilinguals and have cognitive and linguistic practices that may differ from monolinguals (May, 2014; Ortega, 2014) or to perceive ELLs' cultural differences as deficits, devaluing the "funds of knowledge" found in individual, home, and community strengths and resources (González, Moll, & Amanti, 2005). Cultural and linguistic misconceptions can arise because, as Roland Barthes once observed, "… if you're a member of the dominant group, your attributes are invisible, as your role in making things the way they are is not noticeable" (Lakoff, 2000, p. 53). Rather than operating from assumptions of cultural neutrality and viewing ELLs through the lens of their own experiences, it is imperative for educators of ELLs to appropriately design and extend instruction and assessment processes that were originally designed for native-English speakers.

One of the more popular approaches in instructional and assessment contexts in recent years is the application of Universal Design for Learning (UDL) principles. Most commonly associated with the work pioneered by the Center for Applied Special Technology (CAST), UDL had been introduced as a strategy for meeting the needs of student diversity rather than relying on "one-size-fits-all" curricula and assessment that are designed for students who have, essentially, uniform interests and abilities.

In its original conception, developers of UDL explained that the principles were

T. Boals (✉) · M. Castro · L. Shafer Willner
University of Wisconsin-Madison,
Madison, WI, USA
e-mail: timothy.boals@wisc.edu

Table 8.1 Disability categories and primary processing categories affected

Disability category	Primary processing category(ies)
Blind	Perceptual, visual
Low vision	Perceptual, visual
Deaf, hard of hearing	Perceptual, auditory
Learning disability: Reading/language	Linguistic
English language learners	Linguistic
Mild mental retardation	Cognitive
Physical disability	Motoric
Dyspraxia/dysgraphia	Motoric
Attention deficit hyperactivity disorder	Executive
Learning disability: Math	Executive
Autism spectrum disorders	Affective
Emotional disturbance	Affective

"designed to succeed with the widest possible range of learners, with explicit consideration of students with disabilities" (Rose & Strangman, 2007, p. 385). However, support for students was addressed using a cognitive neuroscience approach and addressed individual differences in learning through "joint action of three broad sets of neural networks in cognition and learning: one that recognizes patterns, one that plans and generates patterns, and one that determines which patterns are important" (Rose & Strangman, 2007, p. 381). The use of a cognitive neuroscience approach can have implications for ELLs. As Shafer Willner and Rivera (2011) observed, the 2009 version of the *Universal Design for Computer-Based Testing Guidelines* employed a cognitive neuroscience approach. In these assessment development guidelines for computer-based testing, ELLs' linguistic needs were bundled with other processing support which would be addressed by the same accessibility features offered to students with hearing disabilities and linguistic processing disabilities (Pearson Educational Measurement, 2009, p. 9). As shown below in Table 8.1, this type of bundling can lead to inappropriate conflation of the normal process of second language development with disability.

The purposes of this chapter are twofold: (a) to suggest that sociocultural framing of UDL would more effectively support ELLs and (b) to examine in greater detail what sociocultural reframing of UDL could look like in assessment activities in which ELLs are participating. Similar to the second language acquisition field that began to take a "social turn" in the 1990s (Kibler & Valdés, 2016), we concur with disabilities researchers who, two decades ago, proposed a similar "social turn" might be taken to more *explicitly* extend UDL beyond its cognitive neuroscience roots to incorporate sociocultural lenses (Andrews et al., 2000; Baglieri, Bejoian, et al., 2011; Baglieri, Valle, Connor, & Gallagher, 2011).

In applying a sociocultural lens (Vygotsky, 1978), we suggest that classroom educators and assessment developers consider how they highlight and connect with students' cultural and historical contexts, including social and physical settings, by providing activities involving dialogic interactions and relationships and using social and cultural tools (including language) to mediate higher functioning. Educators can provide students with improved access to the cultural assumptions embedded in speech, text, and activity used in schooling and connect to and build on student linguistic and cultural repertoires. Educators can use UDL, not just as a cognitive tool but also to provide culturally situated multiple pathways to support the access of all students, especially those from non-dominant linguistic and cultural backgrounds.

Because UDL is being framed increasingly in the research literature using sociocultural and historical framing (e.g., Connor & Valle, 2015), it is important to clearly understand why approaches for ELLs based on cognitive neuroscience framing could be improved if they were socially, culturally, and historically situated. We use the first section of the chapter to provide background information to more clearly define the characteristics associated with ELLs and the history of both success and inequity ELLs have experienced in the American educational system. Keeping this history in mind, we then examine how assumptions of cultural neutrality are commonly used to construct a deficit-oriented narrative around ELLs. The social construction of deficit models in the education of ELLs has resulted in continuous social and economic marginalization of many ELLs.

Unique Characteristics of ELLs in the United States

The rationale for extending cognitive neuroscience approaches using a sociocultural perspective begins with an understanding of the unique characteristics of ELLs. ELLs are one of the fastest-growing segments of public school enrollment in the United States, increasing 60% in the last decade, as compared with 7% growth of the general student population (US Department of Education/National Center for Educational Statistics, 2012). Nationally, twice as many ELLs are enrolled in elementary schools (3.3 million) compared with ELLs in middle and high schools (1.6 million; National Center for Educational Statistics, 2015). Although six of the largest states currently have the largest ELL enrollment (CA, TX, FL, NY, IL, CO), over the past 15 years, many states in the Midwest, West, and Appalachia have been experiencing even larger percentage growth in their ELL K-12 student population relative to the total school population (Ruiz Soto, Hooker, & Batalova, 2015). By 2025, demographers predict that nearly one out of every four students in US public schools will be classified as an ELL (Hodgkinson, 2008).

The ELL population falls into roughly three categories: local populations born in the United States, new arrivals (consisting of refugee and immigrant students), and migrant students. In contrast to popular perception, the majority of ELLs in American schools are not new arrivals; nearly half of ELLs are second-generation Americans, and almost another quarter are third-generation Americans (Editorial Projects in Education, 2009). Indeed, even the vast majority of children of immigrants to the United States are native-born, with most adult immigrants having their children after arriving in the United States (Capps et al., 2005). As a result, 85% of the pre-kindergarten to 5th grade ELL students and 62% of the 6th to 12th grade ELL students are born in the United States (Zong & Batalova, 2015).

During the past decade, educators have grown more aware of the complexity of who ELL students are and of the unique circumstances that impact their academic and linguistic performances. Historically, educators have recognized ELLs as students who are in the process of learning English. However, more recently, educators and researchers have begun to recognize ELLs as a "group" that is characterized by a dynamic, temporary designation, differing in quality of prior schooling, socioeconomic status, and other factors. Some ELLs begin school with strong academic backgrounds and others with little to no formal schooling (Espinoza & Lopes, 2007; Short & Fitzsimmons, 2007). Most recently, concerns have emerged related to what is perceived as ELL student performance challenges, resulting in the creation of two additional labels for ELL students whose English acquisition/development process is nonnormative: (a) students who, based on summative, large-scale assessment performance measures in particular, continue to be classified as ELL well beyond 6 years (so-called long-term ELLs or "long-termers") (Olsen, 2010) and (b) students with limited or interrupted formal education (SLIFE) (DeCapua, Smathers, & Tang, 2009). Later analyses in this chapter will address concerns with these labels.

ELL Access to Schooling: A History of Inequity and Lack of Access

The policy and educational history of ELLs in US schools has been characterized by ongoing inequity and lack of access to education. Lack of equitable educational opportunities to ELL and other students from non-dominant backgrounds and controversies over the use and maintenance of native languages have led to a number of lawsuits around due process and the equal protection clauses of the 14th Amendment. In the early 1970s, court cases focused on issues surrounding free and appropriate education (FAPE), with cases building support for access to meaningful, comprehensible classroom experiences, not just access to educational facilities and resources.

In 1974, the core points of the Lau v. Nichols court decision were codified into federal policy, with the US Department of Education's Office of Civil Rights creating the Lau Remedies, which confirmed that public schools and State educational agencies (SEAs) must act to overcome language barriers that impede equal participation by students in their instructional programs. While Title VII Bilingual Education Act regulations applied only to federally funded programs, the Lau Remedies applied to all school districts and functioned as standards requiring de facto compliance (Wright, 2010). Further cases, such as the 1981 Castañeda v. Pickard case, established a three-prong test to evaluate whether educational officials had set up a program to ensure "appropriate action to overcome language barriers" be taken through well-implemented programs informed by theory, provided with resources, and assessed after the "legitimate trial" period (Castañeda vs. Pickard 1981, p. 1). Most recently, federal civil rights policy has stated that "all students must have equal access to a high-quality education and the opportunity to achieve their full academic potential" (US Department of Justice, US Department of Education, 2015).

Ideas around equal opportunity for all students have been further developed in the 1994, 2001, and 2015 reauthorizations of the Elementary and Secondary Education Act (ESEA). The 2001 reauthorization of ESEA (No Child Left Behind) made more explicit the language needs of ELLs and ways for addressing those needs: It required ELP standards that were aligned with the achievement of the core content areas (which was a major step forward in promoting content and language integration). The 2015 reauthorization of ESEA, the Every Student Succeeds Act (ESSA, 2015), maintains basic components of accountability while devolving much of the control in defining what accountability will look like back to states and local schools. ESSA also moved accountability for ELLs from Title III to Title I, placing it within a larger department responsible for student success of other groups, a large department which, historically, did not deal with issues related to language and culture. However, in an era of college-and-career-ready standards, an era which emphasizes the role of language and literacy development more than ever before, ESSA draws increased attention to the intersection of two subgroups (ELLs and students with disabilities). This leads to questions of how accessibility (and UDL processes) might be enhanced to ensure that accessibility for all really means all.

The challenge of distinguishing between language difference and a specific learning disability continues to be a central topic of concern among researchers and educators working with ELLs (Klingner & Artiles, 2006). In states or districts with high populations of ELLs, there has been a long history of overrepresentation among ELLs in special education, particularly at the secondary school level (Artiles, Rueda, Salazar, & Higareda, 2005; Linn & Hemmer, 2011; Sullivan, 2011). Underrepresentation of ELLs is often evident in the primary grades and is particularly prevalent among early education students (Samson & Lesaux, 2009). This suggests that young ELLs who could potentially benefit from special education are not being referred to receive such services and may not be receiving early interventions that could help prevent later school difficulties.

Limitations Associated with Achievement Gap Analyses

It is common to frame ELL participation in large-scale assessments using achievement gap analyses. In this section, we first explore student achievement using currently available indicators of socioeconomic status (SES). We then raise linguistic, cultural, and equity questions about these analyses. We conclude with the recommendation to consider achievement gap data also in relation to student opportunity to learn and viewing ELLs also in relation to their assets.

The prevailing narrative used with achievement gap analyses of ELLs is that, more than a decade after the passage of NCLB (2002), ELLs – especially those with disabilities – continue to be some of the lowest-scoring account-

Table 8.2 Spring 2015 NAEP mathematics assessment: 8th grade composite scale scores for ELLs and students with disabilities.

Mathematics assessment: gap in average composite scale scores	4th grade	8th grade
Students (no disabilities, not ELL)	246	289
Students with disabilities (not ELL)	220	249
ELLs (no disabilities)	222	251
ELLs with disabilities	197	224

ability subgroup on large-scale assessments. As illustrated in Table 8.2, a common way to illustrate the achievement gap narrative is to use annual "snapshot" data from the 2015 National Assessment of Education Progress (NAEP) (U.S. Department of Education/National Center for Educational Statistics, 2016). An initial, high-level pass through the data set of ELLs' composite scale scores (displayed by grade level) appears to confirm ever-widening performance gaps as ELLs, especially those with disabilities, progress from elementary school to middle school (i.e., 4th grade to 8th grade).

Yet, when developing a narrative around the student achievement gap of ELLs, care should be taken not to frame it using only ELL status. Over the past four decades, family income has increasingly become a dominant factor, correlated to other family characteristics and access to resources that are important for children's development and schooling (presence of two parents, both with college degrees) (Reardon, 2013, p. 2). In his original analysis, Reardon (2011) explains:

> The income achievement gap (defined here as the average achievement difference between a child from a family at the 90th percentile of the family income distribution and a child from a family at the 10th percentile) is now nearly twice as large as the black-white achievement gap. Fifty years ago, in contrast, the black-white gap was one and a half to two times as large as the income gap.. ... Family income is now nearly as strong as parental education in predicting children's achievement. (pp. 1–2).

Since the ELL student population is more likely to live in poverty (Zong & Batalova, 2015), it is not surprising to see those ELLs with lower socioeconomic status (as denoted within the NAEP data by eligibility for the National School Lunch Program[1]) as showing lower composite scale scores in the 2015 8th grade NAEP we are examining. Yet, by unpacking this data set, it appears that students who are identified with disabilities and/or have ELL status have lower composite scale scores than the general student population who "only" have lower socioeconomic status.

As shown in Table 8.3, the addition of ELL and disabilities status to lower socioeconomic status appears to further intensify the achievement gap. On the 2015 8th grade NAEP, the general student population has average scale scores of 300; students with eligibility for the National School Lunch Program (but not having either disabilities status or ELL status) have average composite scale scores of 276. Students who are not eligible for the National School Lunch Program but are either ELLs or identified as having a disability scored lower (263 for ELLs vs. 257 for students with disabilities). Both groups' composite scale scores on the 2015 NAEP lower further when examining their data in relation to eligibility for the National School Lunch Program (249 for ELLs vs. 238 for students with disabilities). Student data that uses all three variables (ELL status, students with disabilities status, and eligibility for the National School Lunch) drops the average student composite scale scores even further (222). Thus, the impact of low socioeconomic status appears to be greatly impacted by the addition of ELL status and disabilities status.

Yet, deeper exploration of gap analysis data using 2015 composite scores from the NAEP raises questions about the impact of systematic structural inequities in the American educational system. ELLs are most likely to be members of non-dominant racial and ethnic minorities and, as a result, are often subjected to deficit labeling. Table 8.4 shows a deeper analysis of the same data set used in the preceding paragraphs, 8th grade NAEP data for ELLs with disabilities, by

---

[1] Note: At this time, no single composite socioeconomic status variable is available with NAEP results. National School Lunch Program Eligibility is one factor for socioeconomic status (US Department of Education/National Center for Educational Statistics, 2012).

Table 8.3 Spring 2015 NAEP mathematics assessment: 8th grade composite scale scores for ELLs and students with disabilities by National School Lunch Program Eligibility

National school lunch program eligibility	ELL	SD		Not SD	
		Average scale score	Standard error	Average scale score	Standard error
Eligible	ELL	222	(1.5)	249	(1.1)
	Not ELL	238	(0.6)	276	(0.3)
Not eligible	ELL	229	(5.7)	263	(2.2)
	Not ELL	257	(0.7)	300	(0.3)
Information not available	ELL	‡	(†)	269	(6.2)
	Not ELL	266	(5.3)	296	(1.4)

† Not applicable
‡ Reporting standards not met. https://nces.ed.gov/datatools/index.asp?DataToolSectionID=4

Table 8.4 Spring 2015 NAEP mathematics assessment: 8th grade composite scale scores by race/ethnicity

Race/ethnicity	ELL	IEP status	Composite scale score
American Indian/Alaska native	X	X	214
Hispanic	X	X	223
Asian	X	X	234
Black[a]	X	——	235
Native Hawaiian/other Pacific islander[a]	X	——	236
American Indian/Alaska native	X	——	249
Hispanic	X	——	249
White[a]	X	——	259
Asian	X	——	271

[a]ELL/IEP data not available for this group

racial and ethnic categories. This data reveals that the "lowest performers" on large-scale assessments like NAEP are invariably students from non-dominant racial and ethnic groups (American Indian/Alaska Native, Native Hawaiian/Other Pacific Islander, Black, and Hispanic ELLs), groups who have experienced systematic structural inequity.

The deeper problem with the achievement gap narrative is that, by focusing on achievement "gaps," achievement differences are framed as a gap between dominant and non-dominant racial and ethnic groups, reinforcing the hegemonic view of dominant groups as the norm and the non-dominant groups as lacking or in need of "fixing." This discourse problematizes students and the groups to which they belong and not the practices that create the lack of accessibility to these groups.

Other problems arise with the achievement gap narrative. While there may be commonalities among a cultural group, it should not be assumed that all members within that group ascribe to or fit certain preordained categories that are often associated with that group.

ELL student performance data are further complicated by issues of language proficiency, age, time in the United States, trauma, lack of formal education, and transience. Most significantly, the temporary nature of ELL identification and related underlying instability within ELL data sets impacts the quality of multi-year analyses. Moreover, the recent trend to use labels such as "long-termer" (long-term ELLs or LTELL), while a convenient shorthand, condenses complex educational challenge and frames them using deficit-oriented measures (Kibler & Valdés, 2016). Indeed, Flores, Kleyn, and Menken (2015) warn, "LTELL has become synonymous with and has replaced terms such as semilingual" (p. 2).

Standards-referenced assessments privilege particular sociocultural values and language use which are not held by non-dominant communities. For example, these assessments are unable to capture the richness of translanguaging practices as students use linguistic resources from more than one language community. As a result, our educational system uses framing that sweeps aside the impacts of cultural, linguistic, and socioeconomic differences on the validity of summative, large-scale assessment scores of these students and instead frames the issue as an individual student problem or deviance.

To summarize, assessment of ELLs' performances is often framed in relation to achievement gaps, that is, the difference between performance targets and student performance. This approach (a) problematizes students and the group to which they belong and not the practices that create the lack of accessibility to some of the groups, (b) treats ELLs as a homogenous group, (c) condenses complex educational challenges and frames them using deficit-oriented measures, and (d) privileges particular sociocultural values and language use which are not held by non-dominant communities. Yet, for students from culturally and linguistically diverse backgrounds, these achievement gaps are cloaked in assumptions of cultural neutrality, with the results from these analyses more often being a measure of students' distance from dominant group norms.

Recognizing ELL Strengths

As the global economy and global communications create rapid change in today's world's social systems and cultures, the field of education has identified communication and intercultural understandings as key in individuals' participation in these new global contexts (Partnerships for Twenty-First Learning, 2016). This recognition has been demonstrated through the inclusion of world languages in the themes that are part of the twenty-first-century educational frameworks. Students who have been identified as ELLs are bilingual and, in some instances, multilingual and continuously negotiate intercultural communication and understandings, which means that they possess the skills needed to participate in global contexts.

Another strength of ELLs associated with their bilingualism is their academic potential. Research has shown significant correlation in studies between bilingualism and academic achievement, cognitive development, metalinguistic awareness, and positive attitudes and beliefs toward others in terms of language learning and other cultures (Bialystok, 2001; Collier & Thomas, 2002). Strong metalinguistic skills have been associated with cognitive flexibility, mental abilities, and divergent thinking (Bialystok, 1986; Díaz & Klinger, 1991; Landry, 1974; Lambert, Tucker, & d'Anglejan, 1973; Peal & Lambert, 1962; Yelland, Pollard, & Mercuri, 1993).

Research has documented that immigrant families demonstrate a pattern of resilience, resourcefulness, behavioral and physical health, and educational assets; members of subsequent generations may face a range of stressors and risks (e.g., poverty, discrimination, fewer years of schooling, and social isolation; American Psychological Association, Presidential Task Force on Immigration, 2012). Even with these stressors, the temptation is to frame all ELLs as problems to solve, thereby ignoring student, family, and community strengths.

We would like to highlight that many stressors are in fact socially constructed and a result of the social, political, and educational systems in which ELLs live and learn. The social construction of limited access to academic achievement for ELLs is apparent in a large-scale longitudinal experimental study that analyzed the effects of a professional development intervention on ELLs' achievement in science (Lee et al., 2008). The results of the study indicated ELLs are capable of performing substantially well on high-stakes tests if teachers have the appropriate pedagogical tools to increase scientific reasoning and literacy among ELLs. Nevertheless, data continue to show chronic achievement differences between ELLs and native-English-speaking children in K-12 US schools (Polat, Zarecky-Hodge, & Schreiber, 2016). The fact that approximately 75% of ELLs in schools are second- or third-generation immigrants who were born in the United States further suggests that these results may be related to the sociocultural circumstances of ELLs, their families, and their communities and not to inherent characteristics of the student population. The social construction of deficit models in the education of ELLs has resulted in the historical underrepresentation of language minority groups in technical and scientific fields (Moschkovich, 2002) as well as continual social and economic marginalization of these groups.

In reframing the challenges that ELLs face in education, we recommend that voices from students and families be at the center of the discussion. In studies in which students' and their families' voices have been included, findings have provided deeper understandings not only about language use but also about effective learning approaches that meet the unique cultural and linguistic challenges ELLs experience (Gregory & Williams, 2000; Martin-Jones & Bhatt, 1998; Tannenbaum & Howie, 2002). Through this lens, the problem is shifted from the student as the actor to our practices, as members of an educational system with the responsibility to provide educational accessibility and opportunity to learn for all students, including ELLs.

Improving ELL Opportunity to Learn by Adding Sociocultural Approaches to Accessibility

For many ELLs, there may be limited opportunity to learn the academic language needed to participate fully in schooling. Escamilla (2015) noted that, rather than viewing student challenges with schooling through a more cognitivist lens, namely, as a problem *within* the child, the problem may be due to the fact that educational institutions are ill-equipped to facilitate the development of academic language and literacy in culturally and linguistically diverse students. Focusing on the "problems" within individual students does not address needed systemic changes and further perpetuates the cycle of performance "gaps" and educational inequity. The "gap" that has beset many students is the opportunity to learn and has socio-institutional roots; it is not just an individual student problem. If a school's mission is to give students access to the most appropriate services in the least restrictive environment, then students should not be taught and assessed using instructional strategies and assessments designed without fully accounting for their unique cultural and linguistic differences. When we fail to make curriculum, instruction, and assessment fully accessible, we end up measuring not a gap in achievement but a psychological distance from what is considered to be the norm.

One solution is to avoid over-reliance on gap analyses of ELL student performance and to balance these analyses with reliable measures of students' opportunity to learn, that is, "the extent to which individuals have had exposure to instruction or knowledge that affords them the opportunity to learn the content and skills targeted by the test" (AERA, APA, & NCME, 2014, p. 56). Research indicates that many students have experienced reduced opportunity to learn needed academic literacy and disciplinary knowledge due to lack of appreciation of the cultural and linguistic resources brought by each student and narrow definitions of academic discourse. These narrow definitions deny the rich sociocultural and linguistic diversity (e.g., fluid use of two or more languages or translanguaging, registers, codes, vernaculars, specialized vocabularies, dialects) that non-dominant students practice in their homes and communities (Escamilla, 2015; Pacheco, 2010).

Accessibility through the UDL lens should leverage teacher instruction, opportunity to learn, and schooling context and connect it to students' historical knowledge, which has been shown to enhance students' achievement outcomes (Epstein, 2009; Gradwell, 2006; Grant, 2003; Ladson-Billings, 2009; Pace, 2011; Saye & The Social Studies Inquiry Research Collaborative, 2013). Studies in which opportunity to learn is operationalized as the degree to which a student experiences classroom instruction, including a variety of approaches that address a range of cognitive processes, teaching practices, and grouping formats, have shown effective in increasing the achievement of ELLs (Abedi & Herman, 2010; Heafner & Fitcheett, 2015). In the second section of this chapter, we turn our attention to an issue that we believe is equally important: accessibility in assessment with ELLs.

In the second section of the chapter, we provide examples of how UDL might be extended in the assessment context using a sociocultural lens. We show how classroom educators and assessment developers might consider highlighting and connecting with students' cultural and historical contexts, including social and physical settings, providing activities that involve dialogic interactions and relationships, and using social and cultural tools (including language) to mediate higher functioning. Educators can provide students with improved access to the cultural assumptions embedded in speech, text, and activity used in schooling and connect to and build on student linguistic and cultural repertoires. Educators can use UDL, not just as a cognitive tool but also to provide culturally situated multiple pathways to support the access of all students, especially those from non-dominant linguistic and cultural backgrounds.

A Case for Accessibility in Teaching and Learning Systems

Historically, language instructional supports have been the focus of various approaches to language development for ELLs (Long, 1985; Wong Fillmore & Snow, 2000). The rationale has been constructed around the belief that all students need to acquire the forms and structures associated with academic learning in order to enhance meaningful participation. Using accessibility as a lens, we seek to expand on the notion of instructional support to shift the focus from interventions to everyday practices. As noted by Zabala (2014), teachers can use accessibility approaches such as UDL to proactively design learning experiences from the outset to provide a greater range of students with multiple pathways to participation and success. These pathways can provide broader and more varied avenues of communication (e.g., nonverbal communication, pictorial and graphic support, arts integration, and technology/multimedia creations and communication) for ELLs to learn along with their non-ELL peers. The benefit of this approach is that, rather than waiting to accommodate student needs after the lesson is designed and delivered or separate from the rest of the class, the use of accessibility principles focuses educators on how these needs can be met during initial design and delivery of the lesson or activity (Russell, Hoffmann, & Higgins, 2009; Russell & Kavanaugh, 2011).

Many scholars have explored how UDL can support student access to the curriculum through the provision of multiple representations and forms of expression (e.g., National UDL Task Force, 2011). This view furthers the realization that ELLs are capable of deep conceptual engagement, even when they are at beginning stages of English acquisition. Beyond multiple means of information presentation and multiple options to express one's understandings, universally designed instruction also relies on various means of engagement by taking into consideration students' interests, needs, and cultural background (Lopes-Murphy, 2012). These culturally sensitive and multimodal approaches to communication reduce learning barriers and scaffold students' successful mastery of content.

Greater awareness of how to improve the accessibility of curriculum and instruction can lead to improved opportunities to address and connect to students' linguistic and cultural repertoires of practice. For example, language researchers have found that teachers who integrated multimodal instruction (visuals, realia, multilingual references/resources, interaction, etc.) were more likely to also have language objectives in addition to the usual content-area objectives. Integrating multimodal instruction was an initial step toward clear identification of language objectives, which led to teachers thinking about the language desired and what must be taught (Lundgren, Mabbot, & Kramer, 2012).

While many educators approach scaffolding from a cognitivist perspective of teaching, learning, and assessment and focus on internal mental processes and metacognitive problem-solving strategies, this approach does not afford an examination of how external interactions during learning shape language use and language acquisition. Learning is not only cognitive in nature but also cultural, social, and situated. We argue that scaffolding can be enhanced if students – especially those from diverse backgrounds – are able to leverage the unique cultural and linguistic experiences to acquire the knowledge and practices needed to participate in the school learning community. These "funds of knowledge" are found in individual, home, and community strengths and resources (González et al., 2005; Wright, 2010).

Opportunity to learn for ELLs requires teachers to explicitly think about how they will create and sustain language- and literacy-rich classrooms whatever content area they teach and how they will "attend to language" as they plan for teaching and learning in their classrooms. A significant percentage of class time needs to include the learner as doing, talking, and writing within and about the content topics, moving beyond listening and short responses where only the teacher demonstrates sustained use of academic language. Moving to student-centered approaches increases student agency and engagement in the learning and greatly improves the climate for academic conversations and literacy development. As teachers, we should remember that the most engaging classrooms allow students to move freely from listening to each other and the teacher to speaking about what they are learning (i.e., practicing their use of the academic register) to reading and writing about the same topics. This is the heart of the language-rich and literacy-rich classroom (Boals, Hakuta, & Blair, 2015; Gee, 2005).

Discussions on the connection between language and content, modeling of learning and motivational processes related to self-efficacy, and understanding of the role of language as a social and political tool can result in opportunities for students' active participation in their own language development. This enhanced language awareness on the part of classroom teachers, when accompanied by related pedagogical practices, can create opportunities for the development of metacognitive and metalinguistic skills and awareness. Thinking about the ways in which one learns and one uses language promotes cognitive flexibility that is useful in cognitive and linguistic development, as well as future learning in classroom and life settings (Diamond et al., 2007).

The role of the educator is critical in designing nurturing environments and in providing students with the tools, knowledge, and skills to participate in instruction and assessment in ways that promote self-efficacy and increased student agency. As students become aware of their need and capability in acquiring language, what we call metalinguistic awareness, a systematic approach to language development is useful to further nurture the process. The process is cyclical and intrinsically connected to content learning, since the content provides the context in which and through which language is learned (Mohan, 1986).

Ongoing dialog with students and agency on when to focus on language and when to focus on content makes the process less stressful and more focused. Clarifying, sharing, and understanding learning intentions and criteria for success, promoted through effective models of formative assessment (Heritage, 2010, MacDonald et al., 2015; Wiliam, 2011), exemplify accessible instruction and assessment. With clear language goals and clear understanding on when and how language will be the focus, students can begin to self-monitor the way they use language. This practice of self-monitoring has been found to lead to enhanced self-regulation, which means that students eventually apply independent effort and begin to adjust learning goals over time to eventually bring their language skills, in this case, into alignment with set expectations (Burnette et al., 2013). Further, self-monitoring and self-regulation have added benefits. Typically, information on language performance is available from annual, standardized, assessments of learning in many schools. Information from ways in which students are using language supplied by them can supplement this data. Annual summative assessment data then can be analyzed along with student- and teacher-collected data to more fully document language use (Gansle & Noell, 2007; MacDonald et al., 2015).

Yet, accessibility is not only achieved through language development. Waiting for students to first acquire a predetermined level of language and literacy skills before exposing them to the core content, especially those elements which involve higher depth of knowledge (DOK) levels, only further diminishes student access to the curriculum (Webb, 1997). As noted in Boals et al. (2015) and Shafer Willner (2014), language is the primary medium through which student content-area knowledge, skills, and abilities are learned and assessed. New standards-related language demands, especially those around DOK level 3 (e.g., draw conclusions, cite evidence, explain, revise) and DOK level 4 (e.g., analyze, recommend, justify), will require all content teachers, not just the ELA and English language learner (ELL) teachers, to devote instructional time to the particular language skills and understandings needed for each content area. In particular, these standards-related language demands will be even more challenging for students who have not yet acquired the necessary academic English register for grade-level lessons and activities (Anstrom et al., 2010; DiCerbo, Anstrom, Baker, & Rivera, 2014). Accessibility for all students, including ELLs, should include both multiple pathways of access and explicit access to more complex language forms. As the cognitive levels of academic lessons and activities increase in complexity and abstraction, the sophistication of the language that students will need to receive, to interact with, and to use to produce content-specific knowledge, skills, and abilities also intensifies.

A Case for Genre-Based Language Choices to Improve Accessibility During Assessment of Learning

Educators can provide students with improved access to the cultural assumptions embedded in speech, text, and activity used in schooling and connect to and build on student linguistic and cultural repertoires. Using a sociocultural lens, the accessibility of language embedded into assessments might be more clearly matched by genre to ensure ELLs are being accurately assessed on the language demands of a particular disciplinary practice. To help its item writers to more easily identify the meaningful, systematic language necessary to meet academic standards, WIDA, a multistate ELL standards and assessment consortium, recently introduced a tool for use with content and language standards called *Key Uses* of academic language (WIDA, 2016).

The *Key Uses* of academic language draw from the most salient expectations of the college- and career-ready standards: *recount*, *explain*, *argue*, and *discuss*. By becoming aware of the different ways students need to use language during content-area instruction, summative test item writers can make more informed decisions as they plan language for test items. Table 8.5 provides an overview and example of the *Key Uses* of academic language.

The *Key Uses* of academic language are part of a deeper shift in how educators are thinking about instruction and assessment for language learners that is socioculturally and linguistically situated. They are designed to help teachers and students think about how messages are presented to particular audiences (peers, community), in particular contexts (social discussion, formal written), and with features of a particular purpose (recount, report, explain, argue).

By taking time to focus on the primary genres of academic language, teachers can prioritize key concepts and ideas to make better instructional decisions that focus on developing the communicative skills necessary for the instructional purpose at hand. *Key Uses* of academic language can provide students with a clearer road map and meaningful, systematic instruction on the particular forms of language that students are expected to develop and use in and across academic contexts. In so doing, this approach acknowledges the fact that the languages or discourses needed for academic subject areas are not culturally neutral nor are they universal.

Table 8.5 Purposes associated with WIDA *Key Uses* of academic language

Key Use	How language is organized and used in this academic context	Instructional purpose associated with *Key Use*
Recount	In a recount, language is organized to display knowledge, to narrate or relate a series of events or experiences. Narratives follow a cultural storytelling pattern. Procedures require precise details with a clear sequence. Information reports are often restatements of facts, organized by headings and subheadings	Recount information through classroom-based questions Retell or summarize narrative or expository text Provide details of a procedure Write information reports
Argue	In an argument, language is organized around a claim supported by evidence. The development of an argument is determined by the audience and purpose. Order for a logical argument and word choice for a persuasive argument are very important in advancing the claim	Logical and persuasive arguments Incorporate and address counter arguments Anticipate future outcomes as a result of the claim and evidence
Explain	In an explanation, language is organized to clarify order or relationships between ideas, actions, or phenomena, specifically by giving an account of how something works or why something is happening. The aim of an explanation is to help readers/listeners comprehend a phenomenon	Cycles (life cycle, water cycle) Systems (government, computers, ecosystems) Phenomenon (volcanic eruptions, migration, pollution, extreme weather formation)
Discuss	A discussion is used to engage in an exploration of a topic and/or various other points of view and implications, often for the purpose of co-constructing knowledge. Oral discussion often takes place through classroom interaction where linguistic patterns are more social and less predictable. Written discussion reflects more formal, structured language	Students need to learn how to use language features to participate in and/or maintain a discussion (questioning, contradicting/disagreeing, summarizing/paraphrasing, and elaboration), turn-taking, and shared social conventions such interrupting, clarifying, expanding, challenging, and taking (and holding) the floor

Conclusions

In this chapter, we have argued that instruction and assessment practices might better improve ELL opportunity to learn, including those of ELLs with disabilities, if accessibility and its most common application, UDL, were to move beyond assumptions of cultural neutrality and associated deficit-based analyses of student performance. We also have argued for a pedagogy that recognizes the language demands associated with content learning, especially but not exclusively, for ELLs who require explicit language instruction and language- and literacy-rich classrooms throughout school. We end this chapter revisiting the initial proposal for a shift from a deficit perspective of ELLs to an asset-based approach to their education.

Leveraging ELLs' linguistic and cultural assets is best achieved through culturally and linguistically sustainable pedagogies. We define culturally and linguistic sustainable pedagogies as the philosophy, method, and practice of teaching using approaches that help sustain students' cultural and linguistic identities. Drawing on the work of Ladson-Billings (1995) and Paris (2012), we encourage all teachers to develop practices that support the value of their students' multiethnic and multilingual histories. As policies and support of twenty-first-century skills become popular, we must remember that students' own linguistic, literate, and cultural pluralism have been and continue to be part of schooling. Instead of ignoring them or treating them as challenges, we invite educators to counter current policies and practices seeking to maintain hegemonic monocultural and monolingual approaches to learning and instead to embrace cultural and linguistic pluralism as additional opportunities to learn and natural accessibility practices.

References

Abedi, J., & Herman, J. (2010). Assessing English language learners' opportunity to learn mathematics: Issues and limitations. *Teachers College Record, 112*(3), 723–746.

American Educational Research Association, American Psychological Association, & National Council on Measurement in Education (AERA, APA, & NCME). (2014). *Standards for educational and psychological testing*. Washington, DC: American Educational Research Association.

American Psychological Association, Presidential Task Force on Immigration. (2012). *Crossroads: The psychology of immigration in the new century*. Retrieved from http://www.apa.org/topics/immigration/report.aspx

Andrews, J. E., Carnine, D. W., Coutinho, M. J., et al. (2000). Bridging the special education divide. *Remedial and Special Education, 21*, 258–260, 267.

Anstrom, K., DiCerbo, P., Butler, F. A., Katz, A., Millet, J., & Rivera, C. (2010). *A review of the literature on academic English: Implications for K–12 English language learners*. Arlington, VA: George Washington University Center for Equity and Excellence in Education.

Artiles, A. J., Rueda, R., Salazar, J. J., & Higareda, I. (2005). Within-group diversity in minority disproportionate representation: English language learners in Urban School districts. *Exceptional Children, 71*(3), 283–300.

Baglieri, S., Bejoian, L., Broderick, A., et al. (2011). [Re] claiming "inclusive education" toward cohesion in educational reform: Disability studies unravels the myth of the normal child. *Teachers College Record, 113*, 2122–2154.

Baglieri, S., Valle, J., Connor, D. J., & Gallagher, D. (2011). Disability studies and special education: The need for plurality of perspectives on disability. *Remedial and Special Education, 32*, 267–278.

Bialystok, E. (2001). *Bilingualism in development: Language, literacy and cognition*. New York, NY: Cambridge University Press.

Boals, T., Hakuta, K., & Blair, A. (2015). Literacy development in academic contexts for adolescent English language learners. In Molle, Sato, Boals, & Hedgsperth (Eds.), *Multilingual learners and academic literacies: Sociocultural contexts of literacy development in adolescents*. New York, NY: Routledge.

Burnette, J. L., O'Boyle, E. H., VanEpps, E. M., Pollack, J. M., & Finkel, E. J. (2013). Mind-sets matter: a meta-analytic review of implicit theories and self-regulation. *Psychological Bulletin, 139*, 655–701. https://doi.org/10.1037/a0029531

Capps, R., Fix, M., Murray, J., et al. (2005). *The new demography of America's schools: Immigration and the no child left behind act*. Washington, DC: Urban Institute.

Castañeda v. Pickard, 648 F. 2d 989 (5th Cir. 1981).

Collier, V. P., & Thomas, W. P. (2002). Reforming education policies for English learners means better schools for all. *The State Education Standard, 3*(1), 30–36. Alexandria, VA: National Association of State Boards of Education.

Connor, D., & Valle, J. (2015). A socio-cultural reframing of science and dis/ability in education: Past problems, current concerns, and future possibilities. *Cultural Studies of Science Education, 10*, 1103–1122.

De Jong, E., & Harper, C. (2005). Preparing mainstream teachers for English language learners: Is being a good teacher good enough? *Teacher Education Quarterly, 32*(2), 101–124.

DeCapua, A., Smathers, W., & Tang, F. (2009). *Meeting the needs of students with limited or interrupted schooling: A guide for educators*. Ann Arbor, MI: University of Michigan Press.

Diamond, A., Barnett, W. S., Thomas, J., & Munro, S. (2007). Preschool program improves cognitive control. *Science, 318*, 1387–1388.

Diaz, R. M., & Klingler, C. (1991). Towards an explanatory model of the interaction between bilingualism and cognitive development. In E. Bialystock (Ed.), *Language processing in bilingual children*. New York, NY: Longman.

DiCerbo, P. A., Anstrom, K. A., Baker, L. L., & Rivera, C. (2014). A review of the literature on teaching academic English to English language learners. *Review of Educational Research, 84*, 446–482. https://doi.org/10.3102/0034654314532695

Editorial Projects in Education. (2009). Broader horizons: The challenge of college readiness for all students. *Education Week's Diploma Count, 28*(34), 1–38.

Epstein, T. (2009). *Interpreting national history. New York*. New York, NY: Routledge.

Escamilla, K. (2015). Schooling begins before adolescence: The case of manual and limited opportunities to learn. In Molle, Sato, Boals, & Hedgsperth (Eds.), *Multilingual learners and academic literacies: Sociocultural contexts of literacy development in adolescents*. New York, NY: Routledge.

Espinoza, L., & Lopes, M. (2007). *Assessment considerations for young English language learners across different levels of accountability*. The Pew Charitable Trust. Retrieved from http://www.pewtrusts.org/en/research-and-analysis/reports/2007/08/11/assessment-considerations-for-young-english-language-learners-across-different-levels-of-accountability

ESSA (2015). every student succeeds act of 2015, pub. l. no. 114-95 § 114 stat. 1177 (2015-2016).

Every Student Succeeds Act of 2015. (2015–2016). Pub. L. No. 114-95 § 114 Stat. 1177.

Flores, N., Kleyn, T., & Menken, K. (2015). Looking holistically in a climate of partiality: Identities of students labeled 'long-term English language learners. *Journal of Language, Identity, and Education, 14*(2), 113–132.

Gansle, K. A., & Noell, G. H. (2007). The fundamental role of intervention implementation in assessing resistance to intervention. In S. R. Jimerson, M. K. Burns, & A. M. VanDerHeyden (Eds.), *The handbook of response to intervention: The science and practice of assessment and intervention* (pp. 244–251). New York, NY: Springer Science Inc.

Gee, J. (2005). Language in the science classroom: Academic social languages as the heart of school-based literacy. In R. Yerrick & W. Roth (Eds.), *Establishing scientific discourse communities: Multiple voices of teaching and learning research*. New York, NY: Psychology Press.

González, N., Moll, L., & Amanti, C. (2005). *Funds of knowledge: Theorizing practices in households and classrooms*. Mahwah, NJ: Lawrence Erlbaum.

Gradwell, J. M. (2006). Teaching in spite of rather than because of, the test. In S. G. Grant (Ed.), *Measuring history: Cases of state-level testing across states* (pp. 157–176). Greenwich, CT: Information Age Publishing.

Grant, S. G. (2003). *History lessons: Teaching, learning, and testing in US high school classrooms*. Mahwah, NJ: Lawrence Erlbaum Associates.

Gregory, E., & Williams, A. (2000). *City literacies, learning to read across generations and cultures*. London, UK: Routledge.

Heafner, T. L., & Fitcheett, P. G. (2015). An opportunity to learn US history: What NAEP data suggest regarding the opportunity gap. *The High School Journal, 98*(3), 226–249.

Heritage, M. (2010). *Formative assessment and next-generation assessment systems: Are we losing an opportunity? National Center for Research on Evaluation, Standards, and Student Testing (CRESST) and the Council of Chief State School Officers (CCSSO)*. Washington, D.C: CCSSO.

Hodgkinson, H. (2008). *Demographic trends and the Federal role in education*. Washington, DC: Center on Education Policy. Retrieved from http://eric.ed.gov/?id=ED503865

Kibler, A., & Valdés, G. (2016). Conceptualizing language learners: Socioinstitutional mechanisms and their consequences. *The Modern Languages Journal, 100*(1), 97–116.

Klingner, J., & Artiles, A. J. (2006). Struggling to learn to read: Emergent scholarship on linguistic differences and learning disabilities. *Journal of Learning Disabilities, 39*(5), 386–389.

Ladson-Billings, G. (2009). *The dreamkeepers: Successful teachers of African American children* (2nd ed.). San Francisco, CA: Jossey Bass.

Ladson-Billings, G. J. (1995). Toward a theory of culturally relevant pedagogy. *American Education Research Journal, 35*, 465–491.

Lakoff, R. (2000). *The language war*. Berkeley, CA: University of California Press.

Lambert, W. E., Tucker, G. R., & d'Anglejan, A. (1973). Cognitive and attitudinal consequences of bilingual schooling. *Journal of Educational Psychology, 65*(2), 141–159. https://doi.org/10.1037/h0034983

Landry, R. G. (1974). A comparison of second language learners and monolinguals on divergent thinking tasks at the elementary school level. *Modern Language Journal, 58*(1/2), 10–15.

Lee, O., Lewis, S., Adamson, K., Maerten-Rivera, J., & Secada, W. G. (2008). Urban elementary school teachers' knowledge and practices in teaching science to English language learners. *Science Education, 92*(4), 733–758.

Linn, D., & Hemmer, L. (2011). English language learner disproportionality in special education: Implications for the scholar-practitioner. *Journal of Educational Research and Practice, 1*(1), 70–80.

Long, M. H. (1985). Input and second language acquisition theory. In S. M. Gass & C. G. Madden (Eds.), *Input in second language acquisition* (pp. 377–393). Rowley, MA: Newbury House.

Lopes-Murphy, S. (2012). Universal design for learning: Preparing secondary education teachers in training to increase academic accessibility of high school English learners. *The Clearing House, 85*, 226–230.

Lundgren, C., Mabbot, A., & Kramer, D. (2012). *Collaborative conversations: Coteaching and other collaborative practices in the EFL/ESL classroom*. New York, NY: Information Age Publishing.

MacDonald, R., Boals, T., Castro, M., et al. (2015). *Formative language assessment for English learners: A four step process*. Portsmouth, NH: Heinemann.

May, S. (2014). Disciplinary divides, knowledge construction, and the multilingual turn. In S. May (Ed.), *The multilingual turn: Implications for SLA, TESOL and bilingual education* (pp. 7–31). New York, NY: Routledge.

Martin-Jones, M., & Bhatt, A. (1998). Literacies in the lives of young Gujarati speakers in Leicester. In *Literacy development in a multilingual context: Cross-cultural perspectives* (pp. 37–50).

Mohan, B. (1986). *Language and content*. Reading, MA: Addison Wesley.

Moschkovich, J. N. (2002). An introduction to examining everyday and academic mathematical practices. In M. Brenner & J. Moschkovich (Eds.), *Everyday and academic mathematics: Implications for the classroom (Journal for Research in Mathematics Education Monograph)* (Vol. 11, pp. 1–11). Reston, VA: NCTM.

National Center for Educational Statistics. (2015). *The condition of education 2015 (NCES 2015-144), English language learners as cited in English language learners: Fast facts*. Washington, DC: Author. Available: https://nces.ed.gov/fastfacts/display.asp?id=96

National Governors Association Center for Best Practices, & Council of Chief State School Officers. (2010). *Application of common core state standards for english language learners*. Washington, DC: Authors.

Available: http://www.corestandards.org/assets/application-for-english-learners.pdf

National UDL Task Force. (2011). *English language learner FAQs*. Wakefield, MA: Author. Retrieved from http://www.udlcenter.org/advocacy/faq_guides/ell#question1

No Child Left Behind Act of 2001. (2002). Pub. L. No. 107–110, § 115, Stat. 1425–2094.

Olsen, L. (2010). *Reparable harm: Fulfilling the unkept promise of educational opportunity for long-term English learners*. Long Beach, CA: Californians Together.

Ortega, L. (2014). Ways forward for a bi/multilingual turn in SLA. In S. May (Ed.), *The multilingual turn: Implications for SLA, TESOL and bilingual education* (pp. 32–53). New York, NY: Routledge.

Pace, J. (2011). The complex and unequal impact of high stakes accountability on untested social studies. *Theory & Research in Social Education, 39*(1), 32–60.

Pacheco, M. (2010). English-language learners' reading achievement: Dialectical relationships between policy and practices in meaning-making opportunities. *Reading Research Quarterly, 45*(3), 292–317.

Paris, D. (2012). Culturally sustaining pedagogy: A needed change in stance, terminology, and practice. *Educational Researcher, 41*(3), 93–97.

Partnerships for Twenty-First Century Learning. (2016). *Framework for 21st century learning*. Washington, DC: Author. Available: http://www.p21.org/our-work/p21-framework

Pearson Educational Measurement. (2009). *Universal design for computer-based testing guidelines*. Retrieved August 25, 2010, from http://www.pearsonedmeasurement.com/cast/index.html. See also June 22, 2009 press release available at http://www.pearsoned.com/pr_2009/062209.htm

PePeal, E., & Lambert, W. (1962). The relation of bilingualism intelligence. *Psychological Monographs, 76*, 1–23.

Polat, N., Zarecky-Hodge, A., & Schreiber, J. (2016). Academic growth trajectories of ELLs in NAEP data: The case of fourth- and eighth-grade ELLs and non-ELLs on mathematics and reading tests. *Journal of Educational Research, 109*(5), 541–553.

Reardon, S. F. (2011). The widening academic achievement gap between rich and poor: New evidence and possible explanations. In G. J. Duncan & R. J. Murnane (Eds.), *Whither opportunity? Rising inequality, schools, and children's life chances* (pp. 91–115). New York, NY: Russell Sage Foundation.

Reardon, S. F. (2013). The widening income achievement gap. *Educational Leadership, 70*(8), 10–16.

Rose, D., & Strangman, N. (2007). Universal Design for Learning: Meeting the challenge of individual learning differences through a neurocognitive perspective. *Universal Access in the Information Society, 5*(4), 381–391.

Ruiz Soto, A., Hooker, S., & Batalova, J. (2015). *States and districts with the highest number and share of English language learners*. Washington, DC: Migration Policy Institute. Available: http://www.migrationpolicy.org/research/states-and-districts-highest-number-and-share-english-language-learners

Russell, M., Hoffmann, T., & Higgins, J. (2009). Meeting the needs of all students: A universal design approach to computer-based testing. *Innovate, 5*(4). Retrieved June 27, 2009, from http://www.innovateonline.info/index.php?view=article&id=676

Russell, M., & Kavanaugh, M. (Eds.). (2011). *Assessing students in the margins*. Charlotte, NC: Information Age Publishing. Abstract retrieved from http://www.infoagepub.com/products/Assessing-Students-in-the-Margin

Samson, J. F., & Lesaux, N. K. (2009). Language-minority learners in special education: Rates and predictors of identification for services. *Journal of Learning Disabilities, 42*(2), 148–162.

Saye, J., & The Social Studies Inquiry Research Collaborative. (2013). Authentic pedagogy: Its presence in social studies classrooms and relationship to student performance on state-mandated tests. *Theory & Research in Social Education, 41*(1), 89–132.

Shafer Willner, L. (2014). *Teacher professional development rationales and resources on how to meet the language demands of new college-and career-ready standards*. San Francisco, CA: Center on Standards and Assessment Implementation. Available: http://csai-online.org/sites/default/files/resource/151/AcadLangResourcesBRIEF_ShaferWillner2014.pdf

Shafer Willner, L., & Rivera, C. (2011). *Are EL needs being defined appropriately for the next generation of computer-based tests?* Article prepared for the National Clearinghouse of English language acquisition (NCELA) AccELLerate newsletter. Washington, DC: NCELA. Retrieved from http://www.ncela.us/files/uploads/17/Accellerate_3_2.pdf

Short, D., & Fitzsimmons, S. (2007). *Double the work: Challenges and solutions to acquiring language and academic literacy for adolescent English language learners*. Washington, DC: Alliance for Excellent Education.

Sullivan, A. (2011). Disproportionality in special education identification and placement of English language learners. *Exceptional Children, 77*, 317–334.

Tannenbaum, M., & Howie, P. (2002). The association between language maintenance and family relations: Chinese immigrant children in Australia. *Journal of Multilingual and Multicultural Development, 23*(5), 408–424.

U.S. Department of Justice and U.S. Department of Education. (2015). *Ensuring English learner students can participate meaningfully and equally in educational programs*. Washington, DC: Author. Available: https://www2.ed.gov/about/offices/list/ocr/docs/dcl-factsheet-el-students-201501.pdf

U.S. Department of Education/National Center for Educational Statistics. (2012). *Improving the measurement of socioeconomic status for the National Assessment of educational progress: A theoretical foundation*. Washington, DC: Author. Available:

https://nces.ed.gov/nationsreportcard/pdf/research-center/Socioeconomic_Factors.pdf

U.S. Department of Education/National Center for Educational Statistics. (2016). *NAEP data explorer*. Washington, DC: Author. Available: http://nces.ed.gov/nationsreportcard/naepdata/report.aspx

Vygotsky, L. S. (1978). *Mind in society*. Cambridge: Harvard University Press.

Webb, N. (1997). Criteria for alignment of expectations and assessments in mathematics and science education. In *Research monograph, no. 8*. Washington, DC: CCSSO.

WIDA. (2016). CAN DO descriptors: Key uses edition. In *Author*. Madison, WI: Board of Regents of the University of Wisconsin. Retrieved from www.wida.us/downloadlibrary.aspx

Wiliam, D. (2011). What is assessment for learning? *Studies in Educational Evaluation, 37*, 3–14.

Wong-Fillmore, L., & Snow, C. (2000). *What teachers need to know about language*. Washington, DC: ERIC Clearinghouse on Languages and Linguistics.

Wright, W. E. (2010). *Foundations for teaching English language learners: Research, theory, policy and practice*. Philadelphia, PA: Caslon Publishing.

Yelland, G., Pollard, J., & Mercuri, A. (1993). The metalinguistic benefits of limited contact with a second language. *Applied Psycholinguisticsm, 14*, 423–444.

Zabala, J. (2014). *Improving educational participation and outcomes for ALL students with universal design for learning and—for some—special education services*. Center for Applied Special Technology (CAST). Atlanta, GA: Conference on Successfully Transitioning Away from the 2% Assessment. Retrieved from http://www.cehd.umn.edu/nceo/AAMAStransition/default.html

Zong, J., & Batalova, J. (2015). *The limited English proficient population in the United States*. Washington, DC: Migration Policy Institute. Available: http://www.migrationpolicy.org/article/limited-english-proficient-population-united-states#Age,%20Race,%20and%20Ethnicity

Confronting the Known Unknown: How the Concept of Opportunity to Learn Can Advance Tier 1 Instruction

Alexander Kurz

Even when students are taught in the same classroom by the same teacher, they are often offered very different opportunities to learn (Kurz, Elliott, Lemons et al., 2014; Rowan & Correnti, 2009; Schmidt, Burroughs, Zoido, & Houang, 2015). These differences in opportunity to learn (OTL) further correlate with differences in student achievement (Kurz, 2011; Schmidt & Burroughs, 2013). According to the *Standards for Educational and Psychological Testing*, OTL must be considered to ensure fair testing practices and prevent "misdiagnosis, inappropriate placement, and/or inappropriate assignment of services" (AERA, NCME, & APA, 2014, p. 57). These are important caveats whenever test score inferences are being made including in the context of response to intervention (RTI), which is predicated on the prevention of academic difficulties through the accurate identification of at-risk students and the timely delivery of effective interventions (Al Otaiba et al., 2014; Compton et al., 2012). Universal screening based on curriculum-based measurement is typically used to determine whether students are responding to high-quality Tier 1 instruction (Fuchs & Vaughn, 2012). This common screening approach, however, has shown unacceptably high rates of false positives (Fuchs, Fuchs, & Compton, 2012). Differences in the provision and accessibility of said "high-quality" instruction represent one factor that could undermine classification accuracy.

Despite the correlation between OTL and student achievement, researchers and practitioners have largely ignored questions about the extent to which Tier 1 screening outcomes could be a function of "low-quality" instruction (Kurz, Elliott, & Roach, 2015; Reddy, Fabiano, & Jimerson, 2013). That is, positive screening results typically suggest two competing inferences: (a) a student's *inadequate response* to high-quality Tier 1 instruction or (b) a teacher's *inadequate implementation* of high-quality Tier 1 instruction. Ruling out the latter inference requires data about the implementation of Tier 1 instruction—a need often acknowledged but rarely addressed in research and practice (Gilbert et al., 2013; Kurz et al., 2015). Knowing that we don't know, of course, makes Tier 1 instructional data the proverbial "known unknown."

The rationale for confronting this known unknown is threefold. First, missing data on Tier 1 instruction represents a threat to fairness and thus potentially impacts the validity of test score inferences (AERA, NCME, & APA, 2014). In addition, reducing the number of false positives (i.e., students receiving Tier 2 who do not really need it) matters greatly in a resource-constrained environment such as public schools (Al Otaiba et al., 2014). Second, ensuring access to high-quality Tier 1 instruction is fundamental to the logic and

A. Kurz (✉)
Arizona State University, Tempe, AZ, USA
e-mail: alexander.kurz@asu.edu

efficacy of all RTI approaches (Fuchs & Vaughn, 2012). In fact, research findings suggest that students' unfettered access to primary prevention leads to fewer students requiring intervention initially and over time (Fuchs, Fuchs, Mathes, & Simmons, 1997; Vaughn et al., 2009), as well as a reduction in special education referrals and placements, with more proportionate representation of minorities, English language learners, and males (Torgesen, 2009; VanDerHeyden, Witt, & Gilbertson, 2007; Wanzek & Vaughn, 2010). Third, documenting the provision and accessibility of high-quality Tier 1 instruction can help educators make data-based decisions to improve "two important determinants of students success: opportunity to learn and quality of instruction" (Fuchs & Vaugh, 2012).

To ensure high-quality Tier 1 instruction as a form of primary prevention, researchers have focused on understanding and operationalizing evidence standards that can be used to identify so-called evidence-based practices (Cook & Odom, 2013; Gandhi, Holdheide, Zumeta, & Danielson, 2016). These laudable efforts, however, have emphasized secondary and tertiary levels of prevention. This omission is likely due to the many challenges of operationalizing and assessing generally effective instruction. Some researchers, however, have suggested that research about OTL holds important implications for addressing these challenges and supporting high-quality Tier 1 instruction (Holdheide, 2016; Kurz et al., 2015).

In this chapter, I argue that the establishment of Tier 1 quality standards and the conceptual expansion of OTL are interconnected, mutually beneficial activities important for truly accessible instruction. To this end, I focus on my conceptual synthesis of OTL (Kurz, 2011) due to its (a) operational definition (Kurz, Elliott, Lemons et al., 2014), (b) application in general and special education (Heafner & Fitchett, 2015; Roach, Kurz, & Elliott, 2015), and (c) measurement via an online teacher log (Kurz, Elliott, Kettler, & Yel, 2014). I begin by reviewing what is known about high-quality Tier 1 instruction and OTL, continue by synthesizing both literature bases to identify potential sources of evidence for high-quality Tier 1, elaborate by highlighting possible measurement options via a case example, and conclude by setting a research and development agenda for Tier 1 OTL.

Tier 1 Instruction

As a multitiered approach to the early identification and support of students with learning and behavior needs, RTI's primary level of prevention (Tier 1) is focused on high-quality instruction and universal screening of all children. Across tiers or prevention levels, struggling learners are provided with interventions at increasing levels of intensity that make instruction more distinctive including students' grouping formats and teachers' skill level (Bradley, Danielson, & Doolittle, 2007; Chard, 2012). According to the high-quality Tier 1 instruction should be characterized by the use of (a) research-based core curriculum materials that are aligned to Common Core or other state standards, (b) data to make instructional decisions (e.g., selection of instructional practices, differentiation of learning activities, use of accommodations, use of problem-solving approaches to identify interventions), (c) teaching and learning objectives that are connected in progression within and across grades, and (d) enrichment opportunities for students who exceed benchmarks. Fuchs et al. (2012) argued that high-quality Tier 1 instruction should feature (a) core programs in reading and mathematics, (b) differentiated instruction, (c) accommodations to ensure accessibility to Tier 1 instruction for virtually all students, and (d) problem-solving strategies to address students' motivation and behavior. Fuchs et al. further acknowledged that the general effectiveness of Tier 1 instructional practices should be derived from research, which does not require the same empirical rigor of validation (via experimental or quasi-experimental studies) as is needed of evidence-based practices.

To determine the extent to which high-quality Tier 1 instruction is being delivered, Metcalf (2012) recommended educators and other multidisciplinary team members review the scope and sequence of their day-to-day instruction and answer the following questions:

> What instructional routines are used? Are the routines consistent from classroom to classroom, general education to special education? Is there evidence of scaffolding and explicit instruction, especially when students are learning something new? Is there evidence of distributed practice of critical skills? Is cumulative review built in on a systematic basis? How much time is allocated? How is that time used (for example, whole group instruction, small group instruction, or independent practice)? Does the pace of the instruction match student needs? Do students have multiple opportunities for response and feedback? Are students actively engaged (that is, are they saying, writing, and doing)? (p. 5).

As such, Metcalf organized high-quality Tier 1 instruction around (a) use of instructional time, (b) emphasis of various instructional practices such as explicit instruction and scaffolding, and (c) student engagement with instructional materials. Moreover, he emphasized the review of ongoing, day-to-day information about classroom instruction.

Gandhi, Holdheide, Zumeta, and Danielson (2016) focused on the following characteristics for purposes of differentiating intervention tiers: (a) approach (i.e., comprehensive, standardized, individualized), (b) group size (i.e., whole class, small group, very small group), (c) progress monitoring (i.e., once per term, once per month, weekly), and (d) population (i.e., all students, at-risk students, students with significant and persistent needs). As evidence to document Tier 1 instruction, they noted comprehensive coverage of critical content and use of instructional practices derived from research. Holdheide (2016) further suggested use of instructional time and screening procedures for documenting the quality of Tier 1 instruction. She identified instructional time, content coverage, and quality of instruction as the defining dimensions of Tier 1 instruction. Holdheide and her colleagues did not suggest, however, what may constitute adequate use of instructional time (e.g., as a percentage of allocated class time) or comprehensive content coverage (e.g., as a percentage of available content standards).

In summary, researchers have identified a variety of characteristics indicative of high-quality Tier 1 instruction. As expected, most of these characteristics address the curricular and qualitative aspects of instruction—the "what" and "how" of a teacher's enacted curriculum. A few researchers also noted temporal considerations (i.e., use of instructional time). To date, these characteristics have lacked an organizing framework as well as operational definitions that address quality as a matter of degree. In other words, what is needed are definitions that go beyond denoting the mere presence of a characteristic (e.g., progress monitoring) by indicating the characteristic's degree of implementation necessary to be considered high quality (e.g., progress monitoring on a weekly basis versus quarterly basis). I argue that the concept of OTL be used to this end for two main reasons: (a) OTL is a well-researched concept with a solid conceptual and empirical basis (see Kurz, 2011); (b) recent advancements in OTL's measurement at the classroom level (e.g., Kurz, Elliott, Kettler et al., 2014; Rowan & Correnti, 2009) can address the next critical step after organizing and operationalizing key characteristics of high-quality Tier instruction, namely, measuring and providing feedback about the extent to which Tier 1 instruction is being implemented with high quality.

Opportunity to Learn

Since the 1960s, researchers have used the OTL acronym to examine a variety of schooling variables and their relationships to student achievement. Due to its continued relevance and applicability, OTL is widely considered a "generative concept" (McDonnell, 1995). That is, OTL has been relevant and applicable for identifying the normative assumptions of policy goals, focusing empirical research on strategies for reaching these goals, and informing ways to measure progress toward these goals. For example, OTL has been used to identify several normative assumptions of standards-based reform such as alignment (Porter, 2002) and access to the general curriculum (Kurz & Elliott, 2011). It has also

Fig. 9.1 Three dimensions of the enacted curriculum that define OTL

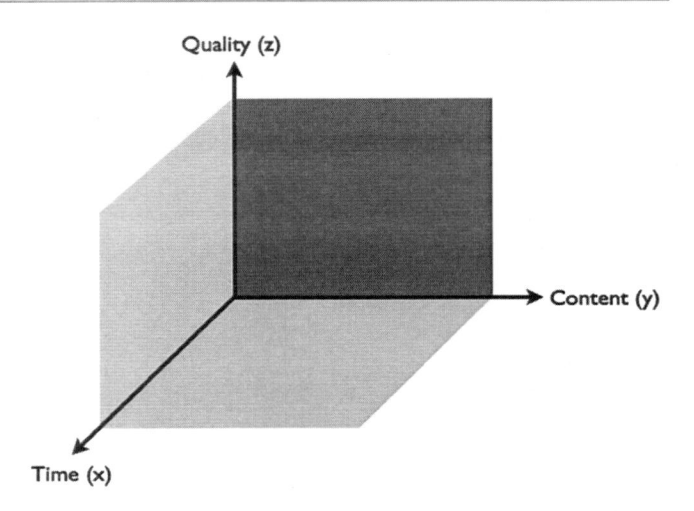

been used to focus empirical research on examining relations between different schooling variables and student outcomes (e.g., Herman, Klein, & Abedi, 2000; Wang, 1998). In addition, several measurement tools of OTL currently hold implications for measuring progress toward certain policy goals (see Kurz, 2011).

I previously reviewed the large variety of OTL variables found in the extant literature focusing on those that showed empirical relations to student achievement (Kurz, 2011) and grouping them into three broad categories related to the time, content, and quality of classroom instruction (e.g., Borg, 1980; Brophy & Good, 1986; Porter, 2002). Based on a review of these three distinct OTL research strands, I provided a conceptual synthesis of OTL that focused on three key dimensions of the enacted curriculum—time, content, and quality—all of which co-occur during instruction (see Fig. 9.1). That is, teachers distribute OTL of what they want students to know and be able to do by allocating instructional time and content coverage to intended objectives using a variety of pedagogical approaches. As such, OTL is considered to be a teacher effect. Teachers provide OTL through their instruction, which is part of the enacted curriculum. The extent to which students engage in that opportunity, of course, is a separate matter. What follows is a summary of the three major OTL research strands I discussed in my earlier work (Kurz, 2011).

Time

The first research strand emerged with John Carroll (1963), who introduced the concept of OTL as part of his model of school learning: "Opportunity to learn is defined as the amount of time allowed for learning, for example by a school schedule or program" (Carroll, 1989, p. 26). Subsequent research on time and school learning (see Borg, 1980; Gettinger & Seibert, 2002) began to empirically examine this OTL conceptualization using general indicators such as *allocated time* (i.e., scheduled time to be allocated to instruction) or more instructionally sensitive indicators such as *instructional time* (i.e., proportion of allocated time actually used for instruction), *engaged time* (i.e., proportion of instructional time during which students are engaged in learning), and *academic learning time* (i.e., proportion of engaged time during which students are experiencing a high success rate).

The amount of time dedicated to instruction has received substantial empirical support in predicting student achievement (e.g., Carroll, 1989; Denham & Lieberman, 1980; Fisher & Berliner, 1985; Walberg, 1988). In a research synthesis on teaching, Walberg (1986) identified 31 studies that examined the "quantity of instruction" and its relation to student achievement. Walberg reported a median (partial) correlation of 0.35 controlling for other variables such as student ability and socioeconomic status. In a meta-analysis on educational effectiveness, Scheerens and Bosker (1997) examined the effect of (allocated) time on student achievement using 21 studies with a total of 56 replications across studies. The average Cohen's *d* effect size for time was 0.39 (as cited in Marzano, 2000). Considering that time usage related to instruction represents one of the best documented predictors of student achievement across schools, classes, student abilities, grade levels, and subject areas (Vannest & Parker, 2010), it is not surprising that research regarding time on instruction continues to this date.

Content

The second research strand emerged with studies that focused on the *content overlap* between the enacted and assessed curriculum (e.g., Comber & Keeves, 1973; Husén, 1967). Husén, one of the key investigators for several international studies of student achievement, developed an item-based OTL measure that required teachers to report on the instructional content coverage for each assessment item via a 3-point Likert scale: "Thus opportunity to learn from the Husén perspective is best understood as the match between what is taught and what is tested" (Anderson, 1986, p. 3682). The International Association for the Evaluation of Educational Achievement (IEA) has conducted several comparative studies of international student achievement, the results of which have supported "students' opportunity to learn the assessed curriculum" as a significant predictor of systematic differences in student performance. This content overlap conceptualization of OTL remained dominant in several other mostly descriptive research studies during the 1970s and 1980s (e.g., Borg, 1979; Winfield, 1993) and continues to date (e.g., Schmidt et al., 1997, 2001). The latter findings based on international studies such as the Second and Third International Mathematics Studies (SIMS, TIMS) as well as the Programme for International Student Assessment (PISA) have established consistent evidence that greater OTL is related to higher student achievement (Schmidt et al., 2015).

Another line of research on content overlap focused on students' opportunity to learn important content objectives (e.g., Armbuster, Stevens, & Rosenshine, 1977; Jenkins & Pany, 1978; Porter et al., 1978). Porter et al., for instance, developed a basic taxonomy for classifying content included in mathematics curricula and measured whether different standardized mathematics achievement tests covered the same objectives delineated in the taxonomy. Porter continued his research on measuring the content of the enacted curriculum (e.g., Gamoran, Porter, Smithson, & White, 1997; Porter, Kirst, Osthoff, Smithson, & Schneider, 1993) and developed a survey-based measure that examined the content of instruction along two dimensions: topics and categories of cognitive demand (Porter & Smithson, 2001). He subsequently developed an *alignment* index (Porter, 2002), which qualified content overlap based on these two dimensions. The findings of Gamoran et al. indicated that alignment between instruction and a test of student achievement in high school mathematics accounted for 25% of the variance among teachers.

Quality

The third and most diverse research strand related to an instructional dimension of OTL can be traced back to several models of school learning (e.g., Bloom, 1976; Carroll, 1963; Gagné, 1977; Harnischfeger & Wiley, 1976). Both Carroll's model of school learning and Walberg's (1980) model of educational productivity, for example, featured quality of instruction alongside quantity of instruction. The operationalization of instructional quality for purposes of measurement, however, resulted in a much larger set of independent variables than instructional time. Most these variables were focused on *instructional practices* related to student achievement. In his research synthesis on teaching, Walberg (1986) reviewed 91 studies that examined the effect of quality indicators on student achievement, such as frequency of praise statements, corrective feedback, classroom climate, and instructional groupings. Walberg reported the highest mean effect sizes for (positive) reinforcement and corrective feedback with 1.17 and 0.97, respectively. Brophy and Good's (1986) seminal review of the process-product literature identified aspects of giving information (e.g., pacing), questioning students (e.g., cognitive level), and providing feedback as important instructional quality variables with consistent empirical support. Additional meta-analyses focusing on specific subjects and student subgroups are also available (e.g., Gersten et al., 2009; Vaughn, Gersten, & Chard, 2000). Gersten et al. (2009), for example, examined various instructional components that enhanced the mathematics proficiency of students with learning disabilities. Gersten and colleagues hereby identified two instructional components that provided practically and statistically important increases in effect size: teaching students the use of heuristics (i.e., general problem-solving strategy) and explicit instruction. In addition, researchers have identified *grouping formats* other than whole class (e.g., Elbaum, Vaughn, Hughes, Moody, & Schumm, 2000) and cognitive expectations for learning, so-called cognitive demands (e.g., Porter, 2002), as important qualitative aspects of instruction. With respect to cognitive expectations, several classification categories ranging from lower-order to higher-order cognitive processes have been suggested, most notably in Bloom's taxonomy of education objectives (Bloom, 1976).

Figure 9.2 compares three classification categories of cognitive process expectations: (a) Webb's Depth-of-Knowledge (DOK) levels (see Webb, 2006), the categories of cognitive demand used as part of the SEC (see Porter, 2002), and the six categories of the cognitive process dimension from the revised Bloom's taxonomy (see Anderson et al., 2001). It should be noted that the latter taxonomy situates all educational objectives within a two-dimensional framework that includes both a knowledge dimension and a cognitive process dimension.

Operational Definition and Measurement

As noted earlier, all three dimensions of the enacted curriculum co-occur during classroom instruction. As such, a comprehensive definition of OTL should include previously discussed OTL indices along each of the three enacted curriculum dimensions: time, content, and quality. Anderson first articulated a merger of the various OTL conceptualizations in 1986: "A single conceptualization of opportunity to learn coupled with the inclusion of the variable[s] in classroom instructional research . . . could have a profound effect on our understanding of life in classrooms" (p. 3686). Following Anderson's suggestion, I developed a conceptual synthesis of OTL, which was subsequently operationalized by defining OTL as "the degree to which a teacher dedicates instructional time and content coverage to the intended curriculum objectives emphasizing higher-order cognitive processes, evidenced-based instructional practices, and alternative grouping formats" (Kurz, Elliott, Lemons et al., 2014, p. 27). Building on the work of Rowan and colleagues (e.g., Rowan, Camburn, & Correnti, 2004; Rowan & Correnti, 2009), Kurz and colleagues conducted several studies measuring OTL via an online teacher log that can collect daily self-report data based on several of the previously discussed OTL indices (see Kurz et al., 2015). The online teacher log specifically incorporates indices related to instructional time, content coverage, cognitive processes, instructional practices, and grouping formats into one assessment.

Historically, researchers have relied on classroom observations and teacher surveys to measure OTL. The variability of classroom instruction, however, presents unique challenges for both options (Rowan & Correnti, 2009). To ensure generalizability of classroom observations, researchers must sample a large number of lessons to make valid inferences about OTL for the entire school year. Due to the high costs associated with this approach, most assessments of OTL rely on teacher surveys, typically conducted at the end of the school year (Porter, 2002). Teacher recall, especially across longer time periods, is subject to recall error (Mayer, 1999; Rowan et al., 2004). Teacher logs represent an alternative approach that is intended to (a) reduce a teacher's response burden by focusing on a discreet set of behaviors, (b) increase accuracy of teacher recall by focusing on a recent time period,

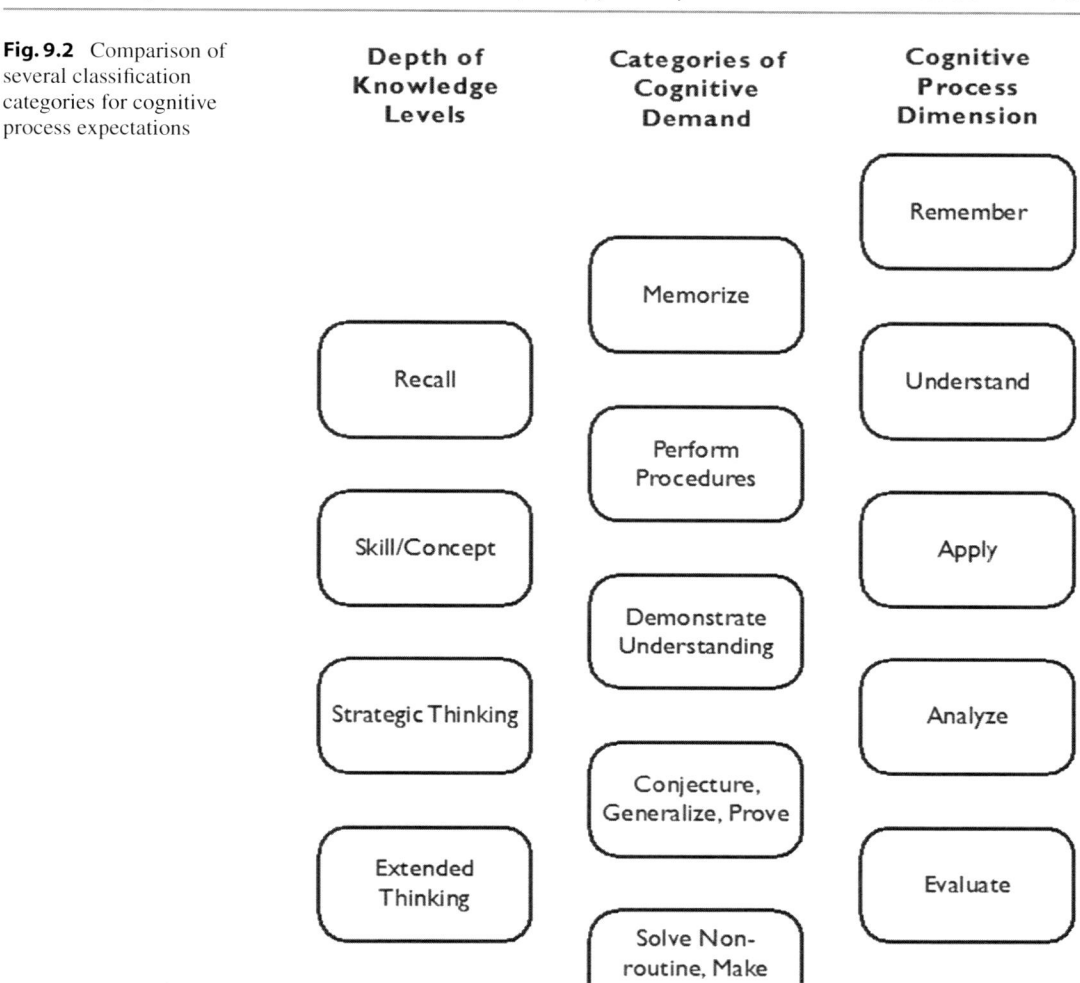

Fig. 9.2 Comparison of several classification categories for cognitive process expectations

Depth of Knowledge Levels	Categories of Cognitive Demand	Cognitive Process Dimension
		Remember
	Memorize	
Recall		Understand
	Perform Procedures	
Skill/Concept		Apply
	Demonstrate Understanding	
Strategic Thinking		Analyze
	Conjecture, Generalize, Prove	
Extended Thinking		Evaluate
	Solve Non-routine, Make Connections	
		Create

and (c) increase generalizability through frequent administrations across the school year (Kurz, Elliott, Lemons et al., 2014).

The online teacher log used by Kurz and colleagues requires teachers to undergo proficiency-based knowledge and skill tests prior to use. The log aggregates daily OTL data into a variety of scores, which have been examined for technical adequacy. Kurz, Elliott, Kettler et al. (2014) provided a summary of initial evidence supporting intended score interpretations for assessing OTL. The summary included multiple sources of evidence: usability, reliability, and validity evidence based on content, responses processes, internal structure, relations to other variables, and consequences of using the measure. More recently, Berkovits, Kurz, and Reddy (2017) provided evidence for the measure's convergent validity with a classroom observational assessment. Table 9.1 adapted from Kurz, Elliott, Kettler et al. (2014) provides details on five major scores provided by the online teacher log called the *Instructional Learning Opportunities Guidance System* (MyiLOGS; Kurz & Elliott, 2012).

Data collection using MyiLOGS has occurred in the context of research studies with incentivized participants as well as part of teachers' regular professional development. Collectively, these

Table 9.1 Enacted curriculum dimensions, OTL indices, and score definitions

Dimension	OTL index	Score definition[a]
Time	Instructional time (IT)	Score between 0.00 and 1.00, which represents the percentage of allocated time used for instruction on standards and custom objectives
Content	Content coverage (CC)	Score between 0.00 and 1.00, which represents the cumulative percentage of academic standards covered for 1 min or more
Quality	Cognitive processes (CP)	Score between 1.00 and 2.00, which represents the percentage of time spent on higher-order cognitive processes +1.00[b]
	Instructional practices (IP)	Score between 1.00 and 2.00, which represents the percentage of time spent on evidence-based instructional practices +1.00[b]
	Grouping formats (GF)	Score between 1.00 and 2.00, which represents the percentage of time spent on individual and/or small group formats +1.00[b]

[a]*Note*: Score definitions are specific to the Instructional Learning Opportunities Guidance System (MyiLOGS; Kurz & Elliott, 2012)

[b]*Note*: The addition of +1.00 is intended to prevent negative user associations with a score of 0

efforts have yielded three important findings: (a) teachers can be trained to provide reliable self-report data when used for self-reflection and professional development; (b) these data can yield valid inferences about their provision of OTL; and (c) their OTL score profiles can be used to establish normative standards (Berkovits, Kurz, & Reddy, 2017; Kurz, Elliott, Kettler et al., 2014; Kurz et al., 2015; Kurz, Reichenberg, & Yel, 2017). Moreover, teachers' OTL scores have shown to be sensitive to job-embedded professional development (i.e., instructional coaching). Controlling for several teacher characteristics and class size, Kurz (2016) reported on coaching status predicting OTL score increases for instructional time (IT), content coverage (CC), instructional practices (IP), and grouping formats (GF). These OTL scores further maintained moderate correlations with median growth scores on benchmark assessments in reading and mathematics ranging from 0.31 to 0.49 (Kurz, 2017).

In summary, researchers have used the concept, definition, and measurement of OTL to describe classroom instruction and its relationship to student achievement. Measurement tools that can be completed on a daily basis such as online teacher logs are capable of capturing the scope and sequence of teachers' day-to-day instruction—an important criterion—if Tier 1 data are to be used formatively (Metcalf, 2012). Several research studies have already provided evidence that OTL data can be used in the context of professional development to drive measurable instructional changes. Research on OTL is thus positioned to confront the known unknown of Tier 1 instruction in several ways: (a) provide data on teachers' use of instructional time, content coverage, and instructional quality, (b) collect these data formatively to drive improvements in Tier 1 instruction, and (c) set quality standards based on these data. As a first step, however, we need to synthesize the discussed RTI and OTL literature relevant to Tier 1 OTL to identify potential sources of evidence for high-quality Tier 1.

Tier 1 OTL

Expectations for what students should know and be able to do must be articulated across all levels of the educational environment. To delineate these levels, researchers have developed curriculum frameworks, which typically emphasize how different curricula relate to the intended curriculum (e.g., Anderson, 2002; Porter, 2002; Webb, 1997). That is, the intended curriculum represents the normative target for all other curricula by defining students' learning objectives (usually by way of subject- and grade-specific standards). Based on this premise, I developed a curriculum framework delineating key curricula at the system, teacher, and student level (see Fig. 9.3).

As shown in the figure, students access the intended curriculum through the teacher's enacted

Fig. 9.3 Curriculum framework that delineates normative function of intended curriculum

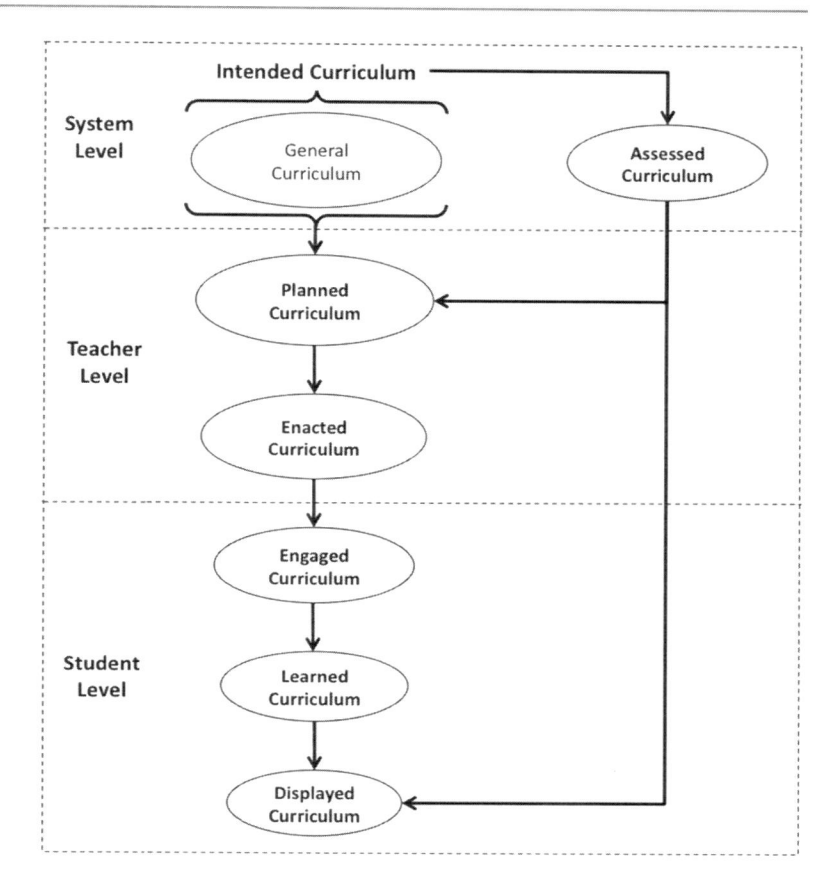

curriculum. The extent to which this happens is captured by OTL along the three dimensions of the enacted curriculum: time, content, and quality. By definition, multitiered support systems are predicated on positing different intended curricula depending on the needs of students. A teacher's enacted curriculum must consequently differ at each level of prevention: primary, secondary, and tertiary. If OTL is to serve as a generative concept for RTI, then OTL must be defined and refined according to each tier: Tier 1 OTL, Tier 2 OTL, and Tier 3 OTL.

The comprehensive definition of OTL provided by Kurz, Elliott, Lemons et al. (2014) was based on empirically supported OTL indices that came out of the three major OTL research strands, which have focused almost exclusively on general instruction provided to the vast majority of students. As such, their OTL definition is most directly applicable to Tier 1 instruction. The OTL scores based on this definition (see Table 9.1) are designed to address several important features of general instruction for students with and without disabilities. Although students with disabilities served in general education under a full inclusion model typically exhibit less severe disabilities, they are still served via an Individualized Education Program (IEP). Both reauthorizations of the IDEA in 1997 and 2004 emphasize the IEP as the central mechanism for detailing a student's access, involvement, and progress in the general curriculum (Karger, 2005). The IEP also documents educational objectives relevant to a student's present levels of performance as well as accommodations and modifications that facilitate the student's access to enacted and assessed curricula (Ketterlin-Geller & Jamgochian, 2011). The IEP thus augments the general curriculum, which is the reason I qualified the curriculum framework displayed in Fig. 9.3 for students with disabilities. That is, I noted that the intended curriculum for students with disabilities is dually determined by both the IEP and the general curriculum (Kurz, 2011). Therefore, measurement of OTL at the enacted curriculum must be able to account for a teacher's time spent teaching the students' IEP objectives in addition to the academic standards that define the general curriculum.

For purposes of Tier 1, assessment of OTL along the time dimension of the enacted curriculum can occur based on any of the aforementioned indices: allocated time, instructional time, engaged time, and academic learning time. While these indices exhibit stronger relations to achievement the more directly they measure student engagement and success, Metcalf's (2012) imperative to measure the scope and sequence of teachers' day-to-day instruction for purposes of high-quality Tier 1 instruction limits the practicality of measuring these more student-centric indices on a daily basis. The instructional time (IT) index, I contend, strikes a reasonable balance between empirical evidence (i.e., the extent to which time indices are predictive of student achievement) and feasible measurement. Moreover, we have evidence that teachers can be trained to estimate their time used for instruction reasonably well by subtracting non-instructional time such as transitions and other interruptions from their allocated time (Kurz, Elliott, Kettler et al., 2014). In addition, the operationalization of IT for measurement purposes via an online teacher log (see Table 9.1) also addresses the previous concern of capturing time spent on both academic standards and custom objectives (i.e., IEP objectives). The score developed by Kurz and Elliott (2012)—IT as the percentage of allocated time used for instruction on standards and custom objectives—further can be interpreted as a measure of efficiency. The IT score does not capture total minutes of instruction but rather how efficiently a teacher can use the allocated time for a particular class (e.g., 60-min mathematics class) for instruction on standards and custom objectives (e.g., 53 min) resulting in a percentage (e.g., IT = 88%).

In the context of RTI Tier 1, researchers have argued for the implementation of a research-based reading or mathematics program that provides instructional objectives and materials aligned to Common Core or other state standards (Fuchs et al., 2012). While IT can capture the amount of time spent teaching intended standards as well as any custom objectives specific to a reading or mathematics program, the time index does not address whether the number of intended standards taught is adequate. In fact, Holdheide (2016) specifically argued for adequate coverage of Tier 1 content. As such, assessment of OTL along the content dimension of the enacted curriculum can be used to address this concern. The content coverage (CC) index of OTL provides a basic measure of the breadth of coverage. MyiLOGS, for example, simply provides a cumulative percentage of academic standards covered (i.e., Common Core State Standards) for at least 1 min or more. This threshold can be adjusted, but it is purposefully set low to avoid construct overlap with the time index.

Thus far, we have identified at least two sources of evidence for high-quality Tier 1 instruction related to the time and content dimensions of the enacted curriculum. Given these are fully aligned with previously established OTL indices, we can use prior research based on these indices to draft operational definitions—short of setting actual standards. For example, large-scale research based on hundreds of teachers across multiple states teaching a variety of subjects and grade levels provided averages for IT ranging between 84% and 94% (Kurz, 2017). At a minimum, we can state that teachers should be able to spend the majority of allocated time on instruction for proposes of high-quality Tier 1 instruction. Looking at content coverage using the same large-scale research, we were able to calculate averages for CC ranging between 54% and 68% (Kurz, 2017). At a minimum, we can make a similar statement, namely, that teachers should be able to cover the majority of subject- and grade-specific content standards for proposes of high-quality Tier 1 instruction.

Assessment of OTL along the quality dimension of the enacted curriculum suggests three sources of evidence of primary prevention: (a) emphasis of higher-order cognitive processes, (b) emphasis of research-based instructional practices, and (c) emphasis of grouping formats other than whole class such as small groups (Kurz, Elliott, Lemons et al., 2014). To develop summative scores, Kurz and colleagues operationalized emphases based on time spent in one of two categories (low-order vs. higher-order cognitive process, non-research-based vs. research-based instructional practices, whole class vs. alternative grouping formats). For the cognitive processes, they used the work by Anderson et al. (2001). For the instructional practices and grouping formats, they focused on practices and formats with empirical support based on meta-analyses (e.g., Elbaum et al., 2000; Gersten et al., 2009). The use of two categories for all three quality-related scores was based on two operating assumptions: (a) teachers who address a range of cognitive processes, instructional practices, and grouping formats during the course of their instruction, and (b) teachers who emphasize higher-order cognitive processes, research-based instructional practices, and alternative grouping formats that improve the quality of students' OTL. Given that the empirical basis for these assumptions is insufficient to single out specific processes, practices, or formats, they argued for a dichotomous grouping. Disaggregated information by each cognitive process, instructional practice, and grouping format is also available.

I contend that the quality index-based cognitive process, instructional practices, and grouping formats remain relevant for purposes of high-quality Tier 1 instruction. But rather than establishing the normative goal of "emphasis" (i.e., majority of time spent in a preferred category), I recommend these quality indices (not their summative scores) be used to operationalize a key characteristic of high-quality Tier 1 instruction noted in the RTI literature: differentiated instruction (e.g., Fuchs et al., 2012). In other words, the use of differentiated instruction represents evidence of primary prevention and is operationalized by the use of different cognitive processes, instructional practices, and grouping formats. The next section provides a brief case example to illustrate some measurement options related to differentiated instruction.

The next critical characteristic of high-quality Tier 1 discussed in the RTI literature that falls under the quality dimensions of the enacted curriculum is the use of instructional accommodations (e.g., Fuchs & Vaughn, 2012; RTI Action Network, n.d.). Instructional accommodations are intended to increase students' access to the enacted curriculum allowing them to learn the same material to the same level of performance as other students in the general education classroom (Ketterlin-Geller & Jamgochian, 2011). More specifically, the teacher should make instructional adaptations to the design and deliver of instruction and associated materials based on presentation, setting, timing/scheduling, or response mode (see Chap. 14 of this volume). This source of evidence of primary prevention could be operationalized based on these adaptation categories and measured via frequency counts using a simple checklist. In fact, Elliott, Kratochwill, and Schulte (1999) developed a detailed assessment accommodations checklist that could be adapted for gathering instructional accommodation evidence.

The final two Tier 1 characteristics that fall under the quality dimensions of the enacted curriculum are the use of universal screening and progress monitoring (Fuchs et al., 2012). As such, high-quality Tier 1 instruction includes brief screening assessments for all students—ideally followed by additional or short-term progress monitoring to confirm risk status and movement in subsequent tiers of prevention (Fuchs & Vaughn, 2012). The Center for Response to Intervention (2014) put forth three criteria for high-quality universal screening:

> (1) screening is conducted for all students (i.e., is universal); (2) procedures are in place to ensure implementation accuracy (i.e., all students are tested, scores are accurate, cut points/decisions are accurate); and (3) a process to screen all students occurs more than once per year (e.g., fall, winter, spring) (p. 1).

For purposes of progress monitoring, teachers should conduct regular assessments to monitor students' academic performance, quantify student rate of improvement or responsiveness to instruction,

Table 9.2 Enacted curriculum dimensions, evidence sources, and operational definitions for high-quality Tier 1 instruction

Enacted curriculum dimension	Evidence of primary prevention	Operational definition
Time	Efficient use of instructional time	Teacher uses the vast majority of allocated class time for instruction
Content	Implementation of a research-based and aligned core program	Teacher fully implements a research-based reading or mathematics program that provides instructional objectives and materials aligned to common core or other state standards
	Comprehensive content coverage	Teacher covers the majority of subject- and grade-specific content standards
Quality	Use of differentiated instruction	Teacher regularly differentiates cognitive process expectations, instructional practices, and grouping formats to address individual needs based on students' background knowledge, readiness for the instructional objective, language skills and abilities, preferences, and interests
	Use of instructional accommodations	Teachers regularly make adaptations to the design and deliver of instruction and associated materials based on presentation, setting, timing or scheduling, and response mode
	Use of progress monitoring	Teachers regularly assess students to monitor academic performance, quantify student rate of improvement or responsiveness to instruction, and evaluate the effectiveness of instruction
	Use of universal screening	Teacher regularly conducts brief screening assessments with all students followed by additional testing or short-term progress monitoring to confirm students' risk status and need for additional interventions

and evaluate the effectiveness of instruction (Fuchs & Vaughn, 2012). The Center for Response to Intervention (2014) also developed two criteria for high-quality progress monitoring:

> (1) progress monitoring occurs at least monthly for students receiving secondary-level intervention and at least weekly for students receiving intensive intervention; and (2) procedures are in place to ensure implementation accuracy (i.e., appropriate students are tested, scores are accurate, decision-making rules are applied consistently). (p. 2).

At this point, I have identified seven sources of evidence for primary prevention that fall along the three dimensions of the enacted curriculum: (a) efficient use of instructional time, (b) implementation of a research-based and aligned core program, (c) comprehensive content coverage, (d) use of differentiated instruction, (e) use of instructional accommodations, (f) use of progress monitoring, and (g) use of universal screening. Table 9.2 includes these evidence sources by each enacted curriculum dimension along with their respective operational definitions.

The operational definitions listed in the table, however, still fall short of setting actual quality standards for high-quality Tier 1 instruction. That is, the operational definitions currently contain qualitative qualifiers (e.g., majority, fully, regularly) rather than quantitative ones. For two dimensions—time and content—I provided quantitative ranges, because I was able to draw from several descriptive OTL studies that can be used to establish some initial base rates. More research is needed, specifically, on base rates regarding the use of differentiated instruction and instructional accommodations. Some suggested frequencies that can quantitatively define "regular" progress monitoring and universal screening are actually available. The Center for Response to Intervention (2014) suggested three universal screenings per year (i.e., fall, winter, spring), and Fuchs and Fuchs (2006) suggested an ideal progress monitoring frequency of every 2 weeks. Next, I provide a brief case example using MyiLOGS and its newly developed lesson planner, easyCBM, and the *Checklist of Learning and Assessment Adjustments for Students* (CLASS; Davies, Elliott, & Cumming, 2016) to show how data on the seven evidence sources can be collected.

Case Example

To illustrate how Tier 1 data collection can occur, I discuss a hypothetical fifth-grade English Language Arts (ELA) classroom. The focus of this brief example is *how* these data can be collected using existing tools. The ELA classroom consists of 28 fifth-grade students who are currently in their third quarter working on a unit that explores examining two texts with similar themes. The units are based on a core reading curriculum. The K-8 curriculum was adopted by the district based on its research-based elements for instructional content (i.e., phonemic awareness, phonics, fluency, vocabulary, comprehension) and instructional design (i.e., explicit instructional strategies, coordinated instructional sequences, ample practice opportunities, aligned student materials). In addition, all curriculum units are aligned to the Common Core State Standards (CCSS). The current unit, which features five mini lessons, addresses four CCSS standards (i.e., RL5.2, RL.5.2, RL.5.3, RL.5.9). The first two standards, RL.5.2 and RL5.3, focus on summarizing texts based on their themes and comparing/contrasting parts of a story such as characters, settings, and events. The teacher intends to cover the first two standards during the first half of the week. The ELA block typically lasts 75 min with Wednesday being an early release day, which shortens the lesson to 45 min. To document evidence of high-quality Tier 1 instruction, the teacher plans and monitors her lessons via MyiLOGS (Kurz & Elliott, 2012), an online teacher log and its newly developed lesson planning feature.

The MyiLOGS lesson planner provides teachers with a monthly instructional calendar that includes an expandable sidebar, which lists all intended objectives for a class. Teachers drag and drop planned objectives that are to be the focus of upcoming lessons onto the respective calendar days. After implementing their lessons, teachers are required to confirm enacted objectives, instructional time dedicated to each objective, and any time not available for instruction at the class level. Figure 9.4 shows an excerpt from the teacher's instructional calendar in MyiLOGS.

Her calendar shows that she intends to cover the current unit on parallel texts and, more importantly, the two content standards RL.5.2 and RL5.3. MyiLOGS also allows her to enter any intended custom objectives under the green "+" sign. She anticipates about 8 min of non-instructional time on Monday and Tuesday and about 5 min of non-instructional time for her early release day. Each day also features a notepad icon, which brings the user to the actual lesson plan. Figure 9.5 shows an excerpt from the teacher's lesson planner in MyiLOGS.

The figure shows the content to be covered on the top left under *Standards* and then several options for three additional lesson elements: *Activities*, *Practices*, and the *Class Roster*. The content standards, student activities, and instructional practices can be dragged and dropped on

Fig. 9.4 MyiLOGS instructional calendar excerpt

Fig. 9.5 MyiLOGS lesson planner excerpt

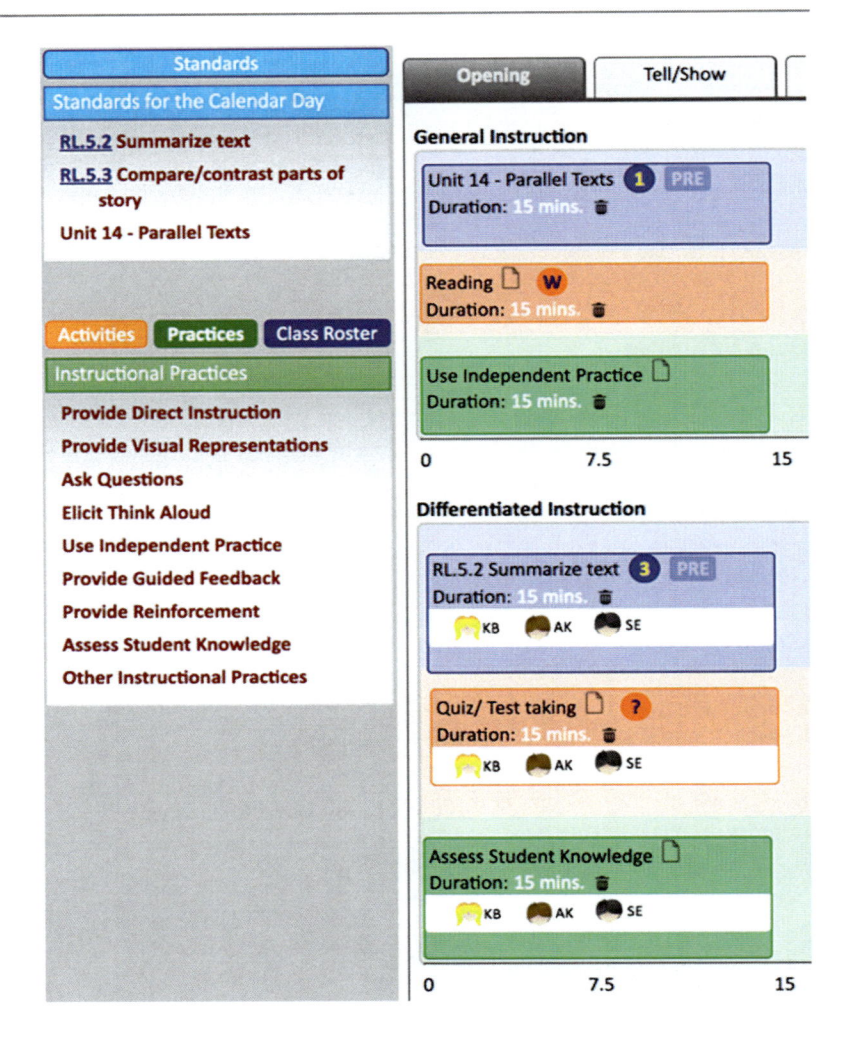

the right-hand side under either *General Instruction* or *Differentiated Instruction*. Several tabs are available for various lesson segments such as *Opening* or *Tell/Show*. These tabs can be customized to whatever lesson plan formats and segments are desired by different school leaders or district requirements. Both spaces allow standards, activities, and practices boxes to be sized according to the intended time frame. In this case, she begins the lesson with 15 min of independent reading on Unit 14, which covers excerpts from "White Socks Only" and "The Story of Ruby Bridges." The Standards box further contains a DOK level indicator, which is focused on recall and reproduction (i.e., Level 1). The Activity box indicates "W" for whole class instruction. All three boxes further contain a text editor, where the details of the lesson plan can be captured. Three students have advanced in their readings during the previous lesson. She decides to move these students directly into a small group assessing their knowledge of theme based on details from both parallel texts. Given that the questions on the quiz require students to think deeply about text details including analysis and judgment, she assigns a Level 3 DOK (i.e., short-term strategic thinking). As can be seen, this online teacher log can be used to capture the scope and sequence of day-to-day instruction.

MyiLOGS further calculates a variety of OTL scores and descriptive information based on the data logged via the lesson planner. The teacher can review over a dozen figures that detail her use of instructional time, implementation of the core program, content coverage, as well as details about her differentiated instruction. Given that allocated time is logged on a daily basis, IT can be calculated accurately. For her class, her average IT score across 107 school days is 89%. Logged time per standard, student activity, and instructional practice further permits the calculation of several additional OTL scores. During 107 school days, for example, she has covered 14 out of 21 units (66%) in the core curriculum with a CC score of 57% for her cumulative coverage of the CCSS reading and writing standards. The current evidence on time and content thus indicates that she is (a) using the majority of her allocated class time for instruction, (b) on track for covering most core curriculum units, and (c) on track for covering the majority of subject- and grade-specific content standards. To better target the remaining CCSS standards, she reviews the MyiLOGS content coverage bar chart that delineates time emphases along all intended standards for the subject and grade in question. Figure 9.6 shows an excerpt of the bar chart, which reveals several content standards yet to be covered.

The newly developed MyiLOGS lesson planner further permits several scores related to differentiated instruction. In addition to MyiLOGS's previous CP, IP, and GF (summary) scores, the lesson planner scores provide information about, and comparisons between, general instruction and any instructional changes logged under the differentiated instruction track. Based on her 107 logged days, for example, she has implemented differentiated instruction (for at least part of her lesson) on 58 days (54%). Based on her logged general instruction time (GET), she specifically provided differentiated instruction during 38% of her GET. Given that the lesson planner requires the assignment of differentiated instruction based on students using the class roster, she further knows that 100% of her students have received some differentiated instruction during the past 107 school days. MyiLOGS provides additional charts that detail the type of instructional differences based on the following categories: (a) content standards, (b) DOK levels, (c) student activities, (d) grouping formats, and (e) instructional practices. The charts are descriptive in as so far as the only document instructional differences. To determine the adequacy of the match between these instructional differences and students' individual needs would require detailed information about students' background knowledge, readiness for the instructional objective, language skills and abilities, preferences, and interests. At a minimum, however, the teacher has

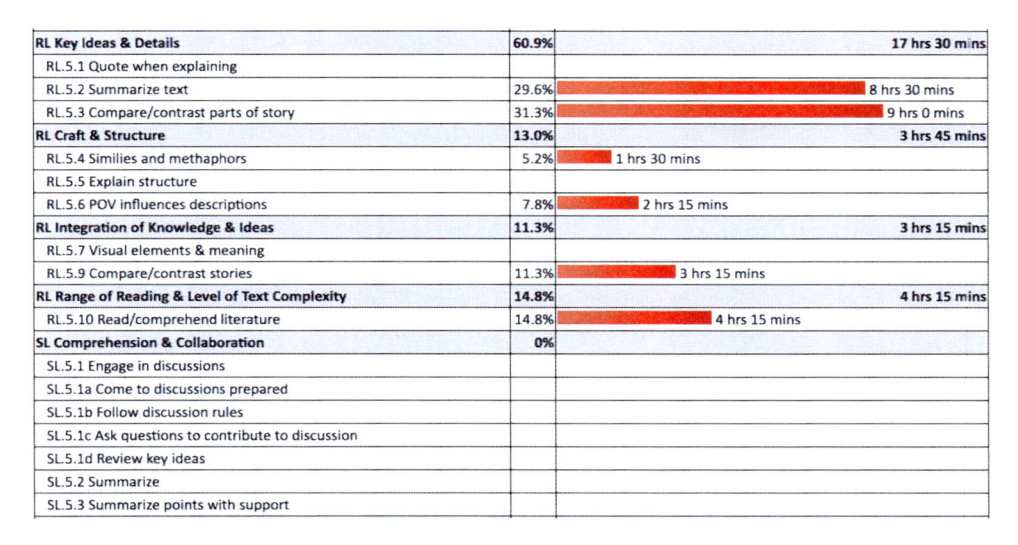

RL Key Ideas & Details	60.9%	17 hrs 30 mins
RL.5.1 Quote when explaining		
RL.5.2 Summarize text	29.6%	8 hrs 30 mins
RL.5.3 Compare/contrast parts of story	31.3%	9 hrs 0 mins
RL Craft & Structure	13.0%	3 hrs 45 mins
RL.5.4 Similies and methaphors	5.2%	1 hrs 30 mins
RL.5.5 Explain structure		
RL.5.6 POV influences descriptions	7.8%	2 hrs 15 mins
RL Integration of Knowledge & Ideas	11.3%	3 hrs 15 mins
RL.5.7 Visual elements & meaning		
RL.5.9 Compare/contrast stories	11.3%	3 hrs 15 mins
RL Range of Reading & Level of Text Complexity	14.8%	4 hrs 15 mins
RL.5.10 Read/comprehend literature	14.8%	4 hrs 15 mins
SL Comprehension & Collaboration	0%	
SL.5.1 Engage in discussions		
SL.5.1a Come to discussions prepared		
SL.5.1b Follow discussion rules		
SL.5.1c Ask questions to contribute to discussion		
SL.5.1d Review key ideas		
SL.5.2 Summarize		
SL.5.3 Summarize points with support		

Fig. 9.6 Excerpt from the MyiLOGS content coverage bar chart

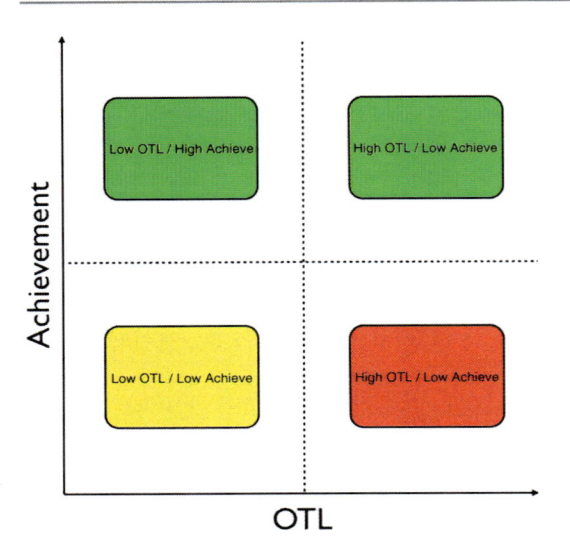

Fig. 9.7 Achievement/OTL chart for instructional priority setting

evidence that she regularly differentiates content standards, DOK levels, student activities, grouping formats, and instructional practices.

MyiLOGS can further provide integration with a curriculum-based measurement called easyCBM to schedule regular progress monitoring and review instructional data alongside student achievement. As such, she knows that she schedules and administers easyCBM probes every 2 weeks to monitor students' academic performance, quantify their rate of improvement or responsiveness to instruction, and evaluate the effectiveness of instruction. In addition, she regularly reviews easyCBM data alongside her content coverage. After each probe, for example, she examines students' achievement data by content domains such as *Key Ideas & Details*, *Craft & Structure*, and *Integration of Knowledge & Ideas* alongside her content coverage as displayed in Fig. 9.6. She therefore knows what content standards were emphasized and the extent to which her students answered items in that domain correctly. Based on the excerpt shown in Fig. 9.6, she knows that she did not yet cover the standards under *Comprehension & Collaboration*. To adjust her scope and sequence of instruction, she follows a simple decision-making chart.

Figure 9.7 shows how she prioritizes content areas. The y-axis refers to student achievement on her curriculum-based measurement. The higher the class or student performance is, the further along the placement on the y-axis. The x-axis refers to OTL for a class or student. The figure highlights two quadrants in green. Both quadrants indicate high student achievement either in the context of high OTL (e.g., extensive content coverage, high use of instructional time) or in the absence of OTL (i.e., student prior knowledge). Either way, these content domains for which we have evidence of high student achievement are not a priority for immediate teaching purposes. Low student achievement, however, prompts her to review OTL data, especially in the context of high OTL.

To gather evidence on instructional accommodations, the MyiLOGS lesson planner further provides the option to complete the CLASS (Davies et al., 2016). The CLASS allows her to log 67 accommodations grouped into eight categories: (a) motivation, (b) scheduling, (c) setting, (d) assistance with directions, (e) assistance prior to testing, (f) assistance during learning or assessment, (g) equipment or assistive technology, and (h) changes in format. These adjustments have their basis in educational instruction, testing standards, and accessible educational practices. Figure 9.8 shows an excerpt from the CLASS, which allows her to record instructional accommodations on an individual basis. While current technology integration does not permit data aggregation such as the percentage of students receiving accommodations or information about the types of accommodations used, the teacher is at least able to document her efforts along key accommodation categories.

As illustrated throughout this case, it is currently possible to document all necessary evidence sources for high-quality Tier 1 instruction with relatively few tools. Further technology integration has the potential to make these efforts even more efficient. As a concluding step, I will summarize my argument and provide some key points for a future research agenda.

Fig. 9.8 Excerpt from the checklist of learning and assessment adjustments for students

Assistance During Learning or Assessment
33 Arrange for a special education teacher or other qualified person to manage learning or assessment
34 Read learning or assessment expectations and content to student
35 Sign learning or assessment expectations and content to student
36 Restate the learning or assessment task with more appropriate vocabulary or define unknown vocabulary
37 Turn pages for the student in learning or assessment
38 Record student's responses (in writing or by audio recording)
39 Provide spelling assistance, where appropriate, during learning or assessment
40 Have teacher sit near student during learning or assessment
41 Use test form with vertically arranged multiple-choice items that have an answer circle to the left of each choice
42 Provide cues such as stop signs or arrows on learning activities or the test form
43 Allow responses to be marked in the learning or test book rather than on a separate answer document
44 Assist the student in tracking learning or test items by pointing to or by placing student's finger on item

Tier 1 OTL: Why, How, and What For?

In most cases, primary prevention at Tier 1 is simply assumed to occur. That is, positive screening results are assumed to represent a student's inadequate response to high-quality Tier 1 instruction. Instructional data about a teacher's enacted curriculum are typically not available and therefore not considered in the interpretation of screening results or subsequent progress monitoring based on formative assessments. In other words, we do not know about the extent to which Tier 1 instruction was actually implemented with high quality. This lack of instructional data undermines the validity of critical test score inferences (i.e., a student's inadequate response to high-quality Tier 1 instruction) and subsequent RTI decisions (i.e., a student's need for additional intervention). Confronting this known unknown is thus essential to maintaining the integrity of RTI at its most fundamental level, namely, ensuring high-quality Tier 1 instruction that can support the vast majority of students.

In recent years, researchers have provided more nuanced descriptions of Tier 1 instruction with the intent to better define characteristics of high quality. The concept of OTL has been used by researchers to examine classroom instruction based on instructional indices along all three dimensions of enacted curriculum—time, content, and quality. In this chapter, I argued that these empirically validated indices and their respective measurement through teacher logs are key to confronting the known unknown of Tier 1 instruction. As such, I used the enacted curriculum (see Fig. 9.1) as an organizing framework to highlight how OTL addresses several, previously unaccounted characteristics of high-quality Tier 1 instruction (i.e., instructional time, content coverage) and to reveal several shortcomings of OTL for capturing high-quality Tier 1 instruction (i.e., core program, differentiated instruction, instructional accommodations, universal screening, progress monitoring). These efforts culminated in seven sources of evidence for high-quality Tier 1 instruction (see Table 9.2) that collectively represent Tier 1 OTL. I further provided operational definitions for each evidence source drawing from previously defined OTL scores. In the case of differentiated instruction, I used multiple OTL scores (i.e., cognitive processes, instructional practices, and grouping formats) to better operationalize measurable differences. I also provided a case example to illustrate how currently available tools can be used to gather evidence for high-quality Tier 1 instruction.

Despite this progress, one may still wonder as to why the concept of OTL should be expanded and refined to represent Tier 1 OTL. First, we need to remember that the concept of OTL originated with the intent to better understand student learning, specifically, student learning as a function of classroom instruction, which is largely under the control of the teacher. Over the years, OTL was used to define and measure the "what" and "how" of classroom instruction. This led to the understanding of OTL as a teacher effect, which provides students access to the intended curriculum through the teacher's enacted curriculum. Much of the current volume, however, argues for a shift from *access to* toward *accessibility of* instruction and testing. As such, we should ensure that any conceptual definition of OTL should not only address access to intended curriculum but also accessibility of the enacted curriculum. The inclusion of differentiated instruction and instructional accommodations thus clarifies that students' opportunity to learn also depends on the extent to which the enacted curriculum accounts for their background knowledge, readiness for the instructional objective, language skills, abilities, preferences, and interest. This necessitates not only changes to general instruction using different practices, cognitive processes, grouping formats, presentations, materials, settings, schedules, or response modes but also changes based on assessment results via screening and progress monitoring.

Evidence for high-quality Tier 1 instruction, while necessary for accurate test score interpretations, nonetheless holds its greatest potential for purposes of instructional improvement of the enacted curriculum. Teachers, especially early career teachers, are often asked to become self-reflective practitioners. Self-reflection, however, requires a framework. We need to know what to reflect upon, and, ideally, we have quantitative information to support our subsequent decisions. Throughout this chapter, I have used the concept of OTL to develop such a framework.

In addition, I have incorporated what is known about high-quality Tier 1 instruction. The proposed evidence sources can guide teachers' instructional improvement efforts and lead to a more seamless integration of data about instruction and student achievement.

Future research and development efforts must address the feasibility and adequacy challenges of Tier 1 OTL. The feasibility challenge stems for the additional time and effort needed to document the various evidence sources. While measurement options are indeed available, they are not well integrated and, in some instances, may even require duplicate efforts (i.e., submitting a paper lesson plan and then logging the lesson plan via the teacher log). Without offering teachers a value-added proposition such as saving time on activities they already do without adding new tasks, it is unlikely that teachers will find the extra time and effort to engage meaningfully with Tier 1 data. Integration of the various tools and clear ways to replace already required tasks (i.e., print options for the lesson planner that provides the format of a traditional lesson plan) is the first step to overcoming the feasibility challenge. The second step is to support teachers in their self-reflection and instructional decision-making. Instructional coaching represents a viable strategy for assisting teachers in these efforts (Joyce & Showers, 2002; Kurz, Reddy, & Glover, 2017). Tier 1 OTL data are complex and require careful decision-making, especially when student background characteristics come into play for purposes of instructional accommodations. Instructional coaches can provide the intensive, job-embedded professional development necessary to use Tier 1 OTL data in the context of goal setting and Tier 1 instructional changes.

To address the adequacy challenge, future research and development efforts must deploy the integrated measurement tools at scale to establish base rates for the various evidence source of Tier 1 OTL across a variety of subjects, grades, as well as additional teacher, student, and school characteristics. Standard-setting methods such as the iterative judgmental policy capturing (JPC) performance-standard-setting procedure could then be used for the multidimensional score profiles (Kurz, Reichenberg, & Yel, 2017) to establish overall standards of quality provision (i.e., ineffective, partially effective, effective, highly effective). At the very least, base rates could be used to translate the qualitative qualifiers (e.g., majority, fully, regularly) of the current Tier 1 OTL definitions into quantitative ones.

Given that high-quality Tier 1 instruction is intended to serve as the primary prevention for the vast majority of the over 50 million K-12 students, the importance of the outlined Tier 1 OTL efforts can hardly be overstated. The current framework provides an initial step. And last but not least, the newly proposed concept of Tier 1 OTL also initiates a fundamental shift in the conceptualization of OTL from addressing students' access to the enacted curriculum toward OTL ensuring the accessibility of the enacted curriculum.

References

Al Otaiba, S., Connor, C. M., Folsom, J. S., Wanzek, J., Greulich, L., Schatschneider, C., & Wagner, R. K. (2014). To wait in tier 1 or intervene immediately. *Exceptional Children, 81*(1), 11–27. https://doi.org/10.1177/0014402914532234

American Educational Research Association, American Psychological Association, & National Council on Measurement in Education. (2014). *Standards for educational and psychological testing.* Washington, DC: Author.

Anderson, L. W. (1986). Opportunity to learn. In T. Husén & T. Postlethwaite (Eds.), *International encyclopedia of education: Research and studies.* Oxford, UK: Pergamon.

Anderson, L. W. (2002). Curricular alignment: A re-examination. *Theory Into Practice, 41*(4), 255–260.

Anderson, L. W., Krathwohl, D. R., Airasian, P. W., Cruikshank, K. A., Mayer, R. E., Pintrich, P. R., … Wittrock, M. C. (2001). *A taxonomy for learning, teaching, and assessing: A revision of Bloom's taxonomy of educational objectives.* New York, NY: Longman.

Armbuster, B. B., Stevens, R. J., & Rosenshine, B. (1977). *Analyzing content coverage and emphasis: A study of three curricula and two tests (Technical Report No. 26).* Urbana, IL: Center for the Study of Reading, University of Illinois.

Berkovits, I., Reddy, L. A., & Kurz, A. (2017). Teacher log of students' opportunity to learn and classroom observation: A preliminary investigation of convergence. Manuscript submitted for publication.

Bloom, B. S. (1976). *Human characteristics and school learning.* New York, NY: McGraw-Hill.

Borg, W. R. (1979). Teacher coverage of academic content and pupil achievement. *Journal of Educational Psychology, 71*(5), 635–645.

Borg, W. R. (1980). Time and school learning. In C. Denham & A. Lieberman (Eds.), *Time to learn* (pp. 33–72). Washington, DC: National Institute of Education.

Bradley, R., Danielson, L., & Doolittle, J. (2007). Responsiveness to intervention: 1997 to 2007. *Teaching Exceptional Children, 39*(5), 8–12.

Brophy, J., & Good, T. L. (1986). Teacher behavior and student achievement. In M. C. Wittrock (Ed.), *Handbook of research on teaching* (3rd ed., pp. 328–375). New York, NY: Macmillian.

Carroll, J. B. (1963). A model of school learning. *Teachers College Record, 64*(8), 723–733.

Carroll, J. B. (1989). The Carroll model: A 25-year retrospective and prospective view. *Educational Researcher, 18*(1), 26–31.

Chard, D. J. (2012). Systems impact: Issues and trends in improving school outcomes for all learners through multitier instructional models. *Intervention in School and Clinic, 48*(4), 198–202. https://doi.org/10.1177/1053451212462876

Comber, L. C., & Keeves, J. P. (1973). *Science education in nineteen countries.* New York, NY: Halsted Press.

Compton, D. L., Gilbert, J. K., Jenkins, J. R., Fuchs, D., Fuchs, L. S., Cho, E., et al. (2012). Accelerating chronically unresponsive children to tier 3 instruction: What level of data is necessary to ensure selection accuracy? *Journal of Learning Disabilities, 45*(3), 204–216. https://doi.org/10.1177/0022219412442151

Cook, B. G., & Odom, S. L. (2013). Evidence-based practices and implementation science in special education. *Exceptional Children, 79*(2), 135–144.

Davies, M. D., Elliott, S. N., & Cumming, J. (2016). Documenting support needs and adjustment gaps for students with disabilities: Teacher practices in Australian classrooms and on national tests. *International Journal of Inclusive Education, 20*(12), 1252–1269. https://doi.org/10.1080/13603116.2016.1159256

Denham, C., & Lieberman, A. (Eds.). (1980). *Time to learn.* Washington, DC: National Institute for Education.

Elbaum, B., Vaughn, S., Hughes, M. T., Moody, S. W., & Schumm, J. S. (2000). How reading outcomes for students with learning disabilities are related to instructional grouping formats: A meta-analytic review. In R. Gersten, E. P. Schiller, & S. Vaughn (Eds.), *Contemporary special education research: Syntheses of the knowledge base on critical instructional issues* (pp. 105–135). Mahwah, NJ: Lawrence Erlbaum.

Elliott, S. N., Kratochwill, T. R., & Schulte, A. G. (1999). *Assessment accommodations guide.* Monterey, CA: CTB/McGraw Hill.

Fisher, C. W., & Berliner, D. C. (Eds.). (1985). *Perspectives on instructional time.* New York, NY: Longman.

Fuchs, D., & Fuchs, L. S. (2006). Introduction to response to intervention: What, why, and how valid is it? *Reading Research Quarterly.* https://doi.org/10.1598/RRQ.41.1.4

Fuchs, D., Fuchs, L. S., & Compton, D. L. (2012). Smart RTI: A next-generation approach to multilevel prevention. *Exceptional Children, 78*(3), 263–279.

Fuchs, D., Fuchs, L. S., Mathes, P., & Simmons, D. (1997). Peer-assisted learning strategies: Making classrooms more responsive to student diversity. *American Educational Research Journal, 34*, 174–206.

Fuchs, L. S., & Vaughn, S. (2012). Responsiveness-to-intervention: A decade later. *Journal of Learning Disabilities, 45*(3), 195–203. https://doi.org/10.1177/0022219412442150

Gagné, R. M. (1977). *The conditions of learning*. Chicago, IL: Holt, Rinehart & Winston.

Gamoran, A., Porter, A. C., Smithson, J., & White, P. A. (1997). Upgrading high school mathematics instruction: Improving learning opportunities for low-achieving, low-income youth. *Educational Evaluation and Policy Analysis, 19*(4), 325–338.

Gandhi, A. G., Holdheide, L., Zumeta, R., & Danielson, L. (2016, February). *Understanding and operationalizing evidence-based practices within multi-tiered systems of support*. Paper presented at the annual Pacific Research Coast Conference, San Diego, CA.

Gersten, R., Chard, D. J., Jayanthi, M., Baker, S. K., Morphy, P., & Flojo, J. (2009). Mathematics instruction for students with learning disabilities: A meta-analysis of instructional components. *Review of Educational Research, 79*(3), 1202–1242.

Gettinger, M., & Seibert, J. K. (2002). Best practices in increasing academic learning time. In A. Thomas & J. Grimes (Eds.), *Best practices in school psychology IV* (Vol. 1, pp. 773–787). Bethesda, MD: National Association of School Psychologists.

Gilbert, J. K., Compton, D. L., Fuchs, D., Fuchs, L. S., Bouton, B., Barquero, L. A., & Cho, E. (2013). Efficacy of a first-grade responsiveness-to-intervention prevention model for struggling readers. *Reading Research Quarterly, 48*(2), 135–154. https://doi.org/10.1002/rrq.45

Harnischfeger, A., & Wiley, D. E. (1976). The teaching–learning process in elementary schools: A synoptic view. *Curriculum Inquiry, 6*(1), 5–43.

Heafner, T. L., & Fitchett, P. G. (2015). An opportunity to learn US history: What NAEP data suggest regarding the opportunity gap. *The High School Journal, 98*(3), 226–249. https://doi.org/10.1353/hsj.2015.0006

Herman, J. L., Klein, D. C., & Abedi, J. (2000). Assessing students' opportunity to learn: Teacher and student perspectives. *Educational Measurement: Issues and Practice, 19*(4), 16–24.

Holdheide, L. (2016, February). *Tier 1 instructional practice: Mixed messages and missed opportunities*. Paper presented at the annual Pacific Research Coast Conference, San Diego, CA.

Husén, T. (1967). *International study of achievement in mathematics: A comparison of twelve countries*. New York, NY: John Wiley & Sons.

Jenkins, J. R., & Pany, D. (1978). Curriculum biases in reading achievement tests. *Journal of Reading Behavior, 10*(4), 345–357.

Joyce, B., & Showers, B. (2002). *Student achievement through staff development*. Alexandria, VA: Association for Supervision and Curriculum Development.

Karger, J. (2005). *Access to the general education curriculum for students with disabilities: A discussion of the interrelationship between IDEA and NCLB*. Wakefield, MA: National Center on Accessing the General Curriculum.

Ketterlin-Geller, L. R., & Jamgochian, E. M. (2011). Accommodations and modifications that support accessible instruction. In S. N. Elliott, R. J. Kettler, P. A. Beddow, & A. Kurz (Eds.), *The handbook of accessible achievement tests for all students: Bridging the gaps between research, practice, and policy*. New York, NY: Springer.

Kurz, A. (2011). Access to what should be taught and will be tested: Students' opportunity to learn the intended curriculum. In S. N. Elliott, R. J. Kettler, P. A. Beddow, & A. Kurz (Eds.), *Handbook of accessible achievement tests for all students: Bridging the gaps between research, practice, and policy* (pp. 99–129). New York, NY: Springer.

Kurz, A. (2016, February). *Measuring Opportunity to learn through a teacher log*. Paper presented at the annual Pacific Research Coast Conference, San Diego, CA.

Kurz, A. (2017, February). *Educational redemption and instructional coaching*. Paper presented at the annual Pacific Research Coast Conference, San Diego, CA.

Kurz, A., & Elliott, S. N. (2011). Overcoming barriers to access for students with disabilities: Testing accommodations and beyond. In M. Russell & M. Kavanaugh (Eds.), *Assessing students in the margins: Challenges, strategies, and techniques* (pp. 31–58). Charlotte, NC: Information Age Publishing.

Kurz, A., & Elliott, S. N. (2012). *MyiLOGS: My instructional learning opportunities guidance system (Version 2) [Software and training videos]*. Tempe, AZ: Arizona State University.

Kurz, A., Elliott, S. N., Kettler, R. J., & Yel, N. (2014). Assessing students' opportunity to learn the intended curriculum using an online teacher log: Initial validity evidence. *Educational Assessment, 19*(3), 159–184. https://doi.org/10.1080/10627197.2014.934606

Kurz, A., Elliott, S. N., Lemons, C. J., Zigmond, N., Kloo, A., & Kettler, R. J. (2014). Assessing opportunity-to-learn for students with and without disabilities. *Assessment for Effective Intervention, 40*(1), 24–39. https://doi.org/10.1177/1534508414522685

Kurz, A., Elliott, S. N., & Roach, A. T. (2015). Addressing the missing instructional data problem: Using a teacher log to document tier 1 instruction. *Remedial and Special Education, 36*(6), 361–373. https://doi.org/10.1177/0741932514567365

Kurz, A., Reddy, L. A., & Glover, T. A. (2017). A multidisciplinary framework of instructional coaching. *Theory Into Practice, 56*, 66–77. https://doi.org/10.1080/00405841.2016.1260404

Kurz, A., Reichenberg, R., & Yel, N. (2017). *Setting opportunity-to-learn standards for effective teaching*. Manuscript submitted for publication.

Marzano, R. J. (2000). *A new era of school reform: Going where the research takes us (REL no. #RJ96006101)*.

Aurora, CO: Mid-continent Research for Education and Learning.

Mayer, D. P. (1999). Measuring instructional practice: Can policymakers trust survey data? *Educational Evaluation and Policy Analysis, 21*(1), 29–45.

Mayer, R. E. (2008). *Learning and instruction* (2nd ed.). Upper Saddle River, NJ: Pearson.

McDonnell, L. M. (1995). Opportunity to learn as a research concept and a policy instrument. *Educational Evaluation and Policy Analysis, 17*(3), 305–322.

Metcalf, T. (2012). *What's your plan? Accurate decision making within a multi-tier system of supports: Critical areas in Tier 1*. Retrieved from http://www.rtinetwork.org/essential/tieredinstruction/tier1/accurate-decision-making-within-a-multi-tier-system-of-supports-critical-areas-in-tier-1

Porter, A. C. (2002). Measuring the content of instruction: Uses in research and practice. *Educational Researcher, 31*(7), 3–14.

Porter, A. C., Kirst, M. W., Osthoff, E. J., Smithson, J. L., & Schneider, S. A. (1993). *Reform up close: An analysis of high school mathematics and science classrooms (final report)*. Madison, WI: University of Wisconsin, Wisconsin Center for Education Research.

Porter, A. C., & Smithson, J. L. (2001). Are content standards being implemented in the classroom? A methodology and some tentative answers. In S. Fuhrman (Ed.), *From the Capitol to the classroom: Standards-based reform in the states. One hundredth yearbook of the National Society for the Study of Education* (pp. 60–80). Chicago, IL: University of Chicago Press.

Porter, A. C., Schmidt, W. H., Floden, R. E., & Freeman, D. J. (1978). *Impact on what? The importance of content covered (Research Series No. 2)*. East Lansing, MI: Michigan State University, Institute for Research on Teaching.

Reddy, L. A., Fabiano, G. A., & Jimerson, S. R. (2013). Assessment of general education teachers' Tier 1 classroom practices: Contemporary science, practice, and policy. *School Psychology Quarterly, 28*(4), 273–276. https://doi.org/10.1037/spq0000047

Roach, A. T., Kurz, A., & Elliott, S. N. (2015). Facilitating opportunity to learn for students with disabilities with instructional feedback data. *Preventing School Failure, 59*(3), 168–178. https://doi.org/10.1080/1045988X.2014.901288

Rowan, B., Camburn, E., & Correnti, R. (2004). Using teacher logs to measure the enacted curriculum: A study of literacy teaching in third-grade classrooms. *The Elementary School Journal, 105*(1), 75–101.

Rowan, B., & Correnti, R. (2009). Studying reading instruction with teacher logs: Lessons from the study of instructional improvement. *Educational Researcher, 38*(2), 120–131.

RTI Action Network, http://www.rtinetwork.org.

Scheerens, J., & Bosker, R. (1997). *The foundations of educational effectiveness*. New York, NY: Pergamon.

Schmidt, W. H., & Burroughs, N. A. (2013). Opening the black box: Prospects for using international large-scale assessments to explore classroom effects. *Research in Comparative and International Education, 8*(3), 236–212. https://doi.org/10.2304/rcie.2013.8.3.236

Schmidt, W. H., Burroughs, N. A., Zoido, P., & Houang, R. T. (2015). The role of schooling in perpetuating educational inequality: An international perspective. *Educational Researcher, 44*(7), 371–386. https://doi.org/10.3102/0013189X15603982

Schmidt, W. H., McKnight, C. C., Houang, R. T., Wang, H. A., Wiley, D. E., Cogan, L. S., & Wolfe, R. G. (2001). *Why Schools Matter: a cross-national comparison of curriculum and learning*. San Francisco, CA: Jossey-Bass.

Schmidt, W. H., McKnight, C. C., Valverde, G. A., Houang, R. T., & Wiley, D. E. (1997). *Many visions, many aims volume 1: A cross-national investigation of curricular intentions in school mathematics*. Dordrecht, Netherlands: Kluwer Academic.

Torgesen, J. K. (2009). The response to intervention instructional model: Some outcomes from a large-scale implementation in Reading First schools. *Child Development Perspectives, 3*, 38–40.

VanDerHeyden, A. M., Witt, J. C., & Gilbertson, D. (2007). A multi-year evaluation of the effects of a response to intervention (RTI) model on identification of children for special education. *Journal of School Psychology, 45*, 225–256.

Vannest, K. J., & Parker, R. I. (2010). Measuring time: The stability of special education teacher time use. *Journal of Special Education, 44*(2), 94–106.

Vaughn, S., Gersten, R., & Chard, D. J. (2000). The underlying message in LD intervention research: Findings from research syntheses. *Exceptional Children, 67*(1), 99–114.

Vaughn, S., Wanzek, J., Murray, C. S., Scammacca, N., Linan-Thompson, S., & Woodruff, A. L. (2009). Response to early reading interventions: Examining higher responders and lower responders. *Exceptional Children, 75*, 165–183.

Walberg, H. J. (1980). A psychological theory of educational productivity. In F. H. Farley & N. Gordon (Eds.), *Psychology and education* (pp. 81–110). Berkeley, CA: McCutchan.

Walberg, H. J. (1986). Syntheses of research on teaching. In M. C. Wittrock (Ed.), *Handbook of research on teaching* (3rd ed., pp. 214–229). New York, NY: Macmillian Publishing Company.

Walberg, H. J. (1988). Synthesis of research on time and learning. *Educational Leadership, 45*(6), 76–85.

Wang, J. (1998). Opportunity to learn: The impacts and policy implications. *Educational Evaluation and Policy Analysis, 20*(3), 137–156.

Wanzek, J., & Vaughn, S. (2010). Is a three-tier reading intervention model associated with reduced placement in special education? *Remedial and Special Education, 32*(2), 167–175.

Webb, N. L. (1997). *Criteria for alignment of expectations and assessments in mathematics and science education (NISE Research Monograph No. 6)*. Madison, WI: University of Wisconsin-Madison, National Institute for Science Education.

Webb, N. L. (2006). Identifying content for student achievement tests. In S. M. Downing & T. M. Haladyna (Eds.), *Handbook of test development* (pp. 155–180). Mahwah, NJ: Lawrence Erlbaum.

Winfield, L. F. (1993). Investigating test content and curriculum content overlap to assess opportunity to learn. *The Journal of Negro Education*, *62*(3), 288–310.

Response-to-Intervention Models and Access to Services for All Students

Todd A. Glover

Decades of federal school reform initiatives have drawn attention to the importance of systematically identifying students' needs and using data to guide decisions about the application of practices with demonstrated efficacy for enhancing learning and behavior (e.g., No Child Left Behind Act, 2001; Individuals with Disabilities Improvement Act, 2004; Every Student Succeeds Act, 2015). During this time, response-to-intervention (RTI) service delivery models have increased in popularity in schools as a means of providing a continuum of supports for all students. By emphasizing early screening of students, the provision of multi-tiered instructional supports, and regular monitoring of progress to identify adjustments to improve intervention effectiveness, RTI service delivery models are proactive in addressing students' needs. They afford significant advantages over traditional "wait to fail" approaches to supporting students with significant difficulties or disabilities, which involved identifying student performance gaps after extended periods of insufficient instruction, often withholding intervention until a discrepancy in students' IQ and achievement could be demonstrated (Fletcher, Coulter, Reschly, & Vaughn, 2004).

Although RTI service delivery models hold great promise with respect to increasing students' access to appropriate instructional practices, they are rarely implemented with the degree of fidelity or explicitness in instructional approach required to ensure that all students receive the support that they need (e.g., Glover, 2017; Glover & DiPerna, 2007). The purpose of this chapter is to introduce RTI service delivery components and organizational structures required to promote all students' access to and participation in practices that allow them to excel in school. The chapter concludes with a discussion of (a) the state of relevant research and (b) evidence-based resources for guiding RTI service delivery that is responsive and accessible to all students.

Service Delivery Components that Promote Accessibility

Within an RTI service delivery framework, at least five primary components facilitate students' access to, and participation in, high-quality instruction: (a) comprehensive student assessment via screening, diagnostic measurement, and progress monitoring, (b) standardized data-based decision-making, (c) multi-tiered implementation of student support based on a continuum of needs, (d) the provision of evidence-based instruction/intervention, and (e) multi-stakeholder involvement in coordinated leadership. Each of

T. A. Glover (✉)
Rutgers University, Piscataway, NJ, USA
e-mail: todd.glover@rutgers.edu

these components is needed to ensure that access is adequately provided.

Comprehensive assessment via screening, diagnostic tools, and progress monitoring. A comprehensive assessment approach that involves screening of all students, diagnostic measurement, and progress monitoring at regular intervals is necessary to identify and address potential instructional needs. By measuring skills or behaviors predictive of student success, screening assessments are used to identify potential areas of concern for individual students early on, as opposed to waiting for students to experience significant difficulties or performance deficits. Through screening and follow-up diagnostic assessment of students identified as potentially at risk, educators are able to determine which instructional practices to prioritize (e.g., Glover & Albers, 2007). For example, in the area of early reading, first grade screening in phonics at the beginning of the school year (e.g., screening via the DIBELS Next Nonsense Word Fluency assessment) is often utilized along with follow-up diagnostic tools (e.g., a phonics inventory) to match instruction to students' skill needs, thus promoting access to differentiated practices that promote immediate skill development.

Likewise, regular monitoring of individual students' progress in response to instruction or intervention is useful for determining whether, over time, students are provided access to the most appropriate instruction (e.g., Fuchs & Fuchs, 2006). For example, if weekly monitoring of a student's phonics skills via the DIBELS Next Nonsense Word Fluency assessment indicates that the student is inadequately responding to a prescribed phonics intervention, this alerts educators to the need for access to an alternative form of student support.

Standardized data-based decision-making Students' access to instruction and/or effective intervention is also promoted through the application of common data-based decision criteria (e.g., Glover & DiPerna, 2007). For example, as illustrated in Fig. 10.1, the use of a standardized decision tree approach to guide student instructional grouping in the areas of early reading helps ensure students are provided with individually appropriate instructional opportunities. Within this example framework, a second grade student who is not meeting beginning-of-year benchmark proficiency at oral reading fluency is assessed to determine whether he or she meets expectations for nonsense word fluency. Based on whether the student meets or exceeds the nonsense word fluency benchmark, he or she is either recommended for a fluency intervention (if benchmark is achieved) or a phonics intervention (if benchmark is not met). Students' specific skill needs are then diagnosed, and those with similar needs are grouped together. Thus, with a standardized decision-making framework, students are afforded access to specific interventions matched to their data-identified needs, rather than grouped into a general category of services (e.g., assigned to a resource room or title services) which may vary in appropriateness.

Multi-tiered support based on a continuum of needs The application of multi-tiered support is also important for promoting students' access to and participation in instruction/intervention. Within an RTI service delivery framework, instruction is provided at a universal level for all students (Tier 1), a targeted level (Tier 2) for groups of students whose needs are not met by Tier 1 services, and an intensive, individualized level (Tier 3) for those that require even more support than what Tier 2 affords. By using data to guide instruction along this continuum, educators are able to assign students to appropriate instructional practices (e.g., Fuchs & Fuchs, 2006; Glover & DiPerna, 2007). For example, in the area of reading, a student who does not meet benchmark expectations and is assigned to a Tier 2 phonics intervention and monitored over time for his response to intervention might receive an individualized, Tier 3 intervention when Tier 2 services do not improve his performance over time. This approach provides instructional support for all students, including those who with a traditional classification model for receiving special education services would not have been eligible for special education services

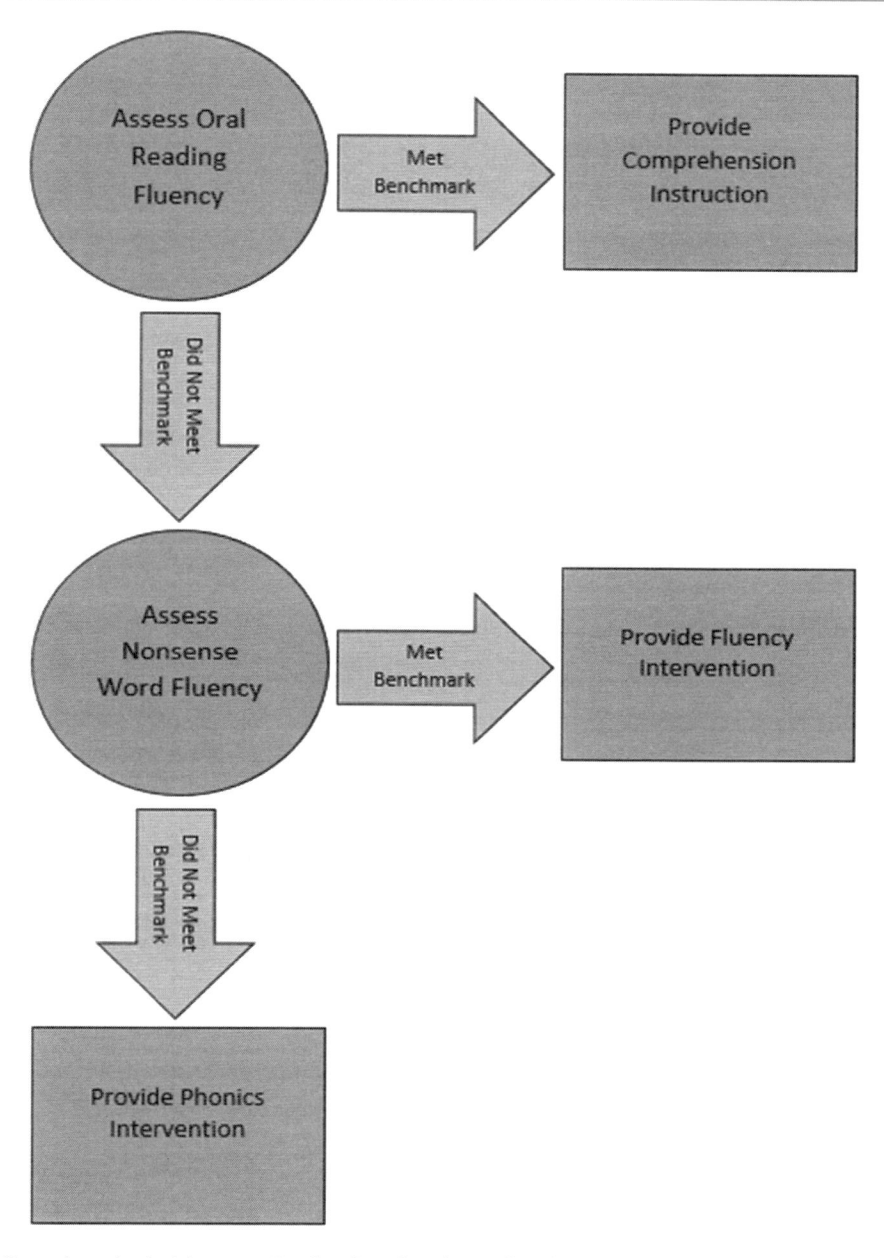

Fig. 10.1 Second grade decision tree for data-based early reading intervention decisions (Adapted from PRESS Research Team, 2013)

(e.g., students performing poorly with IQ and achievement tests scores too close to one another for the students to be eligible for services). Thus, the provision of data-guided instruction and intervention at multiple tiers helps to maximize access to services based on a wide range of needs.

A primary factor that differentiates the multi-tiered approach within an RTI framework from other service delivery models is its focus on the provision of a continuum of supports that enable students not only to access instruction but also to be active participants. Multi-tiered service delivery within an RTI framework is designed to address the needs of students with a large range of academic difficulties, including those with moderate to significant disabilities who may require specialized interventions to meet their learning needs. As Fuchs and Fuchs (2016) have observed, intervention provision within an RTI service delivery approach involves more systematic adaptation of instruction based on students' needs than what is typically offered through routine teacher variations in materials or grouping arrangements or specialized adaptations such as co-teaching, accommodating the curriculum, and universal design approaches. Although such approaches offer frameworks for considering ways to foster student engagement by presenting information in multiple ways and accommodating multiple means of student action and expression, they offer less guidance in considering how to systematically coordinate and address multiple students' individual skill needs.

As highlighted by Fuchs and Fuchs (2016), intervention within a multi-tiered approach is provided by specialists who apply different skills with different students. Tier 2 intervention is delivered by a specially trained practitioner in a different manner than universal practices provided in Tier 1, addressing specific skill needs with greater frequency and duration. Within this framework, Tier 3 intervention is further individualized and intensified by highly trained specialists to match individual needs identified by student data.

Provision of evidence-based and specialized instruction/intervention Although the use of assessments, data-based decision rules, and a multi-tiered system of support is critical for guiding instructional practices, it is the instructional practices and interventions themselves that are primarily responsible for advancing student performance. Within an RTI service delivery framework, provision of instruction and interventions with demonstrated evidence of their effectiveness increases the likelihood that students are granted access to the most appropriate form of support (e.g., Fuchs & Fuchs, 2006; Glover & DiPerna, 2007).

In contrast to commonly advocated inclusionary practices that focus primarily on the receipt of instruction in inclusive settings that expose students with and without significant learning difficulties or disabilities to the same educational content (e.g., co-teaching, push-in instruction, universal design for learning), student support within an RTI framework focuses on the provision of specialized interventions matched to students' individual skill needs. As Fuchs and colleagues note, neither *location* nor *exposure* equates to students' access to or participation in instruction (Fuchs et al., 2015). Within an RTI framework, instruction/intervention is explicit and designed to promote student attention, participation, and motivation through teachers' engagement in direct explanations, modeling, repeated guided and independent practice, regular feedback, and application in multiple contexts to promote transfer of knowledge and skills (e.g., Fuchs et al., 2008, 2015).

Multi-stakeholder involvement in coordinated leadership Finally, the involvement of multiple stakeholders with complementary roles and expertise (e.g., classroom teachers, specialists, and administrators) in systematic and coordinated scheduling and provision of assessment, data-driven decision-making, and instruction and intervention for RTI service delivery promotes greater access to appropriate and high-quality educational practices than has traditionally been afforded by departmentalized and disjointed systems of general and special education. For example, in schools where an administrative leader works with elementary classroom teachers, assessment coordinators, reading specialists, and interventionists to coordinate schoolwide data-driven instruction to students across classrooms and grades based on their individual reading skill needs, the likelihood is increased that students are afforded access to the appropriate reading support (e.g., Parisi, Ihlo, & Glover, 2014).

Organizational Considerations for Promoting Access to High-Quality Instruction for Students

Although core components of RTI service delivery have the potential to promote access for all students to instruction that is matched to their needs, effective implementation of supports for students requires that such components be delivered with fidelity and maintained over time. Unfortunately, given the complexity of training needs and integration of systems of assessment and intervention support, many schools are inadequately prepared for service delivery implementation (e.g., Glover, 2010; Glover, 2017). Fixsen, Blase, and their colleagues (e.g., Fixsen & Blase, 2008) have identified eight key implementation drivers or engines of change necessary for advancing and sustaining new practices and programs: recruitment and staff selection, training, coaching, fidelity/performance assessment, data decision systems, facilitative administrative supports, systems intervention, and adaptive leadership. As noted previously, several of these drivers are core components of RTI service delivery systems. However, five drivers warrant additional attention with respect to their integral role in ensuring that RTI service delivery is effective in promoting access for all students to high-quality instruction: facilitative administrative support, leadership, training, coaching, and fidelity/performance assessment.

Facilitative administrative support and team-based leadership Unfortunately, many schools are ineffective in promoting students' access to high-quality instruction via an RTI service delivery model because they adopt procedures for implementing specific practices without developing fully coordinated and integrated systems. Facilitative administration is needed to ensure that school policies, procedures, structures, and cultures support all students' access to the core components of RTI service delivery (e.g., Fixsen & Blase, 2008; Glover, 2017). For example, in the area of reading, school guidelines and operating procedures could reiterate the need to identify and support *all* students. To help ensure that students receive appropriate individualized reading intervention, policies and structures (e.g., school scheduling) could be aligned to ensure that reading instruction occurs during a common period across classrooms for students with like skill needs.

Team-based leadership guided by a strong leader that is adaptive in championing the integration of RTI service delivery in the context of barriers (e.g., insufficient training, time) and enablers (e.g., teacher buy-in, data supporting increased student performance) and proficient in managing technical aspects of implementation (e.g., core service delivery components) is also helpful for ensuring that all students are able to access high-quality instruction (e.g., Fixsen & Blase, 2008; Glover, 2017). To meet students' needs, effective team leaders must be able to engage and guide multiple stakeholders (e.g., classroom teachers, specialists, and administrators) in coordinating implementation within and across classroom settings and grade levels. For example, to effectively promote the development of all students' reading skills, team leaders might coordinate multiple interventionists' involvement in small-group instructional sessions targeting specific skills needs (e.g., reading specialist teaching phonics instruction, school psychologists working with students on fluency skills, paraprofessionals teaching reading comprehension strategies).

Professional development via training with job-embedded coaching Student access to high-quality instruction is also greatly impacted by faculty and staff training. Given the complexity of RTI service delivery, school personnel often must acquire new skills related to administration of assessments, data literacy, student instructional grouping, intervention selection and provision, and the measurement of students' progress. In addition to receiving workshop-based foundational training, job-embedded coaching has been found to increase the knowledge, skills, and perceived self-efficacy of school personnel implementing RTI service delivery. For example, Glover and Ihlo (Glover, 2017; Glover & Ihlo, 2015) found that relative to personnel in schools where no coaching was provided for RTI service delivery, teachers and interventionists who received regular coaching in the application of data-based decision-making and provision of a toolkit of research-based reading interventions exhibited higher-quality data-driven intervention decisions, resulting in greater performance benefits for students with a variety of significant reading skill needs.

Implementation fidelity assessment Finally, regular monitoring of the fidelity of RTI service delivery implementation is needed to determine whether students are able to access the support that they need. Formative use of implementation data on each service delivery component (e.g., assessment, data-based decision-making, intervention provision, etc.) is useful for identifying gaps in deploying student supports. For example, in the area of early reading, monitoring the consistency with which data-based decision rules are applied is helpful for uncovering whether students' needs are correctly being identified, and monitoring intervention implementation is important for determining whether all students are provided with the instruction that they require. Within a RTI service delivery framework, consideration of implementation fidelity in addition to student performance is critical for determining whether to continue an existing instructional practice (e.g., when there is high fidelity and positive student growth), encourage better implementation (e.g., when there is low fidelity and limited student growth), or change or modify the instructional approach (e.g., when there is high fidelity and limited student growth) (e.g., Parisi et al., 2014).

Promoting Student Access Via RTI Service Delivery: State of the Research

Existing research on components of RTI service delivery (e.g., research on student screening and progress monitoring, the application of data-based instructional decisions, and the impact of multi-tiered intervention supports) provides valuable insights about the utility of this framework for promoting students' access to high-quality instruction. However, additional investigations are also needed to determine how to ensure that (a) accessibility is afforded to *all* students and (b) schools have adequate capacity to implement service delivery with fidelity and maximal opportunities for impact.

Existing research support Existing research on screening and progress monitoring to guide instructional decisions, the impact of multi-tiered intervention supports, and training supports for school personnel in the implementation of assessment and intervention practices provides an emerging empirical basis for the effectiveness of RTI service delivery in increasing students' access to appropriate instruction.

Research on screening and progress monitoring to guide instructional decisions As Fuchs and Fuchs (2006) noted, over 200 empirical studies provide evidence of the reliability and validity of curriculum-based measurement (CBM), the approach utilized by most screening and progress monitoring assessments of academic skills within an RTI service delivery framework. In contrast to other forms of standardized assessment (e.g., standardized achievement tests, classroom observations), CBM-based screening and progress monitoring approaches focus on assessing student performance on discrete skills over time. CBM approaches have been found to be especially useful for investigating the performance of students with intensive needs for whom other forms of measurement would not be adequately sensitive to changes in performance (Fuchs, Compton, Fuchs, & Bryant, 2008). The sensitivity and specificity of CBM approaches in assessing early reading have received considerable research attention (Ardoin, Christ, Morena, Cormier, & Klingbeil, 2013; Fuchs, Fuchs, & Compton, 2004; Jenkins, Hudson, & Johnson, 2007).

Although research on the impact of specific accommodations for CBM approaches within an RTI framework is in its infancy, CBM approaches have been used to reliably assess specific skill needs of students both without and with disabilities, including students with specific learning disabilities and intellectual and cognitive disabilities (e.g., Allor, Mathes, Roberts, Jones, & Champlin, 2010; Deno, Fuchs, Marston, & Shin, 2001; Lemons et al., 2013; Tindal et al., 2003). By determining appropriate assessment approaches and expected rates of growth for those with and without disabilities for specific skills, such studies have been instrumental in providing evidence for the appropriateness of CBM assessments in guiding instructional decisions for students with a wide variety of needs.

Research on the impact of multi-tiered intervention supports Additional research has investigated the performance of students (including those with disabilities) who have received instruction within specific tiers of intervention, especially in the area of early reading (e.g., Vaughn, Wanzek, Linan-Thompson, & Murray, 2007). Systematic reviews have found benefits associated with multiple small-group interventions targeting daily skill instruction for students with and without disabilities (e.g., Burns, Appleton, & Stehouwer, 2005; Elbaum, Vaughn, Hughes, & Moody, 2000). Likewise, meta-analytic research in the area of reading has found that intensive, individualized interventions provide performance increases for students with severe learning difficulties and identified learning disabilities (e.g., Burns et al., 2005; Gersten et al., 2009; Kavale & Forness, 2000).

Research on training supports for school personnel Finally, given that students' access to high-quality instruction is significantly impacted by school personnel's proficiency in implementing complex assessment and intervention practices with fidelity, research on professional development with job-embedded coaching has begun to emerge. Although training teachers in data-based decision-making (e.g., Shapiro, 2016) or the implementation of targeted or individualized interventions (e.g., Vaughn, Linan-Thompson, & Hickman, 2003; Vernon-Feagans, Kainz, Hedrick, Ginsberg, & Amendum, 2013) has been found to benefit early skill development for students with and without disabilities, there have been limited investigations of the approaches required to best support school personnel in promoting students' access to the instruction that they require. A data-driven coaching model investigated by Glover, Ihlo, and their colleagues via a randomized trial (Glover, 2017; Glover & Ihlo, 2015) provides promising evidence in support of the impact of job-embedded professional development with coaching on (a) teachers' fidelity of implementation of RTI service delivery practices in the area of early reading and (b) the performance of students, including those with severe learning difficulties and identified learning disabilities. This coaching model involved support for data-based decision-making, instructional grouping, and the implementation of a toolkit of research-based interventions. Three primary components of this model included (a) an emphasis on the learning environment within teachers' classrooms; (b) enrollment of teachers via modeling, designated opportunities for practice, and feedback; and (c) the use of a formalized data-driven implementation framework for advancing coaching and instructional support. Relative to control participants, school personnel exhibited greater knowledge and application of RTI service delivery practices. Importantly, students with significant academic needs in coached teachers' classrooms benefitted from greater access to individualized interventions and boosts in academic performance in the areas of alphabetic principal and phonics, word attack, and reading fluency.

Additional need for research Despite promising findings from published studies of RTI service delivery components, there is still an ongoing need for additional research. A comprehensive discussion of future research needs for RTI service delivery is provided elsewhere (e.g., Burns et al., 2005; Glover & DiPerna, 2007) and is beyond the scope of this chapter. However, three areas of research are needed to better inform the utility of specific approaches for increasing students' access to appropriate instructional supports—research on (a) decision-making criteria across assessments, (b) interventions for students who persistently do not respond to instruction, and (c) core components necessary for teacher professional development to support high-fidelity service delivery.

Research on decision-making criteria across assessments Although CBM approaches have been used to reliably assess specific skill needs for students both without and with disabilities (e.g., Allor et al., 2010; Deno et al., 2001; Lemons et al., 2013; Tindal et al., 2003), additional work is needed to determine (a) the influence of accommodations for CBM approaches for students with special needs (e.g., assistive technology, extended time, etc.) on assessment validity and (b) variations in expected rates of growth for those with and without disabilities based on specific assessment approaches.

Further, although several approaches to data-based decision-making for determining students' skill needs and responsiveness to intervention have been found to be useful, the decisions that result from the use of specific measures and decision-making criteria vary substantially. For example, in the area of early reading, Fuchs and colleagues (Fuchs, Compton, et al., 2008) found that the percentage of students identified as not responding to Tier 2 intervention differed depending upon the decision-making criteria used. For example, in a study contrasting methods, they found that a dual discrepancy method (whereby the rate and level of student performance are taken into account) yielded 8.6% of students, a slope discrepancy approach (whereby a students' rate of progress is compared to a normative cut score) yielded 7.6% of students, and normative post-intervention decisions yielded 4.2% of students. This variation is of significant concern, because it demonstrates inequities in the identification of students' instructional responsiveness. Additional research is needed to compare alternate approaches with respect to their utility in determining students' response to intervention, to ensure that they are afforded access to the right instructional supports. This research will require that common criterion measures be used to investigate psychometric properties (e.g., sensitivity and specificity) and that common decision-making criteria (e.g., duel discrepancy, slope discrepancy) be applied across assessment approaches.

Research on interventions for unresponsive students Although, overall, the RTI service delivery framework holds great promise with respect to systematically identifying needs of all students and providing a continuum of need-based supports, additional research is needed to investigate intervention alternatives for those who do not respond to intervention, including some students with significant disabilities. Fuchs and colleagues (e.g., Al Otaiba & Fuchs, 2002; McMaster, Fuchs, Fuchs, & Compton, 2005) identified variables associated with unresponsiveness in the area of reading, such as phonological awareness encoding problems, phonological memory difficulties, and/or attention or behavior concerns. In addition, they and others (e.g., O'Connor, 2000) have examined the influence of multiphased interventions that increase in intensity to maximize students' response. These studies have resulted in mixed results; additional research is needed to determine how to best meet the need of select students for whom existing interventions are ineffective.

Research on core components of teacher professional development Finally, although emerging research supports the impact of accompanying workshop-based professional development with job-embedded coaching support for school personnel (e.g., Glover, 2017), very little is known about required aspects of the coaching process. Future research is needed to determine the influence of specific components of coaching on students' (a) access to appropriate instruction and (b) academic performance. Additional experimental studies should explore variations in coaching to determine which components are vital for producing the desired benefits for students.

Evidence-Based Resources for Promoting Access to High-Quality Instruction and Intervention Supports

Although research continues to evolve, there are now substantial resources available to support school personnel in implementing RTI service delivery practices that promote access for all students to high-quality instruction and intervention. In addition to presenting a comprehensive overview of core service delivery components, the National Center on Response to Invention website (www.rti4success.org) provides information on numerous research-based implementation considerations. An implementation checklist and rubric are also available from this website which can be used to monitor the integrity of RTI service delivery to ensure that key components of service delivery are provided to promote high-quality and equitable data-based instructional decisions and intervention implementation for all students.

The National Center on Intensive Intervention website (http://www.intensiveintervention.org/)

also provides access to extensive resources on data-driven approaches for providing intensive intervention matched to students' specific needs. The website houses many practical implementation tools and charts for evaluating the quality of assessment tools and data-based decision criteria and intervention effectiveness.

Additional resources are now available to assist school personnel in the selection and implementation of appropriate interventions. For example, the Florida Center for Reading Research website (http://www.fcrr.org/) provides access to access to numerous free intervention materials, along with guides to assist with determining for whom various activities are appropriate. Likewise, student assessment and intervention guides and materials from the Path to Reading Excellence in School Site (PRESS) reading intervention framework can be ordered for a reasonable cost from the Minnesota Center for Reading Research website (http://www.cehd.umn.edu/reading/). The Technical Assistance Center on Positive Behavioral Interventions and Supports website (https://www.pbis.org/) also provides a comprehensive set of resources on data-driven approaches for supporting positive student behavior. The website houses practical tools such as implementation checklists and intervention guides that can assist school personnel in promoting students' access to appropriate behavioral supports.

Closing Considerations

Despite the need for ongoing research on RTI service delivery approaches that promote students' access to high-quality instruction and intervention, an emerging database of empirical evidence suggests that components of an RTI service delivery framework hold great promise with respect to identifying students' individual needs and implementing practices that increase the likelihood of their success. It is hoped that this chapter's focus on service delivery components and organizational considerations for promoting access to high-quality instruction will present a useful context for considering the utility of RTI service delivery in

meeting students' needs. Further, it is hoped that the research discussion provided herein will help to provide a framework for critically considering aspects of implementation. As indicated by an abundance of research and available implementation resources, there is a reason to be optimistic about students' access to appropriate supports within an RTI service delivery framework.

References

Al Otaiba, S., & Fuchs, D. (2002). Characteristics of children who are unresponsive to early literacy intervention: A review of the literature. *Remedial and Special Education, 23*, 300–316.

Allor, J. H., Mathes, P. G., Roberts, J. K., Jones, F., & Champlin, T. M. (2010). Teaching students with moderate intellectual disabilities to read: An experimental examination of a comprehensive reading intervention. *Education and Training in Autism and Developmental Disabilities, 45*, 3–22.

Ardoin, S. P., Christ, T. J., Morena, L. S., Cormier, D. C., & Klingbeil, D. A. (2013). A systematic review and summarization of the recommendations and research surrounding curriculum-based measurement of oral reading fluency (CBM-R) decision rules. *Journal of School Psychology, 51*, 1–18.

Burns, M. K., Appleton, J. J., & Stehouwer, J. D. (2005). Meta-analysis of response-to-intervention research: Examining field-based and research-implemented models. *Journal of Psychoeducational Assessment, 23*, 381–394.

Deno, S. L., Fuchs, L. S., Marston, D., & Shin, J. (2001). Using curriculum-based measurement to establish growth standards for students with learning disabilities. *School Psychology Review, 30*(4), 507–524.

Elbaum, B., Vaughn, S., Hughes, M., & Moody, S. (2000). How effective are one-to-one tutoring programs in reading for elementary students at risk for reading failure? A meta-analysis of the intervention research. *Reading Research Quarterly, 92*, 605–619.

Every Student Succeeds Act of 2015, 20 U.S.C § 6311. et seq. (2015).

Fixsen, D. L., & Blase, K. A. (2008). *Drivers framework*. Chapel Hill, NC: The National Implementation Research Network/Frank Porter Graham Child Development Institute/University of North Carolina.

Fletcher, J. M., Coulter, W. A., Reschly, D. J., & Vaughn, S. (2004). Alternative approaches to the definition and identification of learning disabilities: Some questions and answers. *Annals of Dyslexia, 54*(2), 304–331.

Fuchs, D., Compton, D. L., Fuchs, L. S., & Bryant, J. (2008). Making "secondary intervention" work in a three-tier responsiveness-to-intervention model: Findings from the first-grade longitudinal reading study at the national research center on learning disabilities. *Reading and Writing: An Interdisciplinary Journal, 21*, 413–436.

Fuchs, D., & Fuchs, L. S. (2006). Introduction to responsiveness-to-intervention: What, why, and how valid is it? *Reading Research Quarterly, 4*, 93–99.

Fuchs, D., & Fuchs, L. S. (2016). Responsiveness-to-intervention: A "systems" approach to instructional adaptation. *Theory Into Practice, 55*, 225–233.

Fuchs, D., Fuchs, L. S., & Compton, D. L. (2004). Identifying reading disabilities by responsiveness-to-instruction: Specifying measures and criteria. *Learning Disability Quarterly, 27*, 216–227.

Fuchs, L. S., Fuchs, D., Compton, D. L., Wehby, J., Schumacher, R. F., Gersten, R., & Joran, N. C. (2015). Inclusion versus specialized intervention for very-low-performing students: What does access mean in an era of academic challenge? *Exceptional Children, 81*(2), 134–157.

Fuchs, L. S., Fuchs, D., Powell, S. R., Seethaler, P. M., Cirino, P. T., & Fletcher, J. M. (2008). Intensive intervention for students with mathematics disabilities: Seven principles of effective practice. *Learning Disability Quarterly, 31*, 79–92.

Gersten, R., Compton, D., Connor, C. M., Dimino, J., Santoro, L., Linan-Thompson, S., et al. (2009). *Assisting students struggling with reading: Response to intervention and multi-tier intervention in primary grades*. Washington, DC: U.S. Department of Education Institute of Educational Sciences.

Glover, T. A. (2010). Key RTI service delivery components: Considerations for research-informed practice. In T. A. Glover & S. Vaughn (Eds.), *The promise of response to intervention: Evaluating current science and practice* (pp. 7–22). New York, NY: Guilford Press.

Glover, T. A. (2017). A data-driven coaching model used to promote students' response to early reading intervention. *Theory Into Practice, 56*, 13–20.

Glover, T. A., & Albers, C. A. (2007). Considerations for evaluating universal screening assessments. *Journal of School Psychology, 45*, 117–135.

Glover, T. A., & DiPerna, J. C. (2007). Service delivery models for response to intervention: Core components and directions for future research. *School Psychology Review, 36*, 526–542.

Glover, T. A., & Ihlo, T. (2015). *Professional development with coaching in RTI reading: A randomized study*. Paper presented at the annual meeting of the National Association of School Psychologists, Orlando, FL.

Individuals With Disabilities Education Act, 20 U.S.C. § 1400. (2004).

Jenkins, J. R., Hudson, R. F., & Johnson, E. S. (2007). Screening for at-risk readers in a response to intervention framework. *School Psychology Review, 36*, 582–600.

Kavale, K. A., & Forness, S. R. (2000). Policy decisions in special education: The role of meta-analysis. In R. Gersten, E. P. Schiller, & S. Vaughn (Eds.), *Contemporary special education research: Synthesis of the knowledge base on critical instructional issues* (pp. 281–326). Mahwah, NJ: Lawrence Erlbaum Associates.

Lemons, C. J., Zigmond, N., Kloo, A., Hill, D. R., Mrachko, A. A., Paterra, M. F., … Davis, S. M. (2013). Performance of students with significant cognitive disabilities on early grade curriculum-based measures of word and passage reading fluency. *Exceptional Children, 79*(4), 408–426.

McMaster, K. L., Fuchs, D., Fuchs, L. S., & Compton, D. L. (2005). Responding to nonresponders: An experimental field trial of identification and intervention methods. *Exceptional Children, 71*(4), 445–463.

No Child Left Behind Act of 2001, Pub. L. No. 107-110, § 115, Stat. 1425. (2002).

O'Connor, R. E. (2000). Increasing the intensity of intervention in kindergarten and first grade. *Learning Disabilities Research & Practice, 15*(1), 43–54.

Parisi, D. M., Ihlo, T., & Glover, T. A. (2014). Screening within a multi-tiered early prevention model: Using assessment to inform instruction and promote students' response to intervention. In R. J. Kettler, T. A. Glover, C. A. Albers, & K. Feeney-Kettler (Eds.), *Universal screening in educational settings: Evidence-based decision making for schools*. Washington, DC: American Psychological Association.

PRESS Research Team. (2013). *PRESS intervention manual*. Minneapolis, MN: University of Minnesota, Minnesota Center for Reading Research.

Shapiro, E. (2016). Evaluating the impact of response to intervention in reading at the elementary level across the state of Pennsylvania. In S. R. Jimmerson, M. K. Burns, & A. M. VanDerHeyden (Eds.), *Handbook of response to intervention: The science and practice of multi-tiered systems of support* (2nd ed.). New York, NY: Springer.

Tindal, C., McDonald, M., Tedesco, M., Clasgow, A., Almond, P., Crawford, L., & Hollenbeck, K. (2003). Alternate assessments in reading and math: Development and validation for students with significant disabilities. *Exceptional Children, 69*, 481–494.

Vaughn, S., Linan-Thompson, S., & Hickman, P. (2003). Response to intervention as a means of identifying students with reading/learning disabilities. *Exceptional Children, 69*, 391–409.

Vaughn, S., Wanzek, J., Linan-Thompson, S., & Murray, C. (2007). Monitoring response to intervention for students at-risk for reading difficulties: High and low responders. In S. R. Jimerson, M. K. Burns, & A. M. VanDerHeyden (Eds.), *The handbook of response to intervention: The science and practice of assessment and intervention* (pp. 234–243). New York: Springer.

Vernon-Feagans, L., Kainz, K., Hedrick, A., Ginsberg, M., & Amendum, S. (2013). Live webcam coaching to help early elementary classroom teachers provide effective literacy instruction for struggling readers: The targeted reading intervention. *Journal of Educational Psychology, 105*, 1175–1187.

Accurate and Informative for All: Universal Design for Learning (UDL) and the Future of Assessment

David H. Rose, Kristin H. Robinson, Tracey E. Hall, Peggy Coyne, Richard M. Jackson, William M. Stahl, and Sherri L. Wilcauskas

Universal Design for Learning (UDL): Principles, Policies, and Practices

The Promise of UDL

The *Universal Design for Learning (UDL) framework* (Meyer, Rose, & Gordon, 2014; Rose & Meyer, 2002) has become increasingly prominent in national (and international) educational policies and practices. The UDL framework has been featured in the National Educational Technology Plan (U.S. Department of Education, Office of Educational Technology, 2016), in the Educational Technology Developer's Guide (U.S. Department of Education, Office of Educational Technology, 2015), and in the Every Student Succeeds Act (ESSA, 2015).

The recent prominence of UDL reflects the increasingly widespread recognition that the UDL principles and guidelines (CAST, 2011; Rose & Gravel, 2013) can guide developers to create educational systems that are more equitable and effective for all learners. That recognition has multiple substantive roots in (a) *theory* (Meyer et al., 2014; Rappolt-Schlichtmann et al., 2013), (b) *practice* (Hall, Meyer, & Rose, 2012; Nelson, 2014; Novak, 2014), and (c) *research* (Daley, Hillaire, & Sutherland, 2014; Rappolt-Schlichtmann & Daley, 2013; Rappolt-Schlichtmann et al., 2013; Reich, Price, Rubin, & Steiner, 2010).

In a world where new knowledge and skills are exploding exponentially, the goal of UDL is not simply to help learners master a specific body of knowledge or specific skills but to master learning itself. Through UDL, educators seek to create expert learners, individuals who—whatever their particular strengths and weaknesses—know how to learn.

To do this successfully in classrooms where student variability is typical, UDL prompts educators to provide options that minimize barriers to learning and maximize the opportunities for every learner to grow. The UDL guidelines are designed to help educators ensure that every learner can succeed through intentionally building flexibility into the learning environment, including the addition of supports and scaffolds. We promote the

---

D. H. Rose · K. H. Robinson · T. E. Hall (✉)
R. M. Jackson · S. L. Wilcauskas
CAST, Wakefield, MA, USA
e-mail: thall@cast.org

P. Coyne
Lexia Learning Systems, Concord, MA, USA

W. M. Stahl
CAST, Wakefield, MA, USA

National Center on Accessible Educational Materials, Wakefield, MA, USA

use of UDL as a design framework infused throughout the design, prototyping, development, implementation, and evaluation process so that curricula, tools, resources, or digital environments are built from the outset to have the flexibility that addresses learner variability. As such, UDL is a powerful framework to ensure educational equity for learners who are often disenfranchised by traditional, "one size fits all" educational activities and products. Three broad principles provide the framework for the UDL guidelines.

1. *Provide multiple means of engagement* (the *why* of learning) means supporting interest, motivation, and persistence. Just as students learn more effectively when they are engaged and motivated, their performance on assessments can be enhanced by increasing engagement.
2. *Provide multiple means of representation* (the *what* of learning) means presenting information and content in different ways and making connections between them. In assessments, the ways in which the items are presented—text, graphs, charts, images, videos, demonstrations, and objects to manipulate—can have a significant impact on how a student performs on an item or an entire assessment.
3. *Provide multiple means of action and expression* (the *how* of learning) means providing different ways for students to work with information and content and to demonstrate what they are learning. In assessments, providing flexible options for ways in which learners can express their skills, knowledge, and understanding results in more accurate assessment results.

The promise of UDL is in ensuring that modern instructional approaches—including their goals, methods, materials, and assessments—will routinely and effectively address the wide range of individual differences among learners. In doing so, UDL has the potential to reduce the inadvertent barriers to learning that many students now face. From a UDL perspective, disabilities are not inherent in individuals but in their interaction with their environments. In that sense, many schools and environments—and many learning media and materials—can be viewed as "disabled" or "disabling."

By providing principled options that optimize choice and self-determination, a UDL approach to learning, including assessment, incorporates flexibility and options in education that provide opportunity for learners to demonstrate strengths and understanding, particularly during assessments. While the current view of assessment is to find out what students are taking away, or not, from an instructional episode, UDL embraces a broader view of assessment: assessment is a means of discovery about learners and their interaction with learning environments and about how learners are progressing toward standards and goals within those environments. This approach identifies challenges and strengths early and often to identify and build on learning successes and address challenges before they become failures.

The Goal of Assessment: From Individuals to Interactions

Assessment in education is used for many purposes, from statewide accountability systems to classroom progress monitoring to individual diagnostics. In most of these applications, the underlying goal is to understand learner skills and knowledge and subsequently improve learning outcomes for students through instruction, practice, and experiences. Whether it is the administrator who seeks to ensure that the district's new curriculum is effective, the teacher who seeks to ensure that daily instruction is meeting the needs of the students, or the student who seeks to know whether he or she has reached his or her own learning goals, assessment plays an essential role. To be effective, assessments need to be timely and ongoing and provide accurate, actionable data to improve instruction for students.

In a UDL approach, the basic purposes of assessment remain the same as in any other approach: providing timely and accurate information to improve learning outcomes. The UDL framework, however, adds a critical emphasis. Because of its foundation in the neuroscience of individual differences, the UDL framework recognizes that optimizing instruction for all students will require flexibility in that instruction, adapting and customizing strategies and tactics to the particular strengths and challenges of each individual learner (Meyer et al., 2014).

In that light, the goal of assessment in a UDL approach is to provide the kinds of information that will improve instruction by customizing it rather than generalizing or standardizing it. For example, in a traditional end-of-the-week spelling test, the teacher will dictate words for the students to write using the correct spelling on a lined sheet of paper. In a UDL approach to assessing spelling skills, writing the words could be one method of response. Alternatives to this traditional approach to assess spelling could include oral spelling of each word to a teacher or proxy, using a keyboard instead of handwriting, student dictation of the word to a scribe, oral spelling into a recording device, audio use of a speech-to-text tool in a digital document, as well as the use of finger spelling in sign language. Using this UDL approach for spelling, the common goal in each mode of expression is to evaluate the sequence and accuracy of letters in the words being evaluated (not rate or accuracy of handwriting on paper). The goal of assessment in UDL practice is not to identify what works in general, across classrooms, districts, or states, but to identify what works in specific, for this child, here and now.

Providing timely and accurate information to improve learning outcomes requires assessments with an emphasis on measuring interactions rather than just individuals. Let us expand upon that a bit.

One of the powerful ideas in UDL is the emphasis on identifying both abilities and disabilities in context rather than in isolation. That is to say, UDL recognizes that a person's capabilities are not something that is entirely resident "in" the individual but rather in the interplay between the individual and their environment (Meyer et al., 2014).

For example, the extent to which a person with a physical disability is limited or not depends as much on the affordances of their environment as on their own physical abilities. Whether a blind or dyslexic student in a history class has a "learning disability" or not often depends on whether there are any alternatives to the printed textbooks that are inaccessible or ineffective for them. Through a UDL lens, then, poor performance could likely be evidence of poor design.

Consequently, where traditional tests and diagnostics tend to focus on identifying weaknesses and disabilities in the individual learner, diagnostics in a UDL approach focus much more on identifying weaknesses and barriers in the design of the learning environment. This only makes sense when there are consequential options available in the learning environment, options that would either reduce obstacles or provide alternative paths. Guided by research in the learning sciences of individual differences and enabled by the flexibility to personalize that modern technologies allow, a UDL learning environment is in fact notable for its options. For example, well-designed digital learning environments are flexible (Bakia et al., 2013; Cavanaugh, Repetto, Wayer, & Spitler, 2013). They can allow teachers to see easily the strengths and challenges of individual students, as well as allow students multiple means and opportunities to show what they know and can do. Rather than making decisions about instruction for the elusive "average" student, flexible supported digital environments can support the learning of all students, including those on the margins, provide just-in-time feedback for students, and give educators the feedback they need to revise and improve instruction.

But the options themselves are not sufficient. What are needed are ways to accurately and continuously measure the effects of those different options and alternatives, to identify what kinds of options are optimal, for whom, at what time, and for what purpose.

To do that effectively, UDL assessments, to the extent possible, should be embedded in the interactions themselves, making it possible to probe whether a different set of options, a different path, and a different design might lead to better learning. Diagnostically, UDL assessments can reveal the "disabilities" within the interactions between the learner and the environment, allowing educators to then reduce the barriers that interfere with some students demonstrating their skills and knowledge, in contrast with others.

Through the UDL lens, then, the goal of assessment is to provide information on the match between individual learners and the learning environment, accurately identifying instructional and learning strengths, challenges (e.g., learners' knowledge and skills), and next steps for educators as well as learners. Assessments are bi-directional: instead of interpreting data through the lens of "what's wrong with the student," assessments interpreted through a UDL lens ask, "What are the learners' knowledge and skills? How does the current environment support learning for students? What barriers or obstacles does the current environment erect, and for whom? What can be changed in the learning environment to allow students to succeed? Most importantly, what can be done to make this learning environment optimal for each of my students?"

The "What" of Assessment: From Narrow to Comprehensive

A UDL approach to assessment assumes the fundamental centrality of emotions in both learning and assessment (Steele, 1997). Consequently, any attempt to measure student skills or knowledge, inevitability and importantly, will always measure emotions as well. Emotional phenomena like the "white coat effect," in which behavior, intentional or not, changes due to the "expert" in the room (e.g. the patient whose blood pressure increases when taken in the doctor's office, or behavior in the classroom changes when the principal enters the room) have been traditionally seen as distractions, annoying emotional intrusions on the "true" measures of cognition, skills, and knowledge in education. In a UDL approach (as well as others), emotions are not seen as distractions from learning, they are at the very center of learning. Recognizing both the positive and negative contributions of those emotions is at the core of accurate and comprehensive assessment.

In addition, the UDL approach also recognizes that students differ widely in the effects of emotion on their performance as well as engagement. Just as in the white coat effect, some students are dramatically responsive to elicitations of anxiety, some much less so. Students with ADHD are positively engaged by novelty and surprise. Students on the autism spectrum respond negatively, with stress reaction or even alarm (Bondy & Frost, 2012). That is the "construct-irrelevant" problem of emotion; emotions have powerful effects, but not the same effects for each student. Any measurement instrument, like the blood pressure cuff, will bring its own emotional effects, effects that are a strong and differential source of variance on "construct-relevant" measures. Those emotions, and the engagement they engender, pose problems for accurate measurement of constructs, like the knowledge of math computations, for example.

There are two ways to "recognize" the effects of emotions on performance. One, such as recognizing the effects of representation and expression that we have just discussed, is to provide options in the means of engagement. Thus, a UDL approach toward assessment would logically include options for how students engage with the assessment instrument, including a range of choices for *what*, *why*, and *how* to respond. More pointedly in the emotional sphere, a UDL approach would provide options specifically focused on the means of engagement. For some students, "high stakes" are positively motivating, and for others they pose a "white coat" intrusion that negatively affects performance. For some, extreme time pressure elevates concentration. For others it depresses it. For some, socially mediated assessment is optimal. For some it is detrimental. Providing options, allowing students to make choices about the conditions for their assessment, is one plausible way to optimize performance and minimize differential threats.

But the real value of options is that they provide opportunities to actually assess the positive or negative effects of various conditions of engagement. Without options and without contrasting conditions, it is impossible to know (or measure) the effects of emotional histories and emotional reactivity on present performance. Certainly, one of the most powerful demonstrations of this effect comes from the dramatic and careful work of researchers like Cohen, Garcia, Apfel, and Master (2006) and Steele (1997). They show convincingly how simple changes in the emotional events or conditions that precede testing, such as having minority students do brief self-affirmation exercises or having them provide demographic information after test taking, can radically change performance.

Consider as just one example, the memorable research on closing the achievement gaps for minority students conducted first by Cohen et al. (2006). In that research and many other replications over both short- and long-term time spans, researchers had students with low expectations do a self-affirmation exercise, merely reflecting on their strengths, interests, or values. That simple intervention—which had nothing to do with the *relevant* constructs being learned—resulted in dramatic achievement gains on both school achievement measures and standardized tests.

In related research, Claude Steele and colleagues demonstrated how easily test scores could be manipulated by inducing stereotype threats—and those threats could be induced by merely having participants identifying their race or gender on a test booklet. In this line of research, the participants include an age range of intermediate grade to college graduate level students of both gender and specifically include individuals from minority groups. The identified threat, based on stereotype, could be reduced by changing when those "minority" reports are collected to after test completion. These and many other carefully crafted experiments show that it is relatively easy to conceive of options—the option to begin testing with a short family history or to delay collecting identifying details—that can have powerful effects on testing performance (Jamieson, Mendes, Blackstock, & Schmader, 2010; Spencer, Steele, & Quinn, 1999; Steele & Aronson, 1995).

The mere availability of these options during assessment is valuable not only because it may reduce interfering emotional side effects but also because it allows us to measure the magnitude and valence of the effects of the options. That is to say, by providing the option to begin with "self-affirmation," one can actually begin to identify and measure (by contrasting performance with and without such an option) the interfering emotional baggage from stereotype threat, learned helplessness, etc.

An addition to the research findings on self-affirmation, stereotype threat, and assessment outcomes, another way to recognize the effects of emotion on performance is to measure emotions themselves as part of a more comprehensive and UDL approach to assessment. Whether emotions are elicited bottom-up by an outside event, e.g., by encountering a snake in your path (fear), or top-down by executive systems, e.g., by anticipating a snake in your path, it is difficult to measure emotion directly. Instead, researchers who study emotion measure one or more of a wide variety of external signals—physiological, linguistic, behavioral, and social—from which they infer an internal psychological construct, an emotion that underlies those peripheral signals. However, these emotional measures have not been applied to traditional academic assessment, often because they are too cumbersome, expensive, or disruptive. Therefore, an important question for educators (and everyone else) is this: how can emotions be accounted for to get more accurate estimates of learner knowledge, understanding, skills, and strategies?

This is a longer topic than we have space to fully address, but two aspects of a UDL approach are worth noting. First, a UDL approach assumes that we are measuring emotions and affect in every assessment: we are inevitably measuring engagement, stereotype threat, learned helplessness, growth mindset, and so forth, even when our assessment item is designed explicitly to measure mathematics. That assumption is important because it encourages a comprehensive view of what kinds of interventions might be adaptive. We assert that, for many students, a failure in expressed knowledge is a symptom of lack of engagement; the most effective interventions or remediation will need to start there, not with review or drill and practice.

Second, it is worth noting the power of technology to assist in the measurement of affect. Two examples will suffice here. From our own work on literacy with students who have a history of failure and all the emotional baggage that comes with that, we have included an explicit self-report of affective response to their reading (National Center for Use of Emerging Technologies, 2016). Each reading is followed by an emotional response screen. Students choose their own reading materials and have the option to indicate their emotional response (see Fig. 11.1). The interactive graphic asks students to reflect on their emotional reactions along two dimensions based on affective science: the

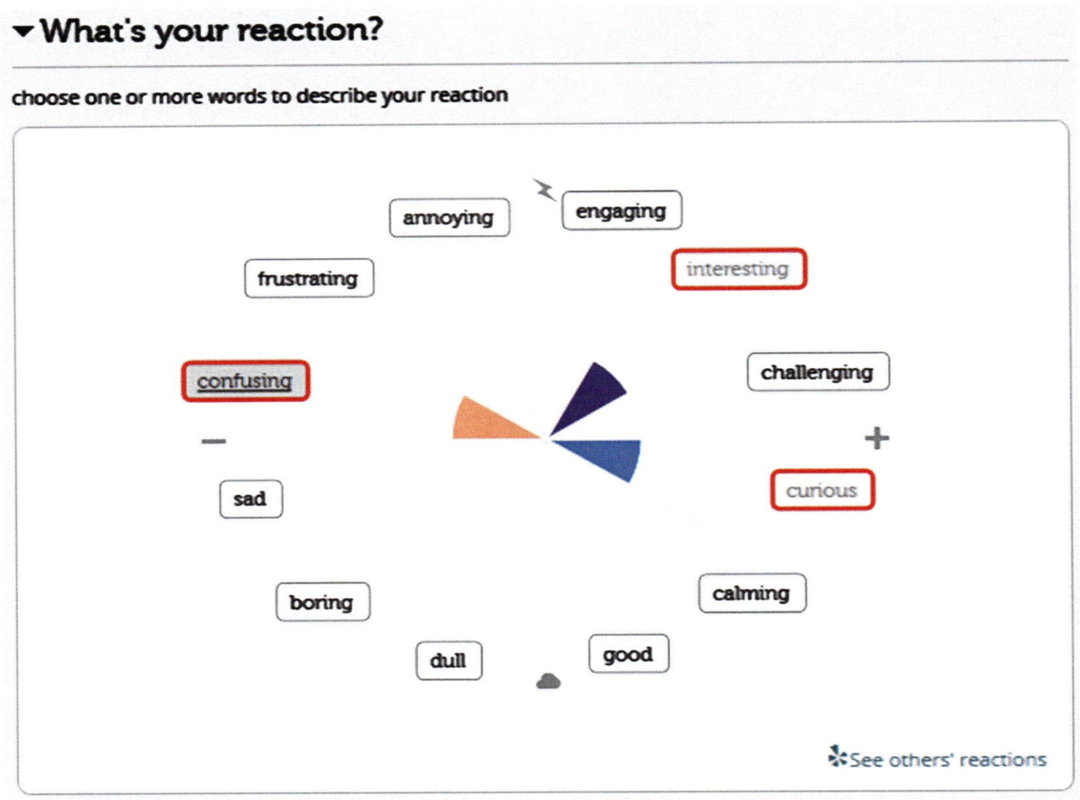

Fig. 11.1 Interactive affective response tool where students can provide emotional reactions to their reading used here in Udio, a CAST web-based tool designed to improve reading comprehension skills for middle school students with disabilities

valence of their emotions and their intensity. Most importantly, after making their own decisions, students may ask to see how their peers have responded to the same article or story. Our research, and that from the Yale Center for Emotional Intelligence, suggests that this act of reflection, and social exchange, provokes students to think about their own emotions, label them more carefully, investigate their sources, and use those emotions as the beginning of conversations with their peers and their teacher (CET, 2016; Ivcevic & Brackett, 2014).

Another example comes from a growing group of researchers who study implicit measures of engagement that are extracted from the ways that students interact with online learning materials (see Baker et al., 2012). These measures are not intrusive or disruptive, usually not even noticeable because they are routinely collected, aggregated, and automatically analyzed from every click or mouseover that learners generate. Using millions of data points, the researchers find particular patterns in the ways that students respond, patterns that are associated with emotional states or levels of engagement. These patterns, the ones that correlate well with self-reports of levels of engagement or emotion, are then used as "automatic engagement detectors." This kind of evaluation of engagement and emotion is still early but promising. The key advantage is that these kinds of embedded and automated measures may eventually supplement traditional formative and summative measurement but with information that is timely enough to inform instruction.

These examples, one implicit and the other explicit, are just two examples of the kinds of measures that are emerging, where technology will enhance our capacity to measure the role of emotion in student learning and performance.

Our point is not that these measures are perfect but that they recognize the centrality of emotion and engagement, in every single kind of learning and its assessment. That recognition is critical in guiding interventions that intend to close achievement gaps and reduce the effects of emotional disabilities and histories.

It should be said that the most commonly administered standardized tests invoke many problems but present a particular challenge from a UDL perspective. The constraints that standardized tests place on representation, expression, and engagement render them inaccurate for many students; they are also very narrow in the kinds of inferences that can be drawn from them, which is the reason they are primarily useful in predicting future testing performance rather than performance in authentic environments. While teachers report a preference for tests because they are the fastest and easiest form of assessment to administer and score, they are more accurate in predicting future test performance than predicting success in authentic environments like college, career, or life.

Assessments that are more accurate and useful must be more comprehensive than the simplifying constraints of testing allows: they should sample more systematically the full range of cognitive and affective abilities that underlie performance in authentic settings. From a UDL perspective, standardized tests may serve only as one component in a more comprehensive assessment system that measures the kinds of things that "expert learners" require: the ability to set effective long- and short-term goals, the ability to develop plans and strategies for complex problem-solving, the ability to choose the most effective media for learning and production, the persistence and resilience to manage distraction and failure, the ability to monitor progress effectively, the capacity to revise plans and strategies in the face of failure, etc. None of these are measured well in a standardized test, but they are the things that will matter most for success outside the classroom.

To conclude this section, accurate and meaningful assessment will require recognizing the representational, expressive, and emotional demands that tests (or other measurements) differentially impose on individuals. Like physicians, educators will have to recognize that their instruments inevitably affect what is being measured. The important point is that more flexible and comprehensive assessment instruments will be more valuable for two reasons: first because they will better identify the actual sources of variance in individual performance and second because they will provide the kinds of information that educators will need to make better instructional decisions by including more about learners and their differences, more about ourselves as instructors and learners, and more about our instructional environments.

The *When* of Assessment: From Extrinsic to Intrinsic

Generally, when we think about assessment, we recall large-scale summative assessments used to measure achievement (knowledge, understanding, skills, and strategies). Unintentionally, these assessments promote a failure model. Large-scale assessments typically occur at the end of an educational episode (a chapter, grading period, or school year) and show performance: successes for sure but failure as well. When and how learners get access to support depend on their performance on these assessments. In fact, they depend on students' nonperformance: a student will usually only qualify for accommodations and support services after (and because) they fail. Since these decisions are based on assessments that typically happen at the end of an academic year, students, teachers, or districts must experience lack of success over a long period of time before any kind of assistance or adjustment of education is provided.

Traditional approaches to address the needs of learners in the margins magnify the challenges related to the typical timing of assessments. Traditional approaches to assessing learners in the margins incorporate diagnostic and prescriptive strategies, where learners are assessed initially to determine how far removed they are from their classmates in terms of achievement measures and in what ways they are struggling as they participate in classroom routines. Once deficits in achievement and information processing are identified, a diagnosis is made, and remedial interventions are prescribed to directly and explicitly teach deficient skills. Such interventions are highly focused in detail and extended over a prolonged period of time. At the end of this period, the learner's performance on the target skills is again measured summatively with the hope that the learner's performance will now resemble the performance of typical peers. In this traditional approach, therefore, assessment occurs prior to instruction and again at the conclusion of instruction for the purpose of measuring instructional effectiveness. While this approach neatly allows for the administration of services so that more than a sufficient amount of time is available to schedule and support an intervention to increase the likelihood of success, if this approach is not successful, a substantial amount of time has passed with little or no assessment feedback or instructional adjustment. Once again, learners, who could only qualify for services because of failure, have the high potential of being failed again.

Readers of this collection are undoubtedly familiar with the distinction between summative and formative assessments. A challenge presented by formative assessments is finding the time to analyze the data that they provide. Whether through pop quizzes, quick check-ins, student-teacher conferencing, or other informal assessments, teachers are collecting data on how well each of their students is doing. And doing this data collection systematically, analyzing, and planning to modify instruction based on data take a lot of time, time which most educators simply cannot find. As a result, the information from these potentially formative assessments lies dormant, and the value of their data to impact instruction and learning is often lost. If educators do not analyze and make instructional adjustments based on this information, formative assessments are, in fact, not formative at all. The value of the feedback that formative assessments can provide is realized only when that feedback is timely enough to inform and motivate change to instruction. This does not happen often in practice. A UDL approach to learning offers a solution.

A UDL approach incorporates assessment throughout instruction in order to provide ongoing, actionable feedback to educators and students before failure takes place, when taking action can make a real difference for all. In a UDL classroom, assessments occur as part of varied and flexible instructional activities. Instructional routines are less likely to be teacher directed, executed in the same manner, or enacted at the same pace. The curriculum is rather highly flexible with many entry points, optional modes of presentation, alternative means of expression, and varied opportunities for interaction. There are so many ways in which learners may engage in such a classroom; learners do not require diagnosis because their wide variability is anticipated and acknowledged in the design of lessons. Extensive use of technology enhances curriculum flexibility allowing participation to be highly personalized. In a UDL classroom, assessment is included as part of the design of the learning experience and is thus inseparable from instruction. Teachers as well as students get ongoing feedback on learning strengths, successes, and areas to work on. Action can, and is, taken long before failure occurs.

In point of fact, the availability of options and choices in the learning environment, the core of any UDL approach, exaggerates the importance of timely assessment. The options are only useful and optimal when enough information is available to guide both teacher and student in choosing among those options effectively. Without that guidance, the options are often merely distractions.

In that context, many current assessment methods, both summative and formative, are too tardy. A key impediment is that these assessments are largely extrinsic to the learning itself. By extrinsic, we mean to say that they are probes or instruments that are designed to follow (in the case of summative measures) or accompany (in the case of formative measures) some kind of learning experience. They are not really embedded in the learning itself, and, as a result, they are not timely or articulate enough to guide that experience. Formative assessments are clearly much more embedded than summative, but the extra effort of scoring, interpreting, providing feedback, etc. is extraneous and limits the timeliness of feedback. For example, when students are doing science investigation, they collect data, analyze it, and use it to draw conclusions and apply scientific principles. If there are problems or inaccuracies with the data students have collected, their ability to accurately analyze, draw conclusions, and connect with science principles is compromised. A UDL approach to this scenario, on the other hand, would provide teachers and learners with an assessment process during the instructional episode: models to check collected data, guides to evaluate the quality of the data collected, and prompts to compare with peers. This allows learners, as they are doing science, to discern which data set provides the most accurate data to analyze and apply to the broader scientific principles, which is the goal of the inquiry science endeavor, thus avoiding misconceptions in science.

New technologies, especially those with UDL designs, are radically changing the possibilities for making assessment methods that are less extrinsic and more intrinsic. It is almost trite to bring up modern interactive games and simulations as examples, but even with their present weaknesses, they demonstrate a much more intrinsic approach to assessment and feedback. Simply put, there is no reason to add extrinsic assessments or tests to most games and simulations or at least to well-designed ones. Those games, in a real sense, are already continuous assessment instruments: they measure progress continuously and can, with good design, continuously provide feedback that is timely enough to inform instructional decision-making, guide individual learning trajectories, and simultaneously reinforce and accelerate engagement. The assessment is not added on, either post hoc or accompanying. The assessment is central to the learning, inseparable from it.

Well-designed learning games are not only eliminating the distinction between assessment and learning, but they are eliminating the distinction between assessment and feedback. What makes games so engaging, even addicting, is that game designers exploit the human nervous system's pervasive compulsion for feedback. One of the surprising things that early anatomists of the human brain discovered is how enormously the brain is wired for feedback: anatomically, the brain has more channels for feedback than for sensation or perception (Farah, 2000). The brain, the learning organ for the body, is in a real sense a beautifully engineered feedback device.

Unfortunately, as we have just noted, traditional schooling is impoverished at providing the quantity or quality of feedback that a learning nervous system wants and needs. A single teacher with 25 students just cannot provide sufficient timely and individual feedback, either summative or formative, to meet the differential needs of each of her students, the feedback that each of them needs and craves. Traditional classroom technologies such as blackboards and books provide little help: they do not provide any feedback at all.

Into this breach come more and more modern interactive learning technologies. Their role is not primarily to instruct or describe in the traditional sense but to engage and envelop students in authentic problem-solving, graduated practice, virtual exploration, and so on. Key to their success is their ability to provide intrinsic, relevant, immediate, and continuous feedback, just what the nervous system needs. Applying UDL principles in the process ensures that the benefits of more intrinsic assessments are equally accurate and helpful for all students.

Who should the Results of Assessments Inform in a UDL Approach?

Traditionally, assessments have been used to inform students, teachers, schools, districts, and states about academic progress. Students get assessment results in the form of a grade to let them know their degree of success in mastering content. Teachers get student and class results to mark the success or failures of their teaching. School and state administrators get assessment results to assess the success or failures of their educational institutions. Assessment results, in short, are usually used to reward or penalize each of these constituencies, long after they could have taken action to inform and improve learning and instruction.

In addition, assessment designers/developers pilot assessments and use those results to evaluate the success of tests or items. Norm-referenced standardized tests are designed to sort students into broad levels of proficiency. A bell curve is the visual representation of standardized assessment designer/developer's goal, and this curve is desired not only on overall results but on individual test items as well. As a result, these tests do not usually include questions on things most students already know, and if not enough students get an item wrong or, in other words, if students are able to figure out concepts and score well, the item is modified to maintain the bell curve. What is the modification? Rather than replacing a mastered concept with a more challenging one, the item is often modified to make the context or language more tricky or obscure, thus throwing more students off and restoring the bell curve. As a result, non-construct-relevant skills such as vocabulary knowledge or decoding skills are often measured rather than construct-relevant ones (Prometric, 2016).

In a UDL approach to assessments, teachers, students and parents, administrators, and assessment designers/developers all need accurate assessments and timely results. However, the goal of assessment results in a UDL approach is not to penalize or confuse but to inform these constituencies so that each can make data-based adjustments to teaching, learning, and assessments. Let's examine each of these groups to see how a UDL approach to assessment results can be used to inform and improve learning for all students.

Teachers A teacher with limited access to assessment results is like an individual who has a savings account without access to deposit and withdrawal information; it is senseless. Assessment results serve as the building blocks of good instruction as each set of results informs the continued development and implementation of good instruction.

Initially, results help teachers identify and develop optimal instructional goals that provide clear direction for what knowledge and skills will be taught. Once goals are established and instruction begins, teachers use feedback, such as formative evaluation, to effectively evaluate and adjust the design of their instructional methods and materials. This cycle provides insights into whether students' learning is maximized and appropriate levels of challenge are provided or adjustments in the selected instructional methods and materials are necessary. When results of measures indicate that the majority of students are struggling, the level of challenge may be too high. On the contrary, if results indicate that students are "flying through" the instructional tasks, the level of challenge may be insufficient. Too much challenge and not enough challenge equally impact student engagement and can result in compromised learning (Vygotsky, 1978). To thwart either of these challenges, instructional techniques should be adjusted to maximize and maintain engagement and learning.

As noted earlier, the most distinctive role of assessment in a UDL approach is not to assay average progress or outcomes but to provide the feedback needed to customize instruction effectively, especially for students in the margins. Results from continuous assessment are critical to inform and influence the amount and types of scaffolds and supports teachers embed in their instructional methods. Providing apt scaffolds and supports ensures appropriate levels of challenge are available for all students and helps maintain persistence and engagement with learning.

Case example: Mr. Devin has a class of 30 students who all use an online literacy environment. Data are collected every time students are logged in. He views these data with one click and sees which students are struggling with embedded summary measures. For each of those students, he clicks a button which turns on embedded hints and exemplars, so the next time these students confront a summary measure, they will have access to the right level of challenge and support. When a student's scores increase, he can click another button which provides students with a more general support. As their scores increase farther, he can gradually release these supports entirely.

Students A central goal of the UDL framework is that all students become expert learners. Expert learners understand who they are in relation to their own learning, are attuned to their learning goals, are able to advocate for what they need to maximize their learning, and will ultimately persist and remain engaged with their own learning. Students who continually struggle or who continually are not challenged enough will find it difficult to persist and remain engaged (Guthrie & Davis, 2003). Assessment results are key to create an optimal mindset for students toward understanding who they are as learners.

When students understand who they are as learners, they are able to build an optimal mindset for learning and to gain an accurate representation of their own abilities related to challenges and preferences (Dweck, 2006). Ultimately, they can identify and use the strategies, supports and scaffolds in order to provide optimal levels of challenge. These skills tie back to the ability to persist and remain engaged in learning tasks as an expert learner.

Case example. Jared uses an online literacy environment for supplemental reading in his ELA classroom. He realizes that he is not performing as well as he would like on embedded summary measures and he would like to improve these scores. The next time that he logs in, he goes to an area where he can access some additional supports. These include videos of how to develop a good summary, some examples and non-examples of good summaries, and pop-up tips which provide details of how to develop a good summary. Jared chooses to view one of the videos that has been scripted and created by one of his peers. Then he opts to display the hints while he completes the embedded summary measure. Both of these help him improve his score. Two weeks later, he only uses the pop-up hints, and then he turns these off 1 week later and completes the measures on his own. During this time, he watches his scores improve.

Parents In a UDL framework, the ultimate goal of assessment is to promote student learning. Parents are key to the success of this goal. Formative and summative assessment results shared with parents support collaboration between parents, teachers, and students, a collaboration that is key to learning success. It is critical that parents are informed about what their child is doing on an ongoing basis so that parents can productively and successfully work with teachers as well as with their own student, to promote learning.

Case example. Paula's sixth grade English language arts teacher sends monthly reports home to all parents; these reports include the results from two to three short formative assessments that have been administered during that month. Paula's parents are grateful that they are able to monitor Paula's progress more frequently than the quarterly report cards allow. Because they receive this feedback, her parents take an active role in supporting her with some tasks that challenge her. In addition, they were able to intervene in January when Paula's grandmother passed away. Her teachers' report showed Paula's parents that her performance that month had declined. Paula's parents wrote a note to her teacher informing her about Paula's grandmother and explained that it may have contributed to Paula's decline in performance that month. As a result, together Paula's parents and teacher were able to provide additional academic and emotional scaffolds in order to support Paula, getting her back to progressing in ELA.

Administrators Assessments are often used by administrators to make decisions that have a life impact such as determining the hiring or firing of teachers or determining whether students receive a high school diploma. In this age of high scrutiny of teacher and student performance through state and national assessments, there have been instances of abuse. For example, there has been at least one report where assessment results were used by teachers and administrators to counsel students to leave school in order that school profiles maintain a desired range of scores. Students were coached to take a GED class to earn their degree instead of remaining in school and taking the state assessments (Stahl, 2006). UDL does not support the use of one type of assessment measure by administrators to determine the fate of any teacher or students' future.

In a UDL framework, administrators use the information provided by ongoing and summative assessments to inform adjustments to curriculum, individual teacher and departmental planning time, professional development, and other aspects of school administration. Armed with assessment data that reveals barriers as well as student and teacher strengths and with a clear goal of improving student learning, administrators can make informed and timely decisions that will promote student growth in skills and understanding.

Case example: Mrs. Fernandez is the head of the Literacy Department for the Bakerside School District. It is summer and she recently received the results of the state assessments for the fifth grade students who have just left to move onto middle school. The information demonstrates that 11% of the students are advanced, 42% are proficient, 28% need improvement and are reading at a basic level, and 19% are failing. Using this information, she decides to research curriculum materials that target struggling readers and to identify long-term opportunities for professional development that focus on struggling readers. She contacts publishers and professional development organizations that provide long-term support for literacy skills as she sets the goal of decreasing the percentage of students who need improvement and who are failing. She arranges several meetings with a group of teachers (some of whom she considers strong and some not quite as strong) to serve as a voice as she moves forward with her decision to investigate new methods and materials to improve literacy.

Test makers/developers Identifying and minimizing barriers and allowing alternate means for students to access relevant constructs are critical part of test developers' work. UDL provides a framework for test makers/developers to design more accurate and useful assessments. UDL guides developers, as well as teachers and other educators, to provide flexibility to ensure that tests are more accurate and useful in measuring the identified constructs. For example, the UDL guidelines suggest that test developers provide multiple means for students to receive information. Text that can be read silently or with a text-to-speech tool, when evaluating non-decoding tasks, is one example of providing this flexibility. In this case, eliminating the construct-irrelevant demand of reading reduces barriers and allows students to more accurately show what they know, better informing teachers, administrators, students, and parents.

In a UDL framework, results inform all constituencies for the same purpose: to promote growth in student learning. With knowledge of assessment results, test makers/developers can also learn more about students, their skills, and their understanding. Test makers/developers are also better able to see the barriers created by assessments and learn who is unintentionally favored by assessment design. Informed by this information, test makers/developers can modify assessment design to increase the accuracy of the assessments themselves (Gordon, Gravel, & Schifter, 2009; Marino et al., 2014; Rose, Hall, & Murray, 2008).

Case example. Assessing mathematics for the New World is a company focused on the development of standardized math assessments. They recently developed a new assessment that included a section on word problems. As part of the instructions, they urged administrators of the measure to read the problems aloud to ensure that students who struggle with reading would not be compromised in their ability to successfully complete the problem because of low decoding skills. This is an example of how to provide options that ensure that construct-irrelevant demands do not render results that represent inaccurate measures of student knowledge, skills, and understanding. In this case, a student who struggles with text decoding has that barrier reduced and can now demonstrate their understanding of the math concept being measured. Clearly, it is critical that test developers identify the construct being measured and minimize barriers by allowing alternative means for students to access the construct.

The Future of Assessment Through a UDL Lens

With the prominent placement of UDL in the Every Student Succeeds Act (ESSA), especially in the sections on assessment, it no longer seems entirely presumptuous to speak of the role of UDL in the future of assessment. With that in mind, we want to close with a bit of presumptuous forecasting, imagining the future of assessment through a UDL lens.

Traditionally, the goals of education have focused on the acquisition of knowledge. Such goals were reasonable when knowledge was scarce, inaccessible, and inequitably distributed. New technologies have radically altered the landscape of knowledge, making it increasingly ubiquitous and instantaneously accessible without keeping it in biological memory. The challenge now is to make knowledge useful, especially in a world where the amount of new knowledge is expanding geometrically and where old knowledge is no longer relevant. The ways that we come to know things have changed, the things that we need to know have changed, and both will change again and again in our lifetimes. The skills we need have changed and will change again and again.

In that modern universe, the ultimate goal of education can no longer be the mastery of specific knowledge or skills but the mastery of learning itself. To prepare students for a future in which they will continually confront new domains of knowledge and new demands for skills, the ultimate goal must be to prepare every student, each in their own individual way, to be *expert learners*.

From a UDL perspective, "expert learners" are:

1. Strategic and goal-directed learners. As they progress on their development path, expert learners can formulate plans for learning, devise effective strategies and tactics for optimal learning, organize resources and tools to facilitate learning, monitor their progress toward mastery, recognize their own strengths and weaknesses as learners, seek out effective mentors and models to guide their learning, and meaningfully reflect upon feedback to adjust their strategies usefully.
2. Knowledgeable learners. Expert learners bring considerable prior, growing, and changing knowledge to new learning; they activate that prior knowledge to identify, organize, prioritize, and assimilate new information; when they lack requisite prior knowledge, they know where and how to find the information they need; they recognize the tools and resources that would help them find, structure, and remember new information; and they know how to transform new information into meaningful and useable knowledge.
3. Purposeful, motivated learners. Expert learners increasingly develop skills to be intrinsically rather than extrinsically motivated to learn, and their goals are focused on mastery rather than performance, they know how to choose and to set challenging learning goals for themselves and how to sustain the effort and resilience that reaching those goals will require, they readily participate in communities of practice to sustain their learning, and they can monitor and regulate emotional reactions that would be impediments or distractions to their success.

Assessments of the future will have to be redesigned to measure expertise that is as rich and comprehensive as this. They will have to be redesigned to measure not whether students "have" knowledge but whether they can find, construct, apply, and evaluate knowledge in new and changing domains and whether they have the motivation and engagement to do any of those things. And they will have to measure those capacities in a way that is accurate for students who are wildly different from one another and for whom the expertise will be developed along widely different paths.

And finally, we shall have to have assessments whose purpose is to recognize, amplify, and celebrate the differences among students as if our future depended on it which, in fact, it will. Those assessments will have to be *universally* designed for learning.

References

Bakia, M., Mislevy, J., Heying, E., Patton, C., Singleton, C., & Krumm, A. (2013). *Supporting K-12 students in online learning: A review of online 1 algebra courses*. Menlo Park, CA: SRI International.

Baker, R. S. J. d, Gowda, S., Corbett, A., & Ocumpaugh, J. (2012). *Towards Automatically DetectingWhether Student Learning is Shallow*. Proceedings of the International Conference on Intelligent Tutoring Systems, (pp 444–453).

Bondy, A., & Frost, L. (2012, May/June). Teaching children to understand changes in routines. *Autism Asperger's Digest*.

CAST. (2011). *Universal design for learning guidelines version 2.0*. Wakefield, MA: Author.

Cavanaugh, C., Repetto, J., Wayer, N., & Spitler, C. (2013). Online learning for students with disabilities: A framework for success. *Journal of Special Education Technology, 28*(1), 1–8.

Cohen, G. L., Garcia, J., Apfel, N., & Master, A. (2006). Reducing the racial achievement gap: A social-psychological intervention. *Science, 313*, 1307–1310.

Daley, S., Hillaire, G., & Sutherland, L. A. M. (2014). Beyond performance data: Improving student help seeking by collecting and displaying influential data in an online middle-school science curriculum. *British Journal of Educational Technology, 47*(1), 121–134.

Dweck, C. (2006). *Mindset: The new psychology of success*. New York, NY: Random House.

Every Student Succeeds Act, E. S. S. (2015). Pub. L. No. 114–95 § 114 Stat. 1177.

Farah, M. J. (2000). *The Cognitive neuroscience of vision*. Hoboken, NJ: Wiley-Blackwell.

Gordon, D. T., Gravel, J. W., & Schifter, L. A. (2009). *A policy reader in universal design for learning* (pp. 209–218). Cambridge, MA: Harvard Education Press.

Guthrie, J. T., & Davis, M. H. (2003). Motivating struggling readers in middle school through an engagement model of classroom practice. *Reading & Writing Quarterly, 19*(1), 59–85.

Hall, T. E., Meyer, A., & Rose, D. H. (2012). *Universal design for learning in the classroom: Practical applications*. New York, NY: Guilford.

Ivcevic, Z., & Brackett, M. A. (2014). Predicting school success: Comparing conscientiousness, grit, and emotion regulation ability. *Journal of Research Personality*. http://ei.yale.edu/publication/predicting-school-success-comparing-conscientiousness-grit-emotion-regulation-ability-2/

Jamieson, J. P., Mendes, W. B., Blackstock, E., & Schmader, T. (2010). Turning the knots in your stomach into bows: Reappraising arousal improves performance on the GRE. *Journal of Experimental Social Psychology, 46*(1), 208–212.

Marino, M. T., Gotch, C. M., Israel, M., Vasquez, E., Basham, J. D., & Becht, K. (2014). UDL in the middle school science classroom can video games and alternative text heighten engagement and learning for students with learning disabilities? *Learning Disability Quarterly, 37*(2), 87–99.

Meyer, A., Rose, D. H., & Gordon, D. (2014). *Universal design for learning: Theory and practice*. Wakefield, MA: CAST Professional Publishing.

National Center on the Use of Emerging Technologies to improve literacy achievement for students with disabilities in middle school. (2016). http://cet.cast.org/

Nelson, L. L. (2014). *Design and deliver: Planning and teaching using universal design for learning*. Baltimore, MD: Brookes Publishing.

Novak, K. (2014). *UDL now!: A teacher's monday morning guide to implementing the common core state standards using universal design for learning*. Wakefield, MA: CAST Professional Publishing.

Prometric. (2016). *Best practices in item development for online testing*. https://www.prometric.com/en-us/news-and-resources/reference-materials/pages/Best-Practices-in-Item-Development-for-Online-Testing.aspx. Accessed 5 Dec 2016.

Rappolt-Schlichtmann, G., & Daley, S. G. (2013). Providing access to engagement in learning: The potential of universal design for learning in museum design. *Curator: The Museum Journal, 56*(3), 307–321. https://doi.org/10.1111/cura.12030

Rappolt-Schlichtmann, G., Daley, S. G., Lim, S., Lapinski, S., Robinson, K. H., & Johnson, M. (2013). Universal design for learning and elementary school science: Exploring the efficacy, use, and perceptions of a web-based science notebook. *Journal of Educational Psychology, 105*(4), 1210–1225.

Reich, C., Price, J., Rubin, E., & Steiner, M. (2010). *Inclusion, disabilities, and informal science learning. A CAISE Inquiry Group Report*. Washington, DC: Center for Advancement of Informal Science Education.

Rose, D. H., Hall, T. E., & Murray, E. (2008). Accurate for all: Universal design for learning and the assessment of students with learning disabilities. *Perspectives on Language and Literacy, 34*(4), 23.

Rose, D. H., & Meyer, A. (2002). *Teaching every student in the digital age: Universal design for learning*. Alexandria, VA: Association for Supervision and Curriculum Development.

Rose, D. H., & Gravel, J. W. (2013). Using digital media to design student-centered curricula. In R. E. Wolfe, A. Steinberg, & N. Hoffmann (Eds.), *Anytime, anywhere: Student-centered learning for students and teachers* (pp. 77–101). Cambridge, MA: Harvard Education Press.

Spencer, S. J., Steele, C. M., & Quinn, D. M. (1999). Stereotype threat and women's math performance. *Journal of Experimental Social Psychology, 35*, 4–28.

Stahl, W. M. (October, 2006). Personal discussion.

Steele, C. M. (1997). A threat in the air: How stereotypes shape intellectual identity and performance. *American psychologist, 52*(6), 613.

Steele, C. M., & Aronson, J. (1995). Stereotype threat and the intellectual test performance of African-Americans. *Journal of Personality and Social Psychology, 69*, 797–811.

U.S. Department of Education, Office of Educational Technology. (2015). *Ed tech developers guide*. Washington, DC. http://ed.tech.gov/developers-guide

U.S. Department of Education, Office of Educational Technology. (2016). *Future ready learning: Reimagining the role of technology in education*. Washington, DC. http://tech.ed.gov/netp/

Vygotsky, L. (1978). Interaction between learning and development. In L. Vygotsky (Ed.), *Mind in society* (pp. 79–91). Cambridge, MA: Harvard University Press.

Item Development Research and Practice

12

Anthony D. Albano and Michael C. Rodriguez

Progressing Toward Accessible Items

Achievement testing in the United States dates back to the 1800s when written exams were used to classify the increasing numbers of children entering the public education system. Early proponents of large-scale testing considered education to be an equalizer in terms of its potential to give students equal opportunities for success (e.g., Mann, 1867). With this objective in mind, standardized achievement tests were used both to screen and place students according to their instructional needs and to evaluate schools, so as to encourage a balanced distribution of educational resources (Office of Technology Assessment, 1992). Thus, from their earliest applications in education in the United States, achievement tests have been associated with fairness and universal access.

Applications of achievement testing today are similar to those from the foundations of public education in the United States. We are still using standardized student achievement tests to screen and place students and, sometimes controversially, to evaluate schools and educators. However, the amount of testing has increased exponentially over the past 200 years, and the makeup and methods of achievement testing have changed dramatically as well. In this chapter we review item development research and practice as it relates to two key changes in achievement testing. The first is a shift in the predominant item response format used, from constructed response to selected response. This shift began in the early 1900s (e.g., Kelly, 1916), as the scale and stakes associated with achievement testing increased and efficiency of administration and objectivity of scoring became priorities. The constructed-response item would later resurge in the form of performance assessments (e.g., Deno, 1985) and other more "authentic" response types (e.g., Hart, 1994), but the majority of tests today still utilize the selected-response format. The second change is an increasing emphasis on validity, especially in terms of accessibility, the extent to which test items allow test takers to demonstrate effectively their knowledge of the target construct (Beddow, Elliott, & Kettler, 2010). The latest edition of the *Standards for Educational and Psychological Testing* (the Standards; AERA, APA, & NCME, 2014) includes a chapter on fairness in testing, with details on the various threats to fairness that must be addressed in the test development process, including the removal of construct-irrelevant barriers to valid test interpretation for all students.

A. D. Albano (✉)
University of Nebraska-Lincoln, Lincoln, NE, USA
e-mail: albano@unl.edu

M. C. Rodriguez
University of Minnesota-Twin Cities,
Minneapolis, MN, USA

Legislation and federal regulations (for a review, see Zigmond & Kloo, 2009) have also increased our attention to issues of inclusion, fairness, equity, and access. Research centers and federally funded research projects have devoted substantial resources to examining the translation of these standards, policies, and issues into research and practice, resulting in a growing literature on item writing for accessibility (e.g., Kettler et al., 2011).

This chapter provides an overview of the fundamentals of item development, especially as they pertain to accessible assessments. Constructed-response and selected-response items are first introduced and compared, with examples. Next, the item development process and guidelines for effective item writing are presented. Empirical research examining the item development process is then reviewed for general education items and items modified for accessibility. Methods for evaluating item quality, in regard to accessibility, are summarized. Finally, recent innovations and technological enhancements in item development, administration, and scoring are discussed.

Current Practice

Constructed-response formats Assessments have historically utilized items and tasks that first presented test takers with a question or prompt, referred to as the item stem, and then required that the test taker construct a response, given orally or in writing. The administrator of the assessment then scored the response or recorded it for later scoring, ideally using a scoring rubric. As discussed below, technology has greatly expanded the available options for presenting, recording responses from, and scoring constructed-response (CR) and other types of assessment items (Williamson, Bejar, & Mislevy, 2006).

A traditional example of a CR item is the essay question, where test takers respond by generating text, either written by hand or typed on a keyboard. Other familiar CR formats include short-answer essays, grid-in responses, computation problems, extended essays such as research papers, and oral reports (for reviews, see Osterlind & Merz, 1994; and Haladyna, 1997). Fill-in-the-blank and cloze procedures can also be considered CR formats, but these are not recommended for general use in educational testing (Haladyna, 1997). Additionally, assessments involving portfolios or work samples, recitals or performances, exhibitions, and experiments may also be categorized broadly as CR tasks; however, these performance assessments require more extensive scoring rubrics and substantially more time to plan, prepare, and administer, and, as a result, they are not well adapted to on-demand testing.

Few attempts have been made to formally categorize the more prevalent CR item formats. Bennett, Ward, Rock, and LaHart (1990) differentiated among item types based on the amount of *openness* permitted in the response process. Openness referred to the extent to which an item allowed for construction as opposed to choice in a response. Judges rated the openness in response for a series of items using an ordinal scale that included (0) multiple-choice items with no openness, (1) selection/identification, (2) reordering/rearranging, (3) substitution/correction, (4) completion, (5) construction, and (6) presentation/performance. Results showed that judges struggled to agree on the categorization of more open response processes. However, agreement overall was high, supporting the idea that item response processes can be distinguished in terms of their openness. The implications of these results for validity were discussed in an edited volume by Bennett and Ward (1991), wherein it is argued that a balance of response openness, consistent with the construct, may be best.

Osterlind and Merz (1994) proposed a taxonomy of CR items based on the multidimensional cognitive abilities involved in the response process (e.g., Hannah & Michaels, 1977; Snow, 1980; Sternberg, 1982). The taxonomy described the response process on three dimensions: (a) the type of reasoning competency used, including factual recall and interpretive, analytical, and predictive reasoning; (b) the nature of the cognitive continuum used, including convergent and divergent thinking; and (c) the kind of response yielded, including open-product and closed-product formats. These dimensions were only discussed from a theoretical standpoint and are yet to be investigated empirically.

There is still no theoretical framework or taxonomic scheme that encompasses the many forms of CR and selected-response (SR) items and performance assessment tasks so as to support meaningful distinctions across response formats. Haladyna and Rodriguez (2013) distinguish between CR items involving objective scoring (e.g., constructing word definitions, where a finite number of responses can be scored with little or no ambiguity) and CR items involving subjective scoring, where human judgment is required (e.g., essay questions). Automated scoring can be used for some types of CR items (Attali & Burstein, 2006; Yang, Buckendahl, Juszkiewicz, & Bhola, 2002). In alternate assessments, alternate forms of CR response are allowable, including verbal responses, drawings, and word lists or construct maps (see Russell & Kavanaugh, 2010).

Selected-response formats Although the SR item type can be used in numerous different formats, the conventional multiple-choice (MC) item is still the most commonly used. Examples of the conventional MC, along with five other SR formats, are shown below (for additional examples, see Haladyna and Rodriguez, 2013). As with the CR format, the SR contains a distinct item stem that outlines the question or task to which the test taker will respond. However, in the SR, two or more response options are also provided, and the test taker is limited to responding by selecting or indicating one or more of these options. In the following examples, the correct response is underlined.

Conventional multiple choice

The content of a vocabulary test item constitutes an accessibility barrier for the test taker when the content involves

A. terms that the test taker is unfamiliar with.
B. skills that are extraneous to the construct measured by the test.

C. cognitive complexity that increases the difficulty of the item.

Multiple true/false

A test is administered with accommodations to some students and without accommodations to others. Do these procedures provide evidence that scores from tests with and without accommodations can be reported on the same scale?

1. Yes/No Accommodations given on the test align with those used during instruction.
2. Yes/No Students receiving accommodations have the same mean test score as students not receiving accommodations.
3. Yes/No A test of measurement invariance indicates that items load on the construct in the same way for both groups of students.

Alternate choice

In general, an item is more effective when it assesses.

A. a single cognitive task.
B. multiple cognitive tasks.

True/false

A test administered with modifications will measure the same construct as a test without. True/False

Matching

Match each item property on the left with the statistic used to estimate it on the right.

1. difficulty	A. mean group differences controlling for ability
2. discrimination	B. correlation with an external criterion measure
3. bias	
4. reliability	C. coefficient alpha if item deleted
5. validity	D. mean response time
	E. correlation with total scores
	F. proportion responding correctly

Complex multiple choice

In general, what are appropriate methods for improving accessibility on a science test?

1. Reducing linguistic complexity.
2. Explaining the meaning of difficult words.
3. Presenting text in large print.

A. 1 and 2.
B. 1 and 3.
C. 2 and 3.
D. All 3.

Choosing an Item Format

Rodriguez (2002) discussed the various considerations to be made when choosing an item response format, including cost, efficiency, reliability, and practical and political issues. In the end, validity is paramount. The appropriate item format or combination of formats is the one that best supports the intended inferences proposed by a test (Bennett & Ward, 1991). Typically, this item format or combination of formats is the one that assesses the intended construct, as defined within a test outline, with the highest level of fidelity.

The main drawbacks of the CR format, in comparison with the SR, are that the CR often requires more time and resources to administer and score, can introduce subjectivity into the scoring process, and has been shown to be less reliable (Wainer & Thissen, 1993). The major strength of the CR is that it can more easily be used to assess complex reasoning and higher-order thinking, as it provides access to a wider range of cognitive functions (Martinez, 1999). As a result, the CR may provide a more direct representation of achievement in a particular domain (Haladyna, 1989). Although the SR can be written to assess higher-order thinking, it is less frequently used in this way (Martinez).

Haladyna and Rodriguez (2013) concluded that the tendency for SR items to assess lower-order thinking is not necessarily a limitation inherent in the item format itself but can instead be attributed to the way SR items are written. Research suggests that, in operational tests, CR items often behave much like SR items without any options (Rodriguez, 1998). As a result, responses from the two formats can be nearly perfectly correlated (Rodriguez, 2003), suggesting that they can be used interchangeably. Thus, when both formats are available to the test developer, the SR format may be the optimal choice.

Item Development Guidelines

The item-writing process is discussed in numerous educational measurement textbooks and book chapters. The *Handbook of Test Development* includes chapters on writing SR items (Rodriguez, 2016), performance tasks and prompts (Lane & Iwatani, 2016), and innovative item formats (Sireci & Zenisky, 2016). Books are also available on *Writing Test Items to Evaluate Higher Order Thinking* (Haladyna, 1997) and *Developing and Validating Multiple-Choice Test Items* (Haladyna & Rodriguez, 2013).

Item development should proceed only after a number of key stages in the test development process have taken place (Downing, 2006). These stages require:

1. Articulation of the purpose of the test, including what is being measured (the target construct), for whom (the target population), and why (the intended score inferences and uses)
2. Description of the standards, learning objectives, or instructional objectives defining what students are expected to know and be able to do with regard to the domain of content for the test
3. Creation of test specifications detailing how the test content is distributed across the test domain, and any subdomains, and the roles of other important features, such as cognitive complexity
4. Communication of this information, along with relevant guidelines and style requirements, to the item writers, who are ideally subject-matter experts

Items are then written collaboratively by subject-matter experts, test developers, sensitivity review committees, and psychometricians, among others. They may also be administered within a pilot test, optionally with feedback from a focus group or cognitive lab, where results from a sample of students can inform revision or removal of certain items. Methods for evaluating item quality are discussed further next.

Here we summarize published guidelines for developing SR and CR items. More detailed guidelines are available for specific grade levels, domains, and student populations, for example, classroom assessment in higher education (Rodriguez & Albano, in press) and language assessment (Schedl & Malloy, 2014). Large-scale testing programs also provide item writers with guidelines, item specifications, and style requirements that are tailored to the particular testing program (e.g., American Institutes for Research, 2009). The guidelines presented here apply broadly to item writing across a variety of domains, with the overarching goal of increasing accessibility for the target population of test takers, including students in need of accommodations.

Selected-response guidelines Haladyna and Downing (1989a, 1989b) developed the first comprehensive taxonomy of SR item-writing guidelines. The taxonomy was later updated and revised based on newer empirical evidence and a meta-analytic review of some of that evidence (Haladyna, Downing, & Rodriguez, 2002). The taxonomy was primarily based on a review of item-writing advice taken from over twenty-four textbooks. The majority of the guidelines reviewed were supported only by logical reasoning and good writing practices; few were based on empirical research. Other taxonomies (e.g., Ellsworth, Dunnell, & Duell, 1990; Frey, Petersen, Edwards, Pedrotte, & Peyton, 2005) corresponded closely with the one presented in Haladyna et al. (2002). Haladyna & Rodriguez (2013) provide the most recent update to the taxonomy.

The SR item-writing guidelines presented here are a compilation of those provided in these other sources. They are organized here, like in Haladyna and Rodriguez (2013), according to concerns with the item content, formatting and style, the stem, and the options.

Content concerns relate to the information and material addressed within an MC item, as outlined in the test and item specifications. In general, items should be carefully constructed to measure relevant and appropriate content and cognitive skills. These content guidelines are largely based on logical argument and the experience of item writers and reactions from examinees. Aside from some general research on clarity and appropriate vocabulary use, there is no specific evidence supporting these guidelines; however, they offer guidance in an area where it is needed.

1. Target one cognitive task in each item, rather than multiple tasks.
2. Use a single type of content in each item, and keep it unique and independent of the content in other items.
3. Assess important content, avoiding content that is trivial, overly specific, or overly general.
4. Use novel material and applications to engage higher-level thinking.
5. Avoid referencing unqualified opinions.
6. Avoid trick items that intentionally mislead students.

Formatting and style concerns relate to the general practice of good writing and its application within the various SR item formats. There is some empirical evidence supporting the general use of most SR formats, including the question, completion, and best answer versions of the conventional MC, the alternate choice, true/false, multiple true/false, matching, and context-dependent item and item set formats; however, some formats, including the complex MC format, may decrease accessibility by introducing construct-irrelevant variance and should not be used (Haladyna et al., 2002).

7. Format the item vertically instead of horizontally, with options listed vertically.
8. Edit and proof all items, including for correct grammar, punctuation, capitalization, and spelling.
9. Minimize the amount of reading required by each item.
10. Keep vocabulary and linguistic complexity appropriate for the target construct and target population.

Writing the stem is an area that extends general style requirements to the stem of the item.

Some research has examined the impact of using negative wording in the stem, which empirical findings suggest should rarely be used.

11. Include the main idea for the item within the stem instead of the options.
12. Word the stem positively, avoiding negative phrasing such as *not* or *except*. When their use cannot be avoided, ensure that they appear capitalized and boldface.

Writing the options is the area with the largest volume of empirical evidence. Issues related to SR options were examined in the first published empirical study of item writing (Ruch & Stoddard, 1925). Since then, numerous studies have explored issues in writing SR options; however, of the guidelines presented here, fewer than half have been studied empirically.

13. Use only options that are plausible and discriminating. Three options are usually sufficient.
14. Ensure that only one option per item is the correct or keyed response.
15. Vary the location of the correct response according to the number of options.
16. Put options in logical or numerical order when possible.
17. Keep options independent; options should not overlap in content.
18. Avoid using the options *all of the above*, *none of the above*, and *I don't know*.
19. Phrase options positively, avoiding negatives such as NOT.
20. Avoid giving clues to the correct response:
    (a) Make options as similar as possible in length, grammatical structure, and content.
    (b) Avoid specific determiners, including always, never, completely, and absolutely.
    (c) Avoid clang associations, options identical to or resembling components of the stem.
    (d) Avoid pairs or triplets of options that clue the test taker to the correct response.
    (e) Avoid blatantly absurd, ridiculous options.
21. Make all incorrect options plausible. Base incorrect options on typical errors of students.
22. Avoid the use of humor.

In the context of testing with accommodations, these guidelines provide for clarity, efficiency in word usage, and good writing practices that should maximize accessibility for the widest audience of examinees. As we read them, most recommendations for improving test accessibility are different versions of good item-writing guidelines.

Constructed-response guidelines As with SR item writing, guidelines for writing CR items are primarily based on logical reasoning and principles of good writing, with limited empirical research supporting their use (less than we have for MC items). Furthermore, as noted above, a variety of CR formats are available, and what specifically constitutes a CR item is not well defined. As a result, guidelines for CR item writing are less developed and less uniform across sources than SR guidelines.

Educational Testing Service (ETS) has published a series of reports examining the quality of CR item formats and scoring methods and the application of CR items (e.g., Sparks, Song, Brantley, & Liu, 2014; Young, So, & Ockey, 2013). The ETS *Guidelines for Constructed-Response and Other Performance Assessments* (Baldwin, Fowles, & Livingston, 2005) recommend that the CR item development process begin with three considerations. First, individuals involved in shaping the assessment should represent the demographic, ethnic, and cultural diversity of the people whose knowledge and skills will be assessed. Second, relevant information about the assessment should be communicated during the early stages of development so that those who need to or wish to know about this information can provide feedback. Third, directions within the assessment should clarify why the assessment is being administered, what the assessment will be like, and what aspects of test taker responses will be considered in scoring. Although these considerations apply generally to all forms of assessment, they speak directly to equity, fairness, and accessibility. They are also reiterated more generally in the Standards (e.g., Standards 3.2 and 4.16; AERA, APA, NCME, 2014).

Numerous textbooks provide practical guidance on writing CR items. These textbooks are primarily written for graduate-level courses in testing and assessment (e.g., Thorndike & Thorndike-Christ, 2011; Popham, 2016). Hogan and Murphy (2007) reviewed 25 books and book chapters on educational and psychological measurement published from 1960 to 2007 and identified 124 recommendations on preparing CR items and 121 recommendations on scoring. A number of recommendations on the preparation of CR items are especially relevant to accessible item writing, including paying attention to testing time and the length of the CR test, avoiding the use of optional items, clearly defining questions or tasks, connecting item content to instructional objectives, assuring items assess more complex processes, avoiding the use of CR items to test recall, and considering the appropriateness of vocabulary, grammar, and syntax given the level of the assessment.

Haladyna and Rodriguez (2013) synthesize the guidelines and recommendations discussed above, and others (e.g., Gitomer, 2007), in the four categories of content concerns, formatting and style concerns, writing the directions/stimulus, and context concerns. The same structure is used here to summarize CR item-writing guidelines.

Content concerns, as with SR items, reference the material covered within the item, and they are best addressed by relying on clear test and item specifications in the item-writing process. The choice of a CR over SR should be justified by the nature of the content and cognitive task assessed, and when CR items with different tasks are used to assess the same content and cognitive tasks, they should do so consistently.

1. Clarify the domain of knowledge, skills, and abilities to be tested.
2. Ensure that the format is appropriate for the intended cognitive task.
3. Ensure that the construct is comparable across tasks.

Formatting and style concerns have to do with improving clarity in the overall presentation of the item, including good writing that is evaluated through review by test developers and subject-matter experts, along with students from the target population, ideally within a pilot test or focus group administration. As we discuss further below, pilot testing is especially key to examining accessibility for students with varying levels of cognitive abilities.

4. Edit and proofread instructions, items, and item formatting.
5. Pilot items and test procedures.

Writing the directions/stimulus refers to the importance of clear communication of the intent of the task to the test taker. When expectations are unclear or ambiguous, the test taker will struggle to construct a response that meets them, regardless of the test taker's knowledge of the construct. Unclear expectations may result from a lack of detail within a task, where key information is left up to interpretation, or a task that is overly complex, perhaps involving multiple requirements. Expectations can often be clarified by including information from the scoring rubric for a CR item within the task itself.

6. Clearly define directions, expectations for response format, and task demands.
7. Provide sufficient information on scoring criteria.
8. Avoid requiring implicit assumptions; avoid construct-irrelevant task features.

Context concerns refer broadly to guidelines for ensuring that the context of an item does not introduce construct-irrelevant features for the target population. These concerns can be addressed by incorporating into the item development and piloting processes input from individuals representing the entire population of test takers.

9. Consider cultural and regional diversity and accessibility for the intended population of test takers.
10. Ensure that the linguistic complexity is suitable for the intended population of test takers.

Like the SR guidelines, the CR item-writing guidelines encourage clarity, efficiency in word usage, and good writing practices that should maximize accessibility for the widest audience of examinees.

Research on Item Development

How often do published test items violate item-writing guidelines? Ellsworth et al. (1990) investigated this question by reviewing over a thousand sample items published in textbooks on testing and measurement. Results were somewhat discouraging. Over 60% of the items reviewed violated one or more guidelines. Roughly 31% of items contained grammatical errors, and about 13% contained redundant information from the item stem within the options. This review highlights the need to be more careful in item development and more critical in item selection. The quality of published items should not be taken for granted. The question that remains is, how do guideline violations impact item development and quality?

As noted above, empirical evidence supporting the item-writing guidelines is limited. The available research on writing SR items is summarized here, along with research on the optimal number of response options.

Evidence on SR development In their original taxonomy of 43 item writing guidelines, Haladyna and Downing (1989b) found that only seven guidelines were supported by empirical evidence. These guidelines included: avoid negative phrasing, use the question or completion format, keep options similar in length, avoid the option *none of the above*, avoid the option *all of the above*, use as many functional incorrect options as are feasible, and avoid complex item formats. The first three of these guidelines had strong support across multiple studies, whereas support for the last four was mixed, including evidence both for and against their use. The guideline receiving the most attention addressed using as many functional incorrect options as possible. As will be discussed further below, results from a more recent study indicate that three functional options should typically suffice.

Extending the work of Haladyna and Downing (1989a, 1989b) and Ellsworth et al. (1990), Rodriguez (1997) conducted a meta-analysis examining the impact of violating a subset of SR item-writing guidelines, as reported in published research. Impact was meta-analyzed in terms of average changes in item difficulty, discrimination, score reliability, and validity. Results were mixed, with any statistically significant effects tending to be small. Findings indicated that using *none of the above* was associated with slightly more difficult items, but did not have a significant effect on discrimination, reliability, or validity. Items with negative wording in the stem were more difficult, and items with the correct option being longer than the others were found to be easier. Use of the complex MC format made items much more difficult and reduced discrimination but did not impact score reliability. Using an open completion-type stem had no effect on any of the metrics examined.

Moreno, Martinez, and Muniz (2006) took a different approach to examining the SR guidelines. Instead of measuring impact in terms of statistics based on test scores, they evaluated a condensed set of 12 guidelines through expert review by two groups of guideline users. These groups included university instructors who had implemented the guidelines in teacher-made assessments and professionals in educational and psychological measurement who had implemented the guidelines in a variety of testing applications. Reviews focused on features such as utility, clarity, coherence, simplicity of phrasing, and overlap within the guidelines themselves. Reviewers generally endorsed the guidelines, though some indicated that they were too restrictive in terms of practical use. Ratings on utility were generally positive. According to professionals, the guideline with the lowest utility pertained to the vertical presentation of response options. Instructors rated utility lowest for the guideline relating to the ordering of response options. Overall, the study documents a unique perspective on the validity of SR guidelines.

Three options are optimal Convention seems to suggest that the minimum number of options in an SR item is four, with even more being preferable for reducing the impact of guessing and increasing item difficulty. Rodriguez (2005) examined this convention in a comprehensive synthesis of empirical evidence spanning 80 years of research. Results indicated that four options are often unnecessary; instead, three tends to be optimal. Moving from five or four options down to three did not negatively impact item or test score statistics. Reducing the number of options to two did have negative effects. Results also showed that the effect of removing an incorrect option depended on how the option was selected to be removed. When options were removed randomly, score reliability decreased significantly. On the other hand, when the least effective incorrect options were removed, reliability was not impacted.

Reducing the number of incorrect response options will necessarily increase the chances of randomly guessing the correct response. Consider a test with 40 items, each having the traditional four options. The probability of a correct response by random guessing is .25, which results in an expected minimum total score of 10/40 items correct. By reducing the number of options per item to three, the probability of a correct response by guessing increases to .33, and the expected minimum total score increases to 13/40. The chances of obtaining a high score by random guessing remain low (e.g., the probability of 24/40 is .00033). However, as the minimum expected total score increases, score precision at the lower end of the scale is expected to decrease, and additional options may be justified if this is a concern.

Reducing the number of incorrect response options can be expected to improve accessibility in at least two related ways. First, fewer options reduce the amount of reading required by each item and by the test overall. Less reading per item allows for additional testing time that can be allocated to additional items. Coverage of the content domain can be improved, and internal consistency reliability can be expected to increase. Second, fewer options reduce the cognitive load for a given item and for the test overall. With fewer options, construct-irrelevant variance due to unnecessary cognitive load is reduced, and the essential components of an item become more accessible to the test taker.

Rodriguez (2005) argued that, in addition to increasing the available testing time per item and reducing cognitive load, fewer response options have the added practical benefit of simplifying the process of item development. Writing plausible incorrect options, especially more than two of them, can be a challenge for item writers. As a result, the fourth and fifth options tend to be of lower quality, with a limited number of test takers selecting them. The most important consideration in writing SR options is to create incorrect options that are representative of common errors or misconceptions of students. When incorrect options are based on common errors or misconceptions, they become more plausible, and they provide more useful diagnostic information.

Research on Accessibility in Item Development

Attention to accessibility in assessment has increased substantially in the past 15 years, especially with the continuation of federal requirements for inclusion of all students, including students with disabilities, in state accountability assessments. Two forms of alternate assessment emerged as a result of these federal requirements: alternate assessments for alternate academic achievement standards (AA-AAS), intended for students with the most severe cognitive impairments, and alternate assessments for modified academic achievement standards (AA-MAS), intended for students with moderate to severe cognitive impairments and persistent academic difficulties. The development and implementation of these alternate assessments led to a growing literature on the development of accessible items. Although current federal regulations (e.g., Every Student Succeeds Act) no longer allow state education accountability systems to include AA-MAS, we have learned a great deal from prior research on this form of testing because of the attention to meeting the needs of students with persistent academic difficulties.

AA-AAS Research has examined several general issues pertinent to accessible item development in AA-AAS. As with general assessments, the test and item specifications used in AA-AAS must demonstrate adequate linkage to the academic standards for a given state. The test and item specifications must represent the standards in terms of both content and cognitive complexity, as appropriate for the target population of students with the most significant cognitive disabilities. Linkage between specifications and state standards is evaluated through an alignment study (e.g., Browder et al., 2004; Ysseldyke & Olsen, 1997).

The alignment process differs for alternate assessment in three main ways (Wakeman, Flowers, & Browder, 2007). First, alternate assessments typically include more performance-based tasks, such as checklists and portfolios, with varying levels of standardization. Second, the content of alternate achievement standards themselves may be less academic than in a general assessment. Third, the content standards may also be under development with implementation ongoing at the classroom level. These issues must be addressed when documenting alignment for AA-AAS.

Marion and Pellegrino (2006, 2009) presented a framework for evaluating validity evidence for AA-AAS based on research by Kane (2006), Messick (1989), and others. This framework covers accessibility issues related to each section traditionally included in a test technical manual, including item and test specifications and item development.

AA-MAS The majority of research on accessible item writing originates in the area of AA-MAS. Although this relatively young form of assessment has been phased out of use by recent federal policy, the lessons learned from research on item-writing for AA-MAS inform the development of more accessible general assessments moving forward. The transition of AA-MAS test-takers to general assessment systems will also require additional research on the appropriateness of accommodations and methods for ensuring fairness and comparability of scores (e.g., Wyse & Albano, 2015).

The research on AA-MAS development and implementation has focused on correctly identifying the target population for the assessment, defining participation levels, examining opportunity to learn within the general education curriculum, and studying the impacts of accommodations and overall results (see the special issue of *Peabody Journal of Education*, Volume 85, 2009). The work of Kettler, Elliott, and Beddow (2009) is especially relevant to accessible item development. This work resulted in the creation of the Test Accessibility and Modification Inventory and related tools (Beddow et al., 2010), a tool for guiding test modifications and improving accessibility. TAMI was developed based on principles of universal design, test accessibility, cognitive load theory, test fairness, test accommodations, and item-writing research (Beddow, 2010).

The TAMI is used to evaluate the accessibility of an item according to (a) the reading passage or other item stimuli, (b) the item stem, (c) visual materials, (d) answer choices, (e) page and item layout, (f) overall fairness, and (g) other aspects pertinent to computer-based tests, as applicable. A series of rubrics are used to rate the accessibility of each of these item elements and provide recommendations for item modifications to improve accessibility. Standard modifications are also provided as a guide. The modifications are intended to ensure the use of effective item-writing guidelines to improve the item by removing sources of construct-irrelevant variance and maximizing accessibility for all students. Cognitive labs are also recommended as a method for developing item and test modifications.

A number of studies demonstrate effective applications of the TAMI to item development. Elliott et al. (2010) and Kettler et al. (2011) describe results from research projects with consortia of states where the TAMI was used to improve modifications within state tests. Findings showed that modifications preserved score reliability and improved performance for the target group of AA-MAS students, in some cases more so than for other students. Rodriguez, Elliott, Kettler, and Beddow (2009) examined further the effects of item modifications on the functioning of incorrect response options. Most often, items were modified to have fewer options, with the least effective incorrect option being removed. In mathematics and reading items, the removal of a response option led to the remaining incorrect options being more discriminating.

Evaluating the impact of item modifications can be complicated by the fact that modifications are typically adapted to a specific item. A single item may also incorporate multiple modifications. It will generally not be appropriate to apply the same modification across all items in a test or to apply any modifications without tailoring them to a given item. As a result, it is difficult to summarize the overall effects of one or more modifications. Still, studies have been able to document positive results for items with accommodations and modifications (Rodriguez, Kettler, & Elliott, 2014).

Evaluating Item Quality

A variety of methods are available for evaluating item quality during the item development process, so as to provide validity evidence supporting the interpretation of scores across student groups (Kettler, et al., 2009). These methods include expert and panel review (e.g., for bias, fairness, sensitivity, and appropriateness of content and cognitive complexity), statistical analyses based on item response data (e.g., item difficulty and discrimination via classical item analysis and item response theory modeling, internal structure via factor analysis), and observations involving samples of test takers (e.g., think-aloud studies, cognitive labs, and surveys on the testing experience). This section describes examples of statistical and observational methods for improving accessibility in item development.

Statistical methods Statistical methods for evaluating accommodations and modifications for accessibility typically involve comparisons of item and test performance across groups of test takers. The focal group of test takers is usually the group for whom accommodations or modifications are designed, and a reference group or control group consists of test takers for whom the accommodations or modifications were not designed. With data from both groups of students, researchers then seek to determine whether or not items or the test function differentially or have different properties for one group compared to the other.

One statistical approach to evaluating performance across groups involves the comparison of exploratory and confirmatory factor analytic models to determine the internal factor structure of an assessment and its invariance over groups. This approach, denoted broadly as testing for measurement invariance, addresses the stability or robustness of the construct underlying an assessment in the presence of potential group differences and changes in the relationships among items and the construct. For example, Cook, Eignor, Steinberg, Sawaki, and Cline (2009) used a factor analytic approach to investigate the effects of a read-aloud procedure on the underlying constructs in a reading comprehension test. Results showed that factorial invariance held for students without disabilities who participated without the read-aloud and students with reading-based learning disabilities with the read-aloud. This finding provides validity evidence in support of the read-aloud, suggesting that scores with and without the procedure may be treated as comparable for different groups of students.

Research on AA-MAS has also demonstrated a statistical result referred to as differential boost (Kettler et al., 2011). Differential boost is a form of differential item functioning, where, for example, students with disabilities perform better on modified items than students without, after controlling for ability differences between the two groups. On an AA-MAS, the presence of differential boost may be desirable. However, Wyse and Albano (2015) note that implementing modified items showing differential boost within an assessment intended both for students with and without disabilities may violate the assumptions of the psychometric model underlying the assessment. Additional work is needed in this area, both addressing the anticipated results of including students with and without disabilities in the same assessment and appropriate methods for examining these results.

Observational Methods

Observational methods allow us to better understand the item response process from the perspective of the test taker (Ericsson & Simon, 1993). The Standards emphasize the importance of evaluating the test taker perspective (e.g., Standard 3.3; AERA, APA, NCME, 2014). These methods involve data collection via focus groups, think-aloud studies, and cognitive labs, where accommodated or modified test items are administered to students from the focal and/or reference groups and the test taker reports on their experience while responding to each item. Survey and interview methods can also be used retrospectively to examine test taker experience after completing the test.

The effective use of cognitive labs has been demonstrated in a number of studies (e.g., Christensen, Shyyan, Rogers, & Kincaid, 2014; Dolan, Goodman, Strain-Seymour, Adams, & Sethuraman, 2011; Kettler et al., 2009; Winter, Kopriva, Chen, & Emick, 2007). Kettler et al. (2009) described the components of a cognitive lab conducted during the development of an AA-MAS. These components included (a) explaining the administration procedures, with guidelines and examples to help test takers verbalize their thought processes, problem-solving strategies, and what information they attended to in each item; (b) audio or video recording of the test administration with verbal cues and reminders given as needed throughout; and (c) asking follow-up questions on the perceived difficulty of each item. Cognitive lab results from Kettler et al. (2009) indicated that students found reading item modifications (e.g., bolding, removing options) to be effective, whereas some math item modifications needed improvement.

Innovations and Technological Advances

Computer-based testing has facilitated the development and administration of new item formats (Sireci & Zenisky, 2016), and improvements in computing technology have led to increasingly more sophisticated computerized adaptive testing and automated scoring algorithms (Laitusis, Buzick, Cook, & Stone, 2010; Williamson et al., 2006). Computers and other assistive devices have been used to administer and enhance accommodations, providing a variety of accessible methods for individuals to respond to test questions. These innovations may improve the fidelity of test content, removing construct-irrelevant variance and improving accessibility. However, they may also introduce new barriers, for example, resulting from unfamiliarity with technology (Dolan et al., 2011), where features within a user interface (e.g., the computer software used in test administration) or the physical interface (e.g., a keyboard or touchpad) may negatively impact student performance.

Items involving reading passages often rely on extended SR items where each sentence in the passage provides an optional response to specific questions. The test can contain questions about a passage, for example, regarding the main idea of a paragraph, and the response is selected by highlighting the appropriate sentence in the reading passage. This format presents a large number of options consisting of the sentences within the reading passage itself, rather than rephrased ideas or statements taken out of context as in the typical SR format. How these features interact and impact accessibility is unknown. Among the many innovative item types examined in the literature, there is little evidence regarding their ability to enhance accessibility.

Other formats include connecting ideas with various kinds of links (dragging and connecting concepts) and other tasks such as sorting and ordering information. The computer environment allows for other innovative response processes, including correcting sentences with grammatical errors or mathematical statements, completing statements or equations, and producing or completing graphical models, geometric shapes, or trends in data. Computers provide a wide range of possibilities. Unfortunately, these formats have been developed without sufficient investigation into their effects on accessibility and fairness. For example, for students with differing levels of manual dexterity, using a mouse to drag and drop objects may present a challenge.

Computer-enabled innovations have been examined in the context of postsecondary and professional exams. Innovations in the GRE and TOEFL have led to numerous studies on impact. Bennet, Morley, Quardt, and Rock (1999) studied the use of graphical modeling for measuring mathematical reasoning in the GRE. The item format of interest involved created graphical representations, for example, by plotting points on a grid and then using a tool to connect the points. Results for graphical representation items were reliable and moderately correlated with the GRE quantitative total score and other related variables. Although examinees agreed that these graphing items were better indicators of potential success in graduate school, they still preferred traditional SR items (a result commonly found when comparing SR and CR items).

Bridgeman, Cline, and Levin (2008) examined how availability of a calculator affected performance on the quantitative section of the GRE. Relatively few examinees used the calculator on any given item (generally about 20% of examinees used the calculator) and the effects on item difficulty were small overall. There were also no effects for gender and ethnic group differences. Previously, Bridgeman and Cline (2000) examined response time for questions on the computer-adaptive version of the GRE, with considerations for impact on fairness. Response time is a critical issue in adaptive tests because examinees receive different items depending on their response patterns. Students who received items with longer expected response times (e.g., items where finding the correct response required more steps) were not found to be at a disadvantage. Gallagher, Bennet, and Cahalan (2000) examined construct-irrelevant variance within open-ended computerized mathematics tasks. They hypothesized that experience with the computer interface might advantage some but not others. Although no evidence of construct-irrelevant variance was detected, some examinees did experience technical difficulties and expressed preference for paper forms of the test. Tasks involving complex expressions appeared to require more time to answer in computer form than in paper form.

In the context of accommodations, assistive technologies have been used effectively in the area of reading test accessibility. The Technology Assisted Reading Assessment (TARA) project seeks to improve reading assessments for students with visual impairments or blindness. The project works in conjunction with the National Accessible Reading Assessment Project (NARAP), through the Office of Special Education Programs and the National Center for Special Education Research. The *Accessibility Principles for Reading Assessments* (Thurlow, Laitusis, Dillon, Cook, Moen, Abedi, & O'Brien, 2009) summarize guidelines for implementation of accessible reading assessments:

1. Reading assessments are accessible to all students in the testing population, including students with disabilities.
2. Reading assessments are grounded in a definition of reading that is composed of clearly specified constructs, informed by scholarship, supported by empirical evidence, and attuned to accessibility concerns.
3. Reading assessments are developed with accessibility as a goal throughout rigorous and well-documented test design, development, and implementation procedures.
4. Reading assessments reduce the need for accommodations yet are amenable to accommodations that are needed to make valid inferences about a student's proficiencies.
5. Reporting of reading assessment results is designed to be transparent to relevant audiences and to encourage valid interpretation and use of these results.

These principles overlap considerably with the elements of the TAMI and foundational concepts in cognitive load theory (see Chapter 13) and good item writing. Guideline 1-A from Thurlow et al. (2009) requires understanding of the full range of student characteristics and experiences, so that item writers produce items with "low memory load requirements" (p. 5). Guidelines 1-B requires application of universal design elements at the test development stage, including "precisely defined constructs; nonbiased items; and simple, clear, and intuitive instructions and procedures" (p. 6). Guideline 2-D suggests developing criteria to specify when visuals are used or removed, recognizing the mixed results in the research literature on the use of visuals to enhance reading assessments. Guideline 3-B addresses item development and evaluation, where the "content and format of the items or tasks may be modified, to some extent, to increase accessibility for all subgroups" (p. 14). This includes the importance of conducting item analysis and think-aloud studies, examining item functioning across relevant subgroups. Guideline 3-C references test assembly, with attention to factors such as "length of a test, the way items are laid out on a page, whether the test is computer-administered" (pp. 14–15). These principles and guidelines are intended to provide direction for improving future test design and the accessibility of current assessments. The principles are a compilation of existing guidance, and the first three principles largely reflect the guidance in the TAMI. The TAMI provides more detailed and explicit direction for item development and modification.

Alternative Scoring Methods

Accessible assessment begins with the development of accessible items, where item-writing guidelines have been followed so as to remove construct-irrelevant variance and ensure that item content and cognitive tasks effectively address the target construct for the target population. Statistical methods can be used to compare item performance and the internal structure of an assessment across groups of test takers, and observational methods can be used to assess accessibility from the test taker's perspective.

Additionally, the scoring method used to evaluate test taker item responses can also be designed to maximize construct-relevant variance.

Traditional standardized test administration and scoring methods have been criticized for neglecting valuable information in the item response process. Whereas traditional methods only evaluate the correctness of a response, incorrect responses may also be useful in assessing the target construct. Attali, Powers, and Hawthorn (2008) investigated the effects of immediate feedback and revision opportunities on the quality of open-ended sentence-completion items. As expected, revising answers resulted in higher scores. However, revising answers also resulted in increased reliability and correlations with criterion measures. These results show that valuable information within incorrect responses can be used to improve an assessment.

There are several alternative scoring methods available for SR items. Most of these methods are intended to capture partial knowledge, a variable that is prevalent and underutilized when assessing students with limited access to the general curriculum and persistent academic difficulties. By ignoring information available within incorrect responses, we lose what little information might be available about students with the most challenging academic learning objectives. For example, the ability to recognize that some options or responses are more correct than others should be rewarded. Levels of correctness could be assessed by allowing students to select more than one possibly correct response so as to obtain partial credit. Another option is to allow students to rate their confidence in the correctness of their answers, where the confidence ratings can be used to weight scores.

Elimination testing was introduced by Coombs, Milholland, and Womer (1956), who allowed students to mark as many incorrect options as they could identify, awarding one point for each option correctly identified, with a deduction if the correct option was identified as incorrect. On a four-option item, this process yielded scores ranging from completely incorrect (scored -3) to completely correct (+3), with partially correct scores in between. A related method allows students to identify a subset of options that includes the correct answer, with partial credit given based on the number of options selected and whether the correct option is in the selected subset. Chang, Lin, and Lin (2007) found that elimination testing provides a strong technique to evaluate partial knowledge and yields a lower number of unexpected responses (guessing that results in responses inconsistent with overall ability, in an item response theory framework) than standard number correct scoring. Bradbard, Parker, and Stone (2004) found that elimination testing provides scores of similar psychometric quality, reduces guessing, measures partial knowledge, and provides instructionally relevant information. They noted that in some college courses, the presence of partial or full misinformation is critical (e.g., in the health sciences), and instructors should be more intentional when developing incorrect response options, so that they reflect common errors and misconceptions and can thereby be used to infer partial understanding. Bush (2001) reported on a method that parallels the elimination procedure except, instead of asking students to select the incorrect options, students may select more than one correct answer and are penalized for selecting incorrect ones. Results indicated that higher-achieving students liked the method (because of the additional opportunities to select plausibly correct options), but lower-achieving students strongly disliked it (primarily because of the negative markings for incorrect selections). Finally, studies have also shown the utility of models allowing students to assign a probability of correctness to each option or to assign confidence to their correct responses. Diaz, Rifqi, and Bouchon-Meunier (2007) argued that when students can assign a probability of correctness to one or more options in an SR item, they are forced to consider all of the options, which provides a more accurate picture of the target construct.

The multiple true/false item is a simple alternative to SR items with complex scoring procedures that incorporate information from incorrect options. As noted above, the multiple true/false item (like an SR item where test takers can *select all that apply*) includes individual statements that resemble response options but that are scored as separate items. The utility of this item type has been demonstrated in a number of recent studies (e.g., Couch, Wood, & Knight, 2015).

Summary

This chapter presents guidelines for the development of CR and SR assessment items, with a summary of evidence supporting their use and a discussion of their application and evaluation with accessible assessments. Overall, the guidelines align well with principles of universal design, including those applied within the TAMI, and they thereby encourage clear, efficient writing practices that can be expected to improve accessibility for the largest audience of examinees.

Although item types are grouped here broadly into the categories of SR and CR, a variety of response formats are available, along with computer-based and technologically enhanced items. The choice of item type and response format should always be based on the purpose of the assessment, with consideration given to the target construct, content domain, and student population. In the absence of a rationale for developing complex CR formats or technological enhancements, research indicates that the traditional SR item formats, in particular the MC item with three options, should be optimal. During the item development process, ideally prior to the operational administration of an assessment, statistical and observational methods should be used to evaluate item quality, especially in high-stakes settings and with new, untested item features and response formats.

Effective item development, following evidence-based guidelines, is critical to accessible assessment. Substantial work has been done to examine and improve the item development process. Moving forward, research should continue to focus on strategies for identifying and evaluating item features and item-writing guidelines that minimize construct-irrelevant variance and maximize accessibility. As technology becomes more prevalent in the classroom, studies must also examine how technological advances can be leveraged to create more accessible assessments.

References

American Educational Research Association, American Psychological Association, & National Council on Measurement in Education. (2014). *Standards for educational and psychological testing*. Washington, DC: American Educational Research Association.

American Institutes for Research. (2009). *Reading assessment and item specifications for the 2009 National Assessment of Educational Progress*. Washington, DC: National Assessment Governing Board.

Attali, Y., & Burstein, J. (2006). Automated scoring with e-rater v.2.0. *Journal of Technology, Learning, and Assessment, 4*(3), 1–30.

Attali, Y., Powers, D., & Hawthorn, J. (2008). *Effect of immediate feedback and revision on psychometric properties of open-ended sentence-completion items (ETS RR-08-16)*. Princeton, NJ: Educational Testing Service.

Baldwin, D., Fowles, M., & Livingston, S. (2005). *Guidelines for constructed-response and other performance assessments*. Princeton, NJ: Educational Testing Service.

Beddow, P. A. (2010). Beyond universal design: Accessibility theory to advance testing for all students. In M. Russell & M. Kavanaugh (Eds.), *Assessing students in the margins: Challenges, strategies, and techniques* (pp. 381–405). Charlotte, NC: Information Age.

Beddow, P. A., Elliott, S. N., & Kettler, R. J. (2010). *Test accessibility and modification inventory, TAMI™ accessibility rating matrix, technical manual*. Nashville, TN: Vanderbilt University. Retrieved at http://peabody.vanderbilt.edu/docs/pdf/PRO/TAMI_Technical_Manual.pdf

Bennett, R. E., Morley, M., Quardt, D., & Rock, D. A. (1999). *Graphical modeling: A new response type for measuring the qualitative component of mathematical reasoning (ETS RR-99-21)*. Princeton, NJ: Educational Testing Service.

Bennett, R. E., & Ward, W. C. (1991). *Construction versus choice in cognitive measurement: Issues in constructed response, performance testing, and portfolio assessment*. Hillsdale, NJ: Lawrence Erlbaum.

Bennett, R. E., Ward, W. C., Rock, D. A., & LaHart, C. (1990). *Toward a framework for constructed-response items*. Princeton, NJ: Educational Testing Service. ED395 032.

Bradbard, D. A., Parker, D. F., & Stone, G. L. (2004). An alternate multiple-choice scoring procedure in a macroeconomics course. *Decision Sciences Journal of Innovative Education, 2*(1), 11–26.

Bridgeman, B., & Cline, F. (2000). *Variations in mean response times for questions on the computer-adaptive GRE general test: Implications for fair assessment (ETS RR-00-07)*. Princeton, NJ: Educational Testing Service.

Bridgeman, B., Cline, F., & Levin, J. (2008). *Effects of calculator availability on GRE quantitative questions (ETS RR-08-31)*. Princeton, NJ: Educational Testing Service.

Browder, D., Flowers, C., Ahlgrim-Delzell, L., Karvonen, M., Spooner, F., & Algozzine, R. (2004). The alignment of alternate assessment content with academic and functional curricula. *The Journal of Special Education, 37*(4), 211–223.

Bush, M. (2001). A multiple choice test that rewards partial knowledge. *Journal of Further and Higher Education, 25*(2), 157–163.

Chang, S.-H., Lin, P.-C., & Lin, Z. C. (2007). Measures of partial knowledge and unexpected responses in multiple-choice tests. *Educational Technology & Society, 10*(4), 95–109.

Christensen, L. L., Shyyan, V., Rogers, C., & Kincaid, A. (2014). *Audio support guidelines for accessible assessments: Insights from cognitive labs*. Minneapolis, MN: University of Minnesota, Enhanced Assessment Grant (#S368A120006), U.S. Department of Education.

Cook, L., Eignor, D., Steinberg, J., Sawaki, Y., & Cline, F. (2009). Using factor analysis to investigate the impact of accommodations on the scores of students with disabilities on a reading comprehension assessment. *Journal of Applied Testing Technology, 10*(2), 1–33.

Coombs, C. H., Milholland, J. E., & Womer, F. B. (1956). The assessment of partial knowledge. *Educational and Psychological Measurement, 16*(1), 13–37.

Couch, B. A., Wood, W. B., & Knight, J. K. (2015). The molecular biology capstone assessment: A concept assessment for upper-division molecular biology students. *CBE – Life Sciences Education, 10*(1), 1–11.

Deno, S. L. (1985). Curriculum-based measurement: The emerging alternative. *Exceptional Children, 52*, 219–232.

Diaz, J., Rifqi, M., & Bouchon-Meunier, B. (2007). Evidential multiple choice questions. In P. Brusilovsky, M. Grigoriadou, & K. Papanikolaou (Eds.), *Proceedings of workshop on personalisation in E-learning environments at individual and group level* (pp. 61–64.) 11th International Conference on User Modeling, Corfu, Greece. Retrieved 25 Sept 2010 from http://hermis.di.uoa.gr/PeLEIGL/program.html

Dolan, R. P., Goodman, J., Strain-Seymour, E., Adams, J., & Sethuraman, S. (2011). *Cognitive lab evaluation of innovative items in mathematics and English/language arts assessment of elementary, middle, and high school students: Research report*. Iowa City, IA: Pearson.

Downing, S. M. (2006). Selected-response item formats in test development. In S. M. Downing & T. M. Haladyna (Eds.), *Handbook of test development* (pp. 287–301). Mahwah, NJ: Lawrence Erlbaum.

Elliott, S. N., Kettler, R. J., Beddow, P. A., Kurz, A., Compton, E., McGrath, D., et al. (2010). Effects of using modified items to test students with persistent academic difficulties. *Exceptional Children, 76*(4), 475–495.

Ellsworth, R. A., Dunnell, P., & Duell, O. K. (1990). What are the textbooks telling teachers? *The Journal of Educational Research, 83*, 289–293.

Ericsson, K. A., & Simon, H. A. (1993). *Protocol analysis: Verbal reports as data (Revised edition)*. Cambridge, MA: MIT Press.

Frey, B. B., Petersen, S., Edwards, L. M., Pedrotti, J. T., & Peyton, V. (2005). Item-writing rules: Collective wisdom. *Teaching and Teacher Education, 21*, 357–364.

Gallagher, A., Bennet, R. E., & Cahalan, C. (2000). *Detecting construct-irrelevant variance in an open-ended, computerized mathematics task (ETS RR-00-18)*. Princeton, NJ: Educational Testing Service.

Gitomer, D. H. (2007). *Design principles for constructed response tasks: Assessing subject-matter understanding in NAEP (ETS unpublished research report)*. Princeton, NJ: Educational Testing Service.

Haladyna, T. M. (1989, April). *Fidelity and proximity to criterion: When should we use multiple-choice?* Paper presented at the annual meeting of the American Educational Research Association, San Diego, CA.

Haladyna, T. M. (1997). *Writing test items to evaluate higher order thinking*. Boston: Allyn & Bacon.

Haladyna, T. M., & Downing, S. M. (1989a). A taxonomy of multiple-choice item-writing rules. *Applied Measurement in Education, 2*(1), 37–50.

Haladyna, T. M., & Downing, S. M. (1989b). The validity of a taxonomy of multiple-choice item-writing rules. *Applied Measurement in Education, 1*, 51–78.

Haladyna, T. M., Downing, S. M., & Rodriguez, M. C. (2002). A review of multiple-choice item-writing guidelines for classroom assessment. *Applied Measurement in Education, 15*(3), 309–334.

Haladyna, T. M., & Rodriguez, M. C. (2013). *Developing and validating test items*. New York: Routledge.

Hannah, L. S., & Michaels, J. U. (1977). *A comprehensive framework for instructional objectives*. Reading, MA: Addison-Wesley.

Hart, D. (1994). *Authentic assessment: A handbook for educators*. Menlo Park, CA: Addison-Wesley.

Hogan, T. P., & Murphy, G. (2007). Recommendations for preparing and scoring constructed-response items: What the experts say. *Applied Measurement in Education, 20*(4), 427–441.

Kane, M. T. (2006). Validation. In R. L. Brennan (Ed.), *Educational measurement* (4th ed., pp. 17–64). New York: American Council on Education, Macmillan.

Kelly, F. J. (1916). The Kansas silent reading tests. *The Journal of Educational Psychology, 7*, 63–80.

Kettler, R. J., Elliot, S. N., & Beddow, P. A. (2009). Modifying achievement test items: A theory-guided and data-based approach for better measurement of what students with disabilities know. *Peabody Journal of Education, 84*, 529–551.

Kettler, R. J., Rodriguez, M. C., Bolt, D. M., Elliott, S. N., Beddow, P. A., & Kurz, A. (2011). Modified multiple-choice items for alternate assessments: Reliability, difficulty, and differential boost. *Applied Measurement in Education, 24*, 210–234.

Lane, S., & Iwatani, E. (2016). Design of performance assessments in education. In S. Lane, M. Raymond, & T. M. Haladyna (Eds.), *Handbook of test development* (2nd ed., pp. 274–293). New York: Routledge.

Laitusis, C. C., Buzick, H., Cook, L., & Stone, E. (2010). Adaptive testing options for accountability assessments. In M. Russell & M. Kavanaugh (Eds.), *Assessing students in the margins: Challenges, strategies, and techniques* (pp. 291–310). Charlotte, NC: Information Age.

Mann, H. (1867). *Lectures and annual reports on education*. Boston: Rand & Avery.

Marion, S. F., & Pellegrino, J. W. (2006). A validity framework for evaluation the technical quality of alternate assessment. *Educational Measurement: Issues and Practice, 25*(4), 47–57.

Marion, S. F., & Pellegrino, J. W. (2009). *Validity framework for evaluation the technical quality of alternate assessments based on alternate achievement standards*. Paper presented at the annual meeting of the national council on measurement in education, San Diego, CA.

Martinez, M. E. (1999). Cognition and the questions of test item format. *Educational Psychologist, 34*, 207–218.

Messick, S. (1989). Validity. In R. L. Linn (Ed.), *Educational measurement* (3rd ed., pp. 13–103). New York: American Council on Education, Macmillan.

Moreno, R. M., Martinez, R. J., & Muniz, J. (2006). New guidelines for developing multiple-choice items. *Methodology, 2*, 65–72.

Office of Technology Assessment. (1992). *Testing in American schools: Asking the right questions, OTA-SET-519*. Washington, DC: US Congress. Retrieved at http://govinfo.library.unt.edu/ota/Ota_1/DATA/1992/9236.PDF

Osterlind, S. J., & Merz, W. R. (1994). Building a taxonomy for constructed-response test items. *Educational Assessment, 2*(2), 133–147.

Popham, J. W. (2016). *Classroom assessment: What teachers need to know*. Boston: Pearson.

Rodriguez, M.C. (1997, March). *The art & science of item writing: A meta-analysis of multiple-choice item format effects*. Paper presented at the annual meeting of the American Educational Research Association, Chicago, IL.

Rodriguez, M.C. (1998, April). *The construct equivalence of multiple-choice and constructed-response items: A random effects synthesis of correlations*.

Paper presented at the annual meeting of the American Educational Research Association, San Diego, CA.

Rodriguez, M. C. (2002). Choosing an item format. In G. Tindal & T. M. Haladyna (Eds.), *Large-scale assessment programs for all students: Validity, technical adequacy, and implementation* (pp. 213–231). Mahwah, NJ: Lawrence Erlbaum Associates.

Rodriguez, M. C. (2003). Construct equivalence of multiple-choice and constructed-response items: A random effects synthesis of correlations. *Journal of Educational Measurement, 40*(2), 163–184.

Rodriguez, M. C. (2005). Three options are optimal for multiple-choice items: A meta-analysis of 80 years of research. *Educational Measurement: Issues and Practice, 24*(2), 3–13.

Rodriguez, M. C. (2016). Selected-response item development. In S. Lane, M. Raymond, & T. M. Haladyna (Eds.), *Handbook of test development* (2nd ed., pp. 259–273). New York: Routledge.

Rodriguez, M. C., & Albano, A. D. (in press). *The college instructor's guide to test item writing*. New York: Routledge.

Rodriguez, M.C., Elliott, S.N., Kettler, R.J., & Beddow, P.A. (2009, April). *The role of item response attractors in the modification of test items*. Paper presented at the annual meeting of the National Council on Measurement in Educational, San Diego, CA.

Rodriguez, M. C., Kettler, R. J., & Elliott, S. N. (2014). Distractor functioning in modified items for test accessibility. *Sage Open, 4*(4), 1–10.

Ruch, G. M., & Stoddard, G. D. (1925). Comparative reliabilities of objective examinations. *Journal of Educational Psychology, 16*, 89–103.

Russell, M., & Kavanaugh, M. (2010). *Assessing students in the margins: Challenges, strategies, and techniques*. Charlotte, NC: Information Age.

Schedl, M. A., & Malloy, J. (2014). Writing items and tasks. In A. J. Kunnan (Ed.), *The companion to language assessment. Volume II: Approaches and development*. Chichester, West Sussex: Wiley-Blackwell.

Sireci, S. G., & Zenisky, A. L. (2016). Computerized innovative item formats: Achievement and credentialing. In S. Lane, M. Raymond, & T. M. Haladyna (Eds.), *Handbook of test development* (2nd ed., pp. 313–334). New York: Routledge.

Snow, R. E. (1980). Aptitude and achievement. In W. B. Schrader (Ed.), *Measuring achievement: Progress over a decade. New directions for testing and measurement* (Vol. 5, pp. 39–59). San Francisco: Jossey-Bass.

Sparks, J. R., Song, Y., Brantley, W., & Liu, O. L. (2014). *Assessing written communication in higher education: Review and recommendations for next-generation assessment (RR-14-37)*. Princeton, NJ: Educational Testing Service. Retrieved at https://www.ets.org/research/policy_research_reports/publications/report/2014/jtmo

Sternberg, R. J. (1982). *Handbook of human intelligence*. Cambridge, MA: Cambridge University Press.

Thorndike, R. M., & Thorndike-Christ, T. (2011). *Measurement and evaluation in psychology and education*. Boston: Pearson.

Thurlow, M. L., Laitusis, C. C., Dillon, D. R., Cook, L. L., Moen, R. E., Abedi, J., & O'Brien, D. G. (2009). *Accessibility principles for reading assessments*. Minneapolis, MN: National Accessible Reading Assessments Projects.

Wainer, H., & Thissen, D. (1993). Combining multiple-choice and constructed-response test scores: Toward a Marxist theory of test construction. *Applied Measurement in Education, 6*, 103–118.

Wakeman, S., Flowers, C., & Browder, D. (2007). *Aligning alternate assessments to grade level content standards: Issues and considerations for alternates based on alternate achievement standards (Policy Directions 19)*. Minneapolis, MN: University of Minnesota, National Center on Educational Outcomes.

Williamson, D. M., Bejar, I. I., & Mislevy, R. J. (2006). *Automated scoring of complex tasks in computer-based testing*. Mahwah, NJ: Lawrence Erlbaum.

Winter, P. C., Kopriva, R. J., Chen, C., & Emick, J. E. (2007). Exploring individual and item factors that affect assessment validity for diverse learners: Results from a large-scale cognitive lab. *Learning and Individual Differences, 16*, 267–276.

Wyse, A. E., & Albano, A. D. (2015). Considering the use of general and modified assessment items in computerized adaptive testing. *Applied Measurement in Education, 28*(2), 156–167.

Yang, Y., Buckendahl, C. W., Juszkiewicz, P. J., & Bhola, D. S. (2002). A review of strategies for validating computer-automated scoring. *Applied Measurement in Education, 15*, 391–412.

Young, J. W., So, Y., & Ockey, G. J. (2013). *Guidelines for best test development practices to ensure validity and fairness for international English language proficiency assessments*. Princeton, NJ: Educational Testing Service.

Ysseldyke, J. E., & Olsen, K. R. (1997). *Putting alternate assessments into practice: What to measure and possible sources of data* (Synthesis Report No. 28). Minneapolis, MN: University of Minnesota, National Center on Educational Outcomes.

Zigmond, N., & Kloo, A. (2009). The "two percent students": Considerations and consequences of eligibility decisions. *Peabody Journal of Education, 84*, 478–495.

Cognitive Load Theory for Test Design

Peter A. Beddow

The 2016 *Standards for Educational and Psychological Testing* (*Standards*: AERA, APA, and NCME) includes a chapter on fairness in testing that describes fairness as a foundational and fundamental validity issue that can influence test scores based on individual and/or group differences that are irrelevant to the construct(s) targeted by the test. The test introduces two subsets of fairness: accessibility and universal design. In testing, the *Standards* define accessibility as the "unobstructed opportunity to demonstrate…standing on the construct(s) being measured"(p.49). Alternately, Beddow, Kurz, and Frey (2011) defined test accessibility as the degree to which a test and its constituent item set permit the test-taker to demonstrate his or her knowledge of the target construct of the test. A universally designed test, as defined in the *Standards*, "reflect[s] the intended construct…minimize[s] construct-irrelevant features that might otherwise impede the performance of intended examinee groups, and maximize[s]…access for as many examinees as possible" (p.50).

In the context of assessment, test accessibility is necessary for ensuring the validity of test score inferences about student learning. When features of the test present access barriers for a portion of the test-taker population, individual, group, and comparative inferences across the tested population (e.g., those made in normative achievement tests) likely will be inaccurate. Proponents of universal design for assessment (e.g., Thompson, Johnstone, and Thurlow, 2002) argue assessments should be designed such that (a) they are inclusive, (b) have clearly defined test constructs, (c) consist of items that are non-biased, (d) they permit accommodations, (e) directions and procedures are clear, and (f) they are maximally readable and understandable. These are important ideals; they do not, however, contain specific guidelines from which a foundation can be built to support the development of accessible assessments.

Beddow et al. (2011) introduced a model of test accessibility that emphasized accessibility as a function of the *test event* as opposed to an attribute of the test itself. He defined the test event as the array of interactions between features of the test and individual test-taker characteristics, arguing that a test may be optimally accessible for one test-taker but may present access barriers for another test-taker. The test event is said to be accessible to the degree the sum of these interactions yields a test score from which subsequent inferences do not reflect the influence of demands other than those intrinsic to the test-taker's demonstration of the target construct.

Beddow argued access skill demands can be categorized into physical, perceptive, receptive,

P. A. Beddow (✉)
Accessible Hope, LLC, Nashville, TN, USA

emotive, and/or cognitive skills. Many of these can be addressed through individualized testing accommodations, and others must be anticipated and controlled by agents outside the actual test event. Beddow et al. (2011) described a theory-driven and evidence-based paradigm of test item development that focused on cognitive skill demands; specifically, the authors suggested by eliminating extraneous cognitive demand from test items, tests can be made more accessible for test-takers with a broad range of abilities and needs.

Beddow, Kettler, and Elliott (2010) examined in detail a similar paradigm for designing accessible tests, introducing a tool called the *Test Accessibility and Modification Inventory* that was developed with the purpose of evaluating and modifying test items with a focus on increasing access for more test-takers, particularly for those identified with disabilities. The *TAMI* was influenced by universal design principles, test and item writing research, and computer and web accessibility principles. In addition, the authors of the instrument consulted research on cognitive load theory (CLT; Chandler & Sweller, 1991; Plass, Moreno, & Brünken, 2010). Since its inception over two decades ago, CLT has found application to the design of instructional materials and learning tasks; until recently, however, few researchers have examined the potential utility of CLT in assessments of student learning.

This chapter examines the practical applicability of CLT to the design of tests for assessing student learning (e.g., achievement tests), with the purpose of addressing the fairness in testing guidelines (e.g., accessibility and universal design) in the *Standards* (2016). The first section provides an overview of CLT, beginning with a discussion of the cognitive forebears of the theory, an examination of Sweller's (2010a) five principles of CLT and its primary assumptions, and an explanation of the three categories of cognitive load as they relate to test design. The final section focuses specifically on current methods of measuring cognitive demand with a focus on their potential application to the measurement of cognitive load during testing.

Origins and Principles of Cognitive Load Theory

In 1948, Claude Shannon introduced a theoretical model of communication in which information is sent through a signal channel to its destination; the amount of information successfully communicated from the source to the destination, Shannon suggested, is a function of the capacity of the transmitter to deliver a clear signal, the amount of noise introduced into the signal across the communication channel, and the capacity of the receiver to accurately distinguish the information from the noise at the destination. This model became known as information theory (Shannon & Weaver, 1949).

In the landmark paper "The Magical Number Seven, Plus or Minus Two: Human Limits of Information Processing," Miller (1956) applied Shannon's theory to human cognition. Miller reported the results of several experiments that he argued suggest there exists a human limitation for information processing – a inherent cognitive bottleneck that prevents the unlimited simultaneous receipt of information. Miller concluded people are able to process a finite number of informational elements, above which there is likely to be a degradation in accuracy (the author proposed a mean of seven with a standard deviation of two).

Miller referred to this upper limit as *channel capacity*, a conclusion that arguably represented the inception of the notion of working memory (also referred to as short-term memory) which has persisted in the field of cognitive psychology for over half a century. Over the past several decades, the mean informational capacity argued by Miller (i.e., seven) has been dismissed by many, but the underlying limitation assumption is widely accepted and continues to stimulate research and influence theory (Baddeley, 1994, 2003; Cowan, 2001).

Sweller (2010a) argued there are five principles that govern the functions and processes of human cognition, particularly when referring to knowledge acquisition: (a) long-term memory store, (b) schema theory, (c) problem-solving and randomness as genesis, (d) novice working memory and narrow limits of change, and (e) environment organizing and linking.

Sweller (2010a) described the long-term memory store as the central structure of human cognition. He argued our understanding of the complex store of information people use to govern their activity is developed slowly over time, and probably has its origins in study of the game of chess. Specifically, he cited researchers who found the only difference between master chess players and less able counterparts was the masters' memory of a store of game board configurations (Simon & Gilmartin, 1973). Indeed, Simon and Gilmartin noted that master players often were able to recall tens of thousands of configurations. Prior to these studies, chess had been understood as an exemplar of the range of human intellectual capacity in that it required sophisticated problem-solving and thought. As such, master players were those who were able to demonstrate the highest degree of cognitive sophistication, and novices were those whose problem-solving and thinking skills were least sophisticated. The fact that long-term memory of board configurations was the strongest predictor of skill level replaced (or at least began to disrupt) the notion that long-term memory was useful to humans only in allowing them to reminisce about the past. In terms of learning theory, long-term memory also has been found to be a predictor of expert-novice differences in other relevant areas.

The borrowing and reorganizing principle explains how long-term memory can be acquired and organized for retrieval. Although most long-term memory involves acquiring knowledge from the knowledge stores of others, the way individuals organize information varies widely. Information is, according to Sweller, "almost invariably altered and constructed" by individuals (2010a, p. 33). Schema theory explains how the alteration and construction of knowledge take place, specifically, by categorizing and bundling multiple elements of information into a single element. For example, the master chess player might determine the next move by recalling moves that lead to advantageous chess board configurations. In this case, the master chess player's problem-solving schema permits him or her to solve a problem by retrieving an information element from long-term memory based on the mode of the solution.

Learning occurs most efficiently when the learner's construction of schema is automated, happening subconsciously as information is processed. For schema construction to be automated, the learner must have a broad enough store of information in long-term memory that single elements can "fit" into schemas without requiring additional cognitive resources. Sweller (2010a) explained the automation of lower-level schemas often is required for the construction of higher-level schemas. He used the example of the automatic processing of letters of the alphabet, which is required for learning how to combine letters into words and sentences and permit reading.

Although schema theory has been criticized many times over the past 30 years, criticisms largely have misunderstood it (Asghar & Winsler, 2000). Several studies on cognitive load effects confirm some of its basic assumptions, namely, that for schematization to happen, individual elements of information are, in essence, "borrowed" from other schema to construct new schema (Sweller, 2010a).

The instructional implications of CLT, therefore, largely apply to how to facilitate the retrieval, or borrowing, of information from long-term memory for the purpose of schematization – or, at least, how to reduce extraneous cognitive demand – thus ensuring the availability of cognitive resources for schematization. Referring to the opportunity of learners to profit from instruction, Sweller (2010a) argued "depending on the schemas that have been acquired, material that is complex for one individual may be very simple for another" (p.42). Since long-term memory storage is varied across individuals, no two learners schematize information in exactly the same way. As well, information may be retained or discarded based on its adaptive value to learners, which implies that schemas change within individuals over time.

The third principle of cognitive load theory is the *problem-solving and the randomness as genesis principle*, which explains how information is generated in the first place. Specifically, while a learner may be able to solve most problems based on long-term memory stores, new problems may have two or more possible solutions; as the learner tests these solutions (i.e., randomly, since no information exists as to their relative value), their effectiveness determines how the new problem and solution will be added to long-term memory. Randomness as genesis will only occur when no definitive information is available to solve a problem, for, Sweller (2010a) argued, "if knowledge is available to us, we are highly likely to use it" (p.36).

The fourth principle, *novice working memory and narrow limits of change*, explains how as schema formations are altered; the amount of change is governed by the learner's working memory. Recalling Miller's (1956) channel capacity theory, a learner can test only a limited number of permutations for any novel problem, because he or she can hold in working memory a limited number of items. Sweller (2010b) argued the limited capacity of working memory ensures adaptive structures of knowledge are not compromised, because large, rapid changes in long-term memory likely will be deleterious to one or more schemas that are useful for problem-solving and other cognitive activities. This concept is central to cognitive load theory, which explains how instruction is most effective when the novice learner is not expected to borrow information from long-term memory that could be presented to them without compromising the objective (i.e., by definition, novices do not possess large stores of information related to the content-at-hand). When instruction requires learners to borrow information from long-term memory, the learner's available working memory is limited and, depending on his or her working memory capacity, the potential to solve novel problems or engage in novel cognitive activities also may be limited.

Sweller's (2010b) fifth principle, *expert working memory and the environment organizing and linking principle*, explains that the primary difference between experts and novices is in the efficiency with which he or she can transfer large amounts of information from long-term memory to be used as a single entity in working memory. An expert is able to organize and link information from long-term memory with environmental information to generate appropriate actions. The novice, by contrast, has reduced ability to organize and link information from long-term memory with environmental information, resulting in less efficient use of working memory and reduced cognitive capacity to generate appropriate actions. The implications of this principle, according to Sweller, are as follows: "the more [knowledge] that is borrowed and the less that learners need to generate themselves, the more effective the instruction is likely to be" (p. 38).

At this point, I should emphasize that CLT research and application heretofore mostly has focused on the implications of the theory to learning (sometimes defined as *useful changes to long-term memory*). It is critical to remain mindful of this fact as our discussion shifts in a moment to consider the implications of CLT to test design. To determine the extent to which the theory of cognitive load as described, investigated, and debated since its conception over two decades ago is applicable to the assessment of student learning, we must examine the relevance of its chief assumptions in the context of this proposed application. These assumptions are the *dual-channel assumption* and the *limited capacity assumption*.

Dual-Channel Assumption The first assumption of CLT is that the human mind processes information for learning through either or both of two channels: the visual and the auditory/verbal. While both channels may receive information simultaneously, CLT assumes the sources and types of information processed through each channel are intrinsically different. Specifically, printed words and images are processed exclusively through the visual channel, and speech and sound are processed exclusively through the auditory channel.

In the case of paper-and-pencil-based tests (PBTs), we can conclude they generally are not subject to the dual-channel assumption of CLT, to wit: with the exception of verbal instructions given by a test proctor or administrator or other audio support (which is supremely more relevant to computer-based tests, as we discuss below), the information-processing demands of PBTs impinge exclusively on the visual channel. Specifically, test-takers are required to read test item stimuli and item stems, interpret visuals, and ultimately to respond through some visual format such as indicating the correct option or recording a written answer on paper. Thus, the discussion of the application of CLT to the design of traditional PBTs largely will be consequentially derived from the limited capacity and active processing assumptions of the theory.

By contrast, the application of CLT to examine computer-based tests (CBTs) is subject to the dual-channel assumption. Sound has been utilized in computer technology since its advent, and sound is now inseparable from the use of computers for many tasks. Many CBTs include sound support such as read-aloud options to accommodate the needs of individual test-takers, such as those with vision or reading problems. Insofar as a test (i.e., paper-based, computer-based, or otherwise) uses sound and visual media in combination to present information to test-takers, the application of CLT to inform the design of the test or the inferences made from results necessarily is subject to the dual-channel assumption.

Limited Capacity Assumption The crux of CLT is the assumption that the cognitive resources available to the human mind for processing information are finite. In the design of instructional materials, the implications of this assumption have led to recommendations such as simplification of visual and auditory information, contiguous rather than simultaneous presentation of information in certain contexts, and elimination of redundancy. This second assumption of CLT is equally applicable to the design of assessment materials, with the single difference (in most cases) being, as mentioned above, the objective of the materials (i.e., instructional materials are designed to produce instructional outcomes, and assessment materials are designed to assess them).

Using the principles and assumptions of CLT as a framework, cognitive load can be categorized into three types: *intrinsic* load, *germane* or *effective* load, and *extraneous* load. Intrinsic load refers specifically to the number of items, or elements, of information that simultaneously must be considered or processed for learning to occur. This is called *element interactivity*. The greater the element interactivity of instruction, the greater the consumption of working memory and the fewer cognitive resources for processing new information (also known as *working memory load*). The second type is the logical opposite of the first: *extraneous* load. Extraneous load refers to the demand for cognitive resources that do not facilitate useful change to the long-term memory store (i.e., learning). CLT research primarily has focused on ways to reduce or eliminate extraneous load in instruction. The third type of cognitive load is *germane* (or effective) load or the demand for cognitive resources that are relevant, or germane, to the acquisition of the knowledge or skill. CLT assumes that as long as effective load in instruction does not exceed the working memory capacity, it facilitates learning; to wit, the more relevant items that can be brought into working memory for schematization, the better; the more opportunities the learner has to "fit" item elements into existing schema, the greater the probability the schematization will occur automatically (i.e., requiring no additional working memory load).

In essence, CLT proponents argue the intrinsic load of instructional tasks is the load required to learn the primary objective(s) of the task, while any germane load demands of the task support the generalization of student learning and/or higher-order thinking – typically a secondary objective of the task (Debue & Van De Leemput, 2014). Thus, depending on the balance and intensity of the task demands, cognitive overload may limit the attainment of either or both of the instructional objectives. Finally, it is generally accepted that the extraneous load demands of instructional tasks should be avoided whenever possible to permit learners to allocate needed cognitive resources to the intrinsic and germane load demands of the tasks.

To apply this model to testing, it is necessary for us to reiterate the essential distinction between instructional tasks and assessment tasks: their objectives. The objectives of learning tasks typically involve the acquisition, retention, and application of knowledge, skills, or abilities. With few exceptions, the objective of testing is to assess or evaluate the extent to which a student has acquired, retained, and/or is able to apply his or her knowledge, skills, or abilities. With regard to applying the triune load model of CLT to the assessment of student learning, this is an important distinction. Instructional tasks arguably can be designed with the deliberate inclusion of both intrinsic and germane load demands, with the intended objective being to promote learning on multiple levels and across multiple contexts. In instructional design, therefore, insufficient or inadequate instruction results in the failure of students to acquire, retain, or apply the target knowledge or skills to the degree intended. By contrast, the primary purpose of assessment tasks is, with few exceptions, to gather information about whether and how much a student has learned. This information is then used to make decisions on many levels. Assessment results often are used to make inferences and high-stakes decisions about student placement, instruction, resource allocation, and personnel performance. Notwithstanding the obvious utility of valid assessment results to facilitate *future* learning, it is rare for an assessment to purpose as its primary objective the promotion of *immediate* learning. The difference is that whereas a failure to achieve the objectives of an instructional task theoretically can be exposed through assessment and often can be remediated through more instruction, a failure to achieve the objective of an assessment is less obvious, and decisions made from test results may be based on false evidence unless test validity problems are diagnosed and ameliorated.

In the following section, I introduce several instructional design strategies that can reduce the potential for cognitive overload and discuss the relevance of these strategies to the design of assessment events (specifically tests and test items). The purpose of this discussion is to examine how CLT may be used to inform the universal design and accessibility of tests and test items in accordance with the fairness in testing guidelines in the *Standards*.

Extraneous Load Reduction Strategies and Their Relevance to Test Design

Chief among the instructional design strategies that can reduce potential cognitive overload and increase the efficacy of instruction is the *worked example*, whereby learners who are led through the process of solving a problem leads to better acquisition than being required to solve an equivalent problem with no such model, especially when problem steps are faded over time (Renkl, Atkinson, & Grosse, 2004). Similarly effective is *completion*, whereby learners are expected to complete partially solved problems. The theory behind these strategies is that extraneous load is reduced when learners are not required to retrieve multiple prior problem solutions or steps from long-term memory, facilitating acquisition of the new solution. In terms of test design, worked examples and completion may be useful for developing problem-solving items in mathematics, science, or other relevant domains. An item that may otherwise require the learner to establish the steps that lead to the step designed to be assessed may be achieved more explicitly through a worked example or completion item.

The *split-attention* effect is also well-researched (Mayer & Moreno, 1998, 2003; Kalyuga, Chandler, & Sweller, 1999; Clark, Nguyen, & Sweller, 2006) and essentially suggests that extraneous load is increased when information necessary for instruction is included outside the field of perception of the learner. The theory is that the learner is required to use *representational holding* to retain information in working memory that must be used later to acquire the targeted knowledge or skill; providing it in advance allows the learner to use greater cognitive resources for the learning task. In terms of item design, the split-attention effect can be avoided by including formulae for solving mathematics equations on the same page as the item itself (or even integrated into the item) as opposed to including them in a reference section of the test booklet or testing system, and by including text-based items near the text to which they relate (e.g., by integrating items into reading passages). Additionally, the results of research on multimedia learning and the split-attention effect indicate when read-aloud or audio supports are used in test-delivery systems or items, extraneous sounds should be minimized (Moreno & Mayer, 2000).

Figure 13.1 consists of a digitally delivered grade 6 mathematics items that exemplify how the worked example strategy can be integrated into item development. Specifically, the item requires the test-taker to generate an equation that can be used to solve a word problem, by dragging and dropping numerals and operations into a boxed region on the screen. The second part of the item requires the test-taker to solve for the missing number. The item facilitates the demonstration of the target skill (namely, generating a simple equation to solve a real-world problem) by providing the necessary numerals and operations (with three distractors) as well as supplying the variable in the correct location. Part B of the problem requires (or permits) the test-taker to use the equation generated in part A to solve the problem. The equation remains on the screen, reducing the need for representational holding (i.e., retaining an "image" of the equation in working memory for use in part B). It should be noted that the inclusion of an on-screen calculator, permitted by many computer-based testing systems, would reduce the impact of the split-attention effect on working memory by eliminating the need for the test-taker to shift attention between the computer screen and a physical calculator or piece of paper.

The *modality* effect is observed when working memory load is increased when multiple sources of information are presented in a single modality (e.g., visual, auditory; Sweller, 2010a). Extraneous load can be reduced by presenting the sources of information in a dual-modality format (e.g., presenting a diagram in a visual format while a person audibly describes what the diagram depicts). With respect to assessment, the modality effect is avoided when test items requiring visuals or diagrams include audio descriptions of the visuals rather than adding text-based descriptions. By using a dual-modality format, the item facilitates the acquisition or retrieval of information required for responding (i.e., extraneous load is reduced by permitting the test-taker to process multiple item elements simultaneously).

The *redundancy* effect refers to cognitive overload resulting from the presence of multiple sources of the same information (Kalyuga, et al., 1999). For example, extraneous load may be increased when a figure necessary for acquiring knowledge contains a text-based title, and simultaneously the title is read aloud. The title of the figure and the audible description of the title are redundant, increasing extraneous load and interfering with learning (Chandler & Sweller, 1991). In terms of test design, items should include necessary information only once. This may require eliminating the titles of graphs when text-based descriptions are present, eliminating auditory descriptions when titles are present, or eliminating text when the same information is presented in an audio-based format.

Similarly, the *seductive detail effect* occurs when information is included that, while not

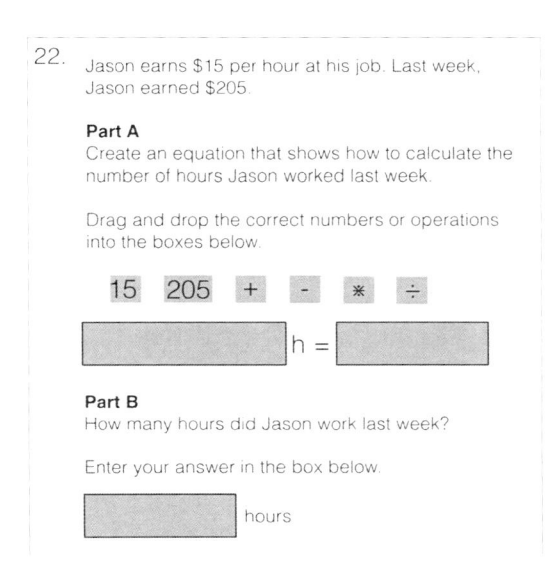

22. Jason earns $15 per hour at his job. Last week, Jason earned $205.

Part A
Create an equation that shows how to calculate the number of hours Jason worked last week.

Drag and drop the correct numbers or operations into the boxes below.

15   205   +   −   ∗   ÷

[ ] h = [ ]

Part B
How many hours did Jason work last week?

Enter your answer in the box below.

[ ] hours

Fig. 13.1 A worked example item

necessarily redundant, distracts the learner from the essential information, potentially requiring him or her to process information that is not requisite for acquiring knowledge. Despite its tangential connection to CLT work, research on *interestingness* – the inclusion of details in text with the purpose of engaging the reader (e.g., Graves et al., 1991) – can inform an understanding of how seductive details might cause cognitive overload during testing and influence test results.

Indeed, for over 100 years, educators have debated the inclusion of nonessential text in reading material (Hidi, 1990). Some advocates have recommended adding some nonessential text to increase interest, while adversaries have pointed to evidence that its inclusion may have a deleterious effect on comprehension. While a full understanding has not been reached, there is considerable research to support the use of caution when considering the inclusion of nonessential material in assessment tasks. At a minimum, the issue warrants a brief review.

In 1913, Dewey admonished educators to avoid attempting to improve educational lessons by including nonessential content with the sole intent of increasing interest. Seventy years later, Graves et al. (1988) conducted a study known as the "Time-Life Study" that became the polestar in a series of studies by several research groups over a decade that investigated the extent to which nonessential text, included only for the purpose of increasing interestingness, increased or decreased reader recall of main ideas. In the Time-Life Study, Graves et al. asked three groups of editors to revise history texts to improve their interest level. Of the three resulting texts, the revisions characterized by the addition of low-importance, high-interest text (seductive details) were (a) rated highest in interest level by readers and (b) recalled to a greater degree than other edits. Subsequent research, however, disconfirmed the hypothesis that seductive details increase recall (e.g., Garner, Alexander, Gillingham, Kulikowich, & Brown, 1991; Graves et al., 1991). Indeed, Garner, Gillingham, and White (1989) found that the addition of seductive details resulted in decreased recall. A subsequent investigation indicated texts that included seductive details took longer to read (Wade, Schraw, Buxton, & Hayes, 1993); thus, the authors theorized that seductive details draw attention away from main ideas to the detriment of reader recall. Sadoski, Goetz, and Rodriguez (2000) found concreteness was the single greatest predictor of text comprehensibility, interest, and recall.

Harp and Mayer (1997) conducted a set of four experiments that provided confirmatory evidence of the seductive detail effect. The authors theorized that seductive details, rather than distracting or disrupting readers, prime inappropriate schemas around which readers then attempt to organize information for later recall. Schraw (1998) found both context-dependent and context-independent seductive details were recalled better than main ideas, but only texts that included context-dependent seductive details took longer to read, and results showed no significant effect of seductive details on reader recall of main ideas. Thus, while Schraw concluded the additional elaborative processing required to comprehend seductive details neither enhanced nor hindered recall, his results confirmed the earlier finding that seductive details increased reading load. We ought to conclude, at a minimum, that test developers consider reducing reading load to the degree possible while preserving the target construct(s) of tests and test items.

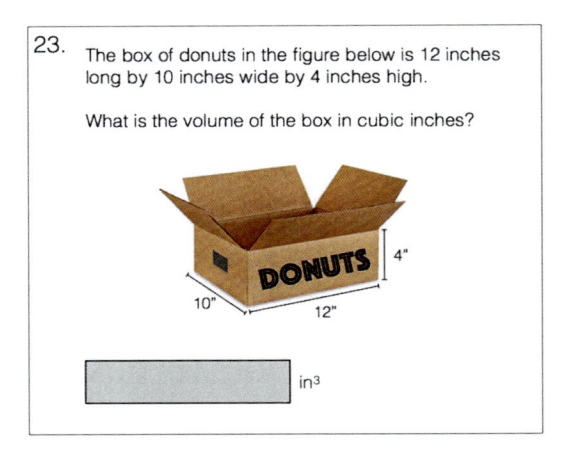

Fig. 13.2 Grade 6 mathematics item with redundant information and seductive details

Figure 13.2 consists of a grade 6 mathematics item that contains redundant information and potentially seductive details. Specifically, the item requires the test-taker to calculate the volume of a box. The item stimulus describes the dimensions of the box, and the figure consists of an image of the box with labels indicating its dimensions (i.e., the dimensions are presented redundantly). Given the figure apparently is included to support responding, the dimensions should be included only next to the figure (i.e., they should not be included in the item stimulus). At best, the redundancy of the box's dimensions increases the reading load of the item; at worst, it increases the amount of information the test-taker loads and processes in working memory, perhaps because the stimulus uses the word "inches" and the figure uses the symbol for inches, creating momentary confusion for a test-taker who may not have a solid grasp on the difference between various forms of measurement notation.

The item also contains what may be considered one or more seductive details. The stimulus refers to the figure as a "box of donuts," and the box is labeled as such. There is no meaningful rationale for including the purpose of the box in the item stimulus or on the figure. Although its inclusion arguably situates the problem in the "real world," it does not contextualize it in a manner that facilitates the demonstration of the target skill (calculating the volume of a rectangular prism). Further, the fact the box is empty notwithstanding its stated purpose of holding donuts may be distracting to the test-taker (hungry or otherwise). Admittedly, the detail does not actually contain information that could lead a test-taker to select an incorrect response, but it may cause the test-taker to expend additional time and/or cognitive resources – perhaps those needed to solve this or another problem on the test. Next, there is the inclusion of the rectangular cutout on the side (perhaps for holding the box). Although this may seem trivial to the vast majority of readers of this chapter, the cutout is neither the correct shade of gray to realistically depict such a cutout nor does it reveal the inside edge of the box as it should. The graphic artist may have included the detail to support the stated use of the box, but the cutout is obviously "photoshopped" and, again, could represent a distraction to test-takers who may tend to take interest in such details.

The *element interactivity* effect is among the most basic of cognitive load effects, but is nonetheless of critical importance (Sweller, 2010a, 2010b). In essence, early CLT research found that instruction that required learners to process a higher number of individual item elements was less effective than instruction that required less element interactivity. In terms of item development, this effect should be considered paramount, as it is directly related to item/test validity. Indeed, inferences based on scores from tests that require high element interactivity may in fact represent measures of working memory, rather than the specific construct(s) they are designed to measure. Although working memory is required for cognitive processing, it is essential that tests control for working memory capacity to the degree possible. Referring once again to the item in Fig. 13.2, three measurement notation formats are used to denote the units of measurement: "inches," double-prime marks, and "in." Since all three are used in the same item, a rationale cannot be made that the item was written to measure the test-taker's understanding of their functional equivalence. The item could be simplified by removing the item stimulus (i.e., "The box of donuts...") and selecting just one of the notations (*in* would do). Following these changes, the measurement construct would be uncompromised and the potential for extraneous element interactivity arguably would be minimized.

It would behoove us to pause here and consider the putative rationale for including all three different ways of notating the unit of measurement in the item contained in Fig. 13.2, namely, if the variations were included for the purpose of teaching the test-taker. Indeed, the functional equivalence of the whole-word, abbreviation, and symbol forms is *germane* to the tested content (i.e., volumetric calculation), even if an understanding of the concept is not required for a correct response. Furthermore, transitive logic could lead the test-taker to deduce the functional equivalence of the notations. The question, then, relates to the purpose of the test: are the test results used solely for evaluation and accountability, or is the process of test-taking, in addition to yielding a measure of knowledge, intended to function as an opportunity for additional learning? That is, does the test have a dual function of evaluating student learning and facilitating the acquisition or mastery of knowledge or skills that are germane to the tested content? The answer is of critical importance, for as we just explored, the design of a test item can (and perhaps *should*) be shaped by the purpose of the item. If the test is intended solely to evaluate student learning, it is imperative the items represent as pure a measure of the target content as depends on the test developers – controlling the demand for cognitive resources to ensure test scores do not include variance that is the result of discrepancies in test-taker working memory capacity. If, however, the test is designed to fit as seamlessly as possible into the learning process (while simultaneously yielding information about student learning), then the items may include non-requisite, germane concepts.

Results from dual-function tests should be interpreted with caution, with the understanding they include content that is not requisite for responding but is intended to support the learning process. Namely, there may be some test-takers for whom the sum of the intrinsic load and germane load of the test exceed the test-taker's cognitive capacity, resulting in either (a) scores from which inferences about learning may be invalid or (b) the failure of the test-taker to profit fully from the opportunity to learn afforded by the test. Optimally, the validation process should include measures of cognitive load to determine the degree to which these threats to validity may operate on test results. In either case (i.e., single- or dual-purpose), test developers should aim to eliminate extraneous load, for it may be deleterious to both learning and test performance and is supportive of neither.

Measurement of Cognitive Load

If a test item either (a) requires cognitive resources for one test-taker that are not required of another or (b) yields results that are in some part reflective of the working memory capacity of the test-taker, we may deduce that inferences made from test results do not represent a valid measure of the target construct of the item for all test-takers. Given decades of CLT research have produced numerous methods of evaluating cognitive demand, it follows some of these measures should be considered for use to measure the cognitive demand of tests and test items, with the purpose of ensuring not only the fairness of test items for all test-takers but their accessibility across the range of the target population.

Brünken, Plass, and Leutner (2003) presented number of measurement approaches, classified by (a) indirect, subjective measures; (b) direct, subjective measures; (c) indirect, objective measures; and (d) direct, objective measures. Indirect subjective measures included posttreatment questionnaires in which learners report mental effort invested in comprehending instructional materials. For example, Elliott, Kettler, Beddow, and Kurz (2010) recommended graphing the correlation between follow-up test-taker-reported cognitive demand and the difficulty of test items using cognitive efficiency plots. Direct, subjective measures may include the use of cognitive labs in which test-takers describe their thoughts and experiences as they respond to test items (e.g., Roach, Beddow, Kurz, Kettler, & Elliott, 2010). The validity of these types of measures has been questioned, however, as differences may reflect individual competency of the respondence or different attentional processes (Brünken et al.).

Indirect, objective measures are the most commonly used measurement method in cognitive load research and typically use knowledge acquisition scores (Brünken et al., 2003). Used in assessment research, such a measure may involve comparing test scores for similar groups on test items that differ on features that are thought to affect cognitive load (e.g., Kettler et al., 2011). Of course, it is critical that these methods control for individual learner traits, which likely will account for the plurality of within-group differences.

Other indirect, objective cognitive load measurement forms involve the analysis of behavioral patterns or physiological conditions and functions, such as time spent engaging materials, navigation errors (e.g., on digitally delivered tests), and eye-tracking analyses. It should be noted, however, that these measures, while objective, may only partially reflect cognitive load, as factors such as attentional or motivational processes may also influence results. Other physiological measures, such as heart rate and pupil dilation, also may be indirectly linked to cognitive load, as may the test-taker's emotional response to items.

Direct, objective measures may include neuroimaging techniques such as positron emission tomography and functional magnetic resonance imaging (fMRI) to measure brain response during task completion. These methods commonly are used to visualize regional brain activation in studies of working memory, but their putative utility for examining more complex learning processes is not yet fully understood (Brünken et al., 2003).

Another promising direct, objective measurement technique that has been used in CLT research is dual-task measurement, where learners complete both an instructional activity and a monitoring task simultaneously (e.g., Chandler & Sweller, 1996; Brünken, Plass, & Leutner, 2004). The theory is that when a secondary task is added, memory load is induced and performance on the primary task is affected. Dependent variables in dual-task measures may range from accuracy to reaction time. A secondary approach would be to measure performance on the secondary task to determine the affect of the primary task on the availability of working memory resources. The dual-task methodology is useful for studying the cognitive load of tests and test items as well, but there are no extant studies where it has been used.

Conclusions and Next Steps

As we have reviewed, CLT has been proposed and studied primarily to inform the design of instructional materials, with a focus on facilitating learning (which is sometimes defined as useful changes to long-term memory). In this chapter, I have examined the potential utility of CLT to inform the design of universally designed, accessible tests and test items for the purpose of ensuring inferences from test results are valid for all test-takers. Specifically, we discussed both of the primary assumptions of CLT: (a) the dual-channel assumption, which states individuals process information primarily through the visual channel and the auditory/verbal channel, and (b) the limited capacity assumption, which states there is an upper limit of working memory, above which an individual cannot effectively process additional information. Both assumptions have relevance not only to participating in instructional tasks but also to participating in assessment tasks such as tests and test items. To the degree individual differences in working memory capacity and/or the ability of individuals to access working memory influence test or test item responses, inferences made from test results should be interpreted not only as reflective of test-takers' knowledge of the target construct(s) but also as measures of working memory. With respect to the fairness in testing guidelines in the *Standards* (2016), such discrepancies potentially pose a "central threat" to test validity, for if the equivalence of the tested construct across the population depends in some part on working memory, the test cannot be considered "an unobstructed opportunity to demonstrate...standing" on the construct. A number of strategies were applied to the design of tests and test items to reduce the potential for cognitive overload – thus increasing the degree to which the test complies with universal design and accessibility guidelines. These strategies included eliminating redundancy, avoiding the use of seductive details, reducing language load, presenting information across two modalities to allow for simultaneous processing, and using worked examples for mathematics problems.

Finally, there is the issue of measuring the mental effort, or cognitive demand, required by tests and test items. To the degree cognitive demand exceeds working memory capacity for a portion of the intended population, a test or test item cannot be considered a pure measure of the target construct because it measures, at least in part, working memory. The intrinsic load of a test should represent the totality of cognitive demand, unless the test is intended as both a learning and an assessment task (in which case inferences from test results should be made with caution, as they may reflect, in part the insufficiency of cognitive resources that were applied to the "assessment" portion of the test). In fact, assessments as lessons should also be considered potentially insufficient opportunities to learn the intended content, for the same reason, namely, students may allocate more resources to doing well on the test, leaving comparatively fewer resources available for learning. For cognitive load to be evaluated, it must be measured. Although subjective, indirect methods are least costly, they also may be the least accurate, as they likely reflect competency levels of the test-takers, attentional differences, or emotional variance. Indirect, objective measures, such as performance outcome measures, may be useful, but they require two variations of any test or test item and some understanding of the features of each that might influence cognitive demand. Further, they are only indirectly linked to cognitive load and are thus impure measures of the construct – for even pupil dilation and heart rate, while potentially correlated with cognitive load, can be influenced by other variables such as test self-efficacy. For this reason, dual-task measurement should be considered as a proxy for direct assessment of cognitive demand. Finally, test developers should consider introducing direct, objective measures such as neuroimaging into the test validation process, although precisely how these measures can be used to understand cognitive load is not yet fully understood and research is needed on how results of these tools should be used to guide the development of tests.

In conclusion, test developers should consider how cognitive load theory may inform test design, with a focus on bridging "the fairness divide" – specifically to ameliorate the differences between test-takers with varying working memory capacities, or for whom tests require greater working memory resources than others. The objective should be to ensure test scores do not reflect measures of working memory, but rather can yield valid inferences regardless of the working memory capacity of the test-taker. For only when working memory differences are controlled during the test event will tests "maximize...access for as many examinees in the intended population as possible" (*Standards*, 2016, p.50).

References

American Educational Research Association, American Psychological Assocation, & National Center for Measurement in Education. (2016). *Standards for educational and psychological testing*. Washington, DC: American Educational Research Association.

Asghar, I., & Winsler, A. (2000). Bartlett's schema theory and modern accounts of learning and remembering. *Journal of Mind and Behavior*, 271–371.

Baddeley, A. (1994). The magical number seven: Still magic after all these years? *Psychological Review*, *101*, 353–356.

Baddeley, A. (2003). Working memory: Looking back and looking forward. *Nature Reviews. Neuroscience*, *4*, 829–839.

Beddow, P. A., Kettler, R. J., & Elliott, S. N. (2010). *Accessibility rating matrix*. Nashville, TN: Vanderbilt.

Beddow, P. A., Kurz, A., & Frey, J. R. (2011). Accessibility theory: Guiding the science and practice of test item design with the test-taker in mind. In S. N. Elliott, R. J. Kettler, P. A. Beddow, & A. Kurz (Eds.), *Handbook of accessible achievement tests for all students* (pp. 163–182). New York: Springer.

Brünken, R., Plass, J. L., & Leutner, D. (2003). Direct measurement of cognitive load in multimedia learning. *Educational Psychologist*, *38*, 53–61.

Brünken, R., Plass, J. L., & Leutner, D. (2004). Assessment of cognitive load in multimedia learning with dual-task methodology: Auditory load and modality effects. *Instructional Science*, *32*, 115–132.

Chandler, P., & Sweller, J. (1991). Cognitive load theory and the format of instruction. *Cognition and Instruction*, *8*, 293–332.

Chandler, P., & Sweller, J. (1996). Cognitive load while learning to use a computer program. *Applied Cognitive Psychology*, *10*, 151–170.

Clark, R. C., Nguyen, F., & Sweller, J. (2006). *Efficiency in learning : Evidence-based guidelines to manage cognitive load*. San Francisco: Jossey-Bass.

Cowan, N. (2001). The magical number 4 in short-term memory: A reconsideration of mental storage capacity. *Behavioral and Brain Sciences, 24*(01), 87–114.

Debue, N., & Van De Leemput, C. (2014). What does germane load mean? An empirical contribution to the cognitive load theory. *Frontiers in Psychology, 5*, 1–12.

Dewey, J. (1913). In H. Suzzalo (Ed.), *Interest and effort in education*. New York: Houghton Mifflin Company.

Elliott, S. N., Kettler, R. J., Beddow, P. A., & Kurz, A. (2010). Research and strategies for adapting formative assessments for students with special needs. In H. L. Andrade & G. J. Cizek (Eds.), *Handbook of formative assessment* (pp. 159–180). New York: Routledge.

Garner, R., Alexander, P. A., Gillingham, M. G., Kulikowich, J. M., & Brown, R. (1991). Interest and learning from text. *American Educational Research Journal, 28*(3), 643–659.

Garner, R., Gillingham, M. G., & White, C. S. (1989). Effects of "seductive details" on macroprocessing and microprocessing in adults and children. *Cognition and Instruction, 6*, 41–57.

Graves, M. E., Slater, W. H., Roen, D., Redd-Boyd, T., Duin, A. H., Furniss, D. W., & Hazeltine, P. (1988). Some characteristics of memorable expository writing: Effects of revisions by writers with different backgrounds. *Research in the Teaching of English*, 242–265.

Graves, M. F., Prenn, M. C., Earle, J., Thompson, M., Johnson, V., & Slater, W. H. (1991). Commentary: Improving instructional text: Some lessons learned. *Reading Research Quarterly*, 110–122.

Harp, S. F., & Mayer, R. E. (1997). How seductive details do their damage: A cognitive theory of interest in science learning. *Journal of Educational Psychology, 90*, 414–434.

Hidi, S. (1990). Interest and its contribution as a mental resource for learning. *Review of Educational Research, 60*, 549–571.

Kalyuga, S., Chandler, P., & Sweller, J. (1999). Managing split-attention and redundancy in multimedia instruction. *Applied Cognitive Psychology, 13*, 351–371.

Kettler, R. J., Rodriguez, M. C., Bolt, D., Elliott, S. N., Beddow, P. A., & Kurz, A. (2011). Modified multiple-choice items for alternate assessments: Reliability, difficulty, and differential boost. *Applied Measurement in Education, 24*, 210–234.

Mayer, R. E., & Moreno, R. (1998). A split-attention effect in multimedia learning: Evidence for dual processing systems in working memory. *Journal of Educational Psychology, 90*, 312–320.

Mayer, R. E., & Moreno, R. (2003). Nine ways to reduce cognitive load in multimedia learning. *Educational Psychologist, 38*, 43–52.

Miller, G. A. (1956). The magical number seven, plus or minus two: Some limits on our capacity for information processing. *Psychological Review, 63*, 81–97.

Moreno, R., & Mayer, R. E. (2000). A coherence effect in multimedia learning: The case for minimziing irrelevant sounds in the design of multimedia instructional messages. *Journal of Educational Psychology, 92*, 117–125.

Plass, J. L., Moreno, R., & Brünken, R. (2010). *Cognitive load theory*. New York: Cambridge University Press.

Renkl, A., Atkinson, R. K., & Grosse, C. S. (2004). How fading worked solution steps works: A cognitive load perspective. *Instructional Science, 32*, 59–82.

Roach, A. T., Beddow, P. A., Kurz, A., Kettler, R. J., & Elliott, S. N. (2010). Incorporating student input in developing alternate assessments based on modified achievement standards. *Exceptional Children, 77*, 61–80.

Sadoski, M., Goetz, E. T., & Rodriguez, M. (2000). Engaging texts: Effects of concreteness on comprehensibility, interest, and recall in four text types. *Journal of Educational Psychology, 92*(1), 85–95.

Schraw, G. (1998). Processing and recall differences among seductive details. *Journal of Educational Psychology, 90*, 3–12.

Shannon, C. E. (1948). A mathematical theory of communication. *Bell System Technical Journal, 27*(379–423), 623–656.

Shannon, C. E., & Weaver, W. (1949). *The mathematical theory of information*. Urbana, IL: University of Illinois Press.

Simon, H. A., & Gilmartin, K. (1973). A simulation of memory for chess positions. *Cognitive Psychology, 5*, 29–46.

Sweller, J. (2010a). Cognitive load theory: Recent theoretical advances. In J. L. Plass, R. Moreno, & R. Brunken (Eds.), *Cognitive load theory* (pp. 29–47). New York: Cambridge University Press.

Sweller, J. (2010b). Element interactivity and intrinsic, extraneous, and germane cognitive load. *Educational Psychology Review*, 1–16.

Thompson, S. J., Johnstone, C. J., & Thurlow, M. L. (2002). *Universal design applied to large scale assessments (Synthesis Report 44)*. Minneapolis, MN: University of Minnesota, National Center on Educational Outcomes.

Wade, S. E., Schraw, G., Buxton, W. M., & Hayes, M. T. (1993). Seduction of the strategic reader: Effects of interest on strategies and recall. *Reading Research Quarterly*, 93–114.

Testing Adaptations: Research to Guide Practice

Leah Dembitzer and Ryan J. Kettler

Introduction

The Individuals with Disabilities Education Act of 1997 and subsequent Individuals with Disabilities Education Improvement Act of 2004 require states to include students with disabilities (SWDs; IDEA, 1997; IDEIA, 2004) in large-scale assessments. To meet this inclusion requirement and provide equitable assessments for students with disabilities, states have used testing accommodations and item modifications. Accordingly, there has been a proliferation of research addressing these trends. The Every Student Succeeds Act of 2016 reinforces this stance, requiring that each state implement high-quality assessments in reading or language arts, mathematics, and science, include all students in those assessments, and provide appropriate accommodations for SWDs. The most recent version of the *Standards for Educational and Psychological Testing* (American Educational Research Association [AERA], American Psychological Association [APA], and National Council on Measurement in Education [NCME], 2014) has given increased clarification on guidelines for testing adaptations conceptualized under fairness concerns. In another recent development, two major federal multistate assessment consortia, namely, the Partnership for Assessment of Readiness for College Careers [PARCC] and the Smarter Balanced Assessment Consortium [SBAC], have promoted a universally designed approach to testing adaptations, aiming to individualize testing adaptations to allow for more equitable assessment. Changes in theory, in practice, and in the research base necessitate a modernization and reconceptualization of the traditional dichotomy between testing accommodations and test modifications. This chapter aims to address this challenge.

Recent Changes in Theory and Practice

The *Standards for Educational and Psychological Testing* (AERA, APA, NCME, 2014) provides an increased emphasis on "fairness." The *Standards* delineates that test-takers may have individual characteristics (including minority status based on language, culture, or disability) that can interfere with the validity of the interpretation of test scores and negatively affect fairness for these individuals. The *Standards* characterizes testing adaptations as a broad range of changes in the standardization of testing, ranging from

L. Dembitzer (✉)
Center for Health Education, Medicine, and Dentistry, Lakewood, NJ, USA

R. J. Kettler
Rutgers, The State University of New Jersey, Piscataway, NJ, USA

accommodations on one end to modifications on the other, and discusses testing adaptations as a possible means of overcoming issues of fairness. This "end-to-end" conceptualization of accommodations and modifications will be discussed in the next section.

PARCC and Smarter Balanced are multistate assessment consortia funded by the federal Race to the Top grant competition (King, 2011). The consortia were tasked with creating assessments that are linked to the common core standards and college and career readiness goals. Both PARCC and Smarter Balanced have a universally designed, more personalized approach to testing accommodations. Both testing systems allow accessibility features and universal tools for all students, as well as specialized additional supports that any student can request, and a last tier of accommodations for students with individualized education plans (IEPs; PARCC, 2013; Smarter Balanced, 2013).

PARCC allows a first level of accessibility features for all students incorporated into the test design and a second level of accessibility features that must be requested in advance. These accessibility features were historically considered accommodations (e.g., text-to-speech for mathematics, changed font); they can now be requested for a SWD by his/her IEP team or for a student without disabilities (SWOD) by a team including student, parent, and teacher. These requests are documented in a Personal Needs Profile (PNP); testing accommodations are also included in the PNP (readers interested in more information on PNPs are directed to Russell's Chap. 16 of the current volume). For the last tier of accommodations, students with an IEP or 504 plan or those who use accommodations regularly in class can be eligible for accommodations. Smarter Balanced has a similar approach, naming the first-level "universal tools," the second-level "designated supports," and the third-level accommodations specifically for SWDs with IEPs or 504 plans. Both PARCC and Smarter Balanced provide recommendations for the appropriate use of accommodations in each content area.

PARCC and Smarter Balanced provide guidelines focused on individual student needs, access, and validity, in line with the recommendations of the standards. However, in many states and districts, teachers and IEP teams tend to recommend more accommodations than necessary, without knowledge of the individualized nature of these decisions (Fuchs et al., 2000; Fuchs, Fuchs, Eaton, Hamlett, & Karns, 2000; Helwig & Tindal, 2003). A further understanding of the current framework for testing adaptations is needed to bridge this gap between research and practice.

Traditional Dichotomy of Accommodations Versus Modifications

Traditionally, testing adaptations were dichotomized as accommodations or modifications. Testing accommodations have been understood to be changes made to external features of a test, with the implication being that test content remained the same. Testing accommodations address a test's setting, scheduling, presentation, and/or response modality to allow students to fairly demonstrate their knowledge (Hollenbeck, 2005). Fuchs, Fuchs, and Capizzi (2005) have categorized testing accommodations by changes in setting, timing, format, and supports. Some examples of testing accommodations given in most states are extra time, read-aloud/audio presentation, response to scribe, and enlarged test format (Bolt & Thurlow, 2004; Christensen, Lazarus, Crone, & Thurlow, 2008; Fuchs et al., 2005). Table 14.1 lists common accommodations allowed and awarded in many states classified by Fuchs et al.'s (2005) categories.

Modifications have been understood as an adaptation to test content itself in order to make test items more accessible to certain populations, possibly implying a change in curricular expectations. Kettler, Elliott, and Beddow (2009) divided common modifications into three categories: (a) modifications to reduce unnecessary language load, (b) modifications for answer choices, and (c) other general modifications that address different access issues. Table 14.2 lists the categories and provides examples of testing modifications.

Table 14.1 Commonly awarded testing accommodations

Categories
Setting
Separate testing location
Small group administration
Individual administration
Timing
Extended time
Extra breaks
Test format
Braille or large print
Audio presentation
Sign directions
Scribe dictation
Supports
Communication devices
Calculator for mathematics tests
Computer for writing

Table 14.2 Examples of modifications by category

Modifications to reduce unnecessary language load
Rewrite to replace pronouns with proper nouns
Simplify sentence and text structure with an emphasis on clarity
Reduce vocabulary load and nonconstruct subject area language
Chunk and segment the text into manageable pieces
Base the item on the construct it is written to measure by removing any trivial content
Minimize the amount of reading necessary by reducing excess text
Replace negatives (e.g., NOT or EXCEPT) with positive wording
Edit the items for errors in grammar, punctuation, capitalization, and spelling
Modifications to answer choices
Eliminate any implausible distractors until as few as three answer choices are possible
Move a central idea that is in the item choices to the item stem
Avoid cuing for a correct or incorrect answer
Place answer choices in a logical order and make them structurally homogenous
Other general modifications
Make items more factual rather than opinion-based
Add white space to make tracking easier
Remove visuals that are not necessary or helpful
Format items to be read vertically
Use bold text for important words

Note Taken from "Modifying achievement test items: A theory-guided and data-based approach for better measurement of what students with disabilities know" by Kettler et al. (2009), Copyright 2009 by Taylor and Francis. Used with permission

Because testing accommodations and modifications are thought to affect students' scores, they are often sought by students and can be controversial (Thurlow, House, Boys, Scott, & Ysseldyke, 2000). CTB/McGraw Hill (2000, 2005) has created three categories of testing accommodations for academic tests with levels of caution needed for interpretation of scores. A *Category 1* accommodation as defined by CTB/McGraw Hill is not expected to influence student performance in a way that would invalidate the standard interpretation of the test scores. For example, a student taking a test alone instead of with a group should not be a concern for test scores. A *Category 2* accommodation may affect student performance, and CTB/McGraw Hill recommends considering the accommodation used when interpreting the scores. Extra time has been classified as a Category 2 accommodation. Lastly, a *Category 3* accommodation is thought to change the construct being studied; therefore, test results from Category 3 accommodations should be interpreted with caution. An example of a Category 3 accommodation is allowing the use of a calculator for a computation test; results from a test event in which this accommodation was allowed should be a concern for score interpretation. CTB/McGraw Hill has considered audio presentation for a reading (decoding) test to be a Category 3 accommodation while audio presentation of other subject matters to be a Category 2 accommodation (CTB/McGraw Hill, 2000, 2005). Modifications historically have been viewed with more skepticism because with the alteration of actual test content, the concern has been that expectations and constructs could change. However, as CTB/McGraw Hill's guidelines indicate, testing adaptations traditionally known as accommodations can also result in changing the construct. Kettler (2015) underscored the importance of categorizing testing adaptations as "appropriate" versus "inappropriate" based on whether the validity of score interpretation is compromised and categorizing accommodations versus modifications based on whether the content is altered.

Theoretical Understanding of Testing

According to the *Standards* (AERA, APA, NCME, 2014), for valid inferences to be drawn from test scores, the test content needs to have been accessible to students (described as "fairness"), the scores need to be reliable, and the test questions need to reflect the content knowledge or construct under study. Without these three components, scores will not yield inferences about student learning of covered material.

Beddow (2012) described test accessibility as the degree to which a test allows examinees to demonstrate their knowledge on a construct. Beddow explained that individual test items are the building blocks of accessibility and must allow entry to the target content being measured without barriers. For example, a handwritten primary source on a history assessment must be legible for its content to be accessible. Accessibility is highly individual and can be depicted as an interaction between the characteristics of a test-taker and features of a test item. If the features of a test item require certain test-taker characteristics that are not intended to be measured, the test is less accessible for students who have impairments in those areas. Accessibility can also be conceptualized as ensuring that test items are not biased toward any subgroup of students, including SWDs (Thompson, Johnstone, & Thurlow, 2002). This broad position on accessibility is taken in the *Standards* chapter on fairness (AERA, APA, & NCME, 2014), with an emphasis on accessibility for all groups with their individual needs. A lack of accessibility causes the inferences drawn from the scores to be less valid, because lower scores can be more reflective of access issues, rather than lesser knowledge of the tested construct (Beddow, 2012).

According to the *Standards*, another contributing factor to ensure valid inferences is a focus on a clearly defined target construct (AERA, APA, & NCME, 2014). Tests are intended to measure constructs, the unseen underlying skills, and knowledge needed to display the targeted competences (e.g., reading skills, mathematical computational skills). Very often, "access skills" are needed for a student to demonstrate his/her knowledge on the target construct of the test. For example, vision is a necessary access skill for a reading test, and reading may be an access skill on a math test. Tests are not designed to measure access skills, but students use these skills to demonstrate their competency on the target constructs. A lack of the level of competence on an access skill necessary for a test constitutes a "functional impairment." Although a test could be designed for maximal accessibility, individual student characteristics and functional impairments can create barriers to the target skills meant to be assessed.

One goal of academic assessment is to obtain accurate estimates of student functioning in a domain. The barrier of a functional impairment in an access skill can compromise the validity of such inferences. Testing adaptations selected to overcome functional impairments can increase the validity of the inferences drawn from the test in this way. However, if accommodations impact the construct being measured, they can negatively affect the validity of inferences drawn from the test scores, rather than positively affecting such inferences (CTB/McGraw Hill 2000, 2005).

Revisions to the *Standards* have refined the definition of accommodations and modifications and have de-emphasized categories of changes. Whether or not the construct was impacted was considered paramount in deciding upon the appropriateness of adaptations. Thus, according to the emphasis placed by the *Standards*, accommodations can be understood as appropriate adaptations that do not alter the target construct of the assessment, and modifications are inherently inappropriate adaptations that alter the target construct.

Individual need of testing adaptations is based on functional impairment or competency in access skills, in conjunction with the defined construct of a test. Determining this need can be complicated because many students exhibit more than one functional impairment, and many tests target multiple constructs.

Review of Research on Testing Accommodations and Modifications

The *Standards* (AERA, APA, & NCME, 2014) requires evidence that a test with adaptations will yield comparable scores to the standard version of the test. Research studies traditionally have used the *differential boost* framework to prove the comparability of scores. A differential boost means that SWDs benefit more from testing adaptations than SWODs do (Fuchs & Fuchs, 2001). Much of the research on testing adaptations has assumed that adaptations are only appropriate if the differential boost criteria can be met. Although SWODs may gain some benefit from testing accommodations as well, Fuchs and Fuchs (2001) considered it fair to allow SWDs to use these accommodations if a differential boost is found. Sireci, Scarpati, and Li (2005) originally suggested a stricter interaction hypothesis of testing accommodations. According to the interaction hypothesis, valid testing accommodations should improve scores for SWDs and not at all for SWODs. In the Sireci et al. review of testing accommodation research, the definition of the interaction hypothesis was revised to make it more similar to the differential boost criteria, due to the lack of support found for their original level of differential effects. Sireci et al. (2005) explained that the interaction hypothesis may not have been found in research due to possible problems with the fairness of assessments toward SWODs. However, reviews of research have found mixed levels of support for the differential boost as well (Cormier, Altman, Shyyan, & Thurlow, 2010; Fuchs et al., 2005; Rogers, Christian, & Thurlow, 2012; Rogers, Lazarus, & Thurlow, 2014; Zenisky & Sireci, 2007).

The research on testing accommodations includes a number of literature reviews. Fuchs et al. (2005) and Sireci et al. (2005) both performed research reviews using the differential boost framework to evaluate accommodations including read-aloud, extra time, and combined packages of accommodations used together. The National Center on Education Outcomes (NCEO) publishes a review of testing accommodation research every 2 years (Cormier et al., 2010; Rogers et al., 2012; Rogers et al., 2014; Zenisky & Sireci, 2007). Overall, the differential boost paradigm had mixed results for all kinds of accommodations with some studies finding a differential boost, some finding a boost for both groups, and some finding no boost for either group. For further discussion of the mixed findings, see Cormier et al. (2010), Fuchs et al. (2005), Rogers et al. (2012, 2014), Sireci et al. (2005), and Zenisky and Sireci (2007).

In the studies that found no differential boost, researchers provided alternate explanations. These explanations generally referred to other forms of validity evidence that would be needed, underscoring the limitation of the differential boost paradigm as a first step in evaluating testing adaptations. For example, Meloy, Deville, and Frisbie (2002) indicated that a lack of student input in pacing and usage of a read-aloud accommodation may have led to their study finding no differential boost. Thus, response process validity about the read-aloud accommodation to pinpoint this issue may be an important step prior to evaluation of differential effects. As another example, Lewandowski, Lovett, and Rogers (2008) theorized that no differential boost was found in their study of the extra time accommodation on a reading comprehension test because the test was speeded. The researchers indicated that content validity evidence would be important before determining the appropriateness of the accommodation. They recommended that tests should remove the timing factor unless it is explicitly stated and understood as a part of the target construct. Although the *Standards* (AERA, APA, & NCME, 2014) recommends studies for differential effects, these studies may be premature before reliability and construct validity evidence are collected. The *Standards* recommends also using other forms of evidence such as small-sample qualitative studies and expert review to ensure the comparability of the constructs. A subset of testing accommodation research focuses on other precursors to inferences, including access, reliability, and construct validity in testing adaptation research (e.g., Elliott et al., 2010; Flowers, Wakeman, Browder & Karvonen, 2009; Lindstrom & Gregg, 2007; Roach, Elliott, & Webb, 2005).

Studies Using Reliability Evidence

Because reliability is a prerequisite to validity, the *Standards* (AERA, APA, & NCME, 2014) enumerates the importance of providing reliability and precision evidence disaggregated for subgroups of students that will take the test. However, most research on testing adaptations has not focused on reliability. Therefore, there are no established expectations for the impact of testing adaptations on reliability indices.

Reliability often is described as the consistency of a set of scores and typically is estimated in testing adaptation research using *internal consistency* (i.e., the degree of cohesiveness among a set of items that are summed to yield the score of a test.) Estimates of internal consistency are relatively easy to obtain because they are calculated on a single set of scores. A limitation of using internal consistency estimates as representation for reliability is that they are based on correlations between subsets of the items that are summed for a score, rather than correlations among total scores, the level used for most test interpretation. Historically, split-half reliability was a popular indicator of internal consistency. To estimate split-half reliability, all the items of a test are subdivided into equal one-half length forms, and then correlations are calculated between scores yielded by the two halves. Coefficient alpha is a computationally intensive extension of split-half reliability; it is the average of all possible split-half reliability estimates among a set of items (Cronbach, 1951). The item level parallel to internal consistency is the item-to-total biserial correlation, which indicates the variance shared between an individual item and the total score from the set, sometimes "corrected" by deleting the item in question from the total score to remove artificial inflation.

Test adaptations should not decrease the internal consistency of a set of scores, and if internal consistency is below the desired criterion for a group of students, test adaptations should increase internal consistency to be above that criterion. This can be quite a challenge, particularly because tests are standardized in large part to maximize the reliability of scores. Adaptations are departures from this standardization used with the intent of further increasing measurement precision, because adaptations that work address barriers that limited reliability, which may be reflected by internal consistency. Thus, an important initial issue regarding test adaptations is whether internal consistency is lacking for a group of students taking the test in non-adapted conditions. Tests designed for SWODs may be less reliable for SWDs for a number of reasons, including that they require access skills that SWDs do not have, as well as that they are centered in difficulty around a population of SWODs. The reauthorization of the Elementary and Secondary Education Act of 1994 required the inclusion of SWDs in large-scale assessment and the disaggregation of their test results. Since score validation is a prerequisite to interpretation, this requirement implies that psychometric evidence relevant to scores should also be disaggregated for SWDs. Providing reliability and validity evidence, particularly including estimates of internal consistency, for SWDs in non-adapted testing conditions assists in addressing the issue of whether any observed differences in mean performance are real or are attributable to error in testing.

The criteria for internal consistency for SWDs are not entirely clear, although there are a few sources of theoretical guidance that should be considered. One is the common heuristic in testing is that internal consistency estimates should exceed 0.80 for low-stakes decisions (e.g., instructional grouping) and should exceed 0.90 for high-stakes decisions (e.g., proficiency). Davidshofer and Murphy (2005) indicated that coefficient alphas in the .80s are moderately high or good and in the .90s are high or excellent. Another theoretical target for the internal consistency of a test for SWDs is the internal consistency of the same test for SWODs. It makes sense from a fairness standpoint that one would expect scores from a test to be equally precise or consistent for SWDs and SWODs. Reliability estimates tend to be lower when the range of scores is restricted, as may be the case with SWDs, possibly making these criteria more difficult to obtain. For cases in which the internal consistency estimates for SWDs are substantially below the heuristics for the decisions being made, or substantially below the estimates for SWODs, the scores are less reliable for this group, and some type of adaptations may be warranted.

Regardless of the criteria that one desires for internal consistency, it is critical that adaptations maintain (or even increase) these coefficients. This is a challenging requirement, however, in standardized testing, because one of the purposes of the standardization is to ensure that the scores yielded by the test are as comparable as possible. Any departure from standard administration (e.g., extra time, calculator, read aloud) introduces the opportunity to additional variance that is not attributable to the construct being measured (i.e., error). Further, because some adaptations are individualized (i.e., accommodations), even the accommodated condition can be different from one SWD to another. This reality underscores the care that must be taken before adapting a test in any way; if there is reasonable doubt about whether an adaptation will lead to better measurement for an individual and comparability to non-adapted scores is desired, the adaptation should not be made.

Kettler (2011a) reviewed technical data from four states that provided psychometric information for both a general assessment and an adapted assessment (CTB McGraw-Hill, 2008; Data Recognition Corporation & Pacific Metrics Corporation, 2008a, 2008b; Louisiana Department of Education, 2008, 2009; Poggio, Yang, Irwin, Glassnap, & Poggio, 2006; Texas Education Agency, 2009). Each report included reliability estimates disaggregated by content area and grade level. The general trend was that while coefficient alpha estimates of the modified assessments were often in the good range, they were usually lower than those of the general (unmodified) assessments (Kettler, 2011b). For modified reading or English/language arts assessments, 21 of 34 estimates exceeded .80. In all 34 comparisons based on state and grade, the estimate for the general assessment was greater than or equal to the estimate for the modified assessment, though many of these differences were small. The difference was greater than 0.10 in 12 of 34 comparisons for reading or English/language arts assessments. For modified mathematics assessments, 18 of 27 estimates exceeded 0.80. The estimate for the general assessment was greater than or equal to the estimate for the modified assessment in 26 out of 27 comparisons. The difference was greater than 0.10 in 11 of 26 comparisons for mathematics. For modified science assessments, four of nine estimates exceeded 0.80. The estimate for the general assessment was greater than or equal to the estimate for the modified assessment in all nine comparisons. The difference exceeded 0.10 in five of nine comparisons for science.

Kettler and colleagues have conducted multiple studies on the impact of testing modifications on the reliability of scores (Elliott et al., 2010; Kettler et al., 2011, 2012). The researchers (Elliott et al., 2010; Kettler et al., 2011) administered short achievement tests in reading and mathematics to eighth grade students ($n = 755$) in four states. Each participant was a member of one of three groups: SWODs, SWDs who would not be eligible for a modified assessment (SWD-NEs), and SWDs who would be eligible for a modified assessment (SWD-Es). Each participant completed the test forms in three conditions; one condition contained original items representative of a general assessment, and the other two conditions contained modified items. In one of the modified conditions, participants read the items silently from a computer screen, and in the other modified condition, the directions, stem, and answer choices were read aloud by voice-over technology. Items in the modified conditions contained 26–28% less words compared to items in the original condition. Because the forms were only 13 items long and coefficient alpha is dependent on the length of a test, the researchers used the Spearman-Brown prophecy formula to project the reliability coefficients of tests with 39 items, a length more typical for large-scale achievement testing. All correlations across groups, conditions, and content areas were between 0.85 and 0.94. Across conditions and content areas, the tests were more reliable among SWODs than among SWD-NEs, and in all but one comparison, the tests were more reliable among SWD-NEs than among SWD-Es. These differences in coefficient alpha were small and nonsignificant. In sum, the tests in the original condition had good to excellent reliability across groups, and the modifications did not change the reliability of the tests (Kettler et al., 2011).

The aforementioned study was replicated for high school biology in a study involving three groups of participants (n = 400) – SWODs, SWD-NEs, and SWD-Es – from three states (Kettler et al., 2012). Each participant completed two 20-item sets of online multiple-choice items. The items were read silently in the original condition and were read aloud using voice-over technology in the modified condition. On average the items in the modified condition contained 30% fewer words compared to items in the original condition. The modification process yielded mixed results regarding internal consistency for SWD-Es. Coefficient alpha for the two sets of items differed greatly in the original condition, raising concerns about comparability of forms. Alpha was reduced for one set of items, and it was increased for the other set. These results underscore the difficulty in systematically improving items by changing content, given that items are unique and a modification that improves one item may negatively affect another.

Some experimental research has addressed the impact of test adaptations on the internal consistency of items. Lindstrom and Gregg (2007) evaluated the Scholastic Aptitude Reasoning Test (SAT®, College Board) with SWODs (n = 2476) in a standard time condition and with SWDs (n = 2476) in an extra time condition. Content areas included critical reading, mathematics, and writing. Reliability estimates were calculated for each of the six combinations yielded by the two groups and three content areas. Reliability estimates were between 0.89 and 0.94 in all combinations. The estimates were highly consistent, varying by less than 0.02 between the two groups within any content area, and scores did not have lower reliability for the SWDs in any of the comparisons within content area.

Cook, Eignor, Sawaki, Steinberg, and Cline (2010) evaluated a fourth grade English/language arts assessment by having the test taken by participants in four separate groups of 500 participants: (a) SWODs under standard conditions, (b) SWDs under standard conditions, (c) SWDs using accommodations (often in packages) from their Individualized Educational Programs (IEPs), and (d) SWDs using a read-aloud accommodation. Internal consistency estimates were low across groups, in part because test forms only included four or five items apiece. Reliability was highest for SWODs in most situations, and accommodations did not systematically improve reliability for SWDs to shrink this gap.

Much more research remains to be conducted on the relationship between reliability and testing adaptations. Some of the studies (Cook et al., 2010; Lindstrom & Gregg, 2007) mentioned in this section also addressed construct validity, a natural consideration to follow reliability and the topic of the next section.

Studies Using Other Indicators of Validity Evidence

Another subset studies on testing adaptations have addressed other indicators of validity, such as evidence based on content, response processes, internal structure, and relations to other variables. According to the *Standards* (AERA, APA, & NCME, 2014), some of these types of validity evidence may be particularly necessary based on the underlying purposes and assumptions of each test.

Evidence Based on Test Content Content validity evidence, also known as construct validity, refers to evidence that the manifest content of the test accurately reflects the underlying construct it is meant to measure. Content validity evidence can include analysis of alignment between items and standards in the content domain, as well as expert review. Content validity is especially important when considering testing adaptations for SWDs because extraneous construct-irrelevant content can be a barrier to this subgroup of students. Adequate analysis of content validity is necessary to ensure fairness and access.

There are not many studies focusing on content validity evidence for tests with adaptations. Some studies have used content validity evidence to examine the alignment of alternate assessments to curriculum standards (e.g., Flowers et al., 2009; Roach et al., 2005; Roach, Niebling, & Kurz, 2008). They have found that this kind of evidence is critical to establishing the validity of alternate assessments.

Dembitzer (2016) examined the content validity of audio presentation and extra time accommodations on a reading comprehension test. Twelfth grade students with and without a functional impairment in reading fluency ($n = 131$) took the test in both an accommodated and nonaccommodated condition. Prior to allowing these accommodations for a functional impairment in reading fluency, a review was conducted of the cognitive targets of the test questions taken from the National Association for Educational Progress (NAEP) and the research base defining the reading comprehension construct. NAEP used target skills of locate and recall, integrate and interpret, critique and evaluate, and a vocabulary to define the construct on their twelfth grade reading comprehension test (NAEP, 2013). As none of these target skills include decoding and fluency skills, the audio presentation and extra time accommodations were deemed appropriate for this test (Dembitzer, 2016). In reviewing the research, Dembitzer (2016) found that reading comprehension in early elementary grades tends to include the constructs of decoding and fluency, while in high school the construct is primarily based on critical thinking. With this content validity evidence, the researcher was able to provide theoretical and empirical evidence for allowing specific accommodations for a specified population taking this test.

Evidence Based on Response Processes When the test interpretation includes assumptions about the process by which test-takers determine answers, validity evidence based on response processes is required. For example, a test measuring reasoning needs to provide evidence that test-takers use reasoning processes rather than step-by-step algorithms to solve problems (AERA, APA, NCME, 2014). Evidence based on response processes requires analysis of individual strategies and processes, which can be done through interviewing, cognitive labs, or objective measures of process such as eye movements, response times, and revision documentation. Evidence based on response processes is also important and relevant in the development on testing adaptations. If the paradigm used for developing testing adaptations involves identifying access skills needed to demonstrate knowledge on target construct, familiarity with the cognitive process inherent in the testing situation is necessary to identify those access skills.

Roach, Beddow, Kurz, Kettler, and Elliott (2010) used a cognitive lab technique to study response processes of eighth grade students completing reading and mathematics items, in both original and modified conditions. The small sample of students ($n = 9$) verbalized their cognitions while taking the test, and researchers found that all students spent less time and made fewer reading mistakes in the modified condition. Specifically for SWDs who were eligible for modified assessments, these changes in time spent and reading mistakes were notable, indicating that their response process in answering the questions was impacted by the modification of items.

Evidence Based on Internal Structure Many tests assess multiple constructs that are thought to be theoretically related and inherently intertwined (e.g., vocabulary and comprehension). Evidence of the internal structure of the test, such as the relationship between components of the test or the way specific items relate to the test as a whole, is necessary to undergird the assumption of interrelated constructs or unidimensional constructs. Item correlations or more complex factor analytic techniques can be used to provide validity evidence based on internal structure. Another way to examine evidence based on internal structure is to study differential item functioning (DIF) to determine whether apparently similar items to the construct receive an overall different response pattern from one subgroup of students. (Due to its incorporation of group status as a second variable, this type of evidence may alternatively be included in the category of validity evidence based on relations to other variables, described later in this section.) For SWDs, this kind of evidence may be necessary in the development of testing adaptations to pinpoint if there are items that require different skills than were assumed.

Lindstrom and Gregg (2007), in their review of the SAT® (College Board), used factor analysis to establish the comparability of internal structure for SWODs in standard time and internal structure for SWDs with extra time. They found that one-factor models for each content area of reading, mathematics, and writing were consistent for both groups. Tests of invariance also showed relative invariance across the groups in all content areas. These findings supported the premise that the constructs are unidimensional for both SWODs in standard time and SWDs with extra time.

Cook et al. (2010) also used factor analysis to test for a two-factor model of reading and writing underlying a fourth grade English/language arts assessment. The tests were conducted across the aforementioned four groups: (a) SWODs under standard conditions, (b) SWDs under standard conditions, (c) SWDs using accommodations from their IEPs, and (d) SWDs using a read-aloud accommodation. The two-factor structure was supported across all four groups, and the model was invariant across groups. These findings supported the claim that the same construct was being measured across groups and conditions.

Cho, Lee, and Kingston (2012) used mixture modeling on matched sample data ($n = 51,591$ and $n = 3452$) to see if DIF was present between SWODs who received non-accommodated testing and SWDs who received accommodations on a mathematics assessment. DIF was computed separately for grades three through eight, and 101 out of 470 items functioned differently for the different groups. They further tested the associations between DIF items and item characteristics. They found that their categorized item difficulty was not different between DIF and non-DIF items, and item discrimination was not related to DIF prevalence. In general, analyses of whether DIF prevalence was related to item type and features were inconclusive. However, in eighth grade more story items than explanation and straightforward items were DIF items, and in fifth grade, most DIF items required one-step calculations, and most non-DIF items required multistep calculations.

The researchers also preformed two-class mixture modeling for each grade to see if SWDs and SWODs fit into groups of accommodations for the DIF items. A large amount of students, however, were classified into the opposite group of their disability status (between 10% and 26% of students who were SWDs). This suggested that some students in the SWD group responded to DIF items more like SWODs. The researchers concluded that although substantial evidence of DIF was found, their results did not provide a consistent explanation for the DIF, which may be due to accommodations or to other factors that were not measured.

Scarpati, Wells, Lewis, and Jirka (2011) used a latent mixture DIF model analysis to explore the factors that may explain the prevalence of DIF for eighth grade students taking a mathematics test with accommodations or without (SWDs $n = 12,268$). The accommodations studied were calculator use and some item presentation accommodations (such as braille, large print, read-aloud directions, electronic e-reader for questions). When examining calculator use, they found 14 out of 34 items displaying a meaningful DIF. In the mixture model, although most calculator users fit into their group of DIF, 19% of calculator users responded more like non-accommodated students. They found that these students had a higher mathematics ability than the 81% of students who fit into their group of DIF. When examining item presentation accommodations, Scarpati et al. found nine out of 34 items with meaningful DIF. Again, a significant percentage of students (36%) did not fit into their predetermined group for DIF, with students with higher mathematics ability functioning more like non-accommodated students on DIF items. The researchers concluded based on these results that although there was significant DIF found, it was more related to mathematics ability in conjunction with accommodation use than accommodation use alone.

Randall and Engelhard (2010) used confirmatory factor analysis and the Rasch model to analyze for the performance of SWODs ($n = 569$) and SWDs ($n = 219$) who took a reading comprehension test in one of three conditions: standard, with a resource guide, or read aloud. They found a one-factor model supported across groups and conditions, as well as factorial invariance across groups. The researchers also found a non-invariant factor structure across conditions and were able to isolate this to two items. The Rasch model also found only one item functioning differentially across groups, underscoring the importance of looking at single items that can be affected when accommodations are offered.

Flowers, Kim, Lewis, and Davis (2011) used DIF analyses to see if computer-based testing items or paper and pencil testing items functioned differently for seventh and eighth grade students with read-aloud accommodations in reading, mathematics, and science ($n = 225$). They found that most items had negligible DIF and did not favor the presentation format. This is an important finding because the e-reader accommodation was found to function similarly to the adult reader accommodation in terms of DIF.

Randall, Cheong, and Engelhard (2011) compared use of a hierarchical generalized linear model to a many-facet Rasch model to investigate DIF on a statewide mathematics problem-solving assessment. Seventh grade students ($n = 868$) were assigned to one of three testing conditions: standard administration, resource guide, or calculator. For both statistical methods, they found only one item differentially easier in the calculator condition, as well as another item biased in favor of SWODs in a standard condition.

Collectively, these studies addressed important questions about internal structure and item functioning for SWDs with accommodations. Generally, internal structure was found to be consistent across groups, with little to no evidence that accommodations changed the internal structure of the test. When examining DIF, some studies found a significant number of items that functioned differently for different groups of students, while other studies found no DIF. The studies that found DIF had much larger sample sizes than those that did not. In the studies in which DIF was found and mixture modeling was used to fit students to the DIF group, there was quite a bit of crossover between SWODs and SWDs, with not all students matching their expected group in terms of DIF. This indicated that the cause of the DIF was not solely accommodation use; there may have been other student characteristics that caused items to function differentially. While steps have been taken to determine whether or not accommodations can cause items to function differentially, more questions have arisen. The presence of DIF is a concern that must be addressed in future research; finding DIF for SWDs that is lessened when accommodations are offered would indicate that the adaptations improved validity.

Evidence Based on Relations to Other Variables When tests include an assumption that the construct should be related to outside criteria or variables, evidence of this relationship must be presented. For testing adaptation research, this has been done by using convergent evidence of concurrent and predictive test-criterion relationships. Convergent evidence indicates that the test construct is related to other constructs that are theoretically positively related (e.g., long division skills and multiplication skills). Test-criterion relationships involve the test score and a set criterion score that are hypothesized to share variance. For example, scores on a classroom measure of reading fluency should share variance with student proficiency scores on a statewide reading test. Test-criterion relationships can be obtained concurrently (i.e., both sets of scores collected at the same time) or predictively (i.e., scores from the predictor variable collected prior to scores from the criterion variable). Validity evidence based on relations to other variables can be critical for SWDs, because it is necessary to see whether or not the relationships function differently for these subgroups of students. To continue the earlier example, it would be important to know whether classroom measures of reading fluency correlate as well with proficiency scores for a sample of SWDs, compared to the correlation for a sample of SWODs. If the correlations are very different within these two samples, testing adaptations may be needed for the test to work comparably for SWDs.

Russell and Famularo (2009) used an online test for eighth grade students ($n = 2365$) to study the effects of modifications on complicated algebra items. The researchers modified each item to create multiple simpler "child" items. Each student was classified as either a *proficiency student* or a *gap student*. Proficiency students were students whose teachers believed they were proficient. Gap students were those whose teachers believed they were at the lowest levels of achievement. The gap students were more successful on the child-modified items than they were on the original items. Specific modifications were differentially effective in different content areas. The researchers found that removing the context of some items may allow some students to achieve proficiency and that simplified items may allow gap students to obtain more correct answers.

The existing research base on testing adaptations is designed to determine whether the underlying constructs of tests are changed in nonstandard administrations. Using the differential boost paradigm has led to very mixed results and raised many questions that may be better addressed using other forms of validity evidence. Although not often characterized this way, differential boost studies are actually addressing a form of validity based on relations to other variables, whereby the additional variables are categorical (i.e., disability group status and accommodation condition) and the relationship of interest is the interaction between group and condition. Studies addressing reliability and other forms of validity evidence have provided direction regarding essential questions about how adaptations can change the testing situation, as well as the evidence needed to allow adaptations. Although much work remains in answering these questions, the theoretical guidelines discussed next can be extremely useful in developing an algorithm for practitioners and test developers to make decisions about adaptations.

Research to Practice: How to Make Decisions About Adaptations

Practitioners and researchers can use the theory and research to make decisions about adaptations that will lead to reliable scores from which valid inferences can be made. The process can be conceptualized in three steps introduced by Kettler (2012): (a) considering the access skills, (b) finding available adaptations, and (c) analyzing the target construct.

The Access Skill Question

The first step to identify appropriate testing adaptations is to answer the access skill question: "Does the student have a functional impairment in an area that is an access skill for the test being considered?" There are steps in answering this question. First, the access skills necessary for this test must be identified. Examples include reading, memory, organizational, or planning skills. Next, it must be determined whether the individual or group under consideration has functional impairments in any of these access skills. This is usually an individual question, and a student's classification in special education does not offer the information needed to answer this question. Likewise, disability category may or may not be indicative of specific functional impairments. For example, learning disability as a category can indicate that a student has a functional impairment in reading fluency, processing speed, working memory, none of the aforementioned, or some combination of the aforementioned. In general, a targeted assessment of student access skills (e.g., through curriculum-based measures, classroom data, or a psychological evaluation) is the most effective way to determine a student's level of impairment in these access skills. To use a simple example to address this question, on a written mathematics test, vision is an access skill. A student who scores low on a vision test and is thus determined to be legally blind likely has a functional impairment that would affect performance on the test.

The Available Adaptation Question

Next, practitioners must ask themselves the available adaptation question (Kettler, 2012): "Are any adaptations available to address the impairment?" There are no complete lists of all adaptations. Some resources with lists of adaptations include the *Assessment Accommodations Checklist* (AAC; Elliott, Kratochwill, & Schulte, 1999), CTB/McGraw-Hill's (2000) *Guidelines for Using the Results of Standardized Tests Administered Under Nonstandard Conditions*, and lists included on websites for many state departments of education. Missing from the research base at this point are empirically supported adaptations to address specific functional impairments, so practitioners need to use professional judgment and peer review to make that determination. To continue the earlier example, adaptations of braille, large print, and audio presentations and responses could be considered to address the needs of a student with a functional impairment in vision.

The Targeted Skills or Knowledge Question

Finally, to address concerns about validity, practitioners must ask themselves the targeted skills or knowledge question (Kettler, 2012): "If selected, will the adaptation or adaptations change the construct being measured by the test?" Answering this question requires clear definitions of the test construct(s) and the aforementioned forms of validity evidence to ensure that no adaptation is undermining what the test is intended to measure. For the student with a visual impairment, a clear definition of the target construct is necessary before selecting an adaptation. For a mathematics test measuring computational skills, braille, large print, or audio presentation could all be appropriate, because none of the adaptations would undermine the target construct. For a mathematics test measuring interpretation of graphs, neither braille nor large print would impact the target skill. Audio presentation may undermine the target construct of interpreting graphs since the audible description of the graphs would necessarily include some interpretation; thus, audio presentation would not be an appropriate adaptation. Figure 14.1 displays a process map for making accommodation decisions.

Conclusions/Recommendations

The individual nature of the interaction between testing adaptations and test-takers is emphasized in the *Standards* (AERA, APA, & NCME, 2014), with a focus on access skills and evidence to show that reliability and construct validity are not compromised. The aforementioned research studies have addressed steps to quantify changes in reliability and validity evidence based on content, internal structure, response processes, and relations to other variables that can be expected with testing adaptations. The studies have incorporated a variety of methods to address the ultimate question of whether test constructs are changed through the use of testing adaptations. In practice, testing adaptations are becoming both more universally available and highly individualized. With new paradigms for testing using a PNP (PARCC, 2013), students are receiving testing adaptation not solely based on disability status or category but based on need. Following updates in theory, research, and practice, some of the traditional assumptions regarding testing adaptations are less central. For example, the traditional dichotomy of whether the test content itself is changed is less relevant in describing an accommodation or modification. A focus on access skills, target constructs, and whether either was changed is a more informative way of categorizing adaptations. Based on the current understanding of validity for testing adaptations, a more helpful categorization is appropriate versus inappropriate. On one end of the continuum exist appropriate accommodations, defined as any change to standard administration (e.g., setting, presentation, or the item itself) that do not change the construct; that is, reliability and validity evidence are only improved with testing adaptations. On the other end of the continuum exist

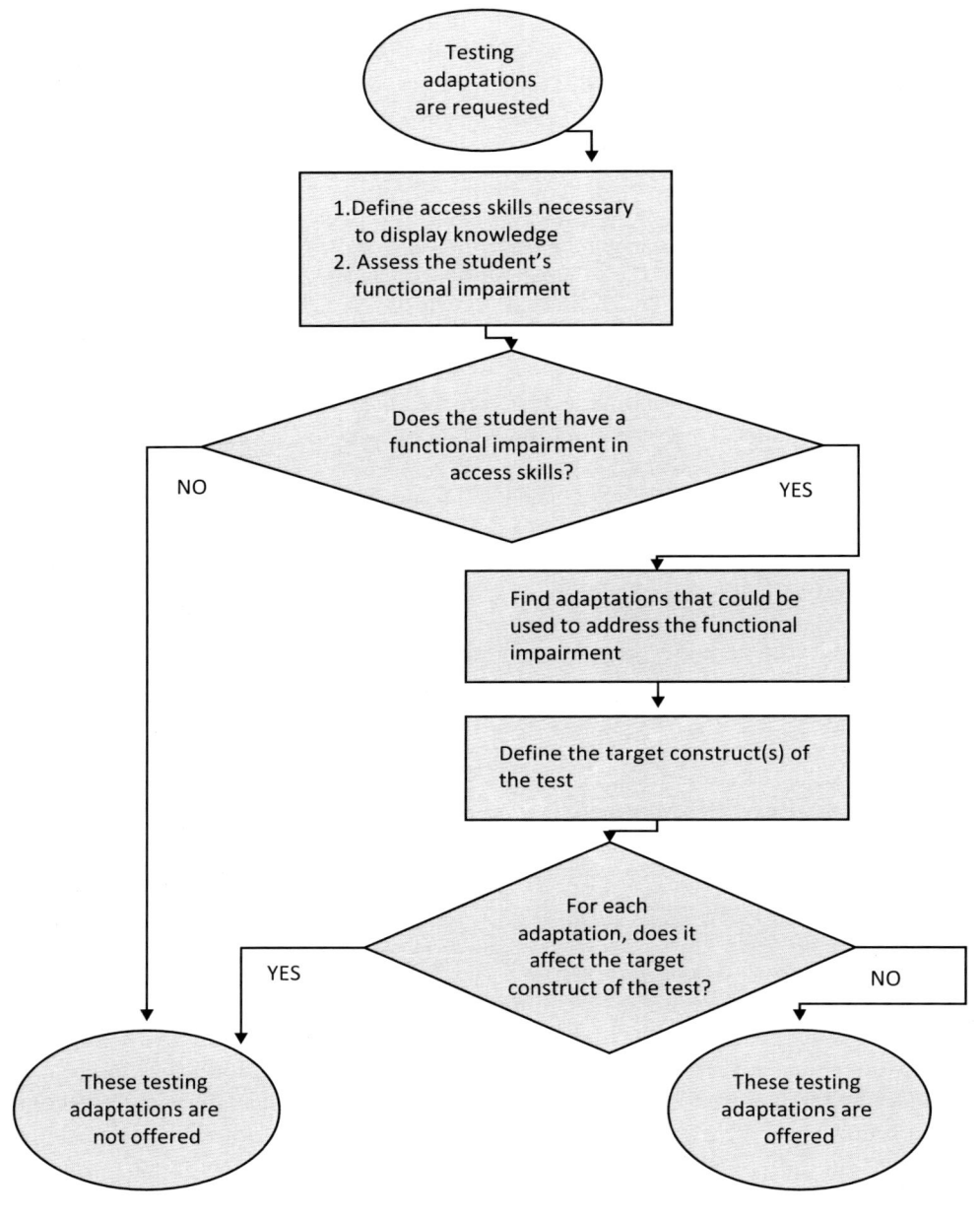

Fig. 14.1 A simple process map may be used for decision-making regarding testing adaptations

inappropriate modifications including any change in standard administration (setting, presentation, or item itself) that does impact the construct, such that the reliability and validity evidence is worsened with the adaptations. These categories of adaptations cannot be generalized from assessment to assessment and across populations, since the construct validity is highly dependent on the interaction between characteristics of the test-taker and the test itself. To that end, the same adaptation may be an appropriate accommodation in one case and an inappropriate modification in another. For example, a third grade student with a functional impairment in working memory using a calculator on a mathematics assessment could be an inappropriate modification, while the same student using a calculator for a mathematics assessment in eighth grade could be an appropriate accommodation, depending on the stated construct at each grade level.

Often reliability and validity evidence remains relatively stable or does not move systematically in either direction, when adaptations are made. It is difficult to know in these situations whether the adaptations are justified. Given the importance of standardized procedures in drawing meaningful interpretations from test scores, the default should be to not use adaptations unless there is evidence that the adaptations address an access skill deficit, allowing the test to better measure that targeted construct. Such an improvement should then be reflected in the reliability and validity evidence.

Another assumption worth examining is the prevalence of using boost analyses and group differences as the primary validity evidence for testing adaptations. Based on the highly individual nature of functional impairments and the multiple forms of validity evidence necessary to ensure the appropriateness of adaptations, differences in group performance, such as differences between achievement of SWDs and SWODs, are a limited indicator of test performance. While any difference in performance between groups should be identified and examined, mean differences may actually reflect true differences in performance between two groups. The use of differential boost to evaluate testing accommodations over the past two decades has focused on group differences, albeit with four data points (SWODs without accommodations, SWDs without accommodations, SWODs with accommodations, and SWDs with accommodations) rather than two data points. Making decisions based on group differences is particularly problematic when comparing SWODs with SWDs, because there are a number of reasonable theoretical explanations for such a gap that do not reflect poor test quality, including: (a) the test is designed to target a skill that is by definition impaired by the students' disabilities, (b) the students have not received the requisite instructional accommodations for their disabilities and have therefore not learned the content addressed by the test, and (c) the SWDs have systematically received instructional programming at a slower pace. Examining differential boost can assist in distinguishing between testing accommodations that address functional impairments and those that function like bonus points; however, evidence of no boost does not mean that there was no improvement in other indicators of validity. Other psychometric evidence such as reliability coefficients, factor analytic indices, and correlations with criterion variables more directly address test quality and can often be calculated and reported in the same studies that feature differential boost. The goal should be to design tests and accommodations that maximize these indices for SWDs or at least assure that they are comparable to the indices yielded by the general assessments without accommodations when taken by SWODs.

A third point to consider is the need for a disability identification or special education status before allowing students to be eligible for an adapted assessment. Put simply, test scores are not directly influenced by disability status. Disabilities are often necessary from a policy standpoint to identify students eligible for accommodations. From an assessment standpoint, not only may the classification of a student as having a disability be meaningless insofar as its impact on assessment results but also the specific classification category. The true determinants of whether an accommodation is helpful are whether the student has functional impairment in an access skill needed for a test, whether an accommodation exists to address that impairment, and whether applying that accommodation will undermine the targeted skills and knowledge of the test. Admittedly, there may be high concurrence rates between certain classifications and certain functional impairments (e.g., attention-deficit/hyperactivity disorder and functional impairments in attention), based on the symptomatology used for diagnosis. However, it is important that adaptations not be considered based on disability classification and that instead the focus is on evidence of functional impairment in access skills.

Lastly, assessment is worth doing, and as such, it is worth doing well! Doing assessment well means giving all groups of students access to scores that reflect underlying educational constructs (e.g., reading, mathematics, science) with the maximum possible precision and accuracy. This is the requirement of the Every Student Succeeds Act of 2016 as stated in its call for high-quality academic assessments for all students, with the explicit acknowledgment that accommodations may be necessary to achieve this goal for some. Therefore, the search for adaptations is important, and evaluating those adaptations to ensure they are improving test quality is equally important. Doing assessment well does not necessarily mean that SWDs will attain scores as high as those attained by SWODs nor does it necessarily mean that they will experience the test in the same way that it is experienced by SWDs; these are both outcomes that may occur to a certain degree due to pursuit of the primary goal, which is that SWDs will receive scores that inform their proficiency and future educational programming to the same degree that the scores received by SWODs meet these goals.

References

American Educational Research Association, American Psychological Association, & National Council on Measurement in Education. (2014). *Standards for educational and psychological testing*. Washington, DC: Author.

Beddow, P. A. (2012). Accessibility theory for enhancing the validity of test results for students with special needs. *International Journal of Disability, Development and Education, 59*(1), 97–111. https://doi.org/10.1080/1034912X.2012.654966

Bolt, S. E., & Thurlow, M. L. (2004). Five of the most frequently allowed testing accommodations in state policy synthesis of research. *Remedial and Special Education, 25*(3), 141–152. https://doi.org/10.1177/07419325040250030201

Cho, H. J., Lee, J., & Kingston, N. (2012). Examining the effectiveness of test accommodation using DIF and a mixture IRT model. *Applied Measurement in Education, 25*(4), 281–304.

Christensen, L. L., Lazarus, S. S., Crone, M., & Thurlow, M. L. (2008). *2007 State policies on assessment participation and accommodations for students with disabilities (Synthesis Report 69)*. Minneapolis, MN: University of Minnesota, National Center on Educational Outcomes.

Cook, L., Eignor, D., Sawaki, Y., Steinberg, J., & Cline, F. (2010). Using factor analysis to investigate accommodations used by students with disabilities on an English-language arts assessment. *Applied Measurement in Education, 23*, 187–208.

Cormier, D. C., Altman, J. R., Shyyan, V., & Thurlow, M. L. (2010). *A summary of the research on the effects of test accommodations: 2007–2008. (Technical Report 56)*. Minneapolis, MN: University of Minnesota: National Center on Educational Outcomes.

Cronbach, L. J. (1951). Coefficient alpha and the internal structure of tests. *Psychometrika, 16*, 297–334.

CTB McGraw-Hill. (2008). *North Dakota state assessments: Fall 2008 administration final technical report*. Monterey, CA: Author.

CTB/McGraw-Hill. (2000). *Guidelines for using the results of standardized tests administered under non-standard conditions*. Monterey, CA: Author.

CTB/McGraw-Hill. (2005). *Guidelines for inclusive test administration*. Monterey, CA: Author.

Data Recognition Corporation, & Pacific Metric Corporation. (2008a). *iLEAP 2008: Operational technical report*. Washington, DC: Author.

Data Recognition Corporation, & Pacific Metric Corporation. (2008b). *LEAP 2008: Operational technical report*. Washington, DC: Author.

Davidshofer, K. R., & Muphy, C. O. (2005). *Psychological testing: Principles and applications*. Upper Saddle River, NJ: Pearson/Prentice.

Dembitzer, L. (2016). *Universal design and accommodations: Accessibility, reliability, and validity* (Doctoral dissertation). Retrieved from ProQuest Dissertations and Theses Global.

Elliott, S. N., Kettler, R. J., Beddow, P. A., Kurz, A., Compton, E., McGrath, D., … Roach, A. T. (2010). Effects of using modified items to test students with persistent academic difficulties. *Exceptional Children, 76*(4), 475–495.

Elliott, S. N., Kratochwill, T. R., & Schulte, A. (1999). *The assessment accommodation checklist*. Monterey, CA: CTB/McGraw-Hill.

Flowers, C., Kim, D. H., Lewis, P., & Davis, V. C. (2011). A comparison of computer-based testing and pencil-and-paper testing for students with a read-aloud accommodation. *Journal of Special Education Technology, 26*(1), 1–12.

Flowers, C., Wakeman, S., Browder, D. M., & Karvonen, M. (2009). Links for academic learning (LAL): A conceptual model for investigating alignment of alternate assessments based on alternate achievement standards. *Educational Measurement: Issues and Practice, 28*(1), 25–37.

Fuchs, L. S., & Fuchs, D. (2001). Helping teachers formulate sound test accommodation decisions for students with learning disabilities. *Learning Disabilities Research and Practice, 16*, 174–181. https://doi.org/10.1111/0938-8982.00018

Fuchs, L. S., Fuchs, D., & Capizzi, A. M. (2005). Identifying appropriate test accommodations for students with learning disabilities. *Focus on Exceptional Children, 37*(6), 1–8.

Fuchs, L. S., Fuchs, D., Eaton, S. B., Hamlett, C. L., Binkley, E., & Crouch, R. (2000). Using objective data sources to enhance teacher judgments about test accommodations. *Exceptional Children, 67*, 67–81.

Fuchs, L. S., Fuchs, D., Eaton, S. B., Hamlett, C. L., & Karns, K. (2000). Supplementing teacher judgments of mathematics tests accommodations with objective data sources. *School Psychology Review, 29*, 65–85.

Helwig, R., & Tindal, G. (2003). An experimental analysis of accommodation decisions on large-scale mathematics tests. *Exceptional Children, 69*(2), 211–225.

Hollenbeck, K. (2005). Validity issues and decisions about testing accommodations. *Assessment for Effective Intervention, 31*(7), 7–17. https://doi.org/10.1177/073724770503100102

Individuals with Disabilities Education Act of 1997. (1997). Pub. L., 101–476, 104 Stat. 1142.

Individuals with Disabilities Education Improvement Act. (2004). Pub. L., 208–446, 118 Stat. 2647.

Kettler, R. J. (2011a). Effects of packages of modifications to improve test and item accessibility: Less is more. In S. N. Elliott, R. J. Kettler, P. A. Beddow, & A. Kurz (Eds.), *Handbook of accessible achievement tests for all students: Bridging the gaps between research, practice, and policy* (pp. 231–242). New York, NY: Springer. https://doi.org/10.1007/978-1-4419-9356-4_13

Kettler, R. J. (2011b). Holding modified assessments accountable: Applying a unified reliability and validity framework to the development and evaluation of AA-MASs. In M. Russell (Ed.), *Assessing students in the margins: Challenges, strategies, and techniques* (pp. 311–334). Charlotte, NC: Information Age Publishing.

Kettler, R. J. (2012). Testing accommodations: Theory and research to inform practice. *International Journal of Disability, Development and Education, 5*(1), 53–66. https://doi.org/10.1080/1034912X.2012.654952

Kettler, R. J. (2015). Adaptations and access to assessment of common core content. *Review of Research in Education, 39*(1), 295–330.

Kettler, R. J., Dickenson, T. S., Bennett, H. L., Morgan, G. B., Gilmore, J. A., Beddow, P. A., ... Palmer, P. W. (2012). Enhancing the accessibility of high school science tests: A multi-state experiment. *Exceptional Children, 79*, 91–106.

Kettler, R. J., Elliott, S. N., & Beddow, P. A. (2009). Modifying achievement test items: A theory-guided and data-based approach for better measurement of what students with disabilities know. *Peabody Journal of Education, 84*, 529–551.

Kettler, R. J., Rodriguez, M. R., Bolt, D. M., Elliott, S. N., Beddow, P. A., & Kurz, A. (2011). Modified multiple-choice items for alternate assessments: Reliability, difficulty, and differential boost. *Applied Measurement in Education, 24*(3), 210–234. https://doi.org/10.1080/08957347.2011.580620

King, J. E. (2011). Implementing the Common Core state standards: An action agenda for higher education. Retrieved from http://www.acenet.edu/news-room/Documents/Implementing-the-Common-Core-State-Standards-2011.pdf

Lewandowski, L. J., Lovett, B. J., & Rogers, C. L. (2008). Extended time as a testing accommodation for students with reading disabilities: Does a rising tide lift all ships? *Journal of Psychoeducational Assessment, 26*(4), 315–324. https://doi.org/10.1177/0734282908315757

Lindstrom, J. H., & Gregg, N. (2007). The role of extended time on the SAT for students with learning disabilities and/or attention-deficit/hyperactivity disorder. *Learning Disabilities Research and Practice, 22*, 85–95.

Louisiana Department of Education. (2008). *LEAP GEE 2008 technical summary*. Baton Rouge, LA: Author.

Louisiana Department of Education. (2009). *iLEAP 2009 technical summary*. Baton Rouge, LA: Author.

Meloy, L. L., Deville, C., & Frisbie, D. A. (2002). The effect of a read aloud accommodation on test scores of students with and without a learning disability in reading. *Remedial and Special Education, 23*(4), 248–255. https://doi.org/10.1177/07419325020230040801

National Assessment of Educational Progress (2013). Reading Framework for the 2013 National Assessment of Educational Progress. Retrieved from: http://nces.ed.gov/nationsreportcard/reading/moreabout.aspx

Partnership for Assessment of Readiness for College and Careers. (2013). Accessibility features and accommodations manual, 1st edition. Retrieved from: http://www.parcconline.org/parcc-assessment-policies

Poggio, A. J., Yang, X., Irwin, P. M., Glasnapp, D. R., & Poggio, J. P. (2006). Kansas assessments in reading and mathematics: Technical manual. Lawrence: University of Kansas, Center for Educational Testing and Evaluation. Retrieved from https://cete.ku.edu/sites/cete.drupal.ku.edu/files/docs/Technical_Reports/2007/irwin2007_KAMM.pdf

Randall, J., Cheong, Y. F., & Engelhard, G. (2011). Using explanatory item response theory modeling to investigate context effects of DIF for students with disabilities. *Educational and Psychological Measurement, 71*(1), 129–147.

Randall, J., & Engelhard, G. (2010). Using confirmatory factor analysis and the Rasch model to assess measurement invariance in a high stakes reading assessment. *Applied Measurement in Education, 23*, 286–306.

Roach, A. T., Beddow, P. A., Kurz, A., Kettler, R. J., & Elliott, S. N. (2010). Incorporating student input in developing alternate assessments based on modified academic achievement standards. *Exceptional Children, 77*, 61–80.

Roach, A. T., Elliott, S. N., & Webb, N. L. (2005). Alignment of an alternate assessment with state academic standards evidence for the content validity of the Wisconsin alternate assessment. *The Journal of Special Education, 38*(4), 218–231.

Roach, A. T., Niebling, B. C., & Kurz, A. (2008). Evaluating the alignment among curriculum, instruction, and assessments: Implications and applications for research and practice. *Psychology in the Schools, 45*(2), 158–176.

Rogers, C. M., Christian, E. M., & Thurlow, M. L. (2012). *A summary of the research on the effects of test accommodations: 2009–2010 (Technical Report 65)*. Minneapolis, MN: University of Minnesota, National Center on Educational Outcomes.

Rogers, C. M., Lazarus, S. S., & Thurlow, M. L. (2014). *A summary of the research on the effects of test accommodations: 2011–2012 (Synthesis Report 94)*. Minneapolis, MN: University of Minnesota, National Center on Educational Outcomes.

Russell, M., & Famularo, L. (2009). Testing what students in the gap can do. *Journal of Applied Testing Technology, 9*(4), 1–28.

Scarpati, S. E., Wells, C. S., Lewis, C., & Jirka, S. (2011). Accommodations and item-level analyses using mixture DIF models. *The Journal of Special Education, 45*(1), 54–62.

Sireci, S. G., Scarpati, S. E., & Li, S. (2005). Test accommodations for students with disabilities: An analysis of the interaction hypothesis. *Review of Educational Research, 75*(4), 457–490. https://doi.org/10.3102/00346543075004457

Smarter Balanced Assessment Consortium. (2013). Usability, accessibility, and accommodations guidelines. Retrieved from: http://www.smarterbalanced.org/wordpress/wp-content/uploads/2013/09/SmarterBalanced_Guidelines_091113.pdf

Texas Education Agency. (2009). *Technical digest 2007–2008*. Austin, TX: Author. Retrieved from http://www.tea.state.tx.us

Thompson, S. J., Johnstone, C. J., & Thurlow, M. L. (2002). *UD applied to large scale assessments (Synthesis Report 44)*. Minneapolis, MN: University of Minnesota, National Center on Educational Outcomes. Retrieved Sept 30, 2013, from http://education.umn.edu/NCEO/OnlinePubs/Synthesis44.html

Thurlow, M., House, A., Boys, C., Scott, D., & Ysseldyke, J. (2000). *State participation and accommodation policies for students with disabilities: 1999 Update (Synthesis Rep. No. 33)*. Minneapolis, MN: University of Minnesota, National Center on Educational Outcomes.

Zenisky, A. L., & Sireci, S. G. (2007). *A summary of the research on the effects of test accommodations: 2005–2006 (Technical Report No. 47)*. Minneapolis, MN: University of Minnesota, National Center on Educational Outcomes.

Promoting Valid Assessment of Students with Disabilities and English Learners

Stephen G. Sireci, Ella Banda, and Craig S. Wells

Promoting Valid Assessment of Students with Disabilities and English Learners

In education, *standardized* tests are used for many purposes such as understanding how well students have mastered the material they have been taught, school and teacher accountability, high school graduation, college admissions, and many other purposes (Sireci & Gandara, 2016). These tests are standardized to ensure students are tested on the same content, with the same test administration conditions and with the same scoring procedures. This standardization is designed to promote fairness in testing by providing a "level playing field" and a common understanding of what was tested and what the test scores mean.

Although standardization has the benefit of providing a common assessment across students, some features of test content or administration may actually interfere with some students' demonstration of their true knowledge, skills, and abilities. This possibility is particularly likely for students with disabilities (SWDs) and English learners (ELs) who may need accommodations to fully understand the tasks required on the assessment, to engage with the assessment, or to provide their responses to assessment tasks. For these reasons, test developers strive to make their tests as accessible as possible for SWDs and ELs. In some cases, promoting accessibility involves providing *accommodations* to the standardized testing situation to maximize the validity of the interpretation and uses of SWDs' test scores (Elliott & Kettler, 2016).

In this chapter, we (a) review validity issues relevant to the assessment of SWDs and ELs, (b) discuss current and emerging practices in test accommodations, and (c) describe methods for evaluating the degree to which test accommodations may facilitate or hinder valid interpretations of students' performance. Throughout our review, we highlight actions test developers, and researchers can take to make tests more accessible and to evaluate the impact of their testing procedures on SWDs and ELs. Assessment of students with severe cognitive disabilities is particularly challenging, and so we also describe some new developments in that area. Given that these developments have a common goal of increasing fairness and accessibility in educational assessment, we begin with a description of fairness issues in educational testing, including some terminology related to fairness and validity issues in assessing SWDs and ELs.

S. G. Sireci (✉) · E. Banda · C. S. Wells
University of Massachusetts Amherst,
Amherst, MA, USA
e-mail: Sireci@acad.umass.edu; Ebanda@umass.edu; Cswells@educ.umass.edu

Fairness and Accessibility in Educational Testing

For over 60 years, three professional associations in the United States—the American Educational Research Association (AERA), the American Psychological Association (APA), and the National Council on Measurement in Education (NCME)—have worked together to develop *Standards for Educational and Psychological Testing*. The most recent version of this document (AERA, APA, & NCME, 2014) defines important terms for understanding fairness issues in testing. In fact, there is an entire chapter in these *Standards* devoted to fairness, and much of that chapter addresses issues in assessing SWDs and ELs.

The first term important for our discussion is *validity*, which the *Standards* define as "the degree to which evidence and theory support the interpretations of test scores for proposed uses of tests" (AERA et al., 2014, p. 11). From this definition it is clear that tests are not inherently valid or invalid, but rather it is the uses of test scores for specific purposes that need to be validated. Validating the use of a test for a particular purpose requires both theoretical support and empirical evidence.

Central to the evaluation of validity is confirming the assessment measures what it is supposed to measure. The "it" that is measured by a test is referred to as the *construct*, because it is created (constructed) from educational or psychological theories. For example, "elementary algebra" is a construct that is assumed to be reflected in students' performance on an algebra test and is operationally defined in the form of algebra test specifications. In evaluating the validity of a test for a particular purpose, the degree to which the test measures the intended construct is fundamental.

The AERA et al. (2014) *Standards* describe five sources of validity evidence that can be used to evaluate the use of a test for a particular purpose. Four of these sources—validity evidence based on test content, response processes, internal structure, and relations with other variables—can be used to evaluate how well the test measures its intended construct. These sources can also be used to evaluate the degree to which accommodations may alter the construct measured (Sireci & Faulkner-Bond, 2015; Sireci, Han, & Wells, 2008). Thus, in addition to confirming that a test generally measures its intended construct, validation also requires confirming the construct is measured with similar quality for all test takers.

Samuel Messick, one of the most prolific and respected validity theorists, claimed that problems in fair and valid assessment arise from either *construct under-representation* or *construct-irrelevant variance*. As he put it, "Tests are imperfect measures of constructs because they either leave out something that should be included…or else include something that should be left out, or both" (Messick, 1989, p. 34).

Construct under-representation refers to the situation where a test measures only a portion of the intended construct and leaves important knowledge, skills, and abilities untested. For example, if English proficiency was operationally defined as reading, writing, speaking, and listening in English, but the test only measured reading in English, the construct of English proficiency would be under-represented by the assessment. *Construct-irrelevant variance* refers to the situation where the test measures other constructs that are irrelevant to the intended construct. Examples of construct-irrelevant variance undermining test score interpretations include when the font used on an assessment is too small for some students to read (i.e., the construct of "vision" affects test performance) or when a student becomes overly anxious when taking a test (i.e., the construct of "test anxiety" affects test performance).

The disabilities possessed by SWDs may interact with the assessment situation to give rise to construct-irrelevant variance in their test scores. Similarly, a lack of full English proficiency may inhibit the performance of ELs on an assessment that is administered in English. When English proficiency is not the construct measured, it may represent a source of construct-irrelevant variance for ELs.[1] To minimize such irrelevancies, testing agencies may provide *accommodations* to the standardized testing situation. The purpose of providing test accommodations is to allow students to demonstrate their performance in a manner such that confounding factors related to their disability or language proficiency are minimized.

There are two terms that distinguish between accommodations that are thought to affect the construct measured by a test and those that are not. Testing *accommodations* refer to changes in the test or test administration condition that are *not* thought to alter the construct measured. Thus, test accommodations attempt to remove construct-irrelevant barriers to students' test performance while maintaining construct representation. Changes that *are* thought to alter the construct measured are referred to as *modifications* (AERA et al., 2014). When a test is modified, the scores from original and modified versions of the test are considered to be too different to be comparable. That is, scores from original and modified versions of a test are considered to be scores from two different tests.

The *Standards* define *fairness in testing* as "a fundamental validity issue and requires attention to detail throughout all stages of test development and use" (AERA et al., 2014, p. 49). It also defines two related concepts involved in fairness: *accessibility* and *universal test design* (UTD). Accessibility is defined as "the notion that all test takers should have an unobstructed opportunity to demonstrate their standing on the construct(s) being measured" (p. 49). UTD is defined as "an approach to test design that seeks to maximize accessibility for all intended examinees" (p. 50).

UTD refers to a principle of test development that considers the needs of SWDs and ELs while the tests are being constructed. The goal of UTD is to make the test and testing situation flexible enough so that accommodations are not necessary (Thompson, Blount, & Thurlow, 2002). Essentially, UTD calls for test construction practices focused on eliminating construct-irrelevant variance and more flexible test administration conditions that would make the provision of test accommodations for SWDs and ELs unnecessary. For example, removing time limits on a test not only benefits students who have information processing disabilities; it has the potential to benefit all test takers, just like closed-captioned television benefits individuals without hearing limitations who are in public places.

Elliott and Kettler (2016) stated that in educational testing, "access is the opportunity for test takers to demonstrate proficiency on the target construct of a test or item" (p. 376). They pointed out that access for SWDs begins in the classroom, and so SWDs and ELs should be given the opportunity to learn the knowledge and skills that are tested. Elliott and Kettler also provided specific examples regarding how UTD principles can be used in test development to increase their access to educational assessments. Many of these examples are reflective of sound test development practices such as reducing unnecessary language load and using only plausible distractors (incorrect response options) on multiple-choice items.

Fairness and Accommodations: The Psychometric Oxymoron

As previously mentioned, test accommodations are often provided to address the problem of construct-irrelevant variance that may arise from standardized testing conditions. If the conditions of a standardized test administration prevent some students from demonstrating their knowledge and skills, those conditions may be considered barriers to valid assessment. For example, the ability to maneuver test materials may introduce construct-irrelevant variance for students with motor disabilities, and the ability to hear would obviously present construct-irrelevant difficulties for hearing-impaired students taking an orally administered exam. Removing those barriers, which is tantamount

---

[1] For tests measuring English proficiency, English proficiency is seen as construct-relevant (Sireci & Faulkner-Bond, 2015). Thus, there are more accommodations available to ELs for subject area tests such as math and science, where the linguistic complexity of items administered in English is considered construct-irrelevant.

to accommodating the administration, is therefore seen as removing construct-irrelevant variance and thus increasing the validity of the interpreted test score.

The counter-side of this issue is that an accommodation may also *introduce* construct-irrelevant variance, if the accommodation changes the construct measured. For example, if a reading test is read aloud to a student, the construct measured may change from "reading proficiency" to "listening proficiency." Therefore, although test accommodations are often granted in the pursuit of test fairness, the degree to which the accommodation promotes validity is directly related to the degree to which the accommodation alters (or does not alter) the construct measured.

The evaluation of construct equivalence across standard and accommodated test administration conditions is an important activity whenever scores from standard and accommodated administrations are intended to be comparable. As described at the beginning of this chapter, tests are standardized to provide uniform conditions (i.e., a level playing field) for all test takers. Changing (accommodating) those conditions leads to a *psychometric oxymoron*—an accommodated standardized test (Sireci, 2005). Therefore, research is needed to understand the degree to which the deviations from standardized testing conditions involved in test accommodations affect score interpretations. Thus, the "construct equivalence" of standard and accommodated test scores is often studied in evaluating the validity of a particular accommodation for a particular student.

In some cases, if a testing agency concludes an accommodation has altered the construct measured, the score report for an accommodated test taker may include a "flag," which indicates the test was taken under nonstandard conditions. (See Sireci, 2005, for a discussion of issues related to flagging scores from accommodated tests.) We address methods for evaluating construct equivalence in a later section of this chapter. Such evaluations are typically used to help determine if changes to testing conditions should be described as "accommodations" or "modifications" and if scores from accommodated or modified tests should be flagged.

Providing Test Accommodations: A Review of Current Practices

There are generally three major groups of students considered for accommodations in assessment in the United States: (a) SWDs (i.e., students with neurological, psychological, or physical impairments), (b) ELs, and (c) ELs with disabilities.[2] SWDs are a heterogeneous group that may require a wide variety of accommodations to access a test. In this section, we describe the different types of accommodations that are currently offered to SWDs and ELs. We tend to go into more depth on accommodations for SWDs, although many of the issues and practices are similar across SWDs and ELs. For a more in-depth discussion of accommodations for ELs, interested readers are referred to Sireci and Faulkner-Bond (2015).

Currently, it is common for states to provide 30 or more types of accommodations on reading, mathematics, and science achievement tests in elementary, middle, and high school for SWDs and ELs who qualified for them (Sireci, Wells, & Hu, 2014). Test accommodations for SWDs can be classified into five categories: timing (e.g., providing extra time or alternative test schedules), response (e.g., allowing students alternative ways to respond to the test, such as using a scribe), setting (changes to test setting), equipment and materials (the use of additional references or devices), and presentation (alternative ways to present test materials). In addition to these five categories, a review of the literature on test accommodations indicates there are both traditional and technology-enhanced accommodations. In Table 15.1, we present a summary of the more traditional accommodations commonly offered to SWDs and ELs based on the five aforementioned accommodation categories (Thurlow, Elliott, & Ysseldyke, 2003). In Table 15.2, we list accommodations provided through technology-enhanced assessments.

---

[2]Students with severe cognitive disabilities represent a fourth group, but their needs are typically beyond what accommodations can provide, and so alternate assessments are typically provided. We describe alternate assessments in a later section of this chapter.

Table 15.1 Traditional accommodations for SWDs and ELs in the United States

Student group	Accommodation category	Examples of available accommodations
SWDs	Presentation	Large print/large font; signing directions, test questions, or reading passages; oral reading of test questions and reading passages in English; repetition/explaining or paraphrasing the directions for clarity (in English); braille; color overlays; templates or place markers; low vision aids; audio amplification devices or noise buffer/listening devices; human/screen reader
	Response	Basic technology applications such as brailler, word processor, or other communication devices with all grammar and spell-check disabled; student marks answers in test booklet; student points to answers; verbal response in English only; scribe; braillewriter; abacus; basic function calculator including braille or talking calculator; adapted writing tools; adapted/lined paper
	Setting	Special education classroom, special or adapted lighting, small group, preferential seating, sound field adaptations, adaptive furniture, individual or study carrel, individual administration and test administered by certified educator familiar to student
	Time/scheduling	Extended time, frequent breaks, optimal time of day for testing, flexibility in the order of administration for content areas, extending sessions over multiple days
ELs[a]	Linguistic	Modified linguistic structures, provision of a glossary, a customized English dictionary, simplified English, bilingual dictionaries or glossaries, tests in the native language, dual-language test booklets, dual-language questions for English passages

[a]ELs may also receive the other accommodations listed for SWD (e.g., extended time)

Table 15.2 Technology-enhanced accommodations for SWDs and ELs

Student group	Accommodation category	Examples of available accommodations
SWDs	Presentation	Screen reader, refreshable braille display, braille note taker, braillewriter, whisper phone, touch screen gestures, closed captioning of multimedia, text-to-speech, ASL video with American Sign Language, magnification, spell-check, line reader mask tool, headphones or noise buffers, highlight tool, general masking, color contrast, bookmark, audio amplification
	Response	Braille notetaker, braillewriter, embedded grade-level calculator, embedded large-print ruler, speech-to-text, word prediction external device, writing tools, notepad, answer masking, bookmark
	Time/scheduling	Extended time
ELs	Presentation	Word-to-word dictionary, mathematics speech-to-text, online translation of mathematics in other languages, text-to-speech for mathematics assessment
	Response	"Pop-up" and "mouse-over" glossary, spell-check

Assessment guidelines for most states contain specific methods to provide accommodations that involve readers, sign language interpreters, and scribes. However, continued concern about intended and unintended interference that is associated with these types of accommodations has led to more and more incorporation of accommodations within computer-based delivery systems, such as those presented in Table 15.2 (Christensen, Braam, Scullin, & Thurlow, 2011; Clapper, Morse, Thompson, & Thurlow, 2005; Hodgson, Lazarus, Price, Altman, & Thurlow, 2012). As more states adopt computer-based assessments, technology platforms will not only transform the efficiency of testing but will also provide an opportunity for more accommodations to be presented as a unit (Russell, 2011).

Computer-based assessments may improve accessibility not just for SWDs and ELs but for all examinees using universal design principles. In addition, administering tests on the computer allows for easier implementation of some accommodations such as screen-reading (read aloud) software, increased font size (large print), and

Table 15.3 Embedded accessibility features provided by Smarter Balanced and PARCC

Accessibility features, Target group	Accommodation category	Smarter Balanced	PARCC
Universal tools/features for all students	Response	Calculator, digital, notepad, highlighter, writing tools	Eliminate answer choices, highlight tool, writing tools
	Presentation	Zoom, strike-through, spell-check, English dictionary, English glossary, expandable passages, global notes, keyboard navigation mark for review, math tools	Audio amplification, bookmark, headphones/noise buffers, line reader mask tool, notepad, pop-up glossary, magnification/enlargement device, spell-check
	Time/scheduling	Breaks	
	Presentation	Color contrast, masking, text-to-speech, translated test directions, translations (glossary), translations (stacked), turn off any universal tools	Answer masking, color contrast, text-to-speech
Accommodations for SWD, EL with SWD, EL	Response	Text-to-speech	Text-to-speech, grade-level calculator
	Presentation	American Sign Language, braille, closed captioning, streamline	Closed captioning of multimedia (video) for ELA/Literacy, American Sign Language video for ELA/Literacy, American Sign Language video for mathematics assessments, Online Transadaptation of the Mathematics Assessment in Spanish

Sources: PARCC (2016), Smarter Balanced (2016)

alternate language versions of test content. The computerized versions of the assessments from the Smarter Balanced and PARCC consortia[3] provide a number of test accommodations that are embedded in their computerized test delivery systems (PARCC, 2017; Smarter Balanced, 2016).

PARCC and Smarter Balanced use different terminology for the same accessibility features

---

[3] Smarter Balanced and PARRC are multistate assessment consortia in the United States that represent groups of states working together to deliver common assessments in reading and mathematics for elementary, middle, and high school students.

provided on their assessment systems. Smarter Balanced uses "universal tools" (for accessibility features available to all students), "designated supports" (for accessibility features available upon recommendation from an adult), and accommodations (for accessibility features available to SWDs, ELs, and ELs with SWDs based on one's IEP and 504 Plan). PARCC on the other hand uses "features for all students," "accessibility features," and "accommodations," respectively. A summary of these accessibility features is presented in Table 15.3.

For ELs, there is often an additional distinction in accommodations between those that provide *direct linguistic support* and those that do

Table 15.4 Summary of recommended accommodations for SWDs from Abedi and Ewers (2013)

Accommodation	Risk
Test administration directions simplified or clarified (does not apply to test questions)	None
Large-print versions/test items enlarged if font is larger than required on large-print versions	None
Customized dictionary/glossary (content-related terms removed)	None
Pop-up glossary (CBT) (content-related terms excluded)	None
Computer use (including word processing software with spell and grammar check tools turned off for essay responses to writing portion of a test)	None
Calculator on mathematics tests (if not part of the focal construct)	None
Calculator on the science tests (if not part of the focal construct)	Minor
Test questions read aloud to student	Minor
Manually Coded English or American Sign Language to present directions for administration	Minor
Manually Coded English or American Sign Language to present test questions	Minor
Braille transcriptions provided by the test contractor	Minor
Audio amplification equipment	Minor
Color overlay, mask, or other means to maintain visual attention	Minor
Special lighting or acoustics; special or adaptive furniture such as keyboards, larger/antiglare screens	Minor
Visual magnifying equipment	Minor
Assistive device that does not interfere with the independent work of the student	Minor
Arithmetic table or formulas (not provided) on the *mathematics* tests if not part of the focal construct	Minor
Math manipulatives on *mathematics and science* tests (if they don't interact with intended construct)	Moderate
Math manipulatives on mathematics tests (if they don't interact with intended construct)	Moderate
Arithmetic table or formulas (not provided) on *science* tests if not part of the focal construct	High

Notes: Adapted from Abedi and Ewers (2013). "Risk" describes the extent to which the accommodation was judged to possibly change the construct measured. "None" means Abedi and Ewers (2013) did not list a level of risk associated with the accommodation

not (Pennock-Roman & Rivera, 2011). Direct linguistic support accommodations are typically "presentation" accommodations and represent changes to the test content such as translation of directions, items, or both or "linguistic simplification" (Abedi, 2007) of text. These types of accommodations are more likely to be granted to ELs on academic content assessments such as math or science, but not on English proficiency or English language arts assessments. *Indirect linguistic support* accommodations are accommodations to test administration conditions such as the setting and timing accommodations provided to SWDs.

In a commissioned study by the Smarter Balanced Assessment Consortium, Abedi and Ewers (2013) convened a panel of five experts on accommodations for both SWDs and ELs to conduct a systematic review of accommodations research and provide recommendations regarding the appropriateness and validity of different types of accommodations. Their recommendations were centered on a belief that:

The goal of an accommodation is to make an assessment more accessible for English language learners and students with disabilities and to produce results that are valid for these students. The intent is NOT to give them an unfair advantage over those who are not receiving that accommodation. (Abedi & Ewers, 2013, p. 4)

Based on a review of the literature and their expertise, Abedi and Ewers had each panelist rate accommodations on two dimensions: (a) whether the accommodation would alter the construct measured by the test or (b) whether the accommodation would make the test more accessible for the students who would need it. They also determined whether each accommodation might improve the performance of *all* students (not just ELs) in a way that would not affect the construct. If so, they listed the accommodation as "access" and concluded the accommodation improved access for all students by reducing construct-irrelevant variance. In Table 15.4 we present a summary of the final ratings for the accommodations for SWDs in Abedi and Ewers (2013). In Table 15.5 we present the results for accommodations for ELs.

Table 15.5 Summary of recommended accommodations for ELs from Abedi and Ewers (2013)

Accommodation	Risk
Traditional glossary with Spanish translations (content-related terms removed)	None
Traditional glossary with Spanish translations and extra time (content-related terms removed)	None
Customized dictionary/glossary in English (content-related terms removed)	None
Customized dictionary in English (content-related terms removed) and extra time	None
Computer-based test (CBT)	None
Pop-up glossary (CBT) (content-related terms excluded)	None
Modified (simplified) English	None
Extra time within the testing day (not combined with another accommodation)	None
Read aloud of test directions in student's native language	Minor
Picture dictionary (alone, combined with oral reading of test items in English, and combined with bilingual glossary)	Minor
Bilingual dictionary	Minor
Test break	Minor
Test in a familiar environment with other ELs	Minor
Small group setting	Minor
Read aloud of test questions (math, science, history/social science) to student by teacher or electronic media	Minor
Spanish translation of test	Moderate
Dual-language translation of test	Moderate
Read aloud of test questions (ELA) to student by teacher or electronic media	High
Commercial dictionary/glossary in English	High

Notes: Adapted from Abedi and Ewers (2013). "Risk" describes the extent to which the accommodation was judged to possibly change the construct measured. "None" means Abedi and Ewers (2013) did not list a level of risk associated with the accommodation

We do not consider the recommendations presented in Tables 15.4 and 15.5 to be absolute or authoritative, in part because Abedi and Ewers defined an accommodation as "effective" if under randomized assignment; SWD (or ELs) had higher scores under the accommodation condition, relative to the standard condition. If scores for both SWD (or ELs) and the reference group (e.g., non-SWD) were higher under the accommodation condition, they concluded the accommodation improved access for all students. Not everyone would agree that higher scores signify increased effectiveness or access, and so we present Abedi and Ewer's recommendations as a good summary of the recent literature relative to specific types of accommodations. We believe they are a good starting point for helping determine which specific accommodations may be appropriate for specific types of students in specific testing situations, but other literature should also be consulted (e.g., Elliott & Kettler, 2016).

Alternate Assessments for Students with Severe Disabilities

There is a subgroup of SWDs with significant cognitive disabilities who require more than accommodations to standard testing conditions to allow them to fully participate in educational assessments. For statewide accountability testing, the states have created *alternate assessment* systems for these students. Students who require alternate assessments are characterized with intellectual disabilities, autism, and multiple disabilities. Alternate assessments are designed for testing students who are unable to take the regular assessment, even when testing accommodations are provided. Alternate assessments allow students with significant cognitive disabilities to be assessed on extended or alternate content standards that are aligned with the overall state standards (Kearns, Towels-Reeves, Kleinert, & Kleine-Kracht, 2011; US Department of Education, 2015). Students with significant cognitive disabilities often need adaptations, scaffolds (i.e., assistance to leaners that include human or computer guides used in the learning process which are removed slowly as the student's competency increases, see Azevedo & Hadwin, 2005), and supports to access the age- and grade-appropriate general curriculum content in different content areas.

Students with significant cognitive disabilities often utilize augmentative and alternative communication devices in school settings because these students have difficulty in expressive and receptive communication. Such devices include all forms of communication (other than oral speech) that are used to express thoughts, needs, wants, and ideas. Accessibility assessment features suggested for these students are therefore mostly technology enhanced and include answer masking, audio player, line reader, magnification, invert color choice, color contrast, color overlay, read aloud with highlighting text-to-speech (text only, text and graphics only, and nonvisual), uncontracted braille, single switch/Personal Needs Profile-enabled, two-switch system, administration via iPad, adaptive equipment used by student, individualized manipulatives, human read aloud, sign interpretation of text, language translation of text, scribe, and partner-assisted scanning (Lee, Browder, Wakeman, Quenemoen, & Thurlow, 2015; Wells-Moreaux, Bechard, & Karvonen, 2015).

Two prominent alternate assessment systems in the United States are *Dynamic Learning Maps* (DLM) and the *National Center and State Collaborative* (NCSC). These two systems represent groups of states (consortia) that have come together to develop common assessments for students with severe cognitive disabilities.

Both DLM and NCSC begin by transforming general curriculum standards, such as the Common Core College and Career Readiness Standards to alternate assessment standards, using appropriate adaptations, scaffolds, and supports. These alternate assessment standards represent the general intent of a curriculum standard in a way that is more appropriate for these students' cognitive functioning and instructional experiences. For example, DLM's "essential elements" are derived from the College and Career Readiness Standards and are aligned to grade level but at reduced depth, breadth, and complexity (Wells-Moreaux et al., 2015). NCSC's "alternate achievement standards" are based on an adapted general age- and grade-appropriate academic content (Herrera, Turner, Quenemoen, & Thurlow, 2015).

Using the Universal Design for Learning (UDL) framework, DLM claims they make their assessments more accessible by providing communication and alternate access tools, like communication boards and alternate keyboards, that students use during instruction (Dynamic Learning Maps, 2013). DLM is an adaptive testing system in that they administer an initial set of test items (module) to all students at the beginning of the assessment to determine students' ability levels. Using this information, the DLM assessment system routes the students to an appropriately challenging subsequent sets of tasks that closely match their knowledge and skills of the grade-level essential elements (Clark, Kingston, Templin, & Pardos, 2014). Students are given sets of reading and writing items (called "testlets"). In mathematics, these testlets are either multiple-choice or technology-enhanced items (e.g., the computer interface allows students to use graphics to display or provide new information when providing responses.) The tests may be taken independently using accessibility features like alternate keyboards, touch screens, or switches or with support from a test administrator depending on each student's information from the IEP, the educator, and the first contact survey information (Wells-Moreaux et al., 2015).

The NCSC assessment system is designed in a way that the students begin with less complex test items with more adaptations, scaffolds, and supports and then move to more complex test items with reduced supports, as appropriate. In elementary mathematics, the assessment concentrates on number operation relations, spatial relations, and measurement; while for middle and high school, the system concentrates on problem-solving with supports that may include definitions and demonstrations. For ELA the system assesses reading (which may be verbal or nonverbal), comprehension, and writing, using supports and scaffolds like introduction to text, rereading, pictures, definitions, and prompts for what to listen for (Herrera et al., 2015). The system mainly uses computer-administered selected-response items for both ELA and mathematics and a few constructed-response items in both subjects across the grade levels. Most adaptions and supports are built into the system and are computer delivered (e.g., alternate keyboard, switches, and hubs), but some may be provided by humans (e.g., a scriber, sign language test administrator, etc.) based on individual needs of the students (National Center and State Collaborative, 2015).

DLM and NCSC exemplify universal test design for a specific population. That is, accommodations and flexible administrations are part of the standardized assessment protocol. Although these assessment systems are atypical in terms of student population, they may lead the way for more accessible general assessments in the future.

Methods for Evaluating Test Accommodations

As we described in an earlier section of this chapter, providing accommodations to SWDs and ELs is done to make tests more accessible to these groups of students and to improve the validity of the actions that are made on the basis of their test scores. However, we also pointed out that accommodations can diminish validity by changing the construct measured or by making the scores across standard and accommodated tests noncomparable. In this section, we discuss statistical methods that can be used to evaluate the comparability of standard and accommodated tests.

Recall that the AERA et al. (2014) *Standards* specified five sources of validity evidence that can be used to evaluate the use of a test for a particular purpose. Although all five sources are relevant to evaluating test accommodations, with respect to evaluating the comparability of scores from accommodated and standardized tests, two sources have been widely used. The first is validity evidence based on relations to other variables; the second is validity evidence based on internal structure.

Validity evidence based on *relations to other variables* refers to traditional forms of criterion-related validity evidence such as concurrent and predictive validity studies, as well as more comprehensive investigations of the relationships among test scores and other variables. Evidence in this category may also include analysis of group differences in test performance that are considered related to the construct measured (e.g., groups that differ with respect to the instruction received).

Examples of test accommodation studies that can be described as gathering validity evidence based on relations to other variables are studies that have evaluated the *interaction hypothesis* (Koenig & Bachman, 2004) and *differential boost*. The interaction hypothesis states that when test accommodations are given to SWDs who need them, their test scores will improve, relative to the scores they would attain from taking the test under standard conditions, *and* students *without* disabilities will *not* exhibit higher scores when taking the test with an accommodation. Thus, the interaction specified in this hypothesis is between student group (SWDs or non-SWDs) and test administration condition (accommodated versus standard). This interaction can be considered in the context of a factorial design in which a within-subject factor (standard or accommodated test administration) interacts with a between-subject factor (student group).

Differential boost (Elliott & Kettler, 2016; Fuchs et al., 2000) represents a more realistic hypothesis of the effectiveness of test accommodations by relaxing the stipulation that students without disabilities will not have score gains in the accommodation condition. According to this hypothesis, if an accommodation is effective, the gains for SWDs will be greater than the gains observed for SWDs. Like the interaction hypothesis, differential boost is evaluated using experimental designs where one factor is student group and the other factor is test administration condition. These studies typically use analysis of variance to evaluate the main and interaction effects. Reviews of differential boost and interaction hypothesis studies can be found in Kettler (2012) and Sireci, Scarpati, and Li (2005) for SWDs and Pennock-Roman and Rivera (2011) for ELs.

Validity evidence based on *internal structure* refers to statistical analysis of item and subscore data to investigate the primary and secondary (if any) dimensions measured by an assessment. Examples of studies in this area include evaluating whether the dimensionality of an assessment is consistent across students who received an accommodation and students who did not. Analysis of "differential item functioning," (DIF) which is a statistical analysis to assess potential item bias, also falls under the internal structure category. Other examples of statistical procedures used to evaluate the equivalence of a test across groups of students defined by SWD or EL status include item response theory (IRT), structural equation modeling (SEM), and multidimensional scaling (MDS) for factor or structure-level analysis (Sireci, 2005). In this section, we briefly describe these procedures.

Differential item functioning (DIF) DIF is mainly used to evaluate whether there is potential bias for or against different groups of students at the item level. DIF occurs when two groups of students (e.g., accommodated and non-accommodated students) have different probabilities of answering an item correctly, after they are matched on the construct of interest. Clauser and Mazor (1998) defined DIF as being present "when examinees from different groups have differing … likelihoods of success on an item, *after they have been matched on the [proficiency] of interest*" (p. 31, emphasis added). The italicized phrase is key to understanding DIF, because it represents an *interaction* between group membership and the likelihood of a particular response on an item, conditional on the attribute measured. The conditioning or "matching" feature is essential to DIF analysis because if two groups differ with respect to their performance on an item, this difference could reflect a valid (true) difference between the groups on the construct measured. However, if individuals from the different groups are matched on the construct measured, then there should be no differences with respect to how they respond to the item. That is, individuals who are equal on the construct measured should have equal probabilities of specific responses to an item. If that property does not hold across groups, the item is said to exhibit DIF.

DIF is a statistical observation and is used to flag items for further review to determine if the source of DIF indicates construct-irrelevant variance (Karami, 2012). Thus, it represents only the statistical part of a two-step process designed to improve testing fairness by identifying problematic test items.

There are many statistical methods for flagging items for DIF. These methods include Mantel-Haenszel, logistic regression, and methods based on IRT. Analyses using these methods give more accurate and precise results when working with large sample sizes for both the focal group (e.g., students with accommodations) and the reference group (e.g., students without accommodations, Hambleton, 2006; Zumbo, 2007). Small sample sizes can be a major limitation when calculating DIF for groups of students defined by accommodation, EL status, or both, because in many cases the numbers of students in these subgroups may be too small for statistical analysis, especially when disaggregated by specific types of accommodations or native languages (Johnstone, Thompson, Bottsfordmiller, & Thurlow, 2008). However these procedures are commonly used in large-scale assessments, such as statewide testing programs or admissions testing programs, sometimes by combining data across a number of years (Bennett, Rock, Kaplan, & Jirele, 1988; Engelhard, Fincher, & Domaleski, 2011). Further information about these methods, such as the statistical calculations and research design issues, can be found in Clauser and Mazor (1988), Hambleton (2006), Sireci and Rios (2013), and Zumbo (1999).

Item response theory (IRT) As mentioned earlier, IRT is one of the statistical models that can be used to evaluate DIF. In addition, IRT can be used to evaluate differences in measurement precision or structure at the total test level. Although the statistical underpinnings of IRT are beyond the scope of this chapter (see Hambleton, 1989, or Hambleton, Swaminathan, & Rogers, 1991, for details), essentially IRT models stipulate one or more dimensions (typically a single dimension) to quantify students' proficiencies. The degree to which the dimensions are consistent across groups is used to evaluate invariance across groups defined by disability, accommodation, English proficiency, and other demographic variables.

One advantage of calibrating and scoring an educational assessment using IRT is that the relationship between total test score and the underlying dimensionality of the assessment can be evaluated graphically using the *test characteristic curve*. In addition, the precision of measurement across the entire score scale can be graphically evaluated using the *test information function*. Test information is similar to the traditional measurement concept of "reliability" in that more information represents better measurement precision. In evaluating the effect of accommodations or other factors on dimensionality or measurement precision, test characteristic curves and item information functions can be computed separately across groups defined by disability, accommodation, EL status, and other demographic variables. These curves and functions are then compared to evaluate their comparability across groups. Thus, IRT provides a flexible means for evaluating the similarity of the measuring instrument across subgroups of students. Potential disadvantages of using IRT in this context are the degree to which the IRT model fits the data for the general population and the size of and variability within the specific subgroups analyzed. Like virtually all statistical procedures, when sample sizes are small and variability is restricted, parameter estimates may not be reliable, which limits the utility of the results.

Multidimensional scaling (MDS) MDS is similar to factor analysis in that it can be used to discover the most salient dimensions underlying a set of items. It is particularly applicable to the evaluation of invariance test structure across subgroups of students because multiple subgroups can be analyzed and compared in the same analysis. MDS computes coordinates for test items (similar to item factor loadings in a factor analysis) on dimensions that best account for the ways in which the examinees responded to the items. MDS models use distance formulae to arrange items within a multidimensional "space" so that items that are responded to similarly by examinees are close together in this space and are distant from items to which students responded differently.

With respect to the multiple-group case, weights for each group are incorporated into the distance model. This procedure, called weighted MDS (WMDS), derives both a common structure that best represents the data for all groups simultaneously and a set of unique weights for each group that can be used to adjust this common structure to best fit the data for each specific matrix. If the weights are similar across groups, the dimensionality of the test is considered invariant across groups. MDS has been used in this way to evaluate the comparability of test structure across subgroups of students defined by various accommodations provided and by EL status (Sireci & Wells, 2010; Sireci, Wells, & Hu, 2014).

Structural equation modeling (SEM) In the context of SEM, evaluation of the internal structure of a test can be examined through confirmatory factor analyses (CFAs). Multigroup CFA can be used to determine whether the same factors are underlying test performance across groups (Kline, 2016).

Several approaches can be taken when using CFA to evaluate the consistency of factor structure across groups of students defined by the accommodations they received, by EL status, or by any other grouping variable. Typically, the evaluation involves three hierarchical steps. The first step is to establish configural invariance, which means the same dimensions (constructs) are measured across groups. The second step evaluates metric invariance by fitting a model in which the factor loadings are constrained to be equal across the groups (but the intercepts or thresholds are unconstrained). Metric invariance tests whether the factor loadings are the same across groups. In the third step, referred to as scalar invariance, a model is fit in which the intercepts, in addition to the factor loadings, are constrained to be equal across groups. Scalar invariance tests whether the factor loadings and item or subscore means (after controlling for overall proficiency) are invariant across groups.

In SEM, model-fit criteria are used to evaluate configural, metric, and scalar invariance. For configural invariance, a chi-square fit statistic may be used to test the hypothesis that the model fits perfectly in the population. Unfortunately, the chi-square test is typically significant because the hypothesis being tested is unrealistic, and we often use very large sample sizes which provide sufficient power even when the model misfit is negligible. Therefore, goodness-of-fit indices are more typically used to determine if the model provides adequate fit. Two commonly used fit indices are the comparative fit index (CFI) and root mean square error of approximation (RMSEA). Values for the CFI greater than 0.95 and RMSEA less than 0.06 are consistent with acceptable model fit (Hu & Bentler, 1999).

In addition to descriptive goodness-of-fit indices of how well the CFA models fit subgroups of students, statistical tests of invariance can also be conducted. Because the metric model is nested within the configural model, metric invariance can be assessed by comparing the fit of the configural and metric models. The difference in chi-square statistics ($\Delta\chi^2$) between the two models is distributed as a chi-square with degrees of freedom (df) equal to the difference in df for each model. The change in CFI (ΔCFI) between the configural and metric invariance models is reported to determine if a statistically significant result is meaningful. A ΔCFI greater than 0.01 may indicate a non-negligible lack of metric invariance (Cheung & Rensvold, 2002). To assess scalar invariance, the fit of the scalar model (i.e., with constraints placed on the factor loadings and intercepts) is compared to the fit of the metric model using the difference in chi-square statistics ($\Delta\chi^2$) and change in CFI (ΔCFI). In general, through CFA, factor loadings, correlations among factors, and item residuals can be constrained to be equal across groups, and then tests can be performed to determine whether relaxing the constraints provides a significant improved model fit (Tippetts & Michaels, 1997).

Comparing IRT, MDS, and SEM approaches to evaluating test structure In this section, we described three statistical approaches that can be used to evaluate whether test accommodations may have affected the construct measured: IRT, MDS, and SEM. These approaches can also be used to evaluate whether the construct differs across subgroups of students defined by other characteristics such as English language proficiency. All three approaches are based in an evaluation of the "internal structure," or dimensionality, of the test. The structure of the test is evaluated with respect to dimensions that characterize students' responses to the items. In IRT and SEM, the fit of the dimension to all groups can be evaluated. SEM also allows for statistical testing of departures from equivalent dimensionality across groups. MDS does not involve statistical tests but offers the advantage of not having to specify a model before conducting the analysis. Thus, MDS is a multigroup exploratory analysis, whereas IRT and SEM are specifying the structure a priori. Each method has strengths and weaknesses. Where possible, we recommend using more than one procedure to evaluate the invariance of test structure across groups of students defined by accommodation or EL status.

Future Directions for Research and Practice

In this chapter, we discussed validity and fairness issues involved in assessing SWDs and ELs, described current practices in providing test accommodations, and described statistical methods that can be used to evaluate the effect of accommodations on the construct measured (at both the item and test structure levels). The statistical methods we discussed can also be used to evaluate the comparability of test structure and item functioning across any subgroups of students, such as ELs. What we have described up to this point are current practices and research methods for facilitating and evaluating fairness issues in assessing SWDs and ELs. In this section, we risk some predictions of how these practices may change in the future.

Although it is hard to predict the future, it is obvious technology is rapidly changing the educational landscape. Technology is rapidly infiltrating the classroom, with students using computers to access instruction, to respond to classroom exercises, and to complete homework assignments. Students are encouraged to use technology to research and solve problems at their own pace, and computerized programs track their progress and alter instruction accordingly. Through these activities and similar educational "games," students receive rewards and can monitor their own progress, as their teachers simultaneously, and seamlessly, monitor their progress. We imagine assessment technology will catch up to instructional technology and that tests will become more tailored and flexible in these "lower stakes" but instructionally important educational settings. The assistive technologies that are used with such educational software should transfer to future educational assessments.

As mentioned earlier, technology is also being used to provide new accommodations to SWDs and ELs (e.g., "pop-up" glossaries) and is being used to provide accommodations more efficiently. We imagine in the future all accommodations can be provided to all students through the use of assessment technology platforms that "load" all accommodations into the system. Relevant accommodations could be accessed by any student who decides they would benefit from them.[4] If this vision is realized, "accommodations" will cease to exist because these accessibility features will be available to all. That is, they will be part of the standardized test administration.

Essentially, that vision is the realization of universal test design and is already evident in the alternative assessment systems represented by DLM and NCSC.

A positive development that we expect to continue into the future is that accommodations to tests are no longer seen as derailing the testing process or sacrificing validity, but rather they are seen as a standard part of the testing process and as a means to increase validity. Since the beginning of this century, almost all of the major admissions testing programs have abandoned the practice of "flagging" the test scores of SWDs if they received extra time to accommodate their disability. At the time of this writing, the ACT, SAT, and LSAT no longer flag the scores from approved, accommodated test administrations involving extended time. Given that these tests are not designed to see how quickly students can answer questions, we see this as a positive development. It further acknowledges the fact that a limitation, be it a physical disability or limited proficiency in a certain language, should not be stigmatized. The reality is we all have disabilities. Some are just more obvious than others. Thus, in the future we hope more attention gets paid to how to make tests more accessible for all students and how to best decide what testing features are optimal for specific students. As Elliott and Kettler (2016) emphasized:

> it is critical to remember that test accessibility refers to an interaction between each individual and each test; thus, a student's disability category is at best a starting point for considering which adaptations might help a test function optimally. (p. 377)

Thus, we hope in the future, researchers assist educators in identifying testing features best tailored for individual students and making those features readily available.

References

Abedi, J. (2007). *English language proficiency assessment in the nation: Current status and future practice*. Davis, CA: University of California, Davis, School of Education.

---

[4] Of course, understanding the available accommodations, and practicing using them, would be important for students, parents, and teachers to know and are likely to be beneficial.

Abedi, J., & Ewers, N. (2013). Smarter balanced assessment consortium: Accommodations for english language learners and students with disabilities a research based decision algorithm.

American Educational Research Association, American Psychological Association, & National Council on Measurement in Education. (2014). *Standards for educational and psychological testing*. Washington, DC: American Educational Research Association.

Azevedo, R., & Hadwin, A. (2005). Scaffolding self-regulated learning and metacognition. Implications for the design of computer based scaffolds. *Instructional Science, 33*, 367–379.

Bennett, R. E., Rock, D. A., Kaplan, B. A., & Jirele, T. (1988). Psychometric characteristics. In W. W. Willingham, M. Ragosta, R. E. Bennett, H. Braun, D. A. Rock, & D. E. Powers (Eds.), *Testing handicapped people* (pp. 1–15). Needham Heights, MA: Allyn and Bacon.

Cheung, G., & Rensvold, R. (2002). Evaluating goodness of fit indexes for testing measurement invariance. *Structural Equation Modeling: A Multidisciplinary Jounal, 9*, 233–245.

Christensen, L. L., Braam, M., Scullin, S., & Thurlow, M. L. (2011). *2009 state policies on assessment participation and accommodations for students with disabilities* (Synthesis Report 83). Minneapolis, MN: University of Minnesota, National Center on Educational Outcomes.

Clapper, A. T., Morse, A. B., Thompson, S. J., & Thurlow, M. L. (2005). *Access assistants for state assessments: A study of state guidelines for scribes, readers, and sign language interpreters* (Synthesis Report 58). Minneapolis, MN: University of Minnesota, National Center on Educational Outcomes.

Clark, A., Kingston, N., Templin, J., & Pardos, Z. (2014). *Summary of results from the fall 2013 pilot administration of the Dynamic Learning Maps™ Alternate Assessment System* (Technical Report No. 14–01). Lawrence, KS: University of Kansas Centre for Educational Testing and Evaluation.

Clauser, B. E., & Mazor, K. M. (1998). Using statistical procedures to identify differential item functioning test items. *Educational Measurement: Issues and Practice, 17*, 31–44.

Dynamic Learning Maps Consortium. (2013). *Dynamic Learning Maps Essential Elements for English language arts. Lawrence, KS: University of Kansas*. Retrieved from: http://dynamiclearningmaps.org/sites/default/files/documents/ELA_EEs/DLM_Essential_Elements_ELA_%28 2013%29_v4.pdf.

Elliott, S. N., & Kettler, R. J. (2016). Item and test design considerations for students with special needs. In S. Lane, T. Haladyna, & M. Raymond (Eds.), *Handbook of test development* (pp. 374–391). Washington, DC: National Council on Measurement in Education.

Engelhard, G., Fincher, M., & Domaleski, C. S. (2011). Mathematics performance of students with and without disabilities under accommodated conditions using resource guides and calculators on high stakes tests. *Applied Measurement in Education, 37*, 281–306.

Fuchs, L. S., Fuchs, D., Eaton, S. B., Hamlett, C. L., Binkley, E., & Crouch, R. (2000, Fall). Using objective data sources to enhance teacher judgments about test accommodations. *Exceptional Children, 67*, 67–81.

Hambleton, R. K. (1989). Principles and selected applications of item response theory. In R. Linn (Ed.), *Educational measurement* (3rd ed., pp. 147–200). New York, NY: Macmillan.

Hambleton, R. K. (2006). Good practices for identifying differential item functioning. *Medical Care, 44*(Suppl. 3), S182–S188.

Hambleton, R. K., Swaminathan, H., & Rogers, H. J. (1991). *Fundamentals of item response theory*. Newbury Park, CA: Sage.

Herrera, A. W., Turner, C. D., Quenemoen, R. F., & Thurlow, M. L. (2015). *NCSC's age and grade–appropriate assessment of student learning (NCSC brief #6)*. Minneapolis, MN: University of Minnesota, National Center and State Collaborative.

Hodgson, J. R., Lazarus, S. S., Price, L., Altman, J. R., & Thurlow, M. L. (2012). *Test administrators' perspectives on the use of the read aloud accommodation on state tests for accountability* (Technical Report No. 66). Minneapolis, MN: University of Minnesota, National Center on Educational Outcomes. Clapper et al. (2005).

Hu, L. T., & Bentler, P. M. (1999). Cutoff criteria for fit indexes in covariance structure analysis: Conventional criteria versus new alternatives. *Structural Equation Modeling, 6*, 1–55.

Johnstone, C. J., Thompson, S. J., BottsfordMiller, N., & Thurlow, M. L. (2008). Universal design and multimethod approaches to item review. *Educational Measurement: Issues & Practice, 27*, 25–36.

Karami, H. (2012). An introduction to differential item functioning. *International Journal of Educational Psychological Assessment, 11*, 56–76.

Kearns, J. F., Towels-Reeves, E., Kleinert, H. L., Kleinert, J. O., & Kleine-Kracht, M. (2011). Characteristics of and implications for students participating in alternate assessments based on alternate academic achievement standards. *Journal of Special Education, 45*(3), 3–14.

Kettler, R. J. (2012). Testing accommodations: Theory and research to inform practice. *International Disability, Development, and Education, 5*(1), 53–66.

Kline, R. B. (2016). *Principles and practice of structural equation modeling*. New York, NY: Guilford Press.

Koenig, J. A., & Bachman, L. F. (Eds.). (2004). *Keeping score for all: The effects of inclusion and accommodation policies on large-scale educational assessments*. Washington, DC: National Academies Press.

Lee, A., Browder, D. M., Wakeman, S. Y., Quenemoen, R. F., & Thurlow, M. L. (2015, August). *AA-AAS: How do our students learn and show what they know? (NCSC brief #3)*. Minneapolis, MN: University of Minnesota, National Center and State Collaborative.

Messick, S. (1989). Validity. In R. Linn (Ed.), *Educational measurement* (pp. 13–103). Washington, DC: American Council on Education.

National Center and State Collaborative. (2015). NCSC assessment policies. Retrieved from www.ncscpartners.org/Media/Default/PDFs/Resources/Parents/NCSCAssessmentPolicies.pdf.

PARCC. (2017). *Accessibility Features and Accommodations Manual*. Parcc Inc. Washington, DC: PARCC Assessment Consortia. Retrieved from http://avocet.pearson.com/PARCC/Home.

Pennock-Roman, M., & Rivera, C. (2011). Mean effects of test accommodations for ELLs and non-ELLs: A meta-analysis of experimental studies. *Educational Measurement: Issues and Practice, 30*, 10–18.

Russell, M. (2011). *Digital test delivery: Empowering accessible test design to increase test validity for all students*. Washington, DC: Arabella Advisors.

Sireci, S. G. (2005). Unlabeling the disabled: A perspective on flagging scores from accommodated test administrations. *Educational Researcher, 34*, 3–12.

Sireci, S. G., & Faulkner-Bond, M. F. (2015). Promoting validity in the assessment of English learners and other linguistic minorities. *Review of Research in Education, 39*, 215–252.

Sireci, S. G., & Gandara, M. F. (2016). Testing in educational and developmental settings. In F. Leong et al. (Eds.), *International test commission handbook of testing and assessment* (pp. 187–202). Oxford: Oxford University Press.

Sireci, S. G., Han, K. T., & Wells, C. S. (2008). Methods for evaluating the validity of test scores for English language learners. *Educational Assessment, 13*, 108–131.

Sireci, S. G., & Rios, J. (2013). Decisions that make a difference in detecting differential item functioning. *Educational Research and Evaluation, 19*, 170–187.

Sireci, S. G., Scarpati, S., & Li, S. (2005). Test accommodations for students with disabilities: An analysis of the interaction hypothesis. *Review of Educational Research, 75*, 457–490.

Sireci, S. G., & Wells, C. S. (2010). Evaluating the comparability of English and Spanish video accommodations for English language learners. In P. Winter (Ed.), *Evaluating the comparability of scores from achievement test variations* (pp. 33–68). Washington, DC: Council of Chief State School Officers.

Sireci, S. G., Wells, C., & Hu, H. (2014, April). *Using internal structure validity evidence to evaluate test accommodations*. Paper presented at the annual meeting of the National Council on Measurement in Education, Philadelphia.

Smarter Balanced. (2016). *Usability, Accessibility, and Accommodations Guidelines*. Retrieved from https://portal.smarterbalanced.org/library/en/usability-accessibility-and-accommodations-guidelines.pdf.

Thompson, S., Blount, A., & Thurlow, M. (2002). *A summary of research on the effects of test accommodations: 1999 through 2001* (Technical Report 34). Minneapolis, MN: University of Minnesota, National Center on Educational Outcomes. Retrieved January 2003 from http://education.umn.edu/NCEO/OnlinePubs/Technical34.htm.

Thurlow, M. L., Elliot, J. L., & Ysseldyke, J. E. (2003). *Testing students with disabilities: Practical strategies for complying with district and state requirements*. Thousand Oaks, CA: Corwin Press.

Tippets, E., & Michaels, H. (1997). *Factor structure invariance of accommodated and non-accommodated performance assessments*. Paper presented at the meeting of the National Council on Measurement in Education, Chicago. Retrieved from http://www.tandfonline.com/.

U.S. Department of Education. (2015). *US department of education FY2015 annual performance report and FY2017 annual performance plan*. Retrieved from: http://www.ed.gov.about/reports/annual/index.html.

Wells-Moreaux, S., Bechard, S., & Karvonen, M. (2015). *Accessibility manual for the dynamic learning maps alternate assessment, 2015–2016*. Lawrence, KS: The University of Kansas Centre for Educational Testing and Evaluation.

Zumbo, B. (2007). Three generations of DIF analyses: Considering where it has been, where it is now, and where it is going. *Language Assessment Quarterly, 4*, 223–233.

Zumbo, B. D. (1999). *A handbook on the theory and methods of differential item functioning (DIF): Logistic regression modeling as a unitary framework for binary and Likert-type (ordinal) item scores*. Ottawa, Canada: Directorate of Human Resources Research and Evaluation, Department of National Defense.

Recent Advances in the Accessibility of Digitally Delivered Educational Assessments

16

Michael Russell

The past 5 years have been exciting for the field of educational testing. The Race to the Top Assessment (RTTA) program provided an impetus, coupled with funding, to enhance state assessment programs. In response, there has been rapid adoption of computer-based testing across a majority of states. A variety of technology-enhanced items (TEI) have been introduced to state testing programs. Several state testing programs have experimented with automated scoring. Many testing programs and test vendors have embraced the concept of interoperability and have begun developing test content and delivery systems that comply with internationally recognized standards. And the concept of accessible test delivery has shifted testing programs from accommodating students with special needs to increasing accessibility for all. This chapter focuses specifically on the impact digital delivery has had on recent advances in the accessibility of educational tests and explores next steps the field is now prepared to take to further advance fair and accurate assessment for all students.

M. Russell (✉)
Boston College, Chestnut Hill, MA, USA
e-mail: russelmh@bc.edu

Brief History of Test Accommodations

Over the past 40 years, there has been considerable controversy about the accessibility of educational assessment. The initial focus on accessible assessment was stimulated by a series of lawsuits in the early 1970s that focused on equal access to education for students with disabilities. This right was first codified in the 1975 Education for All Handicapped Act [Public Law (PL) 94–142] and later bolstered in the 1990 Americans with Disabilities Act [PL 101–336]. During that time period, concerns about accessibility focused largely on students with physical and visual disabilities. Over time, the population of students for whom concerns were identified expanded to students with learning disabilities, language processing needs, attention and stimulus needs, auditory needs, and most recently students who are English language learners.

In each case, advocacy has focused on a subpopulation of students with common characteristics (e.g., students who are blind or have low vision, students with dyslexia, students who communicate in sign, etc.). In response to concerns about a given subpopulation of students, assessment programs created provisions that allowed assessment instruments to be altered, through what has become known as a test accommodation, so that test content was more accessi-

© Springer International Publishing AG 2018
S. N. Elliott et al. (eds.), *Handbook of Accessible Instruction and Testing Practices*,
https://doi.org/10.1007/978-3-319-71126-3_16

ble for a specific subpopulation of students. While this gradual evolution resulted in increased participation and improvements in the measurement of students with specific needs, the reactive approach of responding to advocacy and, in some cases, legal action produced an uncoordinated piecemeal approach to accessibility that tended to pit the needs of subgroups of students against the financial and administrative interests of testing programs. As a result, approaching accessibility through test accommodations proved to be expensive and, in many cases, controversial.

The expense arose primarily from the need to change or retrofit an existing instrument and in the process revisit the intent of each item to assure that any changes did not alter the knowledge or skill measured by the item. In effect, for each accommodation provided, all items had to be reexamined, and changes to the item that would make it more accessible for a given population of student were specified. The changes were then executed, effectively creating an alternate version of the item. As an example, for students who were blind braille readers, an item might be presented in braille form. For students who communicate in American Sign Language (ASL), the item might be translated to ASL, and video of the item might be developed. In this process, the alternate version of the item was examined carefully to assure that the knowledge, skill, or ability measured by the item was not changed by the alternation. In some cases, this process identified parts of an item that could not be made accessible. As an example, it may not be possible to create a tactile version of a complex diagram that accompanies an item. In such cases, a simplified version of the diagram might be created and then presented in tactile form. In other cases, this process identified some items that could not be appropriately modified, the removal of which complicated the scoring and reporting process. By addressing accommodations after the original item was finalized, this process was an expensive endeavor that often had secondary effects on the administration, scoring, and reporting of tests administered under different conditions.

For a period of time, the provision of test accommodations resulted in scores for students who received accommodations being flagged, reported separately, or not included in school or classroom averages. In some cases, students who required accommodations were excluded entirely from participating in assessment programs. More recently, federal policies codified in the Individuals with Disabilities Education Act and No Child Left Behind Act have effectively eliminated the practice of flagging and have greatly reduced exclusion. Nonetheless, the provision of test accommodations remains an expensive component of an assessment program.

Universal Design and Assessment

During the early 2000s, the concept of universal design was introduced to the field of educational testing. The concept of universal design focuses on "the design of products and environments to be usable by all people, to the greatest extent possible, without the need for adaptation or specialized design" (Center for Universal Design (CUD), 1997). Rather than creating a single solution, universal design has come to embrace the concept of allowing users to select from multiple alternatives. As Rose and Meyer (2000) emphasize, "Universal Design does not imply 'one sizes fits all' but rather acknowledges the need for alternatives to suit many different people's needs…the essence of [Universal Design] is flexibility and the inclusion of alternatives to adapt to the myriad variations in learner needs, styles, and preferences" (pg. 4). A critical component of universal design is anticipating the needs of different people and building in options that make a product accessible to people with those different needs. In effect, this approach to building flexibility into a product contrasts sharply with the traditional approach to test accommodations which relied on reacting to requests and then retrofitting a test.

Over the past 15 years, efforts to apply principles of universal design to the development and delivery of educational assessments have helped improve the quality with which access is provided to students with a variety of needs (Dolan, Hall, Banerjee, Chun, & Strangman, 2005; Thompson, Thurlow, & Malouf, n.d.). This expansion from meeting the needs of specific subgroups of students to supporting all students led to the development of the accessible test design model (Russell, 2011; Russell, Higgins, & Hoffmann, 2009). When applied throughout the development and delivery on an assessment instrument, accessible test design enables an assessment program to capitalize on the flexibility that digital technologies offer to tailor the presentation of content, interactions with that content, and methods of recording the outcome of those interactions based on the specific needs of each individual student. Adoption of accessible test design led to integrating accessibility supports into test delivery systems and the creation of alternate forms of test content during item development. In turn, the need to create efficient and standardized methods of producing and delivering digital test content led to the development of the Question and Test Interoperability – Accessible Portable Item Protocol (QTI-APIP) standard (IMS Global Learning Consortium, 2015; Russell, Mattson, Higgins, Hoffmann, Bebell, & Alcaya, 2011) and detailed guidelines for making test content accessible for test takers with a variety of accessibility needs (Measured Progress/ETS, 2012a, 2012b, 2012c). The RTTA then provided a mechanism to carefully consider policy implications resulting from this new approach to accessibility and to build assessment programs that better capitalized on these emerging methods.

Accessible Test Design

Accessible test design provides a model that allows assessment programs to specify methods for flexibly tailoring the presentation of test content, the interaction with that content, and finally the provision of a response for an assessment item such that the influence of nontargeted constructs is minimized for each individual student. As depicted in Fig. 16.1, the accessible test design model begins by defining the access needs of each individual student. These needs are then used to align the presentation and interaction with the test with the student access needs by (a) presenting specific representational forms of the item content specified in the item itself (e.g., text, braille, sign, audio, alternate language, etc.), which are stored as item content resources, and (b) activating specific access tools, such as a magnifying glass or color contrast, embedded in a test delivery system. Through this interaction with item content and the delivery system, the administration of an assessment item is tailored to maximize the measurement of the intended construct and minimize the influence of unintended constructs.

Flexibly tailoring a student's experience with an assessment item depends on the access needs of each student and may require adaptations to the presentation of item content, the interaction with that content, the response mode, or the representational form in which content is communicated.

Flexible Presentation of Content

As Mislevy et al. (2010) explained, several different representational forms can be used to present instructional or test content to a student. To enable a student to recognize and process content, the form used to present that content may need to be tailored based on the student's need. As an example, a student who is blind cannot access content presented in print-based form. However, when that same content is presented in braille, the content becomes accessible for the student if the student is a braille reader. Reading aloud content, presenting text-based content in sign language, braille, tactile representations of graphical images, symbolic representations of text-based information, narrative representations of chemical compounds (e.g., "sodium chloride" instead of "NaCl") or mathematical formulas, and translating to a different language are all forms of alternate representations. And each of these alternate representations becomes an item content access resource for a given item.

For a paper-based test, alternate representations often require the development of different versions or forms of the materials or the use of translators or interpreters who present alternate representations to the student. In a digital environment, alternate representations of con-

Fig. 16.1 Accessible test implementation model

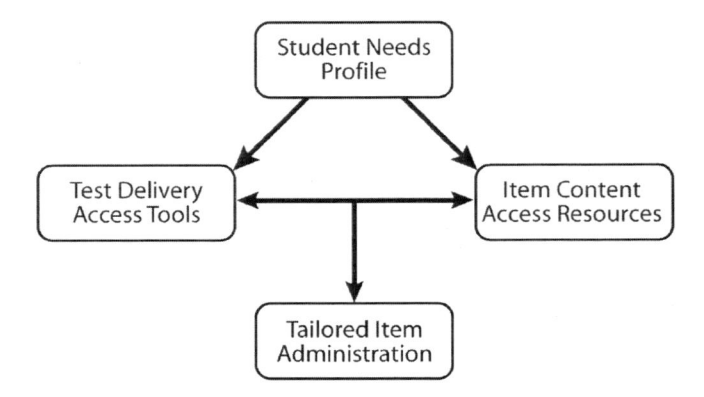

tent can be built into item information, and a digital test delivery system can then tailor the representational form presented to examinees based on their individual needs.

Tailored Delivery of Content

Capitalizing on the flexibility of computer-based technologies, computer-based test delivery interfaces can tailor the delivery of assessment items and tasks based on each individual's access needs. To do so, principles of universal design play an important role in designing systems that can personalize the testing experience based on each individual student's needs. In effect, personalization requires a system to match the representational form (i.e., content resource) and/or the functioning of an accessibility tool (e.g., magnification or read aloud tool) to the needs of a given test taker.

As an example, NimbleTools® was a universally designed test delivery system that embeds several different accessibility and accommodation tools within a single system. A few examples of accessible tools include read aloud of text-based content, oral descriptions of graphics and tables, magnification of content, altered contrast and color of content, masking of content, auditory calming to support sustained concentration, signed presentation of text-based content, and presentation of text-based content in braille (Russell, Hoffmann, & Higgins, 2009). The availability and functionality of these supports were tailored to each student's user profile thus creating a single system that flexibly responded to the needs of each user.

For students who have not been identified with one or more access needs, an accessible test delivery interface delivers content using a standard computer-based delivery interface. For students who need a given accommodation or set of accommodations, a proctor/teacher settings tool is used to customize the tools available for each student. As the student performs an assessment, she/he is able to use available tools as needed. This flexibility allows assessment programs to customize the delivery interface to meet the specific needs of each student and for the student to then use specific tools as needed for each item on the assessment task.

Since its use for operational state test delivery in 2008, many of the embedded supports provided by NimbleTools, coupled with profiles that adapt the functionality of these supports based on each student's accessibility needs, have been integrated into other test delivery systems including those used for PARCC, Smarter Balanced, National Center and State Collaborative (NCSC), and other individual state testing programs. The development of multiple systems that capitalize on embedded accessibility supports to tailor test delivery is among the most significant advances in accessible assessment.

Personal Accessibility Needs (PNP) Profile

In addition to a test delivery interface with embedded access tools and items that contain accessibility specifications, the final element required to make a task accessible for a given user is a student access profile. An access profile

ID	C Spoken	D Magnification	E Color_Contrast	F Color_Overlay	G Extended_Time	H
2340506	0	0	0	0	0	
2340759	1	0	1	0	1	
2356012	0	0	0	0	0	
2371265	0	1	0	0	1	
2386518	0	0	0	0	0	
2401771	0	0	1	0	1	
Fig. 16.2 Sample access profile

defines the access needs for a given student and indicates which tools and/or representational forms should be made available for the student as she/he performs a test. The profile might also specify settings, such as magnification levels, color contrasts, or default representational forms preferred by the student. As an example, Fig. 16.2 depicts access profile settings, stored in a spreadsheet, for a small group of students. In this example, the first row lists five accessibility supports that can be assigned to each student. The first student has no supports assigned. The second student has three supports assigned, including spoken (i.e., having text-based content read aloud), color contrast (i.e., changing the fore- and background color in which text is displayed to alter contrast), and extended time.

Once defined, an access profile interacts with both the delivery interface and the item content. The interaction with the delivery interface focuses on specific tools or features embedded in the interface, activates those tools and features that are defined in the profile, and, in some cases, controls the exact settings for those tools and features. The interaction with the item content focuses on which of the specific representational forms embedded in the item should be presented to a given student in order to meet his/her specific need. The access profile effectively controls the behavior of the interface and the components of an item that are presented to the student. The result is a single unified test delivery that is tailored to meet the specific access needs of each individual student. While NimbleTools was the first system to employ a student access profile, test delivery systems used by several testing programs, including PARCC, Smarter Balanced, Minnesota, and NCSC, now employ user profiles to define the access needs for each student.

Standardizing Accessibility

As more testing programs implemented principles of accessible test design and test vendors modified their systems to support a full range of embedded accessibility supports, an important concern emerged regarding the ability to transfer assessment content seamlessly across item authoring, item banking, and test delivery platforms (aka interoperability). Interoperability of test content is particularly concerning for state assessment programs that change vendors and must transfer digital versions of their test items between vendors' item banking and test delivery systems.

To address this concern, in 2010 the state of Minnesota led a collaboration of other state assessment programs, computer-based testing experts, and interoperability experts to develop a standardized method for encoding accessibility information in test items. Rather than develop a completely new standard, the collaborative extended the Question and Test Interoperability (QTI) standard (IMS, 2015). QTI is a technical specification introduced in the early 2000s and used by several testing vendors to encode item content and metadata in a standardized digital format. The collaboration extended QTI by creating a standardized method for adding accessibility information to a QTI item. In addition, a standardized method for storing information about a given student's accessibility needs in a personal needs profile (PNP) was developed. This new method for encoding accessibility information was termed the Accessible Portable Item Protocol standard (IMS Global Learning Consortium, 2014) and when implemented in conjunction with QTI is referred to as QTI-APIP.

In a sense, QTI-APIP is similar to HTML in that it provides a method for tagging item content. The tags are then used by a computer program as content is presented to a test taker. As an example, QTI includes tags that indicate whether content is part of an item prompt, answer options, or stimulus materials. APIP includes tags that allow an item author to associate accessibility information with item content (e.g., an audio file that reads aloud the prompt). In addition, APIP includes tags that specify which accessibility information is to be presented to different users. For example, for a student who is blind, an APIP inclusion tag may specify that an audio file that contains a description of an image should be presented to the test taker. By combining QTI and APIP tags, several different accessibility needs can be addressed within a single item file. A test delivery system can then use the tags to determine which elements within the item file to present to a test taker based on his/her accessibility needs.

Several of the RTTA-funded assessment consortia, as well as individual state assessment programs, implemented the QTI-APIP standard. The standard is now housed and maintained within the IMS Global Learning Consortium and continues to evolve to meet new accessibility needs. While initial implementation of QTI-APIP was more expensive than developing proprietary items, experience and efficiencies in item develop software have streamlined the process and have contributed to widespread adoption of the standard. In turn, this adoption has greatly increased the adoption of accessible test design and improved the accessibility of state assessment instruments.

Guidelines for Accessible Test Content

Another important advance that occurred over the past 10 years is the development of comprehensive and detailed guidelines for accessible test content. While states have long had documents that articulated policies regarding which students were eligible for a given accommodation and guidelines for how a given accommodation was to be delivered by a school or test proctor, little guidance about accessibility was provided during the actual development of test content. With the introduction of the concept of alternate representations of test content came a need to specify how specific content was to be presented in an alternate form. Today, detailed guidelines provide very specific guidance on the presentation of test content in audio form, tactile form, signed form, and in a translated form (Measured Progress/ETS, 2012a, 2012b, 2012c, 2012d). As an example, the Smarter Balanced Assessment Consortium (Measured Progress/ETS, 2012a) provided 85 pages of detail on how specific mathematics content, such as multiplication symbols, coordinate pairs, algebraic functions, matrices, and Venn diagrams, are to be presented or described in an audio form. As one example, Fig. 16.3 displays the audio guideline for how to refer to a box found in a mathematics item.

Guidelines like these help establish common practices during instruction and during testing for the representation of content in alternate forms and standardize accessibility during assessment. When well designed, they also help ensure that the construct intended to be measured by an item is preserved when content in presented in alternate form, which aids test validity.

Accessibility Policies

A final advance is the expansion of state policies guiding test accessibility. Again, for many years, states have developed policies regarding eligibility requirements for specific test accommodations. Often, these policies pointed schools and teachers to a student's individualized education program (IEP) and specified that a student was eligible for an accessibility support only if their IEP specified that such a support was needed. In this way, test accommodation policies were effectively an extension of IEP plans.

Today, accessibility policies have expanded from meeting the needs of students as specified in their IEPs, effectively meeting a legal requirement,

Fig. 16.3 Smarter Balanced guideline for audio presentation of an empty box

Empty/Unknown Boxes (☐, [?])

Example 1

4+2x= ☐

Example 2

3+y= [?]

Audio Guideline

    a.   Refer to an empty box in a formula or equation as "box."

    b.   Refer to a box with a question mark in it as "unknown box."

Application of Audio Guideline

Example 1

Nimble/Oregon/Georgia/Connecticut

Four plus two x equals box.

Example 2

Nimble

Three plus y equals unknown box.

to providing guidance on making tests accessible to all students. With the integration of accessibility supports into test delivery systems and the embedding of alternate representations of test content into each item, coupled with locally provided supports (e.g., quiet setting, assistive technologies, etc.), these accessibility policies have become considerably more sophisticated. As an example, both Partnership for Assessment of Readiness for College and Careers (PARCC) (2015) and Smarter Balanced (2015) took a three-level tiered approach to their accessibility policies. As Fig. 16.4 shows, this tiered approach begins by defining the accessibility supports that are available to all students regardless of whether the student has an IEP or has previously been defined with an accessibility need. PARCC terms this tier *Features for All*, while Smarter Balanced names it *Universal Tools* (NCEO, 2016). In effect, the supports that fall into this category are analogous to the tools available in most software programs that allow a user to modify the size of text that is displayed on a screen or controls that allow one to adjust the brightness of a display.

The use of these supports is believed to have no relationship with the construct being measured and is intuitive and thus is available to all students.

The second category focuses on a subset of supports that also have no relationship with the tested construct but which may require prior experience to use without creating increased cognitive load. PARCC terms these supports *Accessibility Features*, and Smarter Balanced calls them *Designated Supports*. Because these tools require prior experience, they must be assigned to a student prior to the start of a test and are then only available to those students to which a tool was assigned. However, because these tools may be used by a wide range of students and are often available in other software applications, the tools can be assigned to any student.

The third category contains tools that must be designated in a student's IEP. Both PARCC and Smarter Balanced term these *Accommodations*. These tools are designed to meet specific accessibility needs that are typically associated with a disability or special need. As an example, presentation

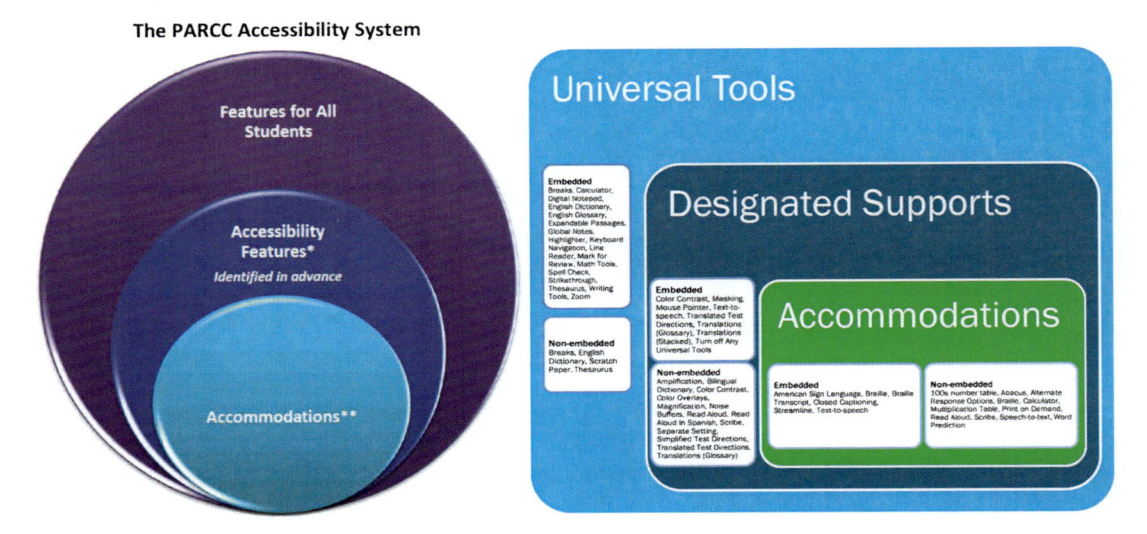

Fig. 16.4 PARCC and Smarter Balanced accessibility frameworks

of content in American Sign Language or in braille both fall into this category. The important aspect of this category is that the support must be specified in the student's IEP and thus is only available to students who have a defined disability or special need.

As noted above, prior to the Race to the Top Assessment programs, almost all state accessibility policies limited the supports available to students to those in the accommodation category. As Fig. 16.4 shows, current policies reflect principles of accessible test design by expanding the availability of accessibility supports to the full population of students.

Summary of Recent Advances

Development and implementation of the Race to the Top Assessment general assessment consortia have been shaky. At its start, more than 40 states were actively involved in the effort to develop next-generation assessment systems. However, political challenges, backlash against the Common Core State Standards, and concerns about state rights (among other issues) eroded participation in the consortia. As of this writing, PARCC's membership has dropped from 25 states (including the District of Columbia) to just 7 members in 2017. Similarly, Smarter Balanced participation dropped from 30 states to 15 in 2016.

Despite this attrition, the effort to develop next-generation assessment systems has had significant impacts on educational testing practices. Arguably, the most noticeable impact has been on accessibility. As described in detail above, adoption of principles of universal design and accessible test design has led to the development of computer-based test delivery systems that support a much wider variety of accessibility needs. The item development process has also evolved to consider accessibility needs from the start and to embed multiple representations of content into items. Adoption of the QTI-APIP standard has helped implement a common approach to including accessibility information in items. Similarly, development of comprehensive guidelines for representing content in different forms has helped standardize practices and create common expectations for students and their teachers. The use of personal needs profiles now allows systems to adapt to the needs of each individual student. And modifications of state policies have broadened access to supports to all students while still ensuring that the specialized needs of students with disabilities, special needs, and English language learners are still met. Given the long battle that began in the early 1970s to ensure that all students could access test instruments and participate in a meaningful way, the advances that have been occurring in the past 5 years are remarkable.

Looking to the Future

Recent advances in the accessibility of digitally delivered tests position the field for a next generation in accessibility. In this section, eight opportunities for advances in accessibility are discussed.

Technology-Enhanced Items

As noted above, several testing programs have begun exploring the use of technology-enhanced items (TEI). In most cases, TEIs take the form of discrete items designed to be answered in a short period of time, much like a traditional multiple choice or short answer item. But, to produce a response, many TEIs require students to manipulate content by dragging and repositioning it on the screen. A common drag-and-drop task may require students to categorize objects by dragging them into a predefined category (e.g., categorizing a list of words as nouns or verbs by moving them into one of two columns). In other cases, an item may ask students to move or reorient an object, such as a line on a graph. In still other cases, multiple objects may need to be manipulated to demonstrate understanding of a given concept. Figure 16.5 displays a concrete example of a TEI that requires students to manipulate line segments to create objects (in this case rectangles to measure understanding of properties of common geometric shapes). Similar items may ask students to manipulate a set of words or images to create a food web or a water cycle.

While these types of manipulations may provide greater insight into student understanding compared to a multiple-choice item, they also introduce potential accessibility barriers. As one example, requiring students to manipulate objects, sometimes with precision, may be challenging for students with fine and gross motor skill needs. Similarly, without knowing the level of precision required to demonstrate understanding of a concept, some students may become focused on aligning objects exactly and, as a result, invest considerable time making very minor and fine-grained manipulations that are not requisite for making an inference about their understanding. For students with vision needs, items that require manipulations may also present challenges when the manipulations require students to visually align or orient objects in an open workspace.

To minimize the influence of these potential construct irrelevant factors, it is important to build tools and methods into the item model that allow students with a variety of needs to interact with the item. As an example, for students who have fine or gross motor needs, methods can be incorporated that allow objects (e.g., line segments in Fig. 16.5) to be selected and maneuvered without the use of a mouse. One method for doing so would allow Tab-Enter manipulation at two levels. At the first or higher level, students would be able to Tab between line segments to select any segment for manipulations. Once selected, students could work at a lower level to perform actual manipulations. Depending on the task, manipulations may include moving the object right, left, up, or down, each of which could be accomplished by tabbing to the desired direction, pressing Enter and pressing Tab to move the object by a predefined amount in the selected direction. For items that require additional types of manipulations, Tab options could allow an object to be rotated in multiple directions, resized, and/or to have its properties altered (e.g., solid versus dotted, arrow head or no arrow head, color, etc.). While performing these manipulations using Tab-Enter is not as efficient as using a mouse, the inclusion of Tab-Enter options ensures that a broader spectrum of students can interact with the item type.

As a further support, interactive items can include "snap" or predefined increment rules. As an example, a snap rule may automatically align the endpoint of two line segments when they are brought into close proximity (e.g., 5 pixels) of each other. Similarly, predefined increments may move line segments a specific number of pixels with each movement (e.g., 10 pixels) or may rotate the object by a predefined number of degrees (e.g., 10 degrees) whether manipulated with a mouse or by Tab-Entering. Predefined rules for manipulating objects can simplify

The line segments shown below can be translated (they can slide) around on the screen, but you cannot rotate (turn) them. Create as many rectangles as you can with the segments (each line segment can only be used once). Then drag the extra segments into the shaded area.

How many rectangles could you make?

[_____] **Type in numbers only**

Explain why you could NOT use the extra segments to make a rectangle.

extra segments

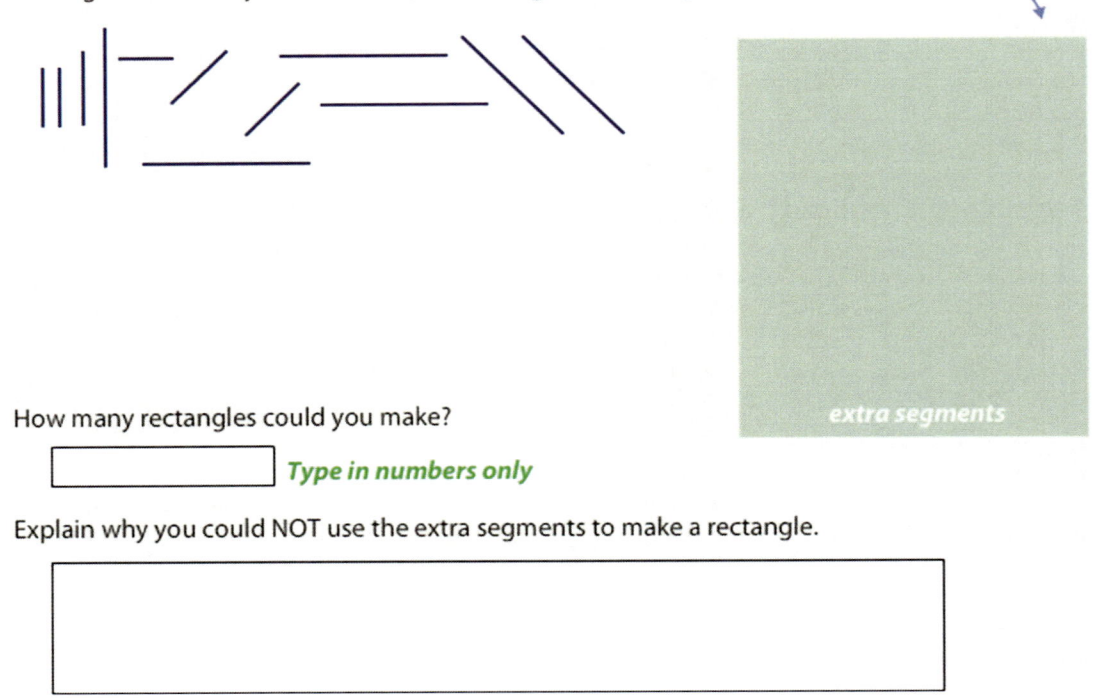

Fig. 16.5 Item requiring the manipulation of line segments

manipulations and support the student's effort to demonstrate knowledge and understanding rather than the process of performing a digital manipulation. As an example, the item depicted in Fig. 16.5 is designed to measure student understanding of the properties of geometric shapes, in this case that a rectangle contains four sides and four right angles such that the two lines forming opposite sides are parallel. To simplify the manipulation, a snap to grid rule might be applied that automatically aligns the ends of two lines when they come within close proximity (say 10 pixels) of each other. Similarly, Tab-Enter might allow the lines to be moved up-down or right-left in 10 pixel increments. Neither of these supports interferes with the knowledge about properties of shapes assessed by this item.

Similar issues must also be considered and addressed for TEIs that require students to produce graphical content (e.g., draw a line or create a diagram) or to work with a simulation. As an example, researchers at Harvard University developed performance assessments designed to measure scientific inquiry that require students to explore and solve problems within a virtual world (Clarke-Midura, Dede, & Norton, 2001). This approach allows a student to apply a variety of data gathering and analytic skills to develop and explore hypotheses. Tasks can also establish complex challenges that simulate problems encountered in the real world yet can embed supports to minimize the influence of construct irrelevant variance. For example, to reduce the influence that content knowledge or familiarity with specific vocabulary has on the measure of scientific inquiry, definitions and examples of vocabulary terms encountered within the virtual environment can be provided to students upon request. Similarly, when students encounter roadblocks or experience difficulty determining how to proceed with an investigation, hints or scaffolded instructions can be built into the system. These supports help maximize the measure of the intended construct and minimize the influence of unintended constructs.

For students with access needs, however, assessment in virtual environments provide additional challenges. For students with vision needs, the visual display of the environment and need to visually identify zones within the environment that can be explored present challenges. For students with reading-support needs, the presentation of dialogues between characters in a text-based format introduces construct irrelevant variance. When sound is used to portray character dialogues, challenges are introduced for students who communicate in sign language. And the abstract nature of a virtual world presents challenges for students who are developing spatial-relations skills or who require concrete representations.

In reality, the challenges presented by assessments conducted in virtual environments are similar to those encountered when more traditional item types are employed to measure a given construct. However, the complexity of the environments, tasks, interactions, and actions that may occur while the student is engaged with the assessment requires careful planning and decisions to provide access for the full spectrum of students who are expected to demonstrate the knowledge and skills measured by the assessment task.

To meet the needs of students who have vision, auditory, or text-processing needs, the assessment systems can be designed to present alternate representations of content encountered during interactions between characters or through information presented during data collection activities. In fact, the methods incorporated in the APIP standards can be applied to assign braille, signed (ASL or signed English), and auditory representations to the text-based information presented on-screen to students. Alternate representations can then be presented to students based on needs defined in the student's access need profile.

For students whose vision needs present challenges to navigating through a virtual environment and for students who encountered challenges with abstract tasks, the manner in which students navigate through an environment can also be altered. While such a change requires careful design, one option is to present the task as a series of options, with each option representing an action a student can take. As an example, when first entering an environment, the task may be designed to allow students to scan the environment to view various features and to then move to a given feature for further investigation. In one version of the Virtual Performance Scientific Inquiry Assessment task, the initial environment allows students to make contact with a person walking on a beach, access a helicopter to transport to a new location, go scuba diving to explore a kelp bed, interact with a scientist, or visit various landmarks such as a dock, a water plant, and a golf course. As the student rotates his/her avatar within the virtual environment, these options become visible, and the student can select them by moving their avatar to their location within the virtual environment. These options, however, could be presented in a menu format, allowing the student to select a given activity. Each activity could then be presented as a set of additional options. As an example, if the student opted to explore the kelp forest, options might include moving to a specific location to make an observation or to collect data. If data collection is selected, the student might then be presented with a list of data collection instruments that are available and so on. For students with vision needs, actions that may require them to observe features presented in the virtual environment can be substituted with reports from an independent observer. By restructuring the task as a series of options, students with visual support needs and students who may have difficulty working within a virtual environment can still gain access to the optional activities associated with the task and to the content provided through those activities. This branching approach to presenting the task may also be preferred by students with motor skill needs who might have difficulty manipulating an avatar in a virtual environment.

Without question, providing these supports requires considerable investment by task developers. However, tools like APIP make the provision of alternate representations feasible as content is developed. Similarly, allowing students to work through tasks using a branching schema does not require additional planning time since this branching structure would be defined while developing the storyboard for the task.

Common Terminology and Methodology

While most state testing programs now employ the concept of a personal needs profile (PNP), the terminology and methods for creating a profile differ considerably across programs. While this might be acceptable if each state administered only one test and always used the same system for delivery, this is not the case. Currently, most states administer at least three large-scale testing programs, one for the general population of students (e.g., PARCC, Smarter Balanced, or a state-specific test), one for students with severe disabilities (e.g., multistate alternate assessment, DLM, or a state-specific assessment), and an English language proficiency test (e.g., ELPA21). In most cases, each of these assessment programs was developed independent of the other, and a separate contractor is employed to oversee administration of the program. As a result, each program has its own vocabulary for personal needs and its own method of recording needs for each student. For teachers who work with students who participate in these multiple assessment programs, this different vocabulary and methodology can be confusing.

As an example, PARCC and Smarter Balanced both employ the concept of an accessibility needs profile. PARCC employs the same terminology used by the international interoperability standards, namely, *Personal Needs Profile* (PNP). In contrast, Smarter Balanced created its own terminology and calls the profile an *Individual Student Assessment Accessibility Profile* (ISAAP). As shown in Fig. 16.4 (above), both groups have also created a three-tiered framework for accessibility. While some of the terminology is the same (e.g., accommodations), some of it differs (e.g., universal tools versus features for all). Moreover, there are differences in the names given to the supports provided by both programs. From a conceptual perspective, the two programs are almost identical: they employ the concept of a needs profile, have the same three tiers, and provide nearly the same supports. Yet, differences in the terminology used by the two programs create a perception that they differ, and this causes confusion for end users.

As programs continue to evolve, it makes sense for the practitioners, policy makers, parents, and the general public to develop fluency with a single set of terms for these various elements of accessibility. As a starting point, it seems reasonable to employ the terminology found in the APIP standards, since these standards have been adopted by several testing companies and testing programs around the world. In addition, it makes sense to establish a common method for deciding which supports are appropriate for a given student and for recording the need in an information system.

Standardization of Accessibility Supports

Today, most test delivery systems provide several accessibility supports. The functionality of these supports, however, differs noticeably among systems. As an example, audio support (aka read aloud) functions in a variety of ways. In some systems, words are highlighted individually as they are read aloud. In other systems, full sentences are highlighted as each word in the sentence is read. In still other systems, no text is highlighted. In some systems, students must click a "play" button to have text read, while other systems allow students to click directly on words or sentences to be read. Similar differences exist for magnification of content, color contrast, delivery of signed versions of content, and the presentation of content in another language. While these differences may seem minor to a lay audience, for students who are accustomed to one system, the change in functionality can cause confusion and increase cognitive load.

Just as methods for encoding item information have been codified through interoperability standards, a similar opportunity exists for standardizing the functionality of accessibility supports. Doing so will require cooperation among test vendors and may require compromise by testing programs. The end result, however, will minimize construct irrelevant variance by eliminating the need for students to adjust to the nuanced functionality of a given delivery systems accessibility supports.

Common Guidelines

Guidelines for creating accessible test content have become considerably more comprehensive and cover a broader array of accessibility needs. However, like the development of personal needs profiles and embedded supports, these guidelines have been developed in isolation by different testing programs. While many guidelines address similar issues, the guidelines for many issues differ across programs. As an example, the New England Comprehensive Assessment Program (NECAP) did not allow numbers in mathematics items to be read aloud while PARCC and Smarter Balanced do. Similarly, when presenting content in American Sign Language, some programs require finger spelling of words associated with a construct (e.g., triangle), while others allow the signed representation of the word to be presented.

For people who do not require content of be presented in an alternate form, these differences may seem trivial. But for end users, these differences can cause confusion and, in some cases, differ noticeably from common classroom practices. To assure continuity in practices across programs, it makes sense to develop common guidelines. Beyond ensuring consistency for students, common guidelines may have a secondary effect of influencing practice in the classroom and standardizing practices across schools, districts, and states.

Assistive Technology

Most test systems embed a variety of accessibility supports. However, there are some supports that cannot reasonably be embedded into a system or which require external technology. As an example, accessing digital content in braille requires the use of a refreshable braille display. Similarly, for a student with fine or gross motor skill needs, selecting or manipulating content may require the use of an alternate input device like eye gaze software or a dual switch mechanism. There are an increasing number and variety of assistive technologies in use by students with special needs. While some systems support a subset of these assistive technologies, many are not supported. To further increase accessibility of assessments, it is important to continue expanding the number and variety of assistive devices that can work in conjunction with test delivery software.

PNP Decision-Making

A PNP is a mechanism for specifying the accessibility needs for a given student when performing an educational test. In one sense, a PNP is similar to an individual education plan: both focus on the accessibility needs for an individual student. What distinguishes a PNP, however, is (a) the concept that all students, regardless of whether or not they have been identified with a disability, may benefit from one or more accessibility supports and (b) the focus on accessibility during assessment. Given the well-established history and use of IEPs, coupled with their focus on students with defined disabilities, it is reasonable for confusion to exist between an IEP and a PNP. Further, given that IEP decisions are typically made by educators with specific training in disabilities and accommodations, it is expected that general education teachers may not be well positioned to make decisions about the access needs during testing for students who do not have an IEP.

To better support educators and, in the process, improve the quality of information specified in each student's PNP, more training and support are necessary. As one example, New Hampshire led an Enhanced Assessment Grant that focused on PNP training (Higgins, Fedorchak, & Katz, 2012). This training included providing all educators with information about universal design and accessibility during testing. Educators were also provided access to a variety of accessibility supports built into a test delivery system. Finally, a digital form was created to collect information from colleagues, students, and potentially parents about each student's perceived accessibility needs. Students were also provided access to practice sessions in which they could experiment with the various accessibility supports prior to providing input via the digital form. Educators then used information collected through the form to make final decisions about each student's PNP. While there were many ways in which this training and input system could be improved, it demonstrated the value of training for improving the quality of decisions about PNPs and greatly increased focus on making individual decisions rather than assigning supports to groups of students based on common characteristics.

Going forward, more research and development are needed to improve the training and tools to which educators have access to support decisions about the assignment of accessibility supports for each individual student. As one example, a system that simulated a testing experience under different accessibility conditions might help educators identify the conditions that are optimal for a given student. This approach was employed by the AIM Explorer (http://aem.cast.org/navigating/aim-explorer.html#.WEhjU6IrKuU). This tool presented reading passages to students and allowed them to alter the visual and reading accessibility supports active, while they interacted with text-based content. The intent was to help educators make decisions about accessibility supports for reading tests and other interactions with text-based content. One challenge with this approach, however, was that the supports provided by the AIM Explorer differed in how they were implemented compared to some testing and learning platforms. If, however, the method used to provide specific accessibility supports were standardized (as suggested above), a tool like the AIM Explorer may provide a powerful support for making accessibility decisions for each student.

Modifying and Fully Embracing the QTI-APIP Standard

Several testing programs and test vendors have embraced the QTI-APIP standard. Many of these groups are also members of the IMS APIP working group, which collaboratively maintains and extends the standard. This effort has greatly increased the speed with which the standard has been adopted and allowed multiple organizations to work together to develop and administer test content in a more efficient manner. As an example, ETS and Pearson both developed item content for PARCC that complied with QTI-APIP and was ported into a common item bank. Similarly, CTB developed content for NCSC that was ported into a system maintained by Measured Progress. While there were hiccups in both cases, the transfer of content was significantly more efficient than what had occurred when vendors used their own proprietary methods for encoding digital items.

Unfortunately, not all major testing programs have embraced a common interoperability standard. In particular, rather than adopt an existing (albeit relatively new at the time) standard, the Smarter Balanced consortium attempted to create its own standard by modifying a vendor's proprietary standard (Smarter Balanced, 2015). While this may have simplified development of content, it has complicated the distribution of content across systems and led to significant challenges administering tests in several states (Molnar & Ujifusa, 2015; Rabe Thomas, 2015; Richards, 2015). Given the growing number of organizations that actively participate in the IMS APIP work group, it seems reasonable for all members of the testing industry to come on board with the standard and contribute to its refinement over time.

Specifically, there are four critical aspects of APIP that must be addressed. First, the method used to encode content in alternate forms requires content to be replicated multiple times within an item file. This greatly expands the size of item files and increases the amount of quality control checks that must occur. A more efficient method of referencing and encoding item content will greatly improve the efficiency of the standard.

Second, in its current form, APIP is an extension to QTI. In part, this relationship contributes to the inefficiency noted above. But it also allows APIP to be treated as an optional component. Modifying QTI such that APIP is an integrated component will increase efficiency while also furthering focus on the accessibility of assessments.

Third, neither QTI nor APIP provides methods for storing content that is used by several third-party assistive technology devices. As an example, refreshable braille displays require access to a Braille ASCII file (BRF) which encodes information about the braille characters to be displayed. Similarly, several text-to-speech tools require access to Digital Accessible Information System (DAISY) file. A better method for incorporating these file types into QTI is needed to increase the variety of assistive technology devices that can be used during testing.

Fourth, QTI was designed to support efficient and accurate transfer of item content across systems. When it was first developed, QTI was agnostic about how content would be delivered to students. As a result, QTI is not effective for specifying how content is to be formatted or laid out on the screen when it is presented to students. At the time, a variety of approaches were being used to create delivery systems including HTML, Flash, and proprietary coding structures. Since then, HTML has become the dominant method for presenting content via the web browsers. Given this development, QTI should support HTML encoding to control the presentation of content across systems. While this initially may have a minimal impact on accessibility, it will help assure consistency and support valid assessment across systems over the long term.

As of this writing, IMS (2015) has formed a committee to explore the development of aQTI, which promises to be the next iteration of QTI-APIP. Addressing these issues through aQTI and encouraging all testing programs to adopt this standard will further advance interoperable delivery of accessible assessments.

Closing Comment

This chapter described several advances in accessibility that have occurred over the past decade. Many of these advances have capitalized on the flexibility of digital technology to embed accessibility content into test items and accessibility supports into test delivery systems. Using information about each student's accessibility needs, digital tests are now able to customize the content presented to students and the access tools available to them as they perform a test.

While interoperability standards have been created to support the exchange of items across systems and guidelines have been developed to inform the creation of specific representational forms of content, these standards and guidelines differ across programs. In addition, the way in which given access supports function, as well as the terminology employed to describe various access supports, differs across programs. As the field moves forward, there is a vital need to create consistency and commonality across programs with respect to the accessibility supports provided, the functionality of those supports, the terminology employed for those supports, and the guidelines and standards used to inform the development and encoding of accessibility information. While standardizing accessibility will require compromise by assessment programs and test vendors, it will solidify these recent advances as standard practice and holds promise to create common practices and expectations across classrooms.

References

Center for Universal Design (CUD). (1997). *About UD: Universal design principles.* http://www.design.ncsu.edu/cud/about_ud/udprincipleshtmlformat.html. Accessed 13 Feb 2009. Archived at http://www.webcitation.org/5eZBa9RhJ

Clarke-Midura, J., Dede, C., & Norton, J. (2001). Next generation assessments for measuring complex learning in science. In D. Plank, J. Norton, C. Arraez, & I. Washington (Eds.), *The road ahead for state assessments.* Cambridge, MA: Rennie Center fro Education Research & Policy.

Dolan, R. P., Hall, T. E., Banerjee, M., Chun, E., & Strangman, N. (2005). Applying principles of universal design to test delivery: The effect of computer-based read-aloud on test performance of high school students with learning disabilities. *Journal of Technology, Learning, and Assessment, 3*(7), 3–32. Downloaded June 21, 2015 from https://ejournals.bc.edu/ojs/index.php/jtla/article/download/1660/1496

Higgins, J., Fedorchak, G., & Katz, M. (2012). *Assignment of accessibility tools for digitally delivered assessments: Key findings.* Dover, NH: Measured Progress.

IMS Global Learning Consortium. (2014). *IMS accessible portable item protocol (APIP): Conformance and certification.* Accessed 15 Dec 2016 from http://www.imsglobal.org/apip/apipv1p0/APIP_CFC_v1p0.html

IMS Global Learning Consortium. (2015). *aQTI v3.0 charter approved.* Downloaded August 4, 2015 from https://www.imsglobal.org/forum/question-test-interoperability-public-forum/133781

Measured Progress/ETS. (2012a). *Smarter balanced assessment consortium: Mathematics audio guidelines.* Downloaded August 4, 2016 from https://portal.smarterbalanced.org/library/en/mathematics-audio-guidelines.pdf

Measured Progress/ETS. (2012b). *Smarter balanced assessment consortium: Guidelines for accessibility for english language learners.* Downloaded August 4, 2016 from https://portal.smarterbalanced.org/library/en/guidelines-for-accessibility-for-english-language-learners.pdf

Measured Progress/ETS. (2012c). *Smarter balanced assessment consortium: Signing guidelines.* Downloaded August 4, 2016 from https://portal.smarterbalanced.org/library/en/signing-guidelines.pdf

Measured Progress/ETS. (2012d). *Smarter balanced assessment consortium: Tactile accessibility guidelines.* Downloaded August 4, 2016 from https://portal.smarterbalanced.org/library/en/tactile-accessibility-guidelines.pdf

Mislevy, R. J., Behrens, J. T., Bennett, R. E., Demark, S. F., Frezzo, D. C., Levy, R., ... Winters, F. I. (2010). On the roles of external knowledge representations in assessment design. *Journal of Technology, Learning, and Assessment, 8*(2). Downloaded December 15, 2016 from http://www.jtla.org

Molnar, M., & Ujifusa, A. (2015, May 4). *Vendors at odds over Nevada testing problems.* Education Week.

National Center on Educational Outcomes. (2016). *Smarter balanced assessment consortium: Usability, accessibility, and accommodations guidelines.* Downloaded August 4, 2015 from https://portal.smarterbalanced.org/library/en/usability-accessibility-and-accommodations-guidelines.pdf

Partnership for Assessment of Readiness for College and Careers. (2015). *PARCC accessibility features and accommodations manual.* Downloaded August 4, 2016 from http://www.parcconline.org/images/Assessments/Acccessibility/PARCC_Accessibility_Features__Accommodations_Manual_v.6_01_body_appendices.pdf

Rabe Thomas, J. (2015, May 20). *Union calls problems with smarter balanced exams 'pervasive'.* The CT Mirror.

Richards, E. (2015, March 26). Latest glitch delays common core exam in Wisconsin. *Milwaukee Wisconsin Journal Sentinel.*

Rose, D., & Meyer, A. (2000). Universal design for learning, associate editor column. *Journal of Special Education Technology, 15*(1), 66–67.

Russell, M. (2011). Accessible Test Design. In M. Russell & M. Kavanaugh (Eds.), *Assessing students in the margin: Challenges, strategies, and techniques.* Charlotte, NC: Information Age Publishing.

Russell, M., Higgins, J., & Hoffmann, T. (2009). *Meeting the needs of all students: A universal design approach to computer-based testing.* Innovate.

Russell, M., Mattson, D., Higgins, J., Hoffmann, T., Bebell, D., & Alcaya, C. (2011). *A Primer to the Accessible Portable Item Profile (APIP) Standards,* Minnesota Department of Education.

Smarter Balanced. (2015). *End of grant report.* Downloaded July 25, 2016 from http://www.smarterbalanced.org/wp-content/uploads/2015/08/SB-EndOfGrantReport-F2.pdf

Thompson, S., Thurlow, M., & Malouf, D. B. (n.d.). *Creating better tests for everyone through universal designed assessments.* Washington, DC: U.S. Department of Education. Downloaded June 3, 2016 from http://www.testpublishers.org/assets/documents/volume%206%20issue%201%20Creating%20%20better%20tests.pdf

Accessibility Progress and Perspectives

17

Stephen N. Elliott, Ryan J. Kettler, Peter A. Beddow, and Alexander Kurz

Over the past decade, progress has been happening with accessibility policies, professional development, and practices across the United States and a number of foreign countries. Much more progress is needed, however, if all students are to benefit from accessible instructional and testing practices. Although we do not have a national or international score card to share at this time, we have a strong sense progress is happening based on the perspectives of the expert authors reporting in this volume.

In this final chapter, we recount and highlight key points from the preceding chapters made about accessibility policies, professional development, and practical tools/frameworks to guide practice. Based on this "progress update," we observe some steps that can be taken to advance instructional and testing practices to make learning more accessible for all students. Although there is a desire to be disruptive in our call for next steps, a strategy for accomplishing a constructive disruption has yet to emerge. This may disappoint some readers, but on balance, it should motivate many others to continue efforts to pursue more accessible schools, instruction, materials, and tests for all students.

Progress Perspectives

The multitalented, experienced authors for this volume have provided us a comprehensive update on efforts to advance the accessibility of instructional and testing practices for all students. Allow us to share some of the highlights from the preceding chapters with the end goal of identifying emerging themes for accessibility research and practices.

Weigert, an experienced leader at the federal level in the United States, in her policy-focused chapter stated that in considering access for SWDs, it is critical to distinguish between policies about content standards and policies about performance standards. Content standards are intended for all students, while performance standards should be at a level that encourages continual progress. She also noted policy debates persist around whether students with significant cognitive disabilities should be taught life skills vs. academic skills and whether public schools should provide students with disabilities a

S. N. Elliott (✉)
Arizona State University, Tempe, AZ, USA
e-mail: steve_elliott@asu.edu

R. J. Kettler
Rutgers, The State University of New Jersey, Piscataway, NJ, USA
e-mail: r.j.kettler@rutgers.edu

P. A. Beddow
Accessible Hope, LLC, Nashville, TN, USA
e-mail: peterbeddow@gmail.com

A. Kurz
Arizona State University, Tempe, AZ, USA
e-mail: Alexander.Kurz@asu.edu

significant educational benefit versus a minimal one. Finally, she noted that promoting equity for SWDs requires the use of within-year assessments that can monitor progress.

Davies, an active researcher and special education leader in Australia, in his chapter on international policies noted the United Nations Convention requires signatories to provide accommodations for students with disabilities that support them with academic and social development. He also noted polices for inclusive practices in instruction and curriculum seem to be accepted more readily than inclusive practices in assessment.

Stone and Cook, both experienced psychometricians with a leading testing/learning enterprise, in their chapter noted that creating accessible tests begins with defining several important properties (e.g., construct, content, format) and continues through every step, and stressed students with a disability or status as a language minority were inspirational to the development of many accessibility features of tests. In the development of a test, these authors suggested evidence should be documented indicating how the characteristics of a diverse population of individuals were taken into consideration in defining or choosing constructs.

Chia and Kachchaf, experienced leaders for multistate large-scale assessment programs, echoed many of the points of Stone and Cook and stressed that a team of experts was needed from the beginning of the test development process to ensure consideration of the needs of a diverse population of students at each step of the development. Specifically, they encouraged one leader at each stage should have expertise in language development, and at least one leader should have expertise in disabilities. They also noted diversity is important among stakeholders, who can provide feedback on assessment design and implementation.

Frey and Gillispies, university-based special education researchers, reported on the access needs of students with disabilities and provided us some hope with research on the status of students with disabilities. Specifically, they noted over the past decade more students with disabilities have been spending more time in general education classrooms, and the rate of achievement growth for students with disabilities as measured by performance on state tests is actually very similar to students without disabilities. These signs of progress were attributed to a number of factors, including the use of inclusive instruction and testing practices.

Beddow, an independent scientist-practitioner, provided us a focused examination of the fast-growing disability group, students with autism. Given the increasing prevalence of autism spectrum disorders (ASD), Beddow suggested it is important that attention be given to cognitive load issues in the design of test events, particularly in terms of eliminating redundancy and other sources of extraneous load and familiarizing students with test-taking procedures, including navigating the test delivery system and using test materials. He also noted that some test events may represent deprivation conditions for many students with ASD. To reduce the impact of the perceived deprivation that may be experienced, test administrators should consider allowing ample opportunity before, after, and even during test events to access preferred stimuli to reduce anxiety for these students.

Boals, Castro, and Wilner, the leadership team of the largest national assessment program for ELL students, provided us a thoughtful examination of accessibility, and in particular the opportunity to learn, from the perspective of English language learners (ELLs), the fastest growing segment of the public school enrollment in the United States. Recognizing the challenge of distinguishing between language difference and special learning disability and noting the rather pervasive achievement gaps with ELLs in comparison to native-speaking students, they contend changes in thinking about these students, and their instruction is in order. Specifically, they contend good teaching for ELL students must involve a sociocultural reframing of UDL principles that emphasizes culturally and linguistically sustainable pedagogies; doing so would help students sustain their cultural and linguistic identities while still learning valued content commonly assessed.

Kurz, a university-based scientist-practitioner, advanced his influential opportunity to learn (OTL) model based on time, content, and quality indices by addressing what is currently known about high-quality Tier 1 instruction. To this end, he reviewed the RTI literature and provided additional quality indices related to the use of differentiated instruction, instructional accommodations, progress monitoring, and universal screening. He then operationalized time, content, and quality indices based on available empirical evidence for purposes of defining and assessing high-quality Tier 1 instruction. Kurz argued that measuring access to high-quality Tier 1 instruction is fundamental to the logic and efficacy of all RTI approaches. His refined OTL model can assist researchers and practitioners in doing so and thereby provide critical instructional data about the provision of high-quality Tier 1 instruction. Such data are important for understanding the extent to which students are responding to primary prevention (i.e., high-quality Tier 1 instruction), determining access to the general curriculum, and guiding instructional improvement efforts.

Glover, another university-based scientist-practitioner, examined the role of accessibility in a response to intervention (RTI) model for supporting the instructional needs of all students. He stressed five aspects of services needed to facilitate students' access to, and participation in, high-quality instruction including (a) comprehensive student assessment via screening, diagnostic measurement, and progress monitoring, (b) standardized data-based decision-making, (c) multitiered implementation of student support based on a continuum of needs, (d) provision of evidence-based instruction and intervention, and (e) multi-stakeholder involvement in coordinated leadership. Each of these components is needed to ensure access is adequately provided. This approach to student support requires substantial teacher professional development, which in many cases has not been achieved, thus limiting access of students to the support levels needed to be effective.

The author team of Rose, Robinson, Hall, Coyne, Jackson, Stahl, and Wilcauskas, all centrally involved in one of the leading educational research and development organizations in the United States, provided us a chapter that takes a close look, and in several ways a new look, at Universal Design for Learning (UDL) and its core principles (i.e., provide multiple means of engagement, provide multiple means of representation, and provide multiple means of action and expression). Within this popular design and learning support framework, they stressed the ultimate goal of education can no longer be the mastery of specific knowledge or skills, but the mastery of learning itself and the preparation of expert learners. This is a big and new challenge for educators, taking accessibility to a new level and requiring massive and sustainable preservice and in-service teacher professional development, consistent with a universal mindset for learning.

Moving from a focus on instruction to one on testing, Albano and Rodriguez, both university-based psychometricians, presented guidelines for the design of accessible tests, with specific guidance for writing items. They emphasized items should target one cognitive task, rather than multiple tasks. They indicated items should be formatted vertically; reading load should be minimized; and vocabulary and linguistic complexity should be commensurate with the target construct and target population. The authors provided specific guidelines for the design of item elements. For example, the item stem should be worded positively, avoiding negative phrasing. When conventional multiple-choice items are used, three options typically are sufficient, and all options should be plausible and discriminating. Only one option should be correct, and the location of the item key should be varied. Response options should not overlap in content and should be ordered numerically or logically when possible. The authors recommended avoiding the use of *none of the above*, *all of the above*, and *I don't know*. The authors also explored some recent computer-enabled innovations that have permitted the use of novel item types such as those requiring graphical modeling, sorting and ordering, and correcting sentences with grammatical errors or mathematical statements. This chapter nicely demonstrates the direct relationship between test items, accessibility, and test performance. Thus, without highly accessible items, the results are likely misleading.

In Beddow's second chapter, the author focused on cognitive load theory (CLT) to explain what likely happens when the cognitive demand of a test or test item exceeds the working memory capacity for a test-taker and indicated that resulting inferences from test scores should not be considered valid. Beddow recommended test developers use advances in cognitive load theory (CLT) to ensure the validity of test score inferences, specifically by eliminating extraneous cognitive load and isolating the intrinsic load of tests and test items. He provided a rich example of how CLT strategies can be used to reduce extraneous cognitive load by eliminating redundancy, avoiding seductive details, reducing language load, presenting information across two modalities to permit simultaneous processing, and using worked examples for mathematics items. As illustrated by Beddow, CLT is a practical theory that has been operationalized to inform test design.

Dembitzer, a school psychologist, and Kettler, a university-based researcher, explored testing adaptations as a means of ensuring fairness and accessibility. These authors recommended test administrators select adaptations only after identifying and verifying the test-taker has a functional impairment in an area that represents an accessibility barrier for the test being considered. Moreover, they argued appropriate adaptations should maintain, or even increase, the internal consistency of a test for the group of students who receive adapted tests. Of greatest importance is the *targeted skills or knowledge question*, as follows: "If selected, will the adaptation or adaptations change the construct being measured by the test?" Answering this question requires clearly articulated constructs and a body of validity evidence based on (a) test content, (b) response processes, (c) internal structure, and (d) relations to other variables.

Sireci, Banda, and Wells, a team of university-based measurement experts, also explored issues of testing accommodations and adaptations, but focused on their use for ELLs. They described fairness and accommodations as "the psychometric oxymoron," whereby some accommodations that are intended to reduce construct-irrelevant variance actually introduce it. Therefore, appropriate accommodations are those that promote validity by ensuring the target construct is unfettered. Only if construct equivalence can be maintained across accommodated and unaccommodated tests can resulting scores be deemed comparable. For ELLs, a distinction often is made between accommodations that provide direct linguistic support, such as translations of directions, test items, etc., and those that represent simplified language. For both types, the same goal remains: to promote the validity of test score inferences without giving an unfair advantage to the accommodated group. The authors also discussed accommodations for test-takers with significant cognitive disabilities (such as alternate assessments) and reviewed methods for evaluating the effects of testing accommodations. They argued that with increasingly rapid advancements in technology changing the assessment landscape, accommodations need not compromise the validity of test results, but rather should be understood as a means to increase validity.

Finally, Russell, a university-based researcher and technology innovator, examined the field of computer-based testing, which arguably has come to maturity in the past decade. He described accessible test design as a means to tailor the presentation of, and interaction with, test content, to ensure nontarget constructs do not influence test results and subsequent inferences. The opportunities for flexibility that are enabled by computer-based test delivery systems exceed those of paper-based tests, which often require different versions of materials for subgroups. Even the need for translators and interpreters can be addressed automatically, significantly reducing resource requirements and increasing the availability of such individualized accommodations. Personal needs profiles (PNPs) can store information for individual test-takers and can be used to toggle various accessibility tools and features. PNPs can interact with the delivery interface and with the test content. Russell also explored the concept of standardized accessibility as a means to prevent having to retrofit tests and test items to meet individual test-taker needs. Ideally, interoperability standards such as Question Test Interoperability (QTI) and the Accessible Portable Item Protocol Standard (APIP) can even permit assessment programs to transfer assessment content across authoring, item banking, and test delivery platforms (e.g., when changing test vendors). Russell explored technology-enhanced items (TEIs), which are discrete items that often require dragging and dropping content into categories, etc. These types of items can provide greater insight into student learning when compared to traditional SR items, but – as Albano and Rodriguez noted – these items also may bring accessibility challenges to bear. Russell argued test developers should ensure tools and methods are built into test systems to allow students with various needs to interact with all items, including TEIs.

Collectively, across the 15 core chapters in this book, we perceived four accessibility progress themes. First, virtually all authors indicate accessibility is now widely seen as a central aspect of educational equity, much more than a set of adjustments or modifications made to instruction or tests to improve the validity of test score inferences. A number of authors noted the growing need to broaden perspectives on the students in need of access, including in particular the growing groups of ELL and students with ASD, as well as the role of cultural and context as part of the conceptualization of accessibility for all students. Many of the authors also indicated accessibility research and practices are being driven effectively by practical theories and principles, such as universal design for learning (UDL) and cognitive load theory (CLT), as well as a new set of professional testing standards conceptualized under the concept of fairness. Finally, a fourth prevalent progress theme is accessibility features need to be built into instruction and testing materials from the beginning. Thus, the notion of *born accessible* is taking root, particularly as more instruction and assessments are being offered in a digitized manner.

Onward

The education of all children is a large and complex enterprise. Education that is accessible for all children must continue to influence this enterprise and, in fact, play a central role in designing key aspects of student support, instructional delivery, and testing practices. We all know children differ in a number of ways, have different strengths and weaknesses, and express different preferences for learning. Thus, it is not surprising that children have different instructional and testing needs. School must be the place – of all the places in children's lives – that adjusts to allow the time, space, and support needed to learn. If schools cannot or will not do this, no other place will.

The conditions for continued growth toward accessible instructional and testing practices for all children are good to great in schools today. That is, educational policies and professional standards and guidelines have helped to create a mindset that accessibility is central to a fair and equitable schooling experience. Professional development efforts are frequently occurring to support educators' use of UDL principles in their daily practices. More tests are born accessible and are more often being delivered in a manner that recognizes individuals' needs without jeopardizing the validity of the resulting scores. More, however, remains to be done in each of these arenas by leaders, teachers, researchers, parents, and students. If the focus on accessible instruction and testing practices continues, education will be better for all of us. Based on the past decade of research and development work reported in this book, we have evidence-based hope this will happen!

Index

A
Ableism, 20
Academic competence evaluation scales, 7
Academic enablers, 7
Accessibility, 189–191, 233
 assessments, 70, 71
 case study, 2, 3
 curriculum and instruction, 127
 defined, 1
 DOK, 129
 educational principle, 1
 formative assessment, 128
 key uses, 129
 language awareness, 128
 learning, 128
 NBT, 2
 needs, 102
 opportunities, 1
 optimal, 1
 strategies and resources, 1
 student-centered approaches, 128
 test, 2
 UDL, 127
Accessibility progress
 academic and social development, 264
 ASD, 264
 child education, 267
 CLT, 266
 cognitive task, 265
 computer-enabled innovations, 265
 constructive disruption, 263
 educational equity, 267
 educational research and development organizations, 265
 ELLs, 264, 266
 high-quality Tier 1 instruction, 265
 instructional and testing practices, 263
 item elements, 265
 life vs. academic skills, 263
 multistate large-scale assessment programs, 264
 national assessment program, 264
 OTL model, 265
 PNPs, 266
 professional development, 263, 267
 progress update, 263
 psychometricians, 264
 student services, 265
 SWDs, 263
 targeted skills/knowledge question, 266
 teacher professional development, 265
 TEIs, 267
 testing accommodations, 266
 university-based special education researchers, 264
Accessibility Rating Matrix (ARM), 9
Accessibility resources, 78, 79, 81, 84, 86, 87
Accessibility support
 accessible test design, 249
 assistive technology, 259
 digital technology, 261
 flexible presentation of content, 249, 250
 guidelines, 259
 implementation model, 250
 interoperability standards, 261
 item development process, 254
 line segments, 256
 next-generation assessment systems, 254
 PARCC and Smarter Balanced, 254
 PNP, 250, 251, 259, 260
 policies, 252–254
 QTI-APIP standard, 260, 261
 sample access profile, 251
 Smarter Balanced guidelines, 253
 standardization, 251, 252, 258, 259
 tailored delivery of content, 250
 TEI, 255–258
 terminology and methodology, 258
 test content guidelines, 252
 universal design and assessment, 248, 249
Accessible computer-based national assessment, *see* Computer-based assessment
Accessible instruction, 136
Accessible Portable Item Protocol Standard (APIP), 252, 267
Accessible test design, 249
Accessible testing, 65–70
Access skill question, 224
Access skills, 95
 appropriate adaptations, 4

Access skills (cont.)
  assumptions, 3
  description, 3
  legislative basis, 12
  three-step process, 4
Accommodation policy, 68, 69
Accommodations, 1, 3, 4, 6, 9, 13, 79, 80, 98
Achievement gap analyses
  family income, 123
  language community, 125
  "long-termer", 124
  NAEP, 123
  NCLB, 122
  SES, 122, 123
  targets and student performance, 125
Achievement testing, 107, 108, 181
Actionable feedback, 174
Advisory Committees, 85
Alternate assessment based on modified academic achievement standards (AA-MAS), 29, 30, 107, 190
Alternate assessments for alternate academic achievement standards (AA-AAS), 27, 69, 189
Alternative assessments, 47, 50, 54
Alternative Scoring Methods, 194–195
American Educational Research Association (AERA), 1, 59, 213, 232
American Psychological Association (APA), 1, 59, 213, 232
American Sign Language (ASL), 83, 86, 248
Americans with Disabilities Act, 68
Anxiety, 109, 110
Applied behavior analysis (ABA), 108, 110, 111
Assessment accommodations checklist (AAC), 225
Assessment design, 85
Assistive technology (AT), 81, 259
Attention-deficit hyperactivity disorder (ADHD), 98
Australia
  assessment policies, 50, 51
  inclusive assessment, 48–50
Autism spectrum disorder (ASD), 264
  ABA, 110, 111
  anxiety, 109, 110
  assessment, 108
  behavioral momentum, 114, 115
  characteristics, 108
  consistency and predictability, 113
  diagnosis, 108
  DSM-V, 108
  DTT, 112
  EBPs, 114
  fluency practice, 114
  hyperspecificity, 114
  prevalence, 108
  schedules, routines and procedures, 113
  testing
    differential reinforcement, 111, 112
    discriminative stimulus, 112
    functional analysis, 111
    problem behavior, 111
    problem behaviors, 111
    requisite skills, 112
    test-taking skills, 114
    test validity, 107
    transitions, 115, 116

B
Behavioral momentum, 114–116
Born accessible, 267
Braille ASCII file (BRF), 261

C
Carroll's model, 139
Case-based instruction, 99
Center for Applied Special Technology (CAST), 119
Channel capacity, 200
Checklist of Learning and Assessment Adjustments for Students (CLASS), 147, 151
China
  assessment policies, 53, 54
  inclusive assessment, 51–53
Classroom connections, 13
Coefficient alpha, 218
Cognitive disabilities, 101
Cognitive labs, 86
Cognitive load theory (CLT), 8, 109, 110, 266, 267
  accessible assessments, 199
  applicability, 200
  channel capacity, 200
  cognitive skill demands, 200
  communication channel, 200
  completion, 204
  dual-channel assumption, 202
  element interactivity, 203
  future learning, 204
  grade 6 mathematics, 207
  human intellectual capacity, 201
  implications, 201
  instructional design strategies, 204
  knowledge acquisition, 200
  learning, 201
  limited capacity assumption, 203
  long-term memory, 201
  objective cognitive load measurement, 209
  origins and principles, 200–204
  PBTs, 203
  principles and assumptions, 200, 203
  proponents, 203
  split-attention effect, 204
  test accessibility, 199
  test event, 199
  test-taker characteristics, 199
Cognitive neuroscience approach, 120
Common Core State Standards (CCSS), 75, 147
Comparative fit index (CFI), 243
Complex multiple choice, 183
Comprehension and collaboration, 150
Computer-based assessments
  accessibility resources, 86

Index 271

AT, 89
cognitive labs, 86
context-specific information, 86, 89
expertise, 85
flexibility
　accessibility resources, 79, 81
　accommodations, 80
　ASL resource, 83
　AT, 81
　color contrast, 80
　english glossaries, 79
　individual student, 79
　ISAAP tool, 81, 83
　translated glossaries, 83, 84
　universal tools, 79
heterogeneity
　assessment resources, 78
　ELA assessments, 78–79
　english proficient, 78
　ethnicity, 77
　gender, 77
ISAAP, 88
language development and disabilities, 88
reviewer feedback, 86
stakeholders, 88
UAAC, 84
UAAG, 88
Computer-based test delivery systems, 254, 266
Computer-based tests (CBTs), 192, 203
Computer-enabled innovations, 193
Confirmatory factor analysis (CFAs), 223, 242
Constructed-response formats, 182
Constructed-response guidelines, 186
Construct-irrelevant variance, 232
Construct under-representation, 232
Construct validity, 220
Content concerns, 187
Content coverage (CC), 144
Content standards, 1, 4–6
Content validity, 220
Context concerns, 187
Conventional multiple choice, 183
Council for Exceptional Children (CEC), 22
CTB/McGraw Hill's guidelines, 215
Cultural neutrality, 119, 120, 125, 130
Curriculum-based measurement (CBM)
　assessments, 24, 162

D
Data-based decision-making, 158
Department of Education (ED), 20
Depth of Knowledge (DOK), 129
DIBELS Next Nonsense Word Fluency
　assessment, 158
Differential boost, 217, 224, 227
Differential item functioning (DIF)
　analysis, 70, 221, 241
Differential reinforcement, 110
Digital Accessible Information System (DAISY), 261

Direct linguistic support, 236
Disabilities Education Act of 1997, 213
Disability category, 120
Discipline-specific language development, 119
Discrete trial training (DTT), 112
Discriminative stimuli, 110, 113
Dual-channel assumption, 202
Dual-function tests, 208
Dynamic learning maps (DLM), 239

E
easyCBM, 150
Educational equity, 267
1975 Education for All Handicapped Act, 247
Educational testing
　accommodations, 233
　construct
　　description, 232
　　irrelevant variance, 232
　　under-representation, 232
　fairness in testing, 233
　modifications, 233
　validity, 232
Educational Testing Service (ETS), 186
Elementary algebra, 232
Elementary and Secondary Education
　Act (ESEA), 21, 75, 122, 218
Element interactivity effect, 203, 207
Elimination testing, 194
Emotional and behavioral disorders (EBD), 98
English Language Arts (ELA), 147, 219
English Language Learner Advisory Committee
　(ELLAC), 84
English language learners (ELLs), 86, 264
　bilingualism, 125
　cultural and linguistic misconceptions, 119
　ESSA, 122
　gap analyses (*see* Achievement gap analyses)
　inclusion, 125
　schooling access, 121, 122
　sociocultural approaches, 120, 126, 127
　teaching and learning systems (*see* Accessibility)
　UDL, 119
　in United States, 121, 125
English learners (ELs), 61, 75, 78
　accommodations, 231, 238
　cognitive disabilities, 231
　educational assessment, 231
　standardization tests, 231
　validity issues, 231
Ethnicity, 77
European Agency for Special Needs and inclusive
　education, 40–42
Every Student Succeeds Act (ESSA), 12, 17, 31–33, 75,
　107, 122, 167, 178, 213
Evidence-based practices (EBPs), 114
Expert working memory and environment
　organizing and linking principle, 202
Extraneous load, 203, 205

F

Fairness and accessible tests
  accommodations and accessibility features, 64
  assessment programs, 70
  computer-/tablet-based test format, 64
  construct-irrelevant variance, 63
  content, 62
  device comparability and input, 64
  disability subtypes/categories, 61
  ELs, 61
  format, 63
  language, 62
  large-scale assessment, 64
  mathematics items, 63
  paper-and-pencil situations, 64, 65
  PARCC, 63
  response mode, 65
  TTS, 63
  universal tools, 63
  validity and score interpretability, 61
Florida Center for Reading Research website, 165
Formatting and style concerns, 185, 187
Free and appropriate education (FAPE), 121

G

General instruction time (GET), 149

H

Handbook of Accessible Instruction and Testing Practices, 12, 13
Handbook of Test Development, 184
Historical test statistics, 115
Hyperspecificity, 114

I

Inclusion
  accommodations, 98, 103
  benefits, 94
  children, 95
  classroom settings, 98
  defined, 94
  employment outcomes, 103
  IEP, 102
  opportunity to learn, 95
  postsecondary education, 102, 103
  summary of performance, 102
  transition research, 103
Inclusive assessment
  accessible and appropriate assessments, 43, 44
  accommodations and adjustments, 47
  all children and young people, 43, 47
  alternate assessments, 47
  Australia, 38, 48–50
  China, 38, 51–53
  comparative studies, 37
  European Agency for Special Needs and inclusive education, 40–42
  macro-policy initiatives, 38
  measure and document areas of relevance, 45, 48
  micro-policy initiatives, 45–46
  national, state and classroom assessment, 43
  OECD, 39, 40
  OTL, 47
  schools and school systems accountability, 37
  special education and inclusive education settings, 37
  Standards for Educational and Psychological Testing, 42, 43
  UNESCO, 39
  United Nations Convention, 38
  United States of America, 46, 47
  universally designed systems, 48
Indirect linguistic support, 237
Individualized Education Program (IEP), 19, 47, 77, 80, 97, 143, 220, 252
Individual Student Assessment Accessibility Profile (ISAAP), 81–83, 258
Individuals with Disabilities Education Act (IDEA), 47, 77, 108, 248
Innovative assessment systems (IAS), 76
Instructional coaching, 152
Instructional Learning Opportunities Guidance System (MyiLOGS), 6, 141
Instructional time (IT), 144
Internal consistency, 218
International Association for the Evaluation of Educational Achievement (IEA), 139
International policies, *see* Inclusive assessment
Interpretation of Achievement Test Scores (IATS) Paradigm, 2, 4–12
Item development process, 185
  AA-AAS, 190
  AA-MAS, 190
  accessibility, 189–191
  constructed-response formats, 182
  CR formats, 182, 184
  fundamentals, 182
  GRE and TOEFL, 193
  incorrect response options, 189
  item-writing process, 184
  legislation and federal regulations, 182
  MC, 183
  multiple true/false item, 195
  SR and CR items, 184, 185
  standardized student achievement tests, 181
  TAMI, 190, 193
Item quality, 191–192
Item response theory (IRT), 241, 242

J

Judgmental policy capturing (JPC), 152

K

Key uses, academic language, 129, 130

Index

L
Large-scale testing, 181
Learning in Regular Classrooms (LRC) program, 52
Least restrictive environment (LRE), 19
Legislation and federal regulations, 182
Limited capacity assumption, 202, 203
Linguistic simplification, 237
Longitudinal Study of Australian Children (LSAC), 51
Long-term memory, 201

M
Macro-policy initiatives, 38
Metric invariance tests, 243
Micro-policy initiatives, 45–46
Minnesota Center for Reading Research website, 165
Modality effect, 205
Motivating operations, 110
Multidimensional scaling (MDS), 241, 242
Multiple-choice (MC) items, 183

N
National Accessible Reading Assessment Project (NARAP), 193
National Assessment of Education Progress (NAEP), 20, 123, 124, 221
National Assessment Program for Literacy and Numeracy (NAPLAN), 49
National Center and State Collaborative (NCSC), 239, 250
National Center on Educational Outcomes (NCEO), 22, 69, 217
National Center on Intensive Intervention website, 164
National Center on Response to Invention website, 164
National Commission on Excellence in Education, 20
National Council on Measurement in Education (NCME), 1, 213, 232
National Disability Insurance Screen (NDIS), 51
National Educational Technology Plan, 167
National Governors Association (NGA), 75
Nationally Consistent Collection of Data on School Students with Disability (NCCDSS), 50
Nemeth code, 63
New England Comprehensive Assessment Program (NECAP), 259
NimbleTools®, 250
2002 No Child Left Behind Act (NCLB), 26, 27, 75, 248
Novice working memory and narrow limits of change, 202

O
Observational methods, 192
Office of Special Education Programs (OSEP), 21
Online smarter mathematics summative assessments
    accessibility resources, 79
    ethnicity, 77
    gender, 77
    LEP, IDEA, 504/low SES, 78
    translated glossaries, 79

Opportunity to learn (OTL), 5–7, 47, 53, 95, 97, 115, 128, 135, 137–142, 265
    See also Tier 1 instruction
Optical character recognition (OCR), 65
Organisation for Economic Co-operation and Development (OECD), 38–40

P
PARCC and smarter balanced assessment, 214
Partnership for Assessment of Readiness for College and Careers (PARCC), 63, 76, 213
Path to Reading Excellence in School Site (PRESS), 165
Peabody Journal of Education, 190
Personal accessibility needs profile, 250, 251
Personal needs profile (PNP), 214, 251, 258, 266
Primary processing categories, 120
Problem-solving and the randomness as genesis principle, 201
Problem-solving process, 99
Program for International Student Assessment (PISA), 39, 139
Psychometric oxymoron, 233, 234, 266

Q
Question and Test Interoperability–Accessible Portable Item Protocol (QTI-APIP), 249
Question Test Interoperability (QTI), 251, 267

R
"Race to the Top" (RTT) assessment initiatives, 30–31, 247
Rasch model, 223
Redundancy effect, 205
Response to intervention (RTI) model, 28, 99, 135, 265
    accessibility, 157–160
    comprehensive assessment approach, 158
    decision-making criteria, 163, 164
    efficacy, 157
    evidence-based and specialized instruction/intervention, 160
    evidence-based resources, 164, 165
    existing research support, 162
    facilitative administrative support and team-based leadership, 161
    guide instructional decisions, 162
    high-quality instruction, 160–162
    implementation drivers/engines, 161
    implementation fidelity assessment, 162
    job-embedded coaching, 161
    multi-stakeholder involvement, 160
    multi-tiered supports, 157–160, 163
    organizational structures, 157
    school personnel, 163
    second grade decision tree, 159
    service delivery models, 157, 165
    standardized data-based decision-making, 158
    teacher professional development, 164
    unresponsive students, 164
Root mean square error of approximation (RMSEA), 243

S

Schema theory, 201
Scholastic Aptitude Reasoning Test, 220
Score comparability, 68
Second International Mathematics Studies (SIMS), 139
Seductive detail effect, 205
Selected-response (SR) formats, 183, 185
Short-term memory, 200
Significant disabilities
 access to testing, 101
 accommodations and supports, 101
 assessment methods, 102
 communication methods, 102
 inclusive settings, 101
 peer support, 101
Smarter Accessibility and Accommodations Framework, 76
Smarter Balanced Assessment Consortium (Smarter Balanced), 63, 77, 90, 213, 237
Sociocultural approaches, 126, 127
Socioeconomic status (SES), 122
Special educational needs (SEN), 52
Special populations, 13
Specific learning disability (SLD), 25
Speech therapy, 108
Split-attention effect, 204
Standards for Educational and Psychological Testing, 10, 42, 43, 61, 62, 135, 181, 213, 232
State testing programs, 247
Statistical methods, 191
Structural equation modeling (SEM), 241–243
Student without disabilities (SWOD), 214
Students with additional needs (SWANs), 49
Students with disabilities (SWDs)
 AA-AAs, 27
 access skills, 95
 access to instruction, 99
 access to testing, 100, 101
 accommodations, 98, 99, 235, 237
 achievement growth, 93
 alternate assessments, 238–240
 assessment policies, 1960s and 1970s, 17, 19, 20
 augmentative and assistive technologies, 28
 "catalogue approach", 25
 CBM, 24
 CEC, 22
 classroom-based formative assessments, 28
 college admissions, assessments, 20
 comprehension reading, 94, 95
 content and performance standards, 23
 Department of Education (ED), 20
 "dynamic" assessment techniques, 25
 educational landscape, 244
 ELs, 231
 ESEA, 21, 27
 ESSA, 17
 "equal playing field", 23
 functional skills, 25
 general education classroom, 24
 goals 2000, 21
 grade-level general education curriculum, 26
 high- and low-performing students, 28
 high-stakes end-of-the-year assessments, 17
 IDEA 2004 and assessments, 25, 28, 29
 IEPs, 95
 inclusion, 93, 94
 instruction and assessment, 95, 244
 item and test structure levels, 244
 legislative milestones, 17
 NAEP, 20
 National Commission on Excellence in Education, 20
 National Longitudinal Transition Study, 21
 "nonstandard" accommodations, 23
 norm-referenced tests, 22
 "out-of-level" assessment, 26
 OSEP, 21
 participation guidelines and sampling plans, 20
 performance-based assessments, 22
 physical disability/limited proficiency, 244
 policy experts, 23
 policy-makers, 23, 24
 probes, use of, 24
 professional development, 100
 "relative contributions", 25
 RTI, 99
 self-contained classrooms, 21
 severe-profound disabilities, 24
 significant disabilities, 101, 102
 Smarter Balanced and PARCC, 236
 special education services, 93
 standards-based accountability movement, 22
 technology-enhanced accommodations, 235
 test fairness, 17
 testing accommodations, 23
 trainable mentally handicapped, 24
Students with Disabilities Advisory Committee (SWDAC), 84
Students with limited/interrupted formal education (SLIFE), 121

T

Targeted skills, 3, 8
Technical Advisory Committee (TAC), 84
Technical Assistance Center on Positive Behavioral Interventions and Supports website, 165
Technology Assisted Reading Assessment (TARA), 193
Technology-enhanced items (TEI), 267
 APIP, 257
 construct irrelevant factors, 255
 drag-and-drop task, 255
 food web/water cycle, 255
 graphical content, 256
 manipulations, 255
 tab-entering, 255
 virtual environment, 256, 257
Test accessibility, 7–11, 199
Test Accessibility and Modification Inventory (TAMI), 9, 200
Test accommodations

Index 275

absolute/authoritative, 238
advocacy, 247
ASL, 248
CFI, 243
computer-based delivery systems, 235
configural and metric models, 243
construct-irrelevant variance, 237
DIF, 241
direct and indirect linguistic support, 237
educational assessment, 247
evolution, 248
goals, 237
interaction hypothesis and differential boost, 240
internal structure/dimensionality, 241, 243
IRT, 242
MDS, 242, 243
physical and visual disabilities, 247
scoring and reporting process, 248
SEM, 242, 243
Smarter Balanced and PARCC consortia, 236
SWDs, 234
universal design principles, 235
validity evidence, 240
Test anxiety, 108, 109
Test characteristic curve, 242
Test-criterion relationships, 223
Test-delivery systems, 113
Test development process, 184
Test event, 199
Test information function, 242
Testing accommodations, 100
Testing adaptations, 9, 10
  AAC, 225
  academic assessment, 216
  accommodations, 214, 225
  CTB/McGraw Hill, 215
  DIF analyses, 223
  functional impairment, 216
  guidelines, 213
  internal consistency, 219
  internal structure, 221
  knowledge question, 225
  modifications, 214
  NAEP, 221
  NCEO, 217
  PARCC and Smarter Balanced, 214
  practitioners and researchers, 224
  reliability and validity, 218, 227
  response processes, 221
  SWD-Es, 220
  SWD-NEs, 220
  SWDs, 214, 218
  SWODs, 217
  test-taker characteristics, 216
  theory and practice, 213–214
Testlets, 239
Test scores, 11, 12, 66–68
Test-taker's cognitive capacity, 208
Test-taking skills, 114
Test validity, 107

Text-to-speech (TTS) rendering, 63
Third International Mathematics Studies (TIMS), 139
Tier 1 instruction
  accessibility, 152
  adequacy challenges, 152
  CCSS, 149
  characterization, 136, 137
  CLASS, 150
  classroom instruction, 137
  cognitive process, 141
  content overlap, 139
  day-to-day instruction, 137
  easyCBM, 150
  ELA classroom, 147
  elements, 147
  enacted curriculum, 138, 142, 146, 151
  evidence-based practices, 136
  feasibility challenges, 152
  formative assessments, 151
  general/differentiated instruction, 148
  GET, 149
  high-quality, 136
  inadequate response and implementation, 135
  instructional priority setting, 150
  instructional time and screening procedures, 137
  instructional types, 149
  integration, 150
  intended curriculum, 143
  K-8 curriculum, 147
  multitiered approach, 136
  MyiLOGS
    content coverage bar chart, 149
    instructional calendar excerpt, 147
    lesson planner excerpt, 148
  operational definition and measurement, 140–142
  opportunity to learn and quality of instruction, 136
  OTL, 135–142
    assessment, 144
    CC, 144
    cognitive processes, 145
    educational environment, 142
    enacted curriculum, 143, 144, 146
    IEP, 143, 144
    instructional accommodations, 145
    intended curriculum, 142
    IT, 144
    large-scale research, 144
    operational definitions, 146
    progress monitoring, 146
    quality-related scores, 145
    research-based reading/mathematics program, 144
    RTI literature, 145
    students with and without disabilities, 143
    universal screening, 145
  quality, 139, 140
  resource-constrained environment, 135
  RTI approaches, 136
  self-reflection, 152
  short-term strategic thinking, 148
  student learning, 152

Tier 1 instruction (*cont.*)
  students' achievement, 150
  test score interpretations, 152
  timing
    academic learning, 138
    allocated, 138
    Cohen's *d* effect size, 139
    engaged, 138
    instructional, 138
    quantity of instruction, 138
    student achievement, 138, 139
  universal screening, 135
Time-Life Study, 206
Translated glossaries, 79, 83
Two-class mixture modeling, 222

U
United Nations Convention, 38
United Nations Educational Scientific and Cultural Organisation (UNESCO), 39
United States of America, 46, 47
Universal design (UD), 76, 248–249
Universal design for assessment (UDA), 8, 9
Universal design for learning (UDL), 6, 62, 96–98, 119, 179, 239, 265, 267
  achievement gaps, 171
  acquisition of knowledge, 179
  administrators, 177, 178
  authentic environments, 173
  automatic engagement detectors, 172
  classrooms, 167
  comprehensive assessment instruments, 173
  construct-irrelevant and relevant problem, 170
  educational institutions, 175
  educational policies and practices, 167
  emotional intrusions, 170
  executive systems, 171
  expert learners, 173
    knowledgeable learners, 179
    purposeful, motivated learners, 179
    strategic and goal-directed learners, 179
  external signals, 171
  from extrinsic to intrinsic, 173–175
  from individuals to interactions, 168–170
  instructional approaches, 168
  interactive affective response tool, 172
  knowledge and skills, 167
  multiple substantive roots, 167
  non-construct-relevant skills, 176
  norm-referenced standardized tests, 176
  parents, 177
  power of technology, 171
  principles, 168
  self-affirmation exercises, 170, 171
  self-determination, 168
  socially mediated assessment, 170
  stereotype threats, 171
  student learning and performance, 172
  students, 176, 177
  teachers, 176
  test makers/developers, 178
  universally design, 179
  white coat effect, 170
Universal design theory, 1, 6, 8
Universal test design (UTD), 233
Universal tools, 79
Universally designed systems, 44, 48, 50
Usability, Accessibility, and Accommodations Committee (UAAC), 84
Usability, Accessibility, and Accommodations Guidelines (UAAG), 80

V
Virtual Performance Scientific Inquiry Assessment task, 257

W
Walberg's model, 139
Webb's Depth-of-Knowledge (DOK), 140
Weighted MDS (WMDS), 242
Working memory load, 203
Writing Test Items to Evaluate Higher Order Thinking, 184
Writing the directions/stimulus, 187

Y
Yale Center for Emotional Intelligence, 172

Printed by Books on Demand, Germany